FROM STALIN TO MAO

FROM STALIN TO MAO

Albania and the Socialist World

Elidor Mëhilli

CORNELL UNIVERSITY PRESS   ITHACA AND LONDON

This publication was made possible in part by a grant from the Barr Ferree Foundation Fund for Publications, Department of Art and Archaeology, Princeton University, and by a grant from the First Book Subvention Program of the Association for Slavic, East European, and Eurasian Studies.

First published 2017 by Cornell University Press
Printed in the United States of America

Library of Congress Cataloging-in-Publication Data

Names: Mëhilli, Elidor, 1981– author.
Title: From Stalin to Mao : Albania and the socialist world / Elidor Mëhilli.
Description: Ithaca : Cornell University Press, 2017. | Includes bibliographical
    references and index.
Identifiers: LCCN 2017022614 (print) | LCCN 2017023206 (ebook) | ISBN
    9781501712234 (epub/mobi) | ISBN 9781501709593 (pdf) | ISBN
    9781501714153 (cloth : alk. paper)
Subjects: LCSH: Albania—Relations—Communist countries. | Communist
    countries—Relations—Albania. | Socialism and culture—Albania. | City
    planning—Albania—History—20th century. | Albania—Civilization—20th
    century.
Classification: LCC DR953.C725 (ebook) | LCC DR953.C725 M45 2017 (print) |
    DDC 303.48/249650171709045—dc23
LC record available at https://lccn.loc.gov/2017022614

Cornell University Press strives to use environmentally responsible suppliers and materials to the fullest extent possible in the publishing of its books. Such materials include vegetable-based, low-VOC inks and acid-free papers that are recycled, totally chlorine-free, or partly composed of nonwood fibers. For further information, visit our website at cornellpress.cornell.edu.

Prindërve

Contents

Illustrations

Acknowledgments

This book required me to look at my place of birth as a strange place, to question what I knew about where I come from. It began at Princeton University, where I had the good fortune to learn from brilliant individuals. Stephen Kotkin, who believed in my project from our very first meeting over a decade ago, has been an inspiration and the best mentor I could have imagined. It was his fierce seminar on Soviet Eurasia that taught me to see dictatorship as a process and how to think like a historian. The courageous Jan Gross has made a deep impression on my thinking about twentieth-century authoritarianism. I have long been grateful for a team-taught seminar on the end of Communist regimes with Adam Michnik. And I was privileged to engage with David Bellos, Gyan Prakash, Anson Rabinbach, and Christine Stansell.

At Princeton's School of Architecture, M. Christine Boyer urged me to take seriously the international history of urbanism, especially as urbanism is neglected more and more these days. The effort to combine the study of power with city planning stems from the fact that back in 2000, I enrolled in an architecture program, only to divert to the study of history and politics shortly thereafter. I am still grateful to those individuals in Ithaca who opened their office doors to a naive eighteen-year-old with unpolished English, saw a glimmer of potential, and steered me the right way: the late Christian F. Otto, D. Medina Lasansky, Sidney Tarrow, Michael P. Steinberg, and Holly Case.

I thank Mark Mazower for his generosity of spirit and mind over the past five years. Arne Westad has been a steady source of support and encouragement. During a Mellon fellowship at the University of Pennsylvania's Humanities Forum, I was lucky to join a small powerhouse group of junior scholars who remain friends and treasured intellectual partners: Laurent Dissard, Rossen Djagalov, Monica Kim, and Noah Tamarkin. Peter Holquist generously invited me to present at the Annenberg Seminar at Penn's Department of History, which prompted revisions to a chapter. Ben Nathans invited me to speak to his graduate seminar, where the critical feedback was first-rate.

In between Princeton, Washington, D.C., Philadelphia, and New York, I have engaged with authors who directly and indirectly have sustained my work: Tarik Amar, David Engerman, James English, Emily Greble, Hope Harrison, Jim Hershberg, Chen Jian, Mark Kramer, Anna Di Lellio, Małgorzata Mazurek, Christian F. Ostermann, Nicholas Pano, Daniel Perez, Kevin M. F. Platt, and Besnik Pula.

There is hardly a better person to discuss Albania's past with than Ardian Vehbiu: *miqësi e vyer për mua*. Daria Bocharnikova, Steven Harris, Vladimir Kulić, Emily Gunzburger Makaš, and Kimberly Elman Zarecor have been valued collaborators in many conferences on socialist-era architecture and urban planning. I also acknowledge many years of discussions with former graduate school colleagues, now professors across the United States and Europe: in particular, Franziska Exeler, Mayhill Fowler, Jeff Hardy, Piotr Kosicki, Kyrill Kunakhovich, and Anne O'Donnell. In Tirana, I incurred large debts to Ana Lalaj, Bujar Hudhri, Ismail Kadare, Gëzim Podgorica, Maks Velo, and countless archivists who had to put up with my endless nagging.

At Hunter College, where I have taught since 2013, I have incredibly supportive colleagues, for whom I am deeply grateful. Dániel Margócsy (now at the University of Cambridge) and Iryna Vushko offered suggestions at an early stage. Manu Bhagavan and Jon Rosenberg have been superb sources of encouragement. In their roles as department chairs, Rick Belsky, Donna Haverty-Stacke, and Mary Roldán ensured that I had everything I needed to succeed. Forever grateful to Catherine Abou-Nemeh, Irena Çomo (and my cool goddaughter Maia, who went on walks with me in Queens), Christienna Fryar (who, among other things, heroically copyedited the text), Nikolce Gjorevski, Christophe Koné, Elona Pira, Eriola Pira, and Arbër Shtëmbari for the big laughs and the memorable get-togethers—from New York to Paris to Corfu—and for every single moment I was not working on this book. *Ju çmoj*.

Travel to nineteen archives would have not been possible without the generosity of many institutions. The Department of History and the Institute for International and Regional Studies at Princeton, a Mellon fellowship at The George Washington University, a Mrs. Giles Whiting Foundation Fellowship, and a postdoctoral fellowship at Columbia University's Harriman Institute facilitated research and writing. A summer grant at the Zentrum für Zeithistorische Forschung, in Potsdam, brought me back to the archives in Berlin. I thank Jan Behrends for seeing potential in my work. A visiting stint with "The Reluctant Internationalists" project, expertly led by the phenomenal Jessica Reinisch at Birkbeck, University of London, was an intellectual privilege. It enabled me to expand research in London, in addition to discussing illiberal internationalism with some of the most exciting young scholars anywhere: Ana Antic, David Brydan, Johanna Conterio, and Dora Vargha.

I am grateful for generous support from Hunter in the form of Presidential Travel Awards, a PSC-CUNY grant, a Shuster Faculty Fund grant, a President's Fund for Faculty Advancement award, and additional research support from the dean's office. Subvention grants from the Barr Ferree Foundation Fund for Publications at Princeton and the Association for Slavic, East European, and

Eurasian Studies facilitated publication. The 2016 Workshop on Authoritarian Regimes at the Hoover Institution, at Stanford, allowed me to dig into fascinating unfamiliar sources. I thank Paul Gregory and Mark Harrison for the opportunity.

A part of the fourth chapter won the Webb-Smith Prize at the Forty-Sixth Annual Walter Prescott Webb Memorial Lecture Series and appeared as "Socialist Encounters: Albania and the Transnational Eastern Bloc in the 1950s" in *Cold War Crossings: International Travel and Exchange across the Soviet Bloc, 1940s–1960s*, ed. Patryk Babiracki and Kenyon Zimmer (College Station: Texas A&M University Press, 2014), 107–33. It is reproduced here, in modified form, with permission. I thank both editors for a sharp reading of that version. At Cornell University Press, Roger Haydon has been an incredibly patient and thoughtful editor.

In the final stages of writing this book, pictures and videos of Joel Mëhilli (age six months) regularly kept crossing the Atlantic Ocean, reaching the island of Manhattan, where they would then pop up on my phone's screen. In them, he banged on coffee tables, giggled deliriously, and made faces, oblivious to the fact that he was lifting his uncle's spirits far away. My parents, to whom this book is dedicated, spent much of their lives under a dictatorship—and then endured decades of post-Communist havoc. They managed to do something that has always seemed improbable and thus astonishing to me: they made a little room, amid cruelty and corruption, to live a life in dignity.

FROM STALIN TO MAO

A NEW WORLD

The foundry's steel door creaks as it opens, revealing Stalin covered in sunlight and pigeon excrement. It is New Year's in Tirana, the Albanian capital. The building rises next to a line of tents that serve as homes for destitute Roma families. Some of the women are washing clothes outside. Stray dogs lurk. Under the former Communist dictatorship, the building was used to manufacture statues of national heroes and party men. Now, decades after the regime's demise, those statues have been locked up in a vast, barren room. Here they are, unceremoniously piled in a corner: Lenin missing an arm, Albanian party boss Enver Hoxha missing a nose, martyrs and anonymous workers rotting away. I recognize this particular Stalin from growing up in this city—the gigantic arm stretched out, the heavy unbuttoned winter coat, the gaze diverted toward some distant part of the globe. I recognize him because he once stood on a pedestal in an industrial suburb just outside the capital—the domain of the defunct Stalin textile mills, a 1950s gift from the Soviet people to the People's Republic of Albania.

The former Stalin mills are ruins now. The road leading to them is dotted with potholes and abandoned car parts. The same vision unfolds across the landscape: car wash after car wash after car wash. Above the tall arched entrance to the Stalin industrial complex, a sign announces that the building can be rented. There is a cell phone number to call. (Presumably, old owners have received their previously confiscated land back.) Where Stalin's tall statue once stood, an empty pedestal still carries a faded red star. Squatters have taken over many of the factory shops, a fact betrayed by the sight of satellite dishes and homemade antennas peeking out of the windows. The battered sidewall of the main administrative building still bears the inscription "1951"—the long-forgotten birth of the Stalin mills. On the opposite side of the road, Soviet-designed housing units for the onetime textile workers look ravaged and pitiful. But on the surface of the exposed brick walls, I can still trace the outline of the balustrades from the original designs. And although the once-celebrated Stalin textile complex died a long time ago, its socialist name lives on. Ask local residents where they live, and they will promptly say, *Kombinat*.

Elsewhere around the city, socialist-era architecture has been disintegrating but is still omnipresent. Shoddy illegal constructions have sprung up without much regard for urban planning principles, green areas, or historic preservation. Inhabitants have added floors to their collective housing blocks, and some have closed balconies or claimed terraces in an effort to create more living space for their crammed families. Residents have learned to customize even the notoriously inflexible prefabricated concrete panels of the 1980s. Virtually no building erected under socialism has survived intact. In the urban chaos and lawlessness that became known as *tranzicion* (transition to capitalism), Tirana has been profoundly reinvented. But some of the best residential areas are still those designed before the 1990s, since they adhered to basic planning principles. As more and more socialist-era buildings get bulldozed and others converted into cafés or poker joints, the "market economy" ushers in colorful but hastily built structures, second-rate imitations of Western architecture, and flamboyant homes for

FIGURE 1.   Stalin in a foundry, Tirana, 2007. Photograph: Elidor Mëhilli.

FIGURE 2.   The unveiling of Stalin at the textile complex in Yzberish, November 1951. Arkivi i Agjencisë Telegrafike Shqiptare (ATSH), Tirana, Albania.

well-connected political families and the shady dealers who bankroll their elections to public office.

It is hard to see all of this and not think of socialism as a vanished civilization. But below the industrial rubble in Albania's overpopulated capital, behind the piles of post-Communist waste and kitsch, and amid the neglected colonies of poverty-stricken Roma families living on top of factory ruins, it is still possible to trace the stubborn material culture of socialism. It is visible inside that warehouse sitting on the edge of Tirana but also in the aging factory-built suburbs of Berlin, Warsaw, Budapest, and Prague. It can be seen in museums and Stalin-themed parks in the Baltic or the televised snapshots from Pyongyang whenever the North Korean regime makes the news. But the ruins tell only part of the story. Underneath the prefabricated blocks, it is also possible to identify the optimism of postwar construction efforts, the revolutionary appeal of a far-reaching social project of remaking individuals by redesigning their environment. Hundreds of thousands of Albanians, after all, still inhabit socialist-era housing, as do millions of others across Eurasia. Socialism disintegrated as geopolitical reality but left behind an unmistakable map of familiar plans, objects, and shared references.

This book analyzes the emergence of these socialist commonalities by telling the story of post-Fascist Albania's path to socialism. In the span of twenty years, the country went from Italian and Nazi occupation (1939–44) to liberation by a native Communist-led army (1944), a brief but dramatic interlude as a Yugoslav satellite (1944–48), and then to a heady decade of wide-ranging borrowings—political advisers, security operatives, brand-new factories, urban plans, school textbooks, ideas, and heresies—from the Soviet Union in the 1950s. The Soviet civilization stood for the bold promise of a new noncapitalist world, but these were also years of profound insecurity for the novice rulers of a small country. They came to speak of Stalin as a powerful ally. They saw in Soviet-style socialism not only a vision of a possible future but also the means to realize the country's aspirations for a place in the world.

Then socialist harmony shattered. The Soviet Union and China quarreled in the early 1960s. Unexpectedly, Albania sided with Mao during this startling Sino-Soviet split that broke the socialist world apart. If the Soviet Union was the anticapitalist alternative to the West, Beijing now claimed to be the guiding voice of anti-imperialism. Having vigorously embraced the Soviet Union, the Albanian party now viciously denounced the post-Stalin leadership in Moscow. From Mussolini to Mao, then, a tiny country (population 1,277,904 in 1953) found itself swept up in the biggest developments of the twentieth century. This turned Albania into a kind of laboratory for transnational collaboration and confrontation during the Cold War, offering an unparalleled angle into the profound contradictions of socialist internationalism, as well as the unforeseen consequences of ideological and personnel exchanges across Eastern Europe and Asia.[1]

Socialism made it possible for someone living on the industrial outskirts of a city like Tirana to find common ground with someone living on the other side of the planet. It came with party central committees, recognizable slogans, surveillance techniques, censorship rituals, a mental map, and a new vocabulary. In Albania, socialism became associated with feats of imagination and engineering, central plans and centrally planned lies, exhausting labor campaigns but also mass literacy, longer lives, and a specific understanding of the world. Connecting countries from the fringes of the Balkans to East Asia, socialism magnified ideological conflicts, turning them into social and cultural crises. It engendered a shared material and mental culture across national borders without ensuring political unity or ultimately, as Albania's history shows, more openness.

Breaks

Two themes run through narratives of Soviet power in Eastern Europe after the Second World War: captivity and failure. The first emphasizes the coercive role of Red Army troops and meddling Soviet operatives. Much of the literature has been consumed with Soviet (and specifically Stalin's) intentions in capturing Eastern Europe.[2] Planned or unplanned, the Soviet Union acquired a sphere of influence, which raised the problem of keeping it. On the other hand, the "people's democracies" of the Eastern bloc were neither of the people nor democratic. It is possible to view them as a sham, a betrayal of possible alternatives to Soviet-style institutions, just as it is possible to dismiss their official rhetoric as self-serving. But no matter how self-serving, Eastern bloc states spent considerable energy in defining themselves and their inhabitants' lives. The people's democracies were actual states with actual institutions, elites, mass organizations, and modes of thinking, speaking, and behaving.

The second theme highlights the myriad failings of Sovietization in the 1950s. Soviet policies backfired in East Germany, Poland, and elsewhere, even as Soviet-style institutions emerged all over. How could something both fail and work? This book tells a story that defies themes of captivity and failure. There was no Red Army to "crush" Albania into submission. There were no secret Soviet operatives in 1945 to run internal affairs. It makes no sense to frame the story in terms of Soviet successes and failures, outside oppression and local resistance—a stubborn dynamic in East European studies. Elsewhere on the continent, there were Communist parties and activists who had spent their adult lives waiting for revolution. As a result, the scholarship dramatizes the struggle between Soviet-backed Communists and well-organized domestic competitors, including other leftists. However, Albania's Communist Party only came into being, hastily, and with Yugoslav backing, two years after the Italian Fascist invasion of 1939. A party materialized not from the spark of old arguments over class struggle but in the shadow of war.

The Communist-led partisan forces—young and amateurish but dogged, energetic, and bold—first insisted on broad anti-Fascist collaboration. Then, after the country fell under German occupation, they effectively framed their opponents as Nazi collaborators. This procession of foreign influences—including Mussolini's Balkan entanglements, Nazi occupation, and Yugoslav wartime tactical advice—brought the Communist Party to power but left Albania under Yugoslav patronage. The Communists boasted that they were on the right side of history. But the party was also painfully aware of its dependence on external forces it could not control. This is why it sided with Stalin in 1948, thus liberating itself from the Yugoslav clutch. The move, however, also detached the country geographically from the Eastern bloc. This crucial fact heightened the leadership's insecurity, and it also encouraged closer contacts with Moscow.

This was a preindustrial country of peasants, shepherds, and a handful of petty shopkeepers. It was overwhelmingly illiterate (some estimates put illiteracy at over 80 percent). It had a majority Muslim population, with important Orthodox and Catholic communities. Born out of war, the Communist Party employed terror against its real and perceived opponents, executing those charged with wartime collaboration and harassing those deemed to have been indifferent to the Communist cause. In other words, by 1945 Communist power was already a fact. The dilemma was this: How to build socialism with a dominant party but no working class? Party leaders may have lacked higher education, but they grasped the basic laws of Marxism-Leninism. This awareness of being economically behind and lacking a class-based foundation for socialism—of defying the laws of history—helps explain the appeal of the Soviet master narrative. To correct this error, the party launched a far-reaching campaign to remake society and create enlightened workers out of illiterate peasants. Forging a working class was not just a precept of ideology; it became a matter of survival.

To understand Communist rule in this corner of Europe, then, it is necessary to spell out how ideology interacted with geopolitical insecurity. The Marxist-Leninist vision of the stages of development (feudalism, capitalism, socialism) held appeal in an isolated country eager to modernize but surrounded by stronger and assertive neighbors. Lacking experience, Albanian officials looked for guidance from the Kremlin. Insecure geopolitically, they embraced Stalinism, sending ambitious youths to universities in Moscow and Leningrad. They saw in a strong dictatorship the promise of national independence (against Yugoslavia and Greece). They oversaw the writing of textbooks, the teaching of Russian in schools, and the expansion of *metoda sovjetike* in industry. Soviet development aid was meant to propel the country from poverty, and Albanian officials used the language of solidarity to acquire credits and defer repayment. They received factories, machines, experts, and consumer goods. Not since the Ottoman Empire had Albania engaged in such large-scale exchange. This time, however, the country's new elite could exploit the resources of the Soviet empire while upholding national independence.

Most analyses of the Cold War ignore Albania.[3] What does exist tends to view the country's history almost exclusively from the angle of nationalism.[4] The breaks with Yugoslavia (1948), the Soviet Union (1960–1961), and eventually with China (1976–1978), along with the later push for isolation, are projected back into earlier history.[5] The result is an aberration within an anomaly (Eastern Europe), a nationalist pathology, a state destined to become a fortress.[6] But other socialist states also flirted with nationalism, and it is not obvious that 1950s and 1960s Albania was any more nationalist than, say, Poland, Romania, Soviet Uzbekistan, or North Korea.[7] Later Communist-era official accounts emphasized national identity, but this does not mean that individuals in Albania could not hold multiple other identities, especially in light of the historic anti-Fascist internationalism of the wartime period.[8] Think, for example, of nascent identities like that of a peasant-turned-worker or a formerly veiled Muslim woman entering a textile factory. Nationalism has long turned into a straitjacket in analyses of the modern Balkans, obscuring the significance and multiple meanings of an internationalist postwar moment.[9]

Accounts of Stalinism typically stem from the Soviet Union or the Eastern European territories occupied by Soviet troops. As a result, Poland, Czechoslovakia, and Hungary have become emblematic of Eastern Europe.[10] Stalin's life, moreover, has served as a blueprint for the story, with the year 1953 (his death) marking a distinct watershed moment in political history. Three years later, the Soviet leader Nikita Khrushchev denounced his predecessor, to the shock of Stalinists around the world, so histories of Stalinism typically end by the mid-1950s. Analyses then invariably turn to the dilemmas of domestic reform, as if reform was the only possible path after Stalin. This book proposes a different story arc. Albania (and others too) clung to Stalinism long after 1956, even as it became clear that this put the Albanian party leadership in an awkward position in Moscow. To look beyond the Soviet Union and its immediate neighbors in Eastern Europe, but also beyond the year 1956, is to bring into view Stalinism's international life.[11]

As a model of state building, the Soviet Union wielded not only the power of industry, which was no small matter for an agrarian country in the Balkans, but the promise of a whole new civilization. The Soviet Union was "a violent experiment in an avowedly noncapitalist modernity," as Stephen Kotkin has put it, "and in an avowedly non-colonial colonialism."[12] It proved challenging enough to try to execute this within the massive Soviet territory, but the Soviet Union also helped create "transnational infrastructure, as well as transnational political habits, transnational economic relations, and transnational ways of behaving."[13] What did this mean for an Albanian party official, an ambitious laborer, or a promising university student in the 1950s? My approach is to see Soviet-Albanian interactions as possibilities for discovery, openings and dead ends, unexpected alignments, and contradictory impulses. It turned out that Albanians did not necessarily have to fully grasp this multifaceted Soviet civilization to understand its power in a post-Fascist setting or to reference it for their own local purposes.

Looking at Stalinism from Europe's margins raises another question: If Stalinism became so circumscribed by presocialist Russian legacies, why could it travel so easily? How could an allegedly retreating and inward-looking Stalinism be so adaptive to unrelated socioeconomic contexts? Stalinism could appeal, adapt, and assume local meaning, including meaning that went against the intentions of Soviet party leaders.[14] When we shift the point of view, the contours of Stalinism change too—not as a purely local process but as a form of rule that could take on a life of its own, far away from the borders of the Soviet Union. At the core, it was a system based on ruthless coercion, party rule, central planning, and a leader cult. But any definition also needs to account for its broad appeal and malleability. In Albania, party authorities vested themselves with the international authority of Stalinism as an alternative to capitalism. Stalinism provided a development formula at home and an opening for an international identity.[15]

Albania's path also shows that there was nothing inevitable about de-Stalinization.[16] Reforming socialism—"normalizing" it, as it were—does not somehow make more historical sense than efforts to entrench Stalinist rule. The Albanian regime stuck to Stalinism *despite* the Soviets. It paid lip service to the Soviet party leader Nikita Khrushchev's rebukes after 1956, but it never gave up repression and terror. It kept executing "party enemies" charged with imaginary crimes. It did not close the labor camps. There was no reconciliation with neighboring Yugoslavia either—no matter how much the Kremlin insisted. The Hungarian uprising in 1956 convinced the Albanian leadership that desirable socialist interactions also came with a price: the Soviet template was productive in a poor country like Albania, but the successes (like the creation of a Soviet-trained administrative, technical, and artistic elite) could be threatening to party rule too. Elsewhere in the Eastern bloc, reform became a rallying cry among committed Communists. In Albania, the idea of reform became associated with hostility to the nation. The country's breakthrough, in other words, came in the form of standing up to the Soviet Union in the name of a distinct Soviet legacy (Stalinism).

Soviet planners did not agree with their counterparts in Tirana about Albania's role in the emerging international socialist economy—a point of contention that preceded similar struggles in the decolonized Third World. When the Soviet and Chinese parties quarreled in 1960, the anxious Albanian party leader saw in Mao's China an opportunity to continue the Stalinist experiment. In response, Moscow lashed out. Soviet advisers disappeared from construction sites, hastily replaced with Chinese experts. But the Soviet-inspired mental and material world of the 1950s did not disappear by decree. Albanian officials used Chinese loans and technology to try to keep up with the rest of the Eastern bloc. They took an interest in Mao's violent "leaps" and also considered opportunities for cooperation in North Korea, Cuba, and across Africa. Albanian Soviet-trained experts continued to draw on their Soviet education, even as their superiors lambasted the "revisionists" in Moscow. Enver Hoxha's regime continued to speak the language of Stalinism but now directed it against the Soviets. This is a story, then, of socialist commonalities that emerged through widespread state-backed efforts in the 1950s and that continued despite the wishes of powerful elites in Moscow or Beijing.

It is also a story of how the Cold War created unexpected possibilities for small states to make big claims. Often mistreated in the international system and neglected in historical overviews of the twentieth century, small states should not be idealized either. They can be as cruel as any big power. Albania's unreconstructed regime, for example, used the Sino-Soviet split to step up its repression and fabricate more enemies. The point is not to show that small states matter but that the Cold War confrontation endowed weak regimes with an outsize ideological significance. The country's breaks with Belgrade and Moscow created unforeseen opportunities for a militant clique, but they also came with risks. They required adjustments in planning and trade. They generated uncertainty at the lower ranks. And they also necessitated the constant rewriting of history. Each break had to be explained ideologically to the population. To address this problem, party ideologues crafted a narrative of betrayal: Yugoslavia had betrayed the Communist cause, whereas Stalin's heirs in Moscow had betrayed Stalinism.

Just as Communist apparatchiks had championed Soviet myths and heroes in the 1950s, so they kept creating more anti-Soviet myths in the 1960s. Put simply, each break created more history—more versions of the past, more justifications for why the future looked uncertain.

Contacts

Socialist states dismantled free markets but also brought millions of people into contact across a vast landmass. Shortly after the Second World War, Communist regimes were in power from Eastern Europe to China. Winston Churchill famously warned of an Iron Curtain ominously connecting the Baltic with the Adriatic. By the 1950s, however, the divide was global. For a while, it seemed that revolution might also spread to the former colonized world.[17] Each of these national roads to socialism had its peculiarities. But the Eastern bloc also invariably featured similarly organized parties and mass organizations, repressive security police methods, and centrally planned economies. Compared with the so-called First World (Western capitalism) and the Third World (decolonized countries), there are far fewer studies of the transnational character of the Second World.[18]

Initially, Communist authorities spoke of a camp (*kamp* in Albanian; *tábor* in Czech; *lager* in German and Bulgarian; *lagărul* in Romanian; *obóz* in Polish), which betrayed the militaristic antagonism of the late 1940s.[19] In 1956, in the wake of the rebellion in Budapest, the Soviet newspaper *Pravda* wrote about a "socialist commonwealth" in an attempt to reclaim the idea of internationalism.[20] The confusion over what to call this sphere reflects the gap between aspiration and reality. Lofty rhetoric notwithstanding, Moscow struggled to create noncapitalist forms of international organization. And though "it suited both communists and anticommunists throughout the Cold War to draw attention to the ideological power of Marxist internationalism," as Mark Mazower writes, "its actual postwar achievements were remarkably small."[21] Somewhere between the aspiration and the dispiriting reality, this socialist sphere kept going on for four decades. From labor campaigns (Stakhanovism) and friendship societies to cultural diplomacy, technical aid programs, industrial prototypes, and city planning schemes, the Soviets encouraged transnational contacts on a large scale.

But they were not alone in doing so. Socialism was bigger than the Soviet Union. And since Albania was the poorest country of the bloc, it increasingly received development aid from the rest of the socialist world too. This turned it into a contact zone between Soviet advisers, East German engineers, Czech energy experts, Bulgarian urban planners, and Hungarian geologists. In addition to a Soviet horizon, then, there was an Eastern bloc horizon, best captured in the circulation of experts, technology, and artifacts. It would be wrong to imagine this as a series of one-way communications. These visitors also came to discover Albania, which entailed ideological and intellectual tasks. They brought their ideas and practices to the country, became frustrated when outcomes did not match the ambitious goals, and struggled to make sense of the fact that the country looked both recognizably socialist and also painfully undeveloped.

Such contacts helped create new knowledge, which often contradicted the regime's rhetoric. Relations with Germans, Hungarians, and Czechs, as we will see, had a tendency to complicate dealings with Soviet planners. In some key industrial sectors, moreover, Czechoslovakia was more advanced than the "homeland of socialism." Getting the most value out of Eastern bloc relations meant assessing these countries' comparative economic advantages and calculating what each of them could furnish (ideally on a "solidarity" basis, meaning free of payment). It meant that planners had to learn to engage with foreign partners, that they had to be socialized in the language of bloc affairs. Were the Albanians supposed to speak to Czechs and Hungarians the way they spoke to Soviet officials? Could they get Moscow to pressure the East Europeans to buy inferior Albanian products? (Later on, the question became how to get the Chinese to fund frenzied industrialization.) These questions were underlined by assumptions about the role of bigger states in an emerging socialist world economy, expectations of solidarity, and enduring frustrations over building socialism in conditions of continued poverty. Disagreements about trade pricing, salaries, and production delays took on political meaning.

This emerging socialist arena provided planners, intellectuals, managers, and workers with a formidable device: comparison. Reports from Bulgaria, East Germany, Azerbaijan, and China filled Albanian newspapers. Delegations from all corners of Eurasia became commonplace. It is true that socialist states increasingly compared themselves with the capitalist West in the 1950s. But there were also comparisons to be made within the socialist sphere. Albania's ranks of educated administrators were modest, which meant that educational opportunities abroad helped make careers. Those who got to travel abroad could forge important professional connections. Socialist cooperation thus encouraged endless comparisons—of wages, material privileges, and standards of living between populations across many time zones. Socialism encouraged these kinds of comparisons, but they came with unexpected consequences. For example, they led to uneasy questions like these: How long would it take for Albania to become like Bulgaria or Hungary (let alone East Germany)? Why were Soviet, Czech, and Polish officials more relaxed in some cultural matters, especially after Stalin's death, than Albanian ones? Party-backed internationalism came to haunt the party.

Some readers may see here a familiar story of development. In fact, thinking about development as stages became popular in many parts of the world during the second half of the twentieth century, as did the idea of skipping stages.[22] Development aid to Albania came with misplaced expectations, translation challenges, logistical hurdles, confusion, high-minded planning, and bitter disappointments. But there were specific aspects to how development played out in a socialist country. There was, for example, the expectation that other socialist states would not behave like capitalist ones (that was the whole point of having socialist relations in the first place). Albanian officials employed this line of reasoning to extract concessions from their foreign partners. The other important aspect of socialist development politics was that technical shortcomings could be masked with ideological modes of reasoning. Decisions and workplace practices that may seem strange to today's reader need to be understood within the context of a planned economy and a system that explicitly rejected cultural domination of one country over another but that found it nevertheless difficult to bridge technical differences between them.

For all the talk of friendship, socialist relations magnified feelings of economic inferiority. Tension emerged between ideas of internationalism on the one hand and specific geopolitical anxieties and conflicting national interests on the other. Because official propaganda so grossly exaggerated the cohesion of the socialist world, the idea of socialist internationalism might seem phony.[23] Badly neglected in much of existing scholarship, the internationalism of illiberal regimes ends up looking like a mask concealing "true" nationalist agendas.[24] But consider that transnational exchange in a rural country was not some abstract notion but came to mean tangible things: cement factories, tractors, brand-new machines, and work routines. Socialist countries established institutional links and created new economic arrangements such as the Council for Mutual Economic Assistance (Comecon), in addition to a military alliance (the Warsaw Treaty Organization). Imperfect and fragmented, the socialist world nevertheless emerged as a reference point and a space of interaction. "Like an empire," Austin Jersild writes, "the socialist bloc was an attempt at forms of integration and cooperation that intentionally blurred the boundaries of the traditional nation-state."[25] Not only did national boundaries persist, but Albania's past also shows how transnational contact could harden them.

To Be Modern

The party-led crusade for socialism was a quest for modernity. "To be 'modern,'" writes Dipesh Chakrabarty, "is to judge one's experience of time and space and thus create new possibilities for oneself."[26] The possibilities for a preindustrial country in the Balkans could be found in the history of Soviet republics seemingly marching into an industrialized future. But the Soviet examples also came with counterexamples in the capitalist West and specific institutional arrangements. Twentieth-century state-driven modernity projects mirrored, engaged, copied, and became entangled with one another. This does not make them indistinguishable, however.[27] Assuming the presence of a powerful state, too, can obscure how *pushteti* (a term that blurs the distinction between state and power, akin to the Russian *vlast'*) actually had to be brought into being in a postwar context.

Thinking about socialism as a form of globalization highlights interdependency without losing sight of local variation and conflict.[28] György Péteri and Michael David-Fox have offered valuable insights on the deeply ingrained sense of superiority that pushed Communist states to engage with the wider world despite the unmistakable Iron Curtain cutting through the continent.[29] Globalization typically brings to mind greater mobility, faster travel, migration, capital circulating across national borders, and the traffic of people and ideas.[30] Many of these aspects were clearly limited under socialism. And yet, from the perspective of Albanian planners, "Soviet experience" was also a model of compressing time and space. Socialist interactions enabled borrowings, just as they facilitated the exchange of assumptions and misunderstandings. As a world-making process, socialism sustained a traffic in people, their ideas, doubts, and economic frustrations. It was not clear how even the most formidable central committee or security police could control exchange on such a large scale. Neither was it clear how countries such as Albania, Poland, the Soviet Union, North Korea, and China could ever form a coherent whole.

In 1959, Nikita Khrushchev promised that national borders would become irrelevant ("as Marxism-Leninism teaches").[31] Two years later, more borders had appeared within the socialist world. The Sino-Soviet schism created a major fault line within the international Communist movement, with complex and often dangerous outcomes for crossing it. All of this made the subversive potential of exchange more problematic for party-states. It is impossible to understand the engagement with China in the 1960s without a full appreciation of the entangled histories of Albanian-Yugoslav and Albanian-Soviet contacts in earlier years. Mao's choices in the 1960s, as we will see, confounded the Albanian party clique. Still, China could serve as a kind of blunt weapon against Moscow. Messy and contradictory, this socialist world defined itself against Western capitalism but also nurtured hostility to the Soviet Union within its own borders.

A strictly domestic approach to this era would miss how global dynamics shaped nationalist choices.[32] A national project, after all, required a constant supply of local and foreign enemies. What better source of enemies than a socialist world constantly engaged in ideological warfare? If individuals can "annex the global into their own practices of the modern," the socialist state provided specific instruments and a concrete language for the task.[33] It invited Albanians to think of themselves as part of a greater world, which begins to explain how individuals in an isolated corner of Europe began to speak in global terms. Party apparatchiks, bureaucrats, planners, youths, and workers had the possibility to engage in the globalizing language of socialism. That language, moreover, could turn against the Soviet Union. Was this not, ironically, a sign of the success of the Soviet civilizational project? It created opportunities for self-definition that the regime in Moscow ultimately could not control.

Much as it can illuminate, the focus on transnational exchange can also be misleading.[34] It is important to specify what could be exchanged and what could not. Who and what could travel? And when? Albania's path in the second half of the twentieth century—from openness and transnational contacts to isolation and autarky—serves as a warning against equating exchange with freedom, or seeing in transnational contacts some kind of inevitable path toward openness to international forces.[35] After all, this was a one-party dictatorship that ruthlessly policed national borders until 1990. The same regime that had fostered exchange in the 1950s later threw individuals in prison on fabricated charges of "contaminating" the nation. The picture that emerges, then, is of an entanglement of nationalism and the globalizing aspects of socialism, a state-directed exchange that created its own unexpected connections, bringing about familiarity but also sharpening differences.

Mussolini to Mao

Albanians made sense of Soviet influences in terms of earlier contacts with Italians, Germans, and Yugoslavs. This book, therefore, begins in 1939, with Mussolini's disastrous bid for a Mediterranean empire, paving the way for the establishment of a Communist party under occupation. The first chapter frames the years 1939–49 as a revolutionary period, exploring wartime military struggles and Yugoslav dependency following liberation. Viewing these processes as interlinked illuminates continuities that are not captured in conventional Cold War chronologies, including the little-known fact that postwar authorities sought to build socialism using Italian engineers stuck in the country after the war. The onset of Communist rule was paradoxical: mobilization to build socialism in a country possessing few workers; a language of enlightenment in the context of predominant illiteracy; radical rejection of the past while recycling Italian Fascist blueprints. After the Stalin-Tito schism of 1948, Albania graduated from being a Yugoslav satellite to becoming Stalin's ally. It was here that Eastern Europe's show trials of the 1950s had their bloody prelude.

The second chapter views socialism as a mental world, following Albanian youths sent to the Soviet Union for training in literature, engineering, and architecture. The encounter with Moscow was awe-inspiring, but exposure to the socialist world could also be alienating. Such contradictory reactions find expression in the lives of two individuals: an aspiring architect shipped to Moscow to learn how to plan the socialist cities of the future, and a young writer sent on a scholarship to absorb the techniques of socialist realism. They both invoked the socialist world in their work, albeit with different consequences. Party-enforced friendship propaganda for the "land of Lenin" was meant to insert Albania into a genealogy of international socialism. It came with rewritten history textbooks, mandatory Russian language courses, and a system of sanctions and rewards.

Such encounters were not one-sided, however. The third chapter also considers those Soviet advisers who came to lift Albania from poverty into socialist plenty. In the 1950s, the Soviet Union also became associated with industrial methods, including Stakhanovism (workers surpassing production norms) as an example of how socialism tried to blur differences between national economies. Socialism came with physical acts that required proper verbal identification and repetition, thus allowing Albanian peasants to make claims about themselves, their past, and their future. "Soviet experience" stood in contrast to "old ways"—presocialist labor techniques, property regimes, traditional conventions and social mores, and religion. Rather than looking at the Soviet-Albanian encounter in terms of oppression and resistance, it is useful to see how it created modes of interpretation. The example of the Stalin textile mills outside Tirana—where

Stalin's massive statue once stood—illustrates how Soviet machines became an Albanian story.[36]

The book's first half views socialism through the optic of war, the struggle for new institutions and identities, and the lived experience of youths, factory workers, and the country's future intellectuals. The second half conceives of socialism as interactions and comparisons that go beyond the Soviet Union. The fourth chapter, for example, traces exchanges between East German, Czechoslovak, Hungarian, and Albanian engineers, economists, geologists, and planners. How could a preindustrial country fit into a more integrated socialist economic space? Who got to determine the terms of exchange? The analysis takes seriously efforts within the Council for Mutual Economic Aid, but it also considers the persistence of bilateral arrangements.

Socialism was also a material reality: buildings, tools, vehicles, and urban plans. Party ideologues spoke of the country as a large construction site. They referred to mass organizations as "levers" (*leva*), or as a "conveyer belt" (*rrip transmisioni*) extending from the highest echelons of the party apparatus down to neighborhoods.[37] Construction sites, in turn, became emblematic of the building of socialism. It is no coincidence that architecture and city planning are evoked by some of the greatest authors writing under or about Communist regimes. Think of Václav Havel's *Redevelopment, or, Slum Clearance*, which centers on the troubles of a group of architects attempting to convert a medieval town into a socialist bloc, or György Konrád's *The City Builder*, a dense meditation of the sickness of the socialist city-civilization, as seen through the eyes of a disillusioned architect.[38] The Albanian author Ismail Kadare, a protagonist in the second chapter, wrote a powerful novel envisioning authoritarianism as an intricate Ottoman palace staffed by a bureaucracy whose job is to survey the subconscious lives of citizens by interpreting their dreams.[39]

Albania's push for planning took on the qualities of an epochal transformation. One problem was that it had no professional city planners. Brand-new Soviet-financed plants and workshops rose, but the cities still looked presocialist. Urban planning had to be invented. The fifth chapter shows how a socialist material culture came about through improvisation. Socialist city planning relied on the adoption of technical solutions from the much-denounced capitalist West. The country borrowed construction technology from the Soviet Union and Czechoslovakia, and these countries, in turn, also borrowed from France, Germany, and Scandinavia. Prefabrication became the socialist buzzword of the late 1950s. Materially, socialism helped produce uniformity on a mass scale. Politically, the socialist world was plagued by disagreements.

The last chapter takes up the Sino-Soviet split in the 1960s, which delivered a major blow to the idea of a harmonious socialist world. The Chinese challenge to

Soviet leadership created an opportunity for the unreconstructed party in Tirana: to retain the essential features of Stalinism but switch from Moscow to Beijing. What happened to Soviet and Eastern bloc borrowings after this dramatic split? What about all the Soviet-trained cadres, who now seemed like a liability? The same exchange mechanisms established with Moscow and the Eastern bloc had to be retooled to conform to a new geopolitical reality. State officials approached Beijing for factories, loans, weapons, and engineers. They also looked to Cuba, North Korea, and newly independent African countries for cooperation.

Speaking in the name of Stalinism, the Albanian regime challenged the homeland of socialism on Soviet terms. This *talking back* to Moscow infuriated the tantrum-prone Nikita Khrushchev, whose handling of the divergences created more backlash. But the Albanian party also became vocal against far-flung China, especially when the latter sought to quell Sino-Soviet flames. This party militancy had been long in the making, but the Soviets and the Chinese did much to feed it. The Soviet Union had launched a bold international socialist project after a total war. Later on, China began to act like a world power too. A small agrarian state along the Mediterranean had no ability to control these dynamics. But neither could these bigger powers control how that small state employed ideology against them.

TEN YEARS OF WAR

World War II has never really ended in Albania.

Harrison Salisbury (1957)

The day after Good Friday, 8 April 1939, residents of Tirana woke up to find themselves under occupation. Rumors about an Italian invasion had been circulating that whole week. On 5 April, Albania's Hungarian-born queen had given birth to a son. Within the span of those two days, King Zog, the Muslim chieftain who had established a royal dictatorship, got an heir and lost the kingdom. Desperate and defeated, he fled to Greece. (He would not step foot into the country again.) "Since yesterday," Mussolini is reported to have said with characteristic exaggeration, "Italy has been turned again into a great empire."[1] With the military occupation complete, Italian officials formed a puppet government and assumed control of the army. The parliament offered the Albanian crown to Victor Emmanuel III. An economic and customs union between the countries followed. Promptly, the Italians also set up a local Fascist party, which took its orders from Rome. But Fascist ambition was no match for Italian capacities. Humiliation ensued. In 1940, Mussolini launched a campaign to invade Greece and failed. Hitler had to come to the rescue; the Wehrmacht attacked Greece the following spring.

Mussolini's occupation set the stage for the establishment of a Communist party in the only Eastern European country that did not have one. To be sure, there had been a number of Communist-leaning activists in the 1920s and 1930s, many of them pushed into exile after Zog's overthrow of the government of Fan Noli (the "red bishop").[2] They had set up the National Revolutionary Committee in Vienna, with support from the Communist International (Comintern). One early Comintern-connected activist was Egypt-born Koço Tashko, a Harvard graduate who became involved with the Vienna committee. Tashko studied at the Lenin Institute in Moscow and then, in 1937, moved to Albania and became leader of a Communist group in the southeastern town of Korçë.[3] There were other such groups around the country, almost all of them quarreling with one another.[4] Two Yugoslav instructors, Miladin Popović and Dušan Mugoša, arrived in 1941 with the task of helping to unite the factions.[5] "We had found a real chaos," Popović later described the domestic scene.[6] After intense campaigning, some activists agreed to join forces and founded the Communist Party of Albania—the official date given as 8 November 1941.

Borrowings from Yugoslav practices were conspicuous from the beginning. Communist-led resistance groups adopted, for example, the wartime motto "Death to Fascism—freedom to the people!" Wartime army-related organizations, similarly, drew from Yugoslav methods. But such borrowings, as we will see, would later become an embarrassment. After the 1948 Stalin-Tito break, Albanian authors would insist that the party had always been native. Yugoslav accounts, in turn, insisted on the Yugoslavs' role.[7] What was supposed to be a historic moment—the founding of a young party of freedom fighters and revolutionaries—fueled accusations, for over half a century, that the Albanian organization had simply been an "appendage" of the mother party in Belgrade. But this controversy is largely a function of later quarrels. In the early 1940s, there was no contradiction in the fact that an inexperienced group could derive its strength from a popular movement for liberation and at the same time borrow extensively from the Yugoslavs, who, for their part, reveled in their organizational superiority.

One participant in the founding meeting of the party was a thirty-three-year-old activist named Enver Hoxha. Son of a Muslim merchant, Hoxha was born in Gjirokastër and briefly studied natural sciences in Montpellier on a state scholarship (issued from the same government he would later vilify). He failed to graduate, however, and moved to Paris and then Brussels, where he worked for the Albanian consulate. In his memoirs, he later claimed to have become active in French Communist circles, an idea that secondary sources have repeated without seeking out any evidence.[8] In reality, Hoxha was a latecomer to Communist interwar activities. Upon his return in 1936, he took up a teaching position at the French lycée in Korçë. There he became friendly with the local Communist faction (where Tashko was active) and, later, in Tirana, he ran a tobacco shop secretly used for party meetings. Not a widely known figure, Hoxha was elected to the provisional Central Committee and took on the role of secretary. Petro Marko, a writer who had volunteered in the Spanish Civil War, only to end up locked in Italian prisons, later recalled that people at the time, including other high-level agitators, did not know much about Hoxha. Like Yugoslav involvement, this fact became fodder for later speculation: Who stood behind this man?[9]

What he may have lacked in experience, Hoxha nevertheless made up for in ambition and appeal: in the Albanian context, he seemed like a vaguely intellectual type, youthful, and a charismatic agitator with a Francophone background (no matter how brief the exposure to the French university had been). He was not leader of any one of the factions, which would have worked to his advantage.[10] As the British recognized, Hoxha was particularly adept at appearing like "a man of moderate views," a mediator between factions.[11] "An attractive person," one 1947 US intelligence report described him, "he makes friends easily and gives the impression of being an accomplished politician."[12] Another confirmed that he was "tall, handsome, athletic," while adding that he was also "determined and aggressive, ambitious, cunning, insincere, and lacking in any fundamental ideals."[13] The clandestine nature of the party proceedings and the urgency of war also likely worked in favor of a quick solution to the problem of selecting a temporary secretary. But Hoxha would prove anything but a provisional choice.

Communist ranks increased thanks to aggressive campaigning and promises of liberty and land reform. Why did peasants in the lowlands mobilize, and, more important, how did the Communists *retain* this popular base? The sociologist Besnik Pula has emphasized institutional and legal centralization showing how the Communist regime reframed "the terms of political conflict from one involving the peasantry and the landowners, to one which found the cause of peasant grievances in the policies of the state."[14] Other domestic forces vying for power included conservative republican opponents, royalists (supporters of the exiled king), liberals, and various landowners alarmed by "the Bolshevik threat." The self-proclaimed nationalists of the National Front (Balli Kombëtar), on the other hand, were made up of agrarian and conservative elements, as well as nationalist proponents of "ethnic Albania" (which included Albanian-inhabited Kosovë/Kosovo). In the pursuit of a "popular front," the Communist Party called a conference in late 1942, out of which came the National Liberation Movement. The Communist elements within the movement, who had the advantage of not being associated with former ruling classes, presented themselves as eager to engage in warfare. The National Front, they would protest, was unwilling to do the same.

British support was another factor in the pursuit of a united front.[15] This took on added significance after Mussolini's fall in the summer of 1943 and the capitulation of Italian troops later that year, which some took to mean that a British intervention might be imminent. Instead, the Germans quickly invaded the country. Like the Italians, they put in place an "independent" government composed of nationalist figures. The Nazis also aggressively exploited the ethnic rallying cry of a "greater Albania," gaining collaborators along the way. They argued that the Reich would sustain Albanian independence in the Balkans, just as Austria-Hungary had supported its exit from the Ottoman Empire. Aware of the importance attached to land reform, a German-language paper emphasized the slogan "Bread for all of Albania."[16] When confronted with mounting partisan resistance, however, particularly along the countryside, Nazi response was ruthless. The Communist-led forces, for their part, lambasted the nationalists of the National Front as collaborators. In this context, the British struggled with the choice of a faction to support. Disagreements among local resistance groups were, as one of their memos put it, "distracting and exasperating."[17]

Some differences among the locals were clear. One British report described the partisans as "young, ill-mannered, fanatical, desperately poor, who perhaps steal on occasions." Ill prepared for sustained fighting, they were nevertheless equipped with determination: "They are sincere, irritatingly, infuriatingly sincere, and, if they are not fighting the Germans, the Germans are fighting them." The nationalists of the Front, on the other hand, did not "possess the fanatical determination of the partisans."[18] Hostility between the partisans and the nationalists escalated into bitter fighting, with the latter invoking German assistance to fight the former.[19] These choices doomed some of the principal non-Communist elements and helped clear the field amid the resistance groups. In the middle of 1944, as they grew more sure of an Allied victory, the expanded Communist-led partisan forces also turned up the violence against the nationalists and pro-Zog elements. British back-and-forth moves, on the other hand, added to suspicions over Allied intentions, based on the fear that London might seek to cooperate with Rome and Athens at the expense of Albanian territorial integrity.[20]

All of this is important for understanding the conflicting impulses that foreign presence created long before the advent of a Communist regime. In November 1944, following German retreat, Hoxha marched into the capital in triumph. Yugoslav organizational guidance, combined with British supplies, but more critically the direction of the anti-Nazi counteroffensive far away from Albania helped propel the partisans to power. Their dogged determination but also some of their opponents' wartime choices allowed the Communists to set the terms for describing what was happening on the ground. They presented themselves as the force of *action*. Their rivals, by comparison, were divided and prone to squabbles. On the one side, there were youthful fighters chanting about the glory of the future. On the other, there were older men, easily stereotyped as bent on restoring past privileges. "The regime was brought to power mainly by the enthusiasm of the youth," observed one British memo.[21] The average age of the army troops, according to witnesses, was about twenty years. The party apparatus was similarly young.[22] Not all nationalists had been Nazi collaborators, but this did not make the youthful charge against them less powerful.

The significance of Communist wartime tactics comes across in a report from Major A. V. Hare, a British officer present in Albania between November 1943 and November 1944. Alongside fighting, the major observed, the Communists placed great emphasis on education and agitprop. "The Party built up a network of political education" within the Front, he wrote, "with the task of explaining the war and the general political situation to every peasant in the zone, in just the way [the Front] wanted it explained." Hare reasoned that a political force that wished to rule in a small destitute country would, by necessity, have to rely on an outside power. The local Communists, he wrote, "naturally look to Russia." But the Communists could also be pragmatic. "In order to check the more natural tendency of the country to look to the Western allies," Hare added, "they employ strong propaganda against us through party cells, while openly maintaining sufficiently friendly relations with us to continue the flow of supplies."[23]

In retrospect, the words seem prophetic. Communist officials came to dominate the Democratic Front (a successor to the National Liberation Movement), which they were at pains to present as a broad-based organization. Joseph Jacobs, the American representative in Tirana, wrote that he had "no illusions" regarding the new regime, which he described as a "sincere, patriotic group of individuals who are going to be difficult to deal with." The officials, he explained, "are ignorant of the science of government, know little of international relations, and are highly sensitive over the fact that, after fighting a common enemy, they have as yet failed to receive any recognition except from Yugoslavia and possibly secret sympathy from the Soviet Union."[24] Belgrade had been the first to recognize Albania's new government, in May 1945. Soviet recognition followed later that year.

In the December 1945 elections, almost all the candidates on the ballot were members of the Democratic Front, and they campaigned in the name of that organization rather than the Communist Party. Party officials were intentional in not extracting the votes through force, but they worked hard to denigrate alternatives to the Front. They did not seek merely votes but verbal commitment and identification with a new social order, casting promises of support for the Front as votes for the "democrats" and hints of wavering as helping the "Fascists" and "foreign-inspired" forces.[25] Desperate for currency, the government nevertheless mobilized anti-Fascist women and youth groups to do canvassing. The chiefs of the various religious communities urged their followers to vote for the Front. The party apparatus carefully screened candidates, engaged local informants, collected rumors, and insisted on door-to-door agitation.[26] As expected, the Front won decisively.

Much of the literature on postwar Albania has highlighted the party's nationalism, which is said to have supposedly trumped its ideology.[27] This presupposes that nationalism and ideology were necessarily distinguishable, which is to say that the approach betrays a narrow definition of ideology. Just as some self-proclaimed nationalist elites had seen themselves as perfectly aligned with Fascist occupation, anti-Fascism could constitute a powerful source in shaping the worldview of a war-born organization.[28] The fervor of the victory against Fascism fed into long-standing anxieties about the country's independence. It was not necessary to have read Lenin to appreciate that the great powers had ignored Albania's national question before.[29] The British were unwilling to cause friction between Greece, Italy, and Yugoslavia on account of Albania. This is not to say that everyone readily went along with the new regime's promises. On the contrary, pockets of anti-Communist resistance persisted for years, including antigovernment rebellions. Some spoke against the regime, sensing the capillary reach of the party and hoping for an Allied intervention. "The Allies will not recognize our government," one rumor went, "because it is a totalitarian government."[30] For others, however, the totalitarian government became precisely an expression of national self-assertion.

It is not easy to write a glorious history of liberation out of such insecure beginnings. Albanian socialist-era history textbooks tried, marking the year 1945 as a kind of "zero hour."[31] The liberation of the country from Fascism became inseparable from the Communist cause. If anything, however, 1945 seems like a middle point. In terms of encounters with foreigners and their planning schemes, state designs, and forced and unforced exchanges of people, the 1940s were years of remarkable continuity. Episodes of forced exchange became routine. People made sense of alliances, property reallocations, and acts of violence on the basis of previous encounters with foreign troops and their plans. The memorialization of the war was immediate: authorities calculated that some twenty-eight thousand men and women had fallen as martyrs (dëshmorë) during the fighting. The number is disputed, but no alternative figure has emerged. War became a story, which is to say that it has invited revision ever since.

A quarter of a century ago, Jan Gross influentially called for expanding the horizon on Communist regimes by reconsidering the Second World War as a "social revolution." He argued that Communist authorities exploited the opportunities created by wartime upheaval to assert a specific kind of authority, crucially defined on the basis of denying the possibility of any alternative vision to their real and imagined rivals.[32] This simple but essential insight helps us understand regimes that seem at once all-powerful and remarkably vulnerable. The war incidentally provided an opening for bringing Albania into the international system. It enabled a small militant organization to use warlike tactics to foment social revolution. There were political opportunities for those cunning enough to seize them. The interplay of domestic dynamics and regional competition in the Balkans, however, also made these years dangerous. Party officials tried to use external actors (British, Yugoslav, Soviet) as leverage or instruments against adversaries. External pressures, on the other hand, further intensified a predisposition toward militancy and conspiratorial thinking.

"Every aspect of Albanian civilization," one author has written, "was measured by the wartime experience." War brought ordinary Albanians into close and violent contact with "foreigners, their ideas, and their guns."[33] In a continent where powerful states disappeared from the map overnight, a tiny country's future was never guaranteed. So insecurity produced a great deal of nationalist talk. But it would be wrong to interpret this kind of insecurity as ideological ambiguity. The Communists, after all, seemed to be the only ones with an answer. They inherited, by default, the political support of the Yugoslavs—"specialists of secretiveness, conspiracy, and subversion," as François Fejtő once put it—which ensured technical aid for building institutions and infrastructure.[34] Even more crucially, the Albanian Communists found themselves on the winning side of the reordering of Europe after Hitler.

Only a few years prior, Benito Mussolini had dreamed of something of a new beginning for Rome's empire. Upon the traces of that ruined vision, the "young, ill-mannered, and fanatical" Communists set out to build socialism.

Socialism with a Fascist Façade

In the backdrop to the rare pictures of partisan troops entering the capital in late 1944 one can discern the stern façades of Fascist-era administrative buildings. Tirana had not been an obvious choice for a capital. An alternative would have been Vlorë, where independence was proclaimed on 28 November 1912, or Shkodër in the north. In the context of constantly shifting borders (at one point or another, the country became host to a procession of Italian, French, Serb, and Greek troops), however, Tirana was a safer choice. Geographically central, it was neither dominated by the southerners (*tosk*) nor subject to northern (*gheg*) clans. It was a kind of meeting ground between mentalities. What it offered in terms of pragmatic politics, however, the city lacked entirely in infrastructure. In February 1920, when it officially became the capital, Tirana resembled a large village. There were not enough proper structures for government offices, so administrators set up their desks in the living rooms of large family villas.

To address the problem, Zog had embarked on an unprecedented building program supported by Italian architects, urban planners, and private contractors. Italians came to Albania to design public showcase buildings like city halls, banks, and ministries, and they also drafted the country's first regulatory urban plan. Struck by the "Oriental life" of the small country, one visitor found a few modern villas in Tirana, "a negligible urban population," and an upper class consisting "mainly of some thirty rich, land-owning families."[35] Lev Pavlovich Sukacev, who had fought with Lavr Kornilov's army in the Russian civil war and who later helped Zog launch a coup in Albania, wrote about lingering "traditional eastern ways" in the country. "You could ride on a plane of the latest type," he later recalled, "or you could ride an ass."[36] A 1925 agreement with Rome established the Società per lo Sviluppo Economico dell'Albania (SVEA, Company for the Economic Development of Albania). SVEA issued a sizable loan for the construction of roads, railroads, and land reclamation projects. The Italians, moreover, set up specialized companies and construction enterprises, whose number expanded in the 1930s.[37]

Count Galeazzo Ciano, Italy's foreign minister and Mussolini's son-in-law, envisioned the country as an outpost for Italy's expanding empire (deliberations supported by the frequently unrealistic, and sometimes fantastical, reports sent by the Italian lieutenant general in Tirana).[38] If Libya served as Italy's fourth shore, Albania would become its fifth (*quinta sponda*). The Italians had opened language courses (under the supervision of the Dante Alighieri Society) well before 1939.[39] But the country's occupation was followed by bolder plans to mobilize more and more Albanians, youths and women in particular. The puppet Fascist Party and the cultural circles propagated the Albanian-Italian bond.[40] Compared with the Nazi racial order for Europe, as Mark Mazower has put it, "Rome placed cultural diffusion ahead of racial purity."[41] To that extent, Italian advisers, journalists, reporters, and scholars descended on the neighboring country across the Adriatic to document local customs and folklore, busy at work in establishing a scientific basis for Italy's relationship to the protectorate.

Central to Italy's Mediterranean pursuits was the idea of *spazio vitale*, a kind of equivalent to the German Lebensraum and something that Fascist authorities presented as central to the future of Italian civilization. This acquired territory around the Mediterranean was not homogenous: different areas corresponded to categories of economic activity within the empire and ethnic hierarchies (according to which, East Africans were inferior to North Africans, and the "Aryan" races were closer to the imperial center). Embedded within the colonial project, Italy's Mediterranean sphere would be characterized by deeper economic integration and an intricate system of institutions aimed at binding to Rome a "first circle" of overseas territories in southern Europe. Within this matrix of territories, Albania fell somewhere between the Italian colonies in Africa and the wartime occupations of 1940–43, which included parts of France, Corsica, southern Slovenia, southwestern Croatia, the Dalmatian coast, Montenegro, most of Kosovë/Kosovo, western Macedonia, and a number of Greek territories.[42]

In devising a system for the occupied territories of the 1940s, Italian administrators constantly spoke of "an Albanian model," which, as Davide Rodogno has shown, would have informed the "new order" (*ordine nuovo*) in other occupied territories. Its features consisted of a "personal union" between the two countries and the establishment of a native Fascist party operating under the Italian party's directives, thus creating the basis of a party-state dualism that would reemerge after the war. This begins to explain why Italian officials (and their local puppets) spent so much time emphasizing Albania's independence within the union. Fascist Party members presented the union as the deepening of a long-existing bond (in fact, power rested directly with the Italian lieutenant general).

Hence Mussolini's slogan for Albania's hall at the second Exhibition of the Fascist Revolution, which connected Fascism to the Ottoman-era warrior Skanderbeg: "The flag of Skanderbeg, which will fly alongside the three colors all over Italy, manifests what kinds of sentiments drive the Italian people vis-à-vis Albania. Fascist Italy will give justice, order, and well-being to the new Albania."[43] From Tripoli's central bank (designed by the Italian architect Armando Brasini) to Tirana's (designed by Vittorio Ballio Morpurgo), the Italian preoccupation with a Mediterranean space became apparent in physical form. Tirana was supposed to be the face of this new Fascist order. Brasini, who worked on Tripoli's urban plan after getting involved with the Ministry of Colonies, turned to planning in Albania.[44] Though mostly unrealized, his ideas for the capital have shaped the city ever since. The most important of these was the decision to create a prominent north-south axis dramatically separating the old quarters from the new developments, a gesture that carried certain similarities with the architect's earlier proposals for Rome.[45]

Brasini also proposed a semicircular government square (Piazza dei Ministeri) centrally located along this axis. In another version, he proposed a full circle of administrative buildings (echoing his plans for the Vatican), but the center ultimately developed according to the semicircular orientation. Unabashedly a classicist, with designs veering toward what an Italian scholar has described as "roman baroque," Brasini's ideas for Tirana were grandiose, given the context.[46] He drafted designs for a royal palace situated along the southern edge of the city, and though state budgets were no match for his vision, his work laid the foundation for other Italian architects and planners who sought to transform Tirana in the 1930s.

One of these was Florestano di Fausto, also a presence in the colonies, who came to Albania under the auspices of the Staccioli construction company. Prior to that, he had been working in the Dodecanese Islands, where he devised a plan for Rhodes and designed numerous public buildings boasting endless arches and Venetian motifs.[47] He worked on an urban plan for Tirana (continuing the work of another Italian, Giulio Bertè) designing a series of governmental buildings along the southern edge of the central square. These were inaugurated to great fanfare in the early 1930s (see figures 3 and 4). In between these structures, di Fausto created a sunken area meant to break the long procession of the boulevard

FIGURE 3. A new order: the Ministry of Justice, Tirana, undated postcard. Arkivi Qendror Shtetëror (AQSH), Tirana, Albania.

and create the illusion of greater height (as we will see, Communist authorities would come to resent this part of the square, which hindered parades). In the late 1930s, his government ensemble in Tirana would be extended around Skanderbeg Square, with the completion of the National Bank building, designed by Morpurgo. Codesigner of the Foreign Ministry edifice in Rome, Morpurgo also designed iconic banks in Durrës and Korçë.

It was the Florentine architect Gherardo Bosio, however, who made the greatest intervention in the Albanian capital. Between 1936 and 1939, Bosio volunteered with the armed forces in Italian East Africa, devising, in the process, urban plans for Gondar, Jimma, Dessie, and Harar.[48] In Addis Ababa, he designed administrative buildings, post offices, and villas. Bosio became increasingly convinced of the need for a central office dealing with architectural design and urban planning in the Italian colonies in East Africa. He then made his way to Albania, entrusted with the task of overseeing urban planning there. Accordingly, he established the Ufficio Centrale per l'Edilizia e l'Urbanistica dell'Albania (Central Office for Construction and Urbanism of Albania), the first central agency to deal with urban planning in the country's history. For years after the war, Communist officials would refer to the Ufficio and its work.

And though Bosio's activities in the country were short-lived (he fell gravely ill and died in 1941), several other architects and engineers continued his work.[49] While retaining and developing Brasini's prominent north-south axis, Bosio zoomed in on the southern half, the Viale del Impero. He planted important administrative buildings on each side, including offices for government staffs, army headquarters, and the accidents and insurance administration. The Dajti Hotel, named after the mountain overlooking the city, was a rectangular structure along the Viale. It was hailed as one of the largest hotels in the Balkans at the time. Bosio conceived it as a total work of art, equipping the interiors with modern furniture, elaborate fixtures, and Venetian lamps. To the south, the massive north-south axis culminated in a monumental ensemble, the Piazza Littoria, created by the Casa del Fascio, the headquarters of the leisure organization Dopolavoro, and the building of the Albanian Youth of the Lictor.

Bosio created façades made of exposed stones and framed by small sculptural elements. His design for the Casa del Fascio had strong echoes of Albania's pavilion at the Fiera del Levante in Bari (which Bosio also codesigned). Both structures made reference to the tall, robust structure of the Albanian *kullë* (fortified tower), though the typical small windows of the pavilion developed into full-blown arched openings at the Casa del Fascio. An Olympic stadium was planned to the right of this ensemble, but the structure remained unfinished for much of the war. Seen from a plane, this urban layout gave the impression of a *fascio*—a bundle of sticks attached to an ax blade—but it is not clear whether this was intentional. Beyond the capital, the Ufficio produced urban plans for Vlorë, Elbasan, Durrës, and Porto Edda (named after Ciano's wife), but its most significant contribution was Tirana's master plan. Envisioned as a city of one hundred thousand inhabitants, Tirana emerged as a hybrid city of extensive gardens, glistening marble, and vernacular low-rises.[50]

Some of Bosio's projects in Africa, particularly the main building of the government square in Gondar (1938), share more than a passing resemblance to designs proposed for the Piazza del Littorio in Tirana.[51] But in many of these cases, his approach to native architectural cultures was ambiguous. He was firmly committed to the civilizational mission of Fascism and sometimes discounted native building traditions as possessing little value. Nevertheless, in Tirana he also sought to preserve "the traces of the Muslim city" but by framing them within a more rational layout of administrative buildings and public squares.[52] While emphasizing green spaces, hygiene, and order, then, the plan for Tirana also incorporated mosques and other "Oriental" elements as interspersed landmarks within the new "civilized" urban profile. Unprecedented for Albania were also the plan's suggestions for zoning, which were nevertheless not taken up by planners until the postwar period.[53]

Design throughout the 1930s and early 1940s reflected, in exaggerated form, the tensions between the various approaches among Italian planners: from Brasini's classicist and eclectic urban panoramas and di Fausto's "folkloristic"

FIGURE 4.   The Ministry of National Economy under construction, Tirana, undated photograph. In the background, the Et'hem Bey mosque and the city's Venetian-style clock tower (*kulla e sahatit*). AQSH.

administrative structures to Bosio's infusion of vernacular elements with Italian rationalism. In Africa or in the Balkans, Italian architects sought to define what an Italian imperial architecture would be, often infusing ideas of *romanità* with local building forms (as they interpreted them). This encounter between the planners and the acquired territories involved much improvisation and divergence, but Bosio also introduced something new in Albania: a total approach to the city. This entailed a move from amateurism to professional authority and greater centralization. His institutional approach to the city created a simple basis for later socialist centralization, which also demanded a comprehensive view of planning.

Scholars have insisted on the failures of Italian planning in Albania. Indeed, on their own terms, the Italians were anything but successful. Alessandro Roselli has shown how Fascist authorities envisioned large returns on their investments, which never materialized. Some of the more ambitious plans for development and colonial settlement were utterly detached from reality. Albania did not go through a full-scale industrialization. Instead, the Italians focused on a few land reclamation projects, public works, and the required infrastructure for their war effort in the Balkans.[54] The self-aggrandizing Fascist project thus failed to enact radical transformation but left in place a number of physical marks. Still, the occupation was only the culmination of longer years of involvement. The Italian legacy was broader than those four years. More than that: Communist authorities, as we will see, utilized Fascist-era infrastructural studies, blueprints, and the labor of Italian technicians well into the postwar years.

Old Plans, New Rules

Presented with many dilemmas, Communist authorities kept the Italian urban plans in place. In November 1945, the Anti-Fascist Council decided to keep Bosio's study in effect until the new government was able to draft an alternative plan "in line with our new conditions and needs."[55] In fact, this plan became the basis for many of the future plans. Similarly, Italian-drafted studies for Durrës, Elbasan, Berat, Vlorë, and Burrel became reference points for planners in the 1950s.[56] A special office within the Ministry of Public Works covered planning (as had been the case with the Ufficio Centrale). Unacknowledged, Bosio's legacy of centralization carried into the improvisations of the postwar years. This was out of necessity. The country had few qualified planners, and the government desperately focused on far more pressing issues, like expropriating the property of well-to-do families, addressing hunger, and providing shelter.

Officials calculated that close to sixty thousand structures had been destroyed during the war, including some thirty-five thousand dwellings but also smaller rural structures, shops, and mills.[57] Of course, there was good reason to exaggerate these figures ahead of filing reparation claims, but even a smaller impact would have been taxing for an ill-equipped government. The simple task of communication between the central government and local prefectures was a challenge. In light of labor and building material shortages, cities pleaded with Tirana for assistance in repairing bridges and roads. The reconstruction campaign, lauded as a turning of the page, in fact necessarily involved recycling of the old. Some officials typed their correspondence on pieces of paper still displaying the insignia of the previous regimes, including the monarchy, crossing out by hand the word "Kingdom" or typing the new names of the ministries on top of the old ones and adding "The Democratic Government of Albania."[58]

In the countryside, change became palpable thanks to the Agrarian Reform (1945–46), completed in a little over a year. Authorities expropriated large holdings (without compensation), olive trees, vineyards, and all private holdings over five hectares. They also restricted land holdings for churches and mosques. Some 172,659 hectares of land went to 70,211 families, who were not permitted to sell or lease it. The following years saw the creation of a number of state-subsidized "cooperatives." Gradually, peasants saw themselves squeezed into a system forcing them to sell produce at set prices or, subsequently, in exchange for industrial goods. This in turn provided incentives to trade in the black market. In the context of promises and pushback, collectivization proceeded slowly. The creation of a collectivist economy required rules, threats, and institutions but also incessant political education.[59]

A wave of property repossessions took over the big cities. For months, partisan forces roamed the residencies of known landowners or traders. Some enterprises formerly headed by Italians effectively continued to operate briefly but in rearranged fashion. The former firms Olivetti and Singer, for instance, merged into one general enterprise with a corresponding state-financed shop.[60] By the middle of 1946, virtually all construction enterprises in the country were nationalized, including cement and brick works, stone quarries, and shops. Government officials also took control of building materials, as evidenced by letters of protest written by some of the owners.[61] Over the following year, textile mills, shops, and cigarette factories suffered a similar fate. From the more advanced Italian companies to tiny family-owned businesses, state representatives took over machines and tools, often on the basis of requests for expropriation submitted by the recently established local committees.

In their letters, local officials argued why such and such owner ought to be subject to expropriation and how the property might be used. In framing their requests, they were careful to raise questions about how the wealth had come about ("off the back of the people"), reasoning that compensation was not, after all, necessary. Private coffee shops could be closed down under the justification that they served as meeting places for anti-Communists and degenerates.[62] In some cases, zealous local authorities went ahead with expropriations and asked for permission from the center only later, or never bothered to formalize their actions at all. At the center, the establishment of Communist rule unfolds as the story of the creation of a domineering central authority. But on the margins, this process was made possible by initiative taking ("in the name of the new people's regime"). Locally, expropriation relied on intimate knowledge of the lives and possessions of neighbors. It created opportunities for settling personal scores, acting out on past jealousies. Reliant on top-down coercion, the new regime was also enabled by these local passions unleashed by the reversal of personal fortunes.

In key areas, the government took steps to centralize production right away. Here too, there was precedent. The corporatism of the Italian occupation and the command economy of the Germans, though short-lived, had already introduced measures to place the economy under government control.[63] The emphasis on coordination and central planning in the 1940s, in other words, was not entirely foreign. By the middle of 1946, there existed a number of manufacturing cooperatives for shoemakers, tailors, steelworkers, painters, and weavers. When compiling guidelines for these cooperatives, Albanian officials simply copied Soviet regulations for production cooperatives (*artels*).[64] Nevertheless, the government also allowed for a limited number of supplies to remain in private hands, especially in areas where it could not immediately satisfy demand. In some areas, in fact, individual activity persisted for many years. By the end of the 1950s, for example, carpentry was still in the hands of individual craftsmen.[65]

In addition to shops and machines, the government sought to take control of the housing stock. Here too, expropriation often became a de facto reality before central government approvals had been issued. Some individuals received compensation, but others did not. Complaint letters sent to the central government by these individuals (petty traders, entrepreneurs, hotel owners, shopkeepers), as well as internal investigations, draw a dramatic picture of contention. They show, for example, that army staffs took over houses as they pleased.[66] Once they occupied the structures, they sought to formally nationalize them. Some local officials confiscated houses, arguing that it would have been impossible to build them under the Zog regime through honest work—and therefore, the owners must have built them by exploiting the local populace.[67] It became incumbent upon residents to prove the legitimate source of the investment. If some had, moreover, refused to support the partisan movement and if they had "poor political standing," in the new socialist parlance, the argument for confiscation grew stronger.[68]

Well into 1948, local council chiefs confiscated housing units after determining that residents had too much living space. They shuffled families from house to house, with no guarantee of retaining previous living arrangements. They also freely confiscated furniture, which was in great demand.[69] Technically, local city officials did not have the right to confiscate private belongings, but internal sources reveal that at least some felt free to circumvent the rules. As the general prosecutor admitted in October 1947, local government officials confiscated properties of arrested individuals even before courts ordered them to do so.[70] After all, the rights of previous owners could be flexible, especially if the occupants were said to have a "reactionary past" or if it could be established that a relative was hostile to "the people's regime."

In September 1947, one soldier named Astrit complained that local housing authorities had decided to take away a room from his family, which consisted of six members sharing a total of two rooms. An investigation deemed the family reactionary because a brother-in-law had escaped to Italy. A rejection of the soldier's complaint followed.[71] Needless to say, families of war veterans were in a better bargaining position. In battling over space, inhabitants also increasingly engaged in self-policing, for example, monitoring how much space others had. Grievance letters received at the Office of the Prime Minister between 1947 and

1949 contain numerous descriptions of similar episodes.[72] Some wrote to complain that they had lost their homes simply for having relatives in prison. Others reported that the housing commission had forcibly brought strangers into their homes. Still others found themselves forced out of the capital under the justification that future urban plans demanded it.

That word—*urbanizimi*—assumed an ominous quality in the postwar years. Officials used the expression *i kap/prek urbanizimi* to convey the fact that future urban planning required resettlement. And there was something appropriately physical and violating in the phrase, since *kap* is "to capture" and *prek* means "to touch." Urban planning thus made an appearance in people's lives as the "grabbing" instrument of power. Political suspects, fallen cadres, relatives of exiles, and former landowning families came to expect physical removal. And because there was no definitive urban plan, the category of undesirables to be removed could expand periodically.[73] In early 1948, the Politburo discussed a Ministry of Interior plan to remove five hundred families ("a category of families that do not need to live here"). The aim was to make room for army officers, Soviet and Yugoslav specialists, and "our people, employed by our State and Party").[74] Housing became entangled in this ongoing social battle. One's past, or family connections, could suddenly erupt into view and cause one's life to be uprooted, just as, for others, the right past and the right connections created opportunities for upward mobility.

The struggle for space took over the capital. The new regime was desperate for space, and it took whatever could be had. Government officials occupied Italian-built administrative buildings, converting leisure facilities built for Fascist youths into Communist youth meeting rooms and staff offices. Some buildings were not finished, but some ministers set up office anyway.[75] Authorities took ownership of Zog's former residences. Other obvious targets were the villas of Italian company bosses, administrators, and local collaborationist politicians but also moneyed landowners in possession of attractive properties. An Italian mission sent to deal with the repatriation of Italians observed with a sense of irritation how Albanian officials handed the best real estate to the diplomatic missions of Yugoslavia and the Soviet Union.[76] The Soviet representative received a ten-room residence that had once housed Tefik Mborja, the former secretary of the Albanian Fascist Party. The Yugoslav mission received former finance minister Fejzi Bey Alizoti's twelve-room villa.[77]

The party higher-ups themselves gravitated toward the southwestern edge of the city, an area that became known as New Tirana. There they snatched up a handful of comfortable villas, which were close to the city center but distant enough to ensure a sense of security. By 1947, virtually all the dwellings containing multiple rooms in the country had been confiscated or repopulated, except for the houses set aside for the leadership, like the residence of former prime minister Koço Kota, which had twelve rooms. Lists of confiscated villas often omitted the names of the new occupants, but it is possible to guess which ones went to the Politburo members, since only a few families were allowed to reside in buildings with multiple rooms.

As houses changed hands, so did personal libraries and valuables, including rare books, paintings, antiques, and religious objects. Some ended up in houses of culture, museums, or public libraries. Officials confiscated the book collection of Stavro Skendi, for example, and the belongings of the Franciscans and Jesuits in Shkodër, even though nobody knew what to do with the latter, and they deteriorated from neglect.[78] As a result of the scavenging, the capital's library, eventually the National Library, increased its holdings significantly. In 1947, officials drafted provisions to protect cultural monuments and archeological remains, but personal possessions were a different matter.[79] Particularly in demand were bronze statues of Mussolini, Victor Emmanuel, and the now reviled king Zog, which the military at one point planned to scrap and use for military equipment. Instead, the newly minted Committee on the Arts and Culture suggested that bronze, which was in short supply, ought to be saved, foreseeing the need to craft statues of Enver Hoxha in the near future.[80]

Along the capital's main boulevard, Bosio's Luogotenenza, originally destined to house the offices of Rome's Fascist administrator, now hosted the Communist government chief (see figure 5). Still under construction at war's end, it was completed with the help of Italian and Yugoslav specialists.[81] (It houses the prime minister's office to this day.) Zog's royal palace, which featured ornate interiors designed by Bosio, was farther away from the city center, nestled in gardens. It became known as the Palace of the Brigades, but Hoxha did not take up residence there. Instead, placed under state administration, the palace hosted important foreign guests and socialist state functions. The buildings of the Dopolavoro organization and the Casa del Fascio had similarly been meant as Fascist showpieces. The needy new regime made use of them anyway—the first housed the people's assembly, and the other eventually became the seat of the state university. Royal residences in Durrës and Shirokë would later serve as summer residences for youths.

Condemning the "propagandistic" architecture of Fascism, Communist authorities lived and worked surrounded by it. They renamed the buildings, draped red flags around the arches and the colonnades, placed red stars on the rooftops, and hung portraits of Stalin on the walls. As we will see, later urban plans for the capital sought to break the Italian heritage and isolate the old traces of a pre-Communist Albania.[82] But in the short term, the party apparatus was desperate to claim the spaces of the old regime. In 1946, Italian functionaries,

FIGURE 5.   Socialism with a Fascist façade: construction of the Luogotenenza building, August 1942. The building later housed the Office of the Prime Minister. AQSH.

who nurtured the myth of Italian benevolence abroad, admitted that some of the Fascist-era constructions "appear to be influenced by propagandist factors." They insisted, however, that this did not "take away from the fact that the program as a whole responded to the country's needs."[83] The Communist leaders would have scoffed at the idea, but their need for space nevertheless was too great.

Architectural continuity was conspicuous, but Italian engineering also informed other showcase projects of the reconstruction years. When the postwar government mobilized workers to drain the Maliq swamp in 1946—one of the showcase projects of the years of *Rindërtim* (Reconstruction)—they relied on the studies and blueprints of an Italian engineer from the 1930s, Angelo Omodeo.[84] Construction officials collected the archives of the former Italian building enterprises, contemplating what could be adopted from preexisting studies. Perhaps Fascist-era façades might be embarrassing, but what about hydraulic studies and technical reports on roads?[85] The joint Albanian-Yugoslav companies set up in the 1940s freely used the Italian materials.[86] Some blueprints had reportedly gotten lost; officials tried to track them down.[87]

It was one thing to keep Fascist-era urban plans and the villas of collaborators and Fascist-era ministers, along with their furniture, their rare books, and the letterhead with the old-regime symbols on the top corner. But the Communist government also continued to rely on Italian personnel for their knowledge and technical skill. So before Yugoslav specialists had shown up in construction sites and well before of any Soviet engineers, it was Italian expertise that would be put to use in the name of post-Fascist state building. The Italians who found themselves stuck in postwar Albania came to embody this uneasy continuity. The imperial exchange that Rome had once promoted now turned, for them, into a form of entrapment.

Italy's Miserable Souls

From Italy's "fifth shore," wartime Albania turned into a theater of Italian humiliation. At war's end, thousands of Italian soldiers still roamed the country. In 1943, there had been some hundred thousand Italians, a third of whom were nonmilitary personnel. By the following year, between twenty and thirty thousand remained.[88] "They are ragged and bare," one Italian military official described his compatriots in late 1944. He admitted that local Albanians had not mistreated them but that living conditions were unforgiving nevertheless. "The hardest works are reserved to Italians in exchange of only nourishment," he wrote, "and very often without nourishment!"[89] Even as soldiers were repatriated, thousands of Italian civilians, engineers, technicians, workers, and craftsmen remained. A diplomatic struggle over their fate ensued. Some of these civilians had arrived in Albania as early as the mid-1920s. Most had come more recently. They included mechanics (one in four) but also geologists, engineers, architects, miners, agricultural workers, and teachers.[90]

These skilled Italians were in demand. During preparations for a constituent assembly in late 1945, for example, government officials signed a contract with a local Italian entrepreneur, Eliseo Canavese, to carry out the construction work, which involved turning a theater hall into a "luxurious" assembly room.[91] On another occasion, the Ministry of Public Works requested the release of an Italian prisoner because, it argued, he was the only person in his specialty in the whole country. There was great need for people like him, the ministry argued, "especially now that construction is booming everywhere."[92] Earlier that year, during a New Year reception in January 1945, a British senior naval liaison officer noted that the Italian-designed Dajti Hotel in Tirana employed Italian staff, who worked under the orders of three Albanian commissars, "none of whom however had ever set foot in a hotel prior to the departure of the Germans."[93] Equally significant for the new regime was a contingent of Italian doctors and sanitary workers staffing the country's hospitals and health clinics.

As reports of arrests and property confiscations reached Rome, Italian diplomats began work on repatriation. In March 1945, Mario Palermo, the Italian

undersecretary for war, discussed the issue with Hoxha. Though Albanian authorities appeared willing to negotiate a deal, they were reluctant to let go of those
specialists who were deemed indispensable for the reconstruction campaign.[94]
The government agreed to issue them regular work contracts. An Italian mission
headed by Ugo Turcato sought to negotiate with the new government, but the
latter felt no urgency to conduct repatriation, drafting detailed lists of workers by specialty and identifying essential and nonessential personnel.[95] Conve-
niently, Albanian government officials used a broad definition of "specialist." At
one point, the Italian representative complained that military doctors could not
be considered specialists, but the Albanian party boss explained that a specialist
could be anyone deemed necessary for Albania's reconstruction.[96] Faced with
obstruction, Rome tried to get the best deal possible. Like the British, the Italians had to come to terms with the fact that dealing with Hoxha's government
had become unavoidable. By early 1946, there were three thousand Italians left
in the country, mostly civilians. Even after another wave of repatriation, Tirana's
government held on to several hundreds.[97]

To create the impression that Italian specialists wished to stay, government
officials pressured them to sign work contracts. Handwritten letters attest, however, that most were desperate to go back to Italy. By March 1948, for example,
there were 138 Italian specialists working in construction, and 90 of them refused
to sign new contracts.[98] Those who refused the contracts had to work without
them. Some requested to go to Italy for only a brief visit, in hopes, perhaps, that
they could trick superiors into granting them temporary leave. A smaller number
tried to negotiate better working terms, likely aware that the government would
not let them depart anytime soon. Aware of the demand for their skills, others
requested the same living conditions enjoyed by Yugoslav specialists.[99] Domenico
Casasola, to take one example, was an urban planner who had arrived in 1940. He
took a different approach, asking for his family to be brought from Italy. Others
similarly refused to sign work contracts in the absence of their families.[100]

Government authorities also encouraged a climate of suspicion and mistrust
around the Italians. Decrees explicitly instructed managers to be strict with the
Italians, but some workers appear to have treated them with respect. A circular from August 1946, for example, noted with concern that Albanian managers
and workers treated Italians and Germans "as if they were nationals of a friendly
allied state, and not of an occupying country that exploited our country and
our people."[101] Officials found it astonishing that Italian and German specialists
received privileges similar to those of Soviet and Yugoslav advisers. Such was
the professional authority some Italians commanded that Albanian workers were
taking orders from them. It was hardly possible to abolish all contact between
Albanians and Italians, but the government deemed too much contact politically

suspicious.[102] The personnel file of one Italian construction expert relayed the kind of suspicion that the government encouraged. "His attitude during the war is unclear," the biographical note clarified, "but nevertheless he must have been pro-Fascist."[103]

Many Albanians hardly recalled Fascism with fondness, but fomenting hatred against Italian specialists was not easy. Much as government superiors tried to depict them as enemies, many Italians and Albanians had created bonds during the war. Some Italians had found shelter in local homes in the mountains or the countryside.[104] Italian soldiers had ended up in a pitiful state, but the specialists still commanded respect. Three months after the government circular of August 1946, in fact, the Ministry of Public Works sent a note to the building enterprise explaining that Italians (and a few Germans) still exercised considerable power in construction. To underscore the seriousness of the problem, the note cited examples of "brutal" behavior by Italian specialists, which was not surprising, it went on, "given the fact that they are remnants of Fascism." Officials instructed that Italians be demoted to nonmanagerial positions. Though the Italians were "dressed in the garb of their profession," the note continued, "they are militants." They were to be treated, thus, as prisoners of war.[105] Indeed, some informants blamed the Italians for delays and unmet construction targets, and they denounced other Albanians who fraternized with them.[106]

The problem of the Italians stuck in Albania encapsulated the main tensions that informed the early Cold War in the Balkans. Turcato's mission was forced to leave the country in January 1946. Rome continued to profess "special interests" in Albania, but obviously it was powerless to affect anything on the ground. Noting an "increasing Soviet penetration" in Albania, one Italian Foreign Ministry memo complained that "those who have not spent a dime are now reaping the ripe fruits."[107] When Hoxha's government broached the subject of reparations, Rome grew even more frustrated. Italy had contributed to turning Albania into a modern state, Italian newspaper editorials insisted, and on the whole, Italian presence in Albania, despite Fascism's absurdities, had proven beneficial for the populace.[108] It was no use approaching Moscow either; the inevitable response, as the Italian mission in Moscow made clear, would be that the Soviet Union could not meddle in the internal affairs of another country.[109]

The Italians dealing with the Communist regime, Turcato wrote to Rome, including himself, were "poor miserable souls who navigate tempestuous and turbid waters."[110] There was more than a hint of cultural arrogance in Turcato's missives describing his interactions with the locals. The Italian personnel, moreover, appear to have been a divided lot, torn by personal conflicts and allegations of corruption. By 1948, the issue of the Italians stuck in Albania had become a contentious political subject in Italy. Alcide De Gasperi, the prime minister, bemoaned the tragic fate of Italian men and women living under Communism. Facing mounting criticism, Italian Communist Party functionaries pleaded with their Albanian counterparts to speed up repatriation.[111] The Albanian regime in turn considered that it might affect Italian elections by sending a small group of Italians back. However, authorities struggled to find "democratic-leaning" individuals within the contingent.

Some Italian specialists kept on sending pleas after promises of repatriation went unfulfilled. Bruno Mozzi, a university-trained architect who had worked in Albania since the early 1940s, submitted a request for repatriation in January 1948. He did not hear back from the Ministry of Foreign Affairs for ten months.[112] Others wrote desperate letters to the government, demanding that it deliver on its repatriation promises. They explained that they had not seen their families for years and that they lived in a "constant state of agony."[113] Government functionaries were unmoved. They argued that keeping the Italians was essential for the country's reconstruction plans, at least until Soviet or Eastern bloc specialists could replace them.[114] In June 1949, the minister of public works wrote to the Politburo that the idea was "to repatriate only those who could be easily replaced." Morale among the Italians left in the country was low, however, and so the minister asked to at least take some steps toward an eventual repatriation. This might motivate them, he argued, to work harder.[115]

Trial and Error

Boastful of its role in the liberation struggle against Italy and Germany, the Albanian party found itself, in 1945, also vulnerable in its subservience to Belgrade. Disagreements had already surfaced in the winter of the previous year, at a party plenum in Berat, where the Yugoslav representative Velimir Stojnić and a number of Albanian delegates argued that the party's wartime tactics had alienated the populace. The Communists had won the war but at what cost? They had been sectarian and vengeful. This emboldened party official Koçi Xoxe to launch an attack against Hoxha, who was humiliated and forced to admit the charges. (Stojnić, on the other hand, earned a seat in Politburo meetings.) An Orthodox tinsmith, Xoxe lacked higher education, reveled in brutality, and despised intellectual types. Unlike virtually all the other high-level officials of the party, which supposedly spoke for the proletariat, Xoxe was actually a member of the working class. Only Hoxha held more party and government posts in the postwar years. In addition to his party duties, Xoxe also served as minister of interior and chief of the security police (later known as Sigurimi). He also oversaw the special 1945 trial against "war criminals," which handed out long prison sentences and execution orders.

Nazi Germany's demise, then, and the ruthless domestic campaign against non-Communists, also ushered in a rivalry within the party echelon. In later years, Hoxha denounced the Berat plenum as Belgrade's tactic of keeping the Albanian leadership divided.[116] The Yugoslav emissaries certainly did not shy from meddling in Albanian affairs, and Stojnić exploited the intraparty tensions. As if these complications were not enough, the thorny issue of the ethnic Albanians living in Kosovë/Kosovo was a source of additional anxiety. The region's future came up repeatedly during the war, and it also came up at the meeting of the political factions in Mukje in August 1943. Some key nationalist figures had insisted on incorporation into Albania. But the Albanian Communist leaders had decided, in accordance with Belgrade's wishes, that the issue ought to be resolved after liberation. After all, would the problem of Kosovë/Kosovo not be solved within the internationalist framework that would link Belgrade and Tirana?

Within the party's leadership, there were also differences on the postwar reforms. In early 1946, one such critic was Sejfulla Malëshova, an intellectual who had spent time in the Soviet Union, where he had been expelled from the Soviet Communist Party as a Bukharinite. Put in charge of culture, education, and propaganda, Malëshova was suspicious of the radical land reform and advocated continued relations with the West. Unlike Hoxha, he was "a scholar rather than a revolutionary," as one US intelligence memo put it.[117] Charged with "opportunism" and "right deviationism," the country's foremost Marxist intellectual spent the rest of his life, after internment, as a provincial storekeeper. In 1946, Hoxha served as prime minister, minister of foreign affairs, and defense minister (in addition to being commander-in-chief and holding his party posts). Whereas intellectuals like Malëshova could be easily eliminated, Xoxe, who headed the security apparatus, continued to wield considerable authority.

The country's constitution, adopted in 1946, was essentially a copy of the Yugoslav one (that one in turn was based on the Soviet blueprint). It enshrined the confiscation of private property and the nationalization of key industries and natural resources. In July of that year, the country signed the Treaty of Friendship and Mutual Assistance with Yugoslavia.[118] Belgrade agreed to provide a substantial credit, to be paid back in Albanian goods. The next step was the creation of joint companies in charge of construction and railroads, oil, mining, electrification, navigation, and trade (as well as an Albanian-Yugoslav bank). An economic agreement laid out plans for coordination in planning, customs, and currency policy. A widely touted postwar project was the construction of the country's first railway line—originally started by the Italians—connecting Durrës with Peqin (and later extended to Elbasan). Thousands of volunteers joined the construction project, and since the majority were youths, the railroad became known as "the railroad of the youth." At the inauguration of the Durrës-Tirana segment in 1948,

FIGURE 6.   Parallel cults: the inauguration of construction work for the Durrës-Tirana railway, 11 April 1948. Enver Hoxha's portrait stands between Stalin and Tito. ATSH.

as shown in a photograph from the time (figure 6), Tito's portrait stood side by side with Hoxha's and Stalin's.[119]

Yugoslav officials took great interest in Albanian oil and minerals, which they could obtain at low prices, while Yugoslav advisers rolled into construction sites. Supervisors, electricians, geometers, and financial advisers came to the country, as did engineers and architects who were supposed to survey the land and issue recommendations for future planning.[120] Delegations traveled to Belgrade tasked with bringing Yugoslav experience on organizational matters and agrarian reform. The railroad construction company alone counted 282 Yugoslav employees by July 1947, including skilled workers.[121] In Belgrade, Albanian students enrolled in university classes in economics, education, and agriculture. Such was the need for technical skill, in fact, that education officials scrapped student requests to study medicine and politics and ordered that they specialize in engineering and construction instead.

The party hailed the agreements with Yugoslavia as the country's path to progress. At a party plenum in December 1946, Hoxha lauded the alliance. "It was very lucky for our country that such a large movement developed in Yugoslavia," he declared, "because in its absence, it would have been very difficult, if not impossible, for us to hold on to power."[122] Newspapers hailed the wartime heroism of the Yugoslav partisans and featured reports on ongoing construction work in Sarajevo or displays at Zagreb's international fair. Radio Korça's program in the spring of 1946, for example, consisted of hours of classical music and film scores but also regular programs aiming to familiarize listeners with "the new Yugoslavia."[123] Serbo-Croatian entered the school curriculum. In fact, Soviet literature and films, which Albanian authorities explicitly sought out, arrived via the Yugoslavs. Belgrade effectively served as Albania's window into the world.

During public manifestations, crowds chanted Tito's name, along with Hoxha's. "When someone shouts a slogan for one of the leaders," an August 1946 report from the Kukës party organization observed, "immediately the people call out for the other leader as well."[124] Later events and the bitter ideological squabbles between Tirana and Belgrade lend the impression of wild exaggeration to such reports. And yet there were obvious reasons for the Albanian regime to feel insecure in 1946. At the Paris Peace Conference, Greece claimed northern Epirus, a southern region within the Albanian borders. (The Soviet Union supported the Albanian delegation instead.)[125] On the occasion of May 1 festivities that year, the party apparatus urged agitators to popularize the slogan "Down with Greek claims against our territorial sovereignty!"[126] Agitators were supposed to foment "popular hatred against saboteurs," linking the work of antiparty elements with the aims of foreign powers seeking to undermine the country's territorial integrity.[127]

This helps explain why the Central Committee urged apparatchiks to emphasize the "distinct character" of relations with Yugoslavia, highlighting common wartime sacrifices and shared ideals. Slogans approved from the central apparatus included the Yugoslav-fashioned "Brotherhood and unity" and "The Alliance, the Economic Convention and, more generally, relations and cooperation between our people and the peoples of New Yugoslavia, are relations of a new type, deeply fraternal and democratic, of a kind that cannot exist between capitalist countries." Another one clarified that between Albanian and Yugoslav peoples there was no "obstacle, neither natural (borders), nor political."[128] Central Committee officials also warned that some people might draw a parallel between economic arrangements with Belgrade and those signed with Fascist Italy before the war. Accordingly, instructions explicitly warned propagandists not to make the comparison.[129] When denouncing landowners, nationalists, and the "Catholic clique," party agitators were similarly supposed to use theater, music, and plain language (në formë muhabeti) so that peasants could understand the party line without being alienated. If local customs required men and women to be seated separately during these discussions, agitators were supposed to respect them.[130]

These were months of hunger, not helped by the cold winter of 1946–47. In Shkodër, in the north, overzealous party cell propagandists claimed that the convention with Yugoslavia would mean greater food rations for everyone, prompting locals to head to the retailers, only to find that no such supplies had in fact materialized.[131] Yugoslav economic advisers pushed their Albanian counterparts for results, and one result was disgruntlement. One memo on the joint companies, for example, mentioned "resistance from various fronts" in meeting common planning objectives.[132] The companies frequently fell short of their targets, giving rise to complaints about delays in shipments from Yugoslavia and inefficient local work practices. Such companies were formally under the leadership of internal councils, but Yugoslav officials complained that Albanian branch ministries actually ran them.

Relations with Yugoslav experts raised technical questions, which, in light of the ideological orientation of the regime, were politically tricky. There were unresolved issues of hierarchy, competencies, and division of labor. In the summer of 1947, Savo Zlatić, the Yugoslav representative, complained to the Albanian party leadership that Albanian cadres were too slow and ineffective in fulfilling the plan.[133] It remained unclear who was in charge at various levels of governance. Moreover, Albanian authorities were not always sure how to categorize the skills of the Yugoslavs for salary purposes.[134] Add to this the presence of Italian and some Soviet specialists, which also complicated tasks like devising comparable salary scales.[135] Albanian officials found some Yugoslav specialists politically suspect and complained that others were irresponsible.[136] Like the Italians, some Yugoslav specialists seem to have been subjected to the same categories of ideological classification as locals—beyond class provenance and work habits, some personnel files linger on their alleged wartime loyalties and whether they had aided the Yugoslav partisans.[137] In other words, speaking the same mutually intelligible conspiratorial language seems to have *facilitated* resentment.

Amid the Yugoslav-Albanian contingent helping with railroad construction, for example, suspicions of willful resistance to achieving construction targets pitted specialists against one another. Yugoslav officials complained that Albanian colleagues had called them "saboteurs." There were also reported rumors that the Yugoslav technicians behaved as "occupiers" in Albania. The party apparatus launched an investigation, warning that some Albanian managers held "incorrect" views about their Yugoslav colleagues.[138] Grueling pressure from above seems to have exacerbated work-site relations, but the party investigation also underscored the political stakes. At the state building enterprise, conflicts arose out of professional and age differences. Investigations showed that specialists had reportedly divided themselves into small rival groups. The Albanian director of the enterprise admitted that because the focus had been on "benefiting from the experience of the Yugoslavs," he had ignored the Yugoslavs' lax attitude. Looking the other way, in other words, had been politically motivated.[139] At the top,

Yugoslav party representatives pressed their Albanian counterparts for accelerating the economic integration of the two countries. Disputes at the lower levels, however, showed that such integration could hardly be achieved by decree.[140]

Hoxha, who longed for direct access to Moscow, got his opportunity to meet Stalin in the summer of 1947. His delegation brought along the party statute and other documents, which, the Soviet hosts told them, contained expressions that showed "immaturity" in the knowledge of Marxism-Leninism. Stalin also recommended changing the party's name to the Party of Labor of Albania, given the demographic reality of the base and the projected industrial future of the country. In response to Hoxha's complaints about insufficient Yugoslav support, Stalin insisted that Albania needed Yugoslavia. The road to Moscow, as the Soviet representative in Tirana would put it, would have to go through Belgrade.[141] Upon his return home, Hoxha delivered a rousing speech to a crowd assembled in the capital. "We saw astonishing things in the Soviet Union," he declared, describing "factories among the greatest and most modern in the world." The Soviet Union was an example of order and discipline and above all, political will. Without the Soviet Union, Albanians would have been haunted by "an ominous fate." They were bound to the Soviets "by blood."[142]

After Hoxha's Moscow visit, Belgrade turned up the pressure on the Albanian leadership. The planning deficiencies and the stalled integration of the two national economies, the Yugoslav representative now claimed, revealed "an anti-Yugoslav line" within the Albanian party.[143] It was a thoroughly Stalinist move, directed at self-proclaimed admirers of Stalinism. The serious charge caused great commotion within the Albanian leadership. Nako Spiru, the young and impressionable chief of the National Planning Commission, shouldered most of the blame for diverging from the Yugoslav path. Confronted by Xoxe's attacks, orchestrated with the help of Zlatić, Hoxha stepped back and let Spiru take the fall. Seemingly alone, Spiru desperately tried to obtain support from the Soviets but then, feeling cornered, committed suicide. Aware of these treacherous dynamics, Hoxha fell in line with Yugoslav demands and professed loyalty to the cause of economic unification—on the financial terms dictated by Belgrade. In early 1948, he vigorously condemned the anti-Yugoslav elements within the party, going so far as even nominating Tito to be secretary of the Albanian party.[144]

Escalating Soviet-Yugoslav tensions in the spring of that year, however, put the Albanian leadership in an increasingly tough position.[145] On the one hand, many Albanian higher-ups did not find it difficult to sympathize with Stalin's accusations that Tito had fostered undemocratic principles. On the other, the charges did not exactly make the Albanians look good, since they had gone along with Yugoslav advice—in fact, they had hailed Yugoslavia as a guarantee for Albania's socialism. Hoxha's tactic, which he would deploy again and again over the years, was to wait as long as possible without openly choosing a side and then profess to have been on the "right" side all along. Indeed, both the Yugoslavs and the Albanians later put forward diverging (and manipulated) versions of the 1948 events.[146] Hoxha presented himself as having stood up to Tito when in fact he had cunningly stepped back to save his own skin.

Such was the pressure that Hoxha even turned against his comrade-in-arms Mehmet Shehu. Born into a middle-class Muslim family, Shehu had studied at the vocational school in Tirana and then in Naples (where he had been expelled for his leftist activities). He then joined the Garibaldi international brigade during the Spanish Civil War and became a member of the Spanish Communist Party. Internment in France followed, as did membership in the French Communist Party, and, after the war, a course of study at the Voroshilov Military Academy in Moscow. In short, Shehu possessed impeccably internationalist credentials, and he also enjoyed a reputation as a tough military man. In early 1948, however, he came under fire for alleged factionalism and for stalling plans for integration with Yugoslavia.[147]

Stalin recalled Soviet military personnel and specialists from Yugoslavia, and Moscow also sought to remove the Soviet specialists stationed in Albania. By April, relations between Tirana and Belgrade had further deteriorated. Hoxha's about-face was sudden, but he made it seem as if Belgrade's plans had become apparent only through Soviet accusations. "The Soviet Union's revelation of this traitorous work," he noted in a government meeting on 30 June, "saved our people from catastrophe. The Soviet Union saved our country for a second time." What would happen to Albania once the Yugoslavs were gone? Hoxha sought to instill confidence. "We will get help," he added, "first and foremost, from the Soviet Union and the people's democracies."[148] All the work that had gone into pursuing economic integration with Yugoslavia was now obsolete. The party ushered in an aggressive campaign of rooting out "pro-Yugoslav" types—merely months after the assaults against supposed "anti-Yugoslav" elements.

The rift between Moscow and Belgrade inaugurated the June 1948 meeting of the Communist Information Bureau (Cominform), which expelled Yugoslavia.[149] Several valuable studies, based on declassified sources, have shed considerable light on the schism. Most authors agree that Yugoslav policy in the Balkans, and especially Tito's moves toward Bulgaria and Albania, alienated the Soviet leader.[150] Particularly aggravating for Stalin was the fact that Tito had failed to consult with Moscow prior to making moves with Bulgaria and Albania, including a tentative effort to send military divisions to Albania in early 1948, with the rationale that they were supposed to offer protection in the event of a Greek attack. (Albania had served as a station point for supplies to guerrilla forces across the border.) Hoxha initially agreed to the Yugoslav proposal but was careful to inform Moscow. Stalin fumed at Tito's audacity.

In a preamble to the vicious show trials that engulfed the Eastern bloc in the late 1940s and early 1950s, Xoxe, the security police chief, submitted to the same kind of gruesome interrogation tactics that he himself had overseen. Declared guilty of conspiring for Belgrade, he was executed by firing squad in June 1949. At this point, and in subsequent moments of geopolitical turmoil, the Albanian party leaders behaved as if they were at war. In a way, they *were* still at war—a war in part of their own making. The party they presided over was essentially a wartime conspiracy. This obsession with internal enemies did not have to be imported from Moscow; it had been present all along. But it would also be wrong to see in this brutal history a reflection of some kind of Balkan ethnonationalism, a trap that many authors have been unable to avoid. After all, the whole Eastern bloc became engulfed in violent purges and social upheaval in the early 1950s. Terror was enabled by a history of internecine violence. Postwar geopolitics, which the leaders of a small state could not control, in turn heightened the sense of ever-present conspiracies.

Conspiracy All Around

Having recently championed Albanian-Yugoslav brotherhood, Communist cadres now faced the task of vilifying Tito's Yugoslavia. Government authorities declared agreements void and confiscated the holdings of the joint companies, including their archives.[151] Yugoslavia, they charged, had enacted a "colonialist" policy against a needy neighbor. Planning failures had been a result of Belgrade's "sabotage"—a charge against Yugoslav railroad specialists that, you will recall, had already come up in 1947, only to be revived.[152] Accordingly, bureaucrats spent considerable time recording the wrongdoings of Yugoslav specialists, assessing the financial damage, and accounting for material losses.[153] During the summer, party cells met to discuss the Yugoslav betrayal.[154] Then, at a plenum in September 1948, the Albanian party leader revised the entire party history of the previous four years, condemning Yugoslav meddling in internal affairs and hailing Stalin's intervention as essential in saving Albania from Tito's plot. It was now necessary to establish the Soviet Union firmly in the hearts and minds of party members. Whereas Mehmet Shehu resumed his duties, Xoxe was singled out for retribution.

This narrative of a sustained conspiracy against the party required the elimination of compromising details. It was necessary, for example, to go through texts and take out embarrassing references or put away publications that contradicted the new party line. Yugoslav books disappeared from library shelves. A government decree specified the list of authors (Tito, Vladimir Dedijer, Milovan Djilas) whose works, in any language, were now banned. Necessarily, Hoxha's own past speeches, which had glorified Yugoslav-Albanian relations, had to be withdrawn—a process supervised by his wife, Nexhmije. Officials also suggested withdrawing official publications—congress proceedings, memoranda, economic plans, textbooks—and virtually anything that might reveal just how far the Albanian party leadership had moved toward a union with Yugoslavia.[155] The schism did not just put the censors in motion. Yugoslav technicians left behind unfinished work. Albanian students enrolled in Yugoslav universities suddenly had to cut their studies short. (Education officials scrambled to reroute them to other Eastern bloc capitals.)[156] With the Yugoslavs gone, according to the French minister in Tirana, "almost the only persons with any technical knowledge still in Albania are 500 Italians who have still not been repatriated." In the face of such difficulties, he predicted turmoil.[157]

On the other side of the Atlantic, US intelligence services also took note of food shortages, crop failures, and the plight of the regime.[158] "The uneducated Albanian people," observed one intelligence report, "having little conception of the way of life of other more advanced peoples, naturally accept without due criticism the statements of the government." Skillfully combining arrogance with ignorance, the report blamed Communist success on "the naturally avaricious, selfish, and vengeful nature of the Albanian."[159] Another piece, written roughly two months later, predicted that the selfish, vengeful, and propaganda-blinded Albanians would, after all, rise up. "Aversion to the present Communist regime of Albania is spreading through all strata of society," it noted. "At the present time, not only the confirmed anti-Communists and the persons without any party allegiances, but also about seventy percent of those who once believed in Communism, are opposed to the regime."[160] That same year, the British and the American intelligence services decided that Albania, now physically isolated from the Communist bloc, offered an ideal setting for rolling back the Soviet sphere through covert operations.

The Western analysts got it wrong. No mass uprising materialized. The regime survived the schism. Discontent, of which there was no shortage, did not morph into mass rebellion. There were several reasons for this. First, by the late 1940s, the regime had solidified its hold over much of the country, which did not mean that propaganda had blinded the inhabitants but that the scope for an alternative form of government had narrowed tremendously. Second, the Stalin-Tito schism incidentally aligned Albania's national independence with the prospect of Soviet-style modernity. Third, the regime blamed its failures and acts of terror on Xoxe, just as it now blamed Belgrade for wanting to colonize Albania, just as

Fascist Italy had sought to do. Charges against the Yugoslavs could be fabricated if necessary, but they seemed plausible, especially given the secrecy shrouding party affairs. Having aided the Albanian Communist cause, Yugoslavia could now serve as an effective scapegoat.

What Western observers also failed to grasp was that while socialist planning necessarily came to Albania with foreigners attached, the idea of social revolution held appeal in a desperately poor country. To be sure, there were constant rumors of power struggles between Hoxha and Shehu, which US intelligence sources picked up and which then resurfaced in scholarly accounts of the postwar period as indications of intraparty struggles. If one desperately looked for indications of resistance to the regime, it was possible to find them. In the early 1950s, Anglo-American covert missions included parachuting agents trained abroad so that they could foment a rebellion, dropping leaflets urging resistance, and broadcasting clandestine radio programs. The results were disastrous: infiltrators ended up being put on trial and humiliated in public. One British observer, who had served as a liaison during the war, wrote that these Anglo-American clandestine efforts merely boosted Hoxha's "long-standing propaganda line about the hostility of the capitalist powers and their nefarious intentions."[161]

It is true that some party officials had come to experience Yugoslav influence as suffocating. But the 1948 schism allowed Hoxha and his supporters to frame Xoxe as a traitor. Just as the Hungarian party chief Mátyás Rákosi, an erstwhile admirer of Tito, had quickly turned into a vicious critic of Tito, so Hoxha gleefully joined the campaign against the Yugoslav leader. The immediate targets, however, were Xoxe and his security apparatus, Sigurimi, which, unsurprisingly, had developed in line with Yugoslav experience. A modest agency, called the Secret Office, had already been established in the 1920s, under Zog (later known as the Political Office). But it was the anti-Fascist struggle that shaped the party's approach to the security apparatus.[162] Mirroring Yugoslav arrangements, the security police had developed as an amateur operative network within the army. At the end of 1944, the People's Defense Department (Drejtoria e Mbrojtjes së Popullit) came into being, along the lines of its Yugoslav counterpart (Odeljenje za zaštitu naroda).[163]

Sigurimi's formal establishment dates from 1946, the year when the Yugoslav State Security Administration (Uprava državne bezbednosti) also came into being. Placed under the Ministry of Interior, it drew its personnel from trusted, and often illiterate, veterans from the partisan contingent.[164] Lacking professional operatives, Sigurimi indulged in informal rampages. A group of security officials moved to the Soviet Union for training in September 1947. Some reports made mention of Soviet security liaisons. The work practices, however, came from Belgrade, as the Politburo itself acknowledged.[165] Hoxha blamed Xoxe for having placed the security apparatus above the party. Sure enough, after the requisite interrogation, Xoxe admitted at his trial that Albanian operatives had intensely copied Yugoslav organizational models. Much of this learning reportedly occurred informally, and it is difficult to substantiate it. But was it surprising that the Albanian security operatives had imitated the Yugoslavs?

Evidence of Yugoslav influence, which the party had vigorously championed, now turned into a liability. The party had to demonstrate its authority over the security police, accordingly launching a reorganization campaign designed to identify suspicious elements within operative ranks. The blame for the excesses of the postwar years, however, fell largely on the shoulders of the slain Xoxe and a minority of rotten cadres. "I can speak with competence on this subject," Mehmet Shehu, who took over as interior minister in 1948, told Chinese visitors many years later. "There are hardly any cases from Koçi Xoxe's days that were handled according to socialist laws."[166] Shehu claimed that Xoxe's operatives had placed under surveillance virtually the entire party leadership. The man had ruled by terror and acted as if the security apparatus had been his personal domain. Things had deteriorated to the point, Shehu claimed, that every "vagabond" employed by the ministry of interior could murder any person at will.

This version of history had a double effect. On the one hand, by way of purging Xoxe, the party establishment admitted the recent practice of fabricated charges and show trials. On the other, the intraparty struggle allowed Hoxha and his collaborators to associate all these crimes with the person of Xoxe (just as Khrushchev would do, years later, with Stalin). The Xoxe-led brutes who had terrorized innocent inhabitants, the new party line went, had not just betrayed the party but also worked against the nation. Hoxha presented himself as intent on curbing abuse and excising infiltrators from the ranks of the security police. In later conversations with the Chinese, Mehmet Shehu admitted that the most important lesson the Albanian leadership had learned in the late 1940s was the necessity of controlling the security police.[167] Hoxha never forgot that lesson.

What Does a Communist Party Do?

Yugoslav tutelage had provided a rudimentary example of governance. With the advisers gone, it now became necessary to devise new rules. Instinctively, Albanian officials rushed to their Soviet counterparts for guidance. The party, which had been in power for years, was still not confident about how a Communist party ought to operate. How did the Central Committee relate to state organs? How could the Central Committee oversee the mass organizations (youth, women, trade unions)? Did party organizations directly supervise production?

What was the job of a general secretary? Who reported to whom within the party apparatus? Then there was the problem of the army, which had followed Yugoslav organizational examples. Should it undergo reorganization? What kind?[168] Such dilemmas reflected a specific condition: a party dictatorship established by an underground movement in the absence of long-standing professional revolutionaries.

In large part, Albanian apparatchiks were doing what was expected of them. They asked the Soviets for guidance on organizational matters. How much of this came about from a sense of freedom from Yugoslav patronage and how much from a sense of fear of getting things wrong is hard to say. Perhaps the people involved could not say either. To obtain the answers, a party delegation traveled to Moscow in February 1949. In addressing the Soviets as instructors, Albanian apparatchiks manifested allegiance, but the fact of the matter was that they also simply did not comprehend how the Soviet party-state functioned at different levels of society. They hardly needed the Soviets to provide them with myths about a liberation war. Neither did they require Soviet guidance in adopting the vicious language ("Tito clique," "Titoite traitors") that engulfed the Eastern bloc in the late 1940s and the early 1950s. They spoke that language already, and they had fought their war. But how to actually govern? Ignorance in organizational matters might have been debilitating, but after the summer of 1948, the Albanian party was again on the right side of history—first anti-Fascism, now Stalinism.

In early 1949, the party chief returned to Moscow for a second meeting with Stalin. Two years earlier he had been told that Yugoslavia was a necessary ally. This time, Hoxha arrived as a staunch ally in the Communist offensive against Tito. Albania's road to Moscow was now clear. Still, Stalin offered more words of caution. Soviet-style policies (collectivization, nationalization of industries), which the Albanian regime had eagerly adopted, had been rushed, he told the visiting delegation. In the context of a poor agrarian country, an alliance with the bourgeoisie was a necessary first step. Albania had very limited arable land; creating kolkhozes there would infuriate the poor peasants. Would Moscow provide Soviet specialists to assist with planning? Yes, but only until the Albanian planners could run their own affairs.

In short, the Albanians were premature Stalinists. Their country was an accidental satellite. For Stalin, backward Albania resembled China, and he offered Hoxha the same advice that he said he had given Mao. It was necessary to tolerate petty traders at first and proceed only later toward the nationalization of all enterprises.[169] Earlier, Mikhail Suslov, in charge of relations with foreign Communist parties, had similarly warned the delegation that Albania could not "mechanically" adopt Soviet policies. Running a party composed of six million members was an entirely different task than running a party of fifty thousand.[170]

The delegation dutifully wrote down what they heard, including the recommendation not to dutifully do what the Soviets did. Then they returned home armed with a loan of 100 million rubles and "Soviet experience" in matters of propaganda and personnel.[171] The following year, the Albanian party chief wrote again to Suslov, asking for more instructions on issues of personnel, competencies, and party discipline.[172]

If the security police had fallen prey to Yugoslav influence, as the new party line went, it was necessary to discipline it. Accordingly, in 1949, Hoxha asked Stalin for permission to send forty security operatives to the Soviet Union for training. The Soviet chief deemed it best to send Soviet instructors to Albania instead. In his pleas, Hoxha betrayed anxiety. He admitted that the Albanian security police still used the ciphering system that it had borrowed from Yugoslavia. This meant that Belgrade could easily decode secret messages.[173] In another meeting with Stalin two years later, Hoxha asked for more Soviet security advisers.[174] Then, in March 1952, the Soviet government decided to admit twenty-five Albanian security police operatives into a one-year-long training course in the Soviet Union. A group of another thirty-five operatives followed after that.[175] Collaboration with security police contacts in the rest of the Eastern bloc similarly expanded. Within a few years, Sigurimi's ranks swelled. In 1948, the apparatus consisted of a staff of 679 officers and civilians. Within two years, it more than doubled.[176]

Compared with Belgrade, Moscow also held the prospect of far greater economic assistance. Accordingly, government officials pleaded for industrial products, railway tracks, replacement parts, factory blueprints, and skilled technicians. Soviet experts were needed in railway and housing construction.[177] Transportation needs were so acute that in the fall of 1948 Albanian trade officials agreed to pay cash for one hundred ZIS trucks.[178] That same year, the Soviet steamship *Pushkin* arrived in the coastal city of Durrës loaded with corn, industrial machines, and agricultural tools. More ships arrived the following months, unloading wheat, steel, tractors, trucks, tools, and tires. One repatriated POW told British diplomats in Belgrade that shelves in the stores had emptied as soon as the Yugoslavs had left the country. Still, clerks had quickly restocked them as soon as Soviet ships had reached the ports.[179] Tirana's military hospital, which treated patients with tuberculosis, reportedly relied on Soviet Russia for quinine, penicillin, and aspirin.[180] "Russian grain, tractors, and ZIS trucks," recalled a local witness decades later, "were received in Albania like gifts falling from heaven" (see figure 7).[181]

Interactions with Moscow reveal a desire to adopt and comply. So what was different from previous relations with Italians and Yugoslavs? Dependency on other states had proven frustrating in the past, but neither Italy nor Yugoslavia had been great powers. Moreover, far from being an immediate threat, Stalin's

FIGURE 7. Boxes of industrial equipment shipped from the Soviet Union arrive in Albania, February 1951. ATSH.

Soviet Union was distant. By the late 1940s, Albania was primed for Soviet-style planning through the Italian and Yugoslav precedents. The country was ready for the fast-track jump to modernity on offer with the Soviet economic model. The crucial difference was that the Stalin-Tito schism incidentally made it possible to assert Albania's independence vis-à-vis a more powerful neighbor. Indeed, it is difficult to understand this early history without an appreciation of the continued existence of an ideological half-brother across the border.

It was possible to erase Yugoslavia from textbooks. It was possible to tear down Tito's photographs and ban Dedijer's texts. It was possible to kill Xoxe and blame his henchmen for abuses and murders. But Yugoslavia did not vanish. Tito's regime did not collapse. In fact, the infusion of Western capital ("in bed with the capitalists!" the Albanian party boss fumed) and, later, the Soviet Union's warming up to Belgrade in the mid-1950s would make that neighbor seem doubly threatening: both as a kind of ersatz West (permissive cultural politics, consumerism, tourism) and—at the same time—as an alternative model of socialism (abandoned collectivization, decentralization, worker self-management). How could one compete with such an opponent? A symbolic defeat of Yugoslavia became even more important precisely because of the blood that had been spilled in the 1940s.

Propelled to power by war, the Albanian party launched the building of socialism with illiterate peasants, convict laborers, and Italian engineers. None of these people made it into the official history of the state-championed reconstruction. The predominantly illiterate former partisans continued to speak the language of war because it had been their only education. One's wartime activities, moreover, became an essential part of one's official history—how the state made sense of the individual.[182] This became even more important in light of the anti-Tito hysteria that enveloped the Eastern bloc in the early 1950s. One's wartime activities thus entered employment records (*karakteristika të punës*), and past actions became a factor for determining eligibility for future posts and hence for upward social mobility. The difference was that after 1948, an additional potentially incriminating aspect of one's biography was also one's attitude toward Yugoslavia.

Seen as a whole, the 1940s emerge as years of maniacal change. Yesterday's friends turned out to have been enemies all along. With the passing of a law, former owners lost properties and found themselves banished from cities. High-placed functionaries found themselves standing before a firing squad, accused of having committed errors that only the previous month had not been errors at all. Fortunes reversed with breathtaking speed. In the spring, the emblems of the Federal People's Republic of Yugoslavia flooded the capital. By autumn, they had disappeared from view. Reversals often involved violence, and newer acts of violence invited the elaboration of more ideological explanations. It is tempting for the historian to go back and point to all the discrepancies and the inconsistencies in the official records of events. It is important, however, to remember that the party's power—a wartime conspiracy that created its own heroic narrative—did not depend on this kind of consistency.

The stakes for being caught on the wrong side of this evolving narrative became evident in the malaria-infested canals of Maliq—recall the draining of the swamps mentioned earlier in this chapter. In 1946, as planned targets had gone unmet, authorities launched a vicious campaign to identify saboteurs in Maliq. Some of the Yugoslav specialists blamed the Italian technicians for "impeding the growth of the Albanian cadres."[183] Local workers, in turn, denounced foreign specialists for "not caring about the property of the Albanian people."[184] On November 8, 1946, the fifth anniversary of the party's founding, ten engineers and technicians, including a married couple and two Italians, stood on trial for sabotage. Six of the accused received death sentences.

Two years later, the Yugoslavs had disappeared from Maliq. Soviet specialists began trickling in. The plan was to build a new sugar refinery where there had been swamps and wasteland before, so Soviet technicians brought blueprints for a workers' town, complete with a house of culture and a movie theater. Here was the ultimate expression of a decade of war: a project that had long preoccupied King Zog (now exiled in Egypt), Italian engineers, and Yugoslav economic advisers now turned into a demonstration of Soviet modernity.[185] The long arduous battle against malaria gave way to a battle against imaginary saboteurs and class enemies. Arshi Pipa was a twenty-eight-year-old poet born in Shkodër who had studied philosophy in Florence in the early 1940s. After the war, he fell afoul of authorities and ended up in the labor camps attached to Maliq. In between the grueling shifts, he recorded scenes of cruelty on tiny pieces of cigarette rolling paper. The Soviets did not need to bring the gulag to this corner of Europe. It was already here, waiting for them:

> Canals like the ones connecting Moscow
> with the Volga, dams and power plants
> and fields that once
>
> were swamps and steppes—proof and testimony
> of what millions of slaves can accomplish.
> Our labor is a smaller replica of all that.[186]

THE DISCOVERY OF A WORLD

Few Albanians have ever seen a Russian except in moving pictures and illustrated magazines and it is a long way indeed from Tirana to Moscow! But on the walls of Albanian villages I have seen pictures, clipped from magazines, of Stalin and the heroic Cossacks, of Uzbeks and Tatars. I have heard old women saying: "The Red Army saved us also."

Il'ia Ehrenburg (1945)

"But you Balkan folk have legends of a different class—they're almost as good as Lithuanian folklore! But what's the use? Socialist realism forbids us to write about them." That was what Maskiavicius used to say, but you couldn't rely on him. He changed his opinions as often as his shirts.

Ismail Kadare, *Twilight of the Eastern Gods*

The Sovietization of Albania is a story of machines. From spinning machinery for cotton mills, freight cars, ZIS and GAZ trucks, tractors, and blueprints to the rise of factories and worker settlements, the Soviets came to be known not by the stomping feet of army troops but through the hum of engines and the wonders of industry. In the 1950s, Albania bore more than a passing resemblance to the Soviet Union of the 1930s. If that resemblance appears almost self-evident in retrospect, it is largely because Albanian party authorities vigorously embraced it. They assumed that the country would go through the trials that the Soviet Union had gone through in previous decades, which in turn affected planning decisions that may otherwise appear out of context. Nothing demonstrated the promise of socialism better than the sight of smokestacks and heavy machines.

But it is also the story of a new horizon: books, film reels, music, theater, images, national costumes, curiosities, unfamiliar references, and distant lands made to appear closer. In short, material exchange (trade) between like-minded regimes went hand in hand with expanding knowledge. In this corner of Europe, international contacts were certainly not new, but they expanded to new places, introducing references to unfamiliar territories all the way to East Asia. Eventually, contacts with this wider world would have to be centrally planned too, although that did not mean that it was possible to determine how borrowing unfolded or that there was no informal interaction beyond the control of party and government authorities. In mapping this mental world of socialism, it becomes necessary to capture the possibilities inherent in the process as well as the unintended consequences.

This socialist horizon looked different depending on who you were and where you stood—different to a Polish worker in ravaged Warsaw, different to a German woman raped somewhere along the Red Army's march to Berlin, different to some ambitious apparatchik in a Central European province, different to an illiterate peasant clinging to a piece of land on the fringes in the Balkans. But virtually everyone came to discover this new horizon in some way. It was enforced by rules, extolled by propaganda, and made part of everyday life. It would be only partially correct to imagine the world of socialism as the territorial stretch of "red states," spanning the eastern half of the European continent, traversing the Ural Mountains and flowing into Asia. It was more than territory. This emerging mental map was a mosaic of texts (including banned texts), ideas, official rites, and associations. For a country like Albania, this kind of contact was unprecedented in scope—of a different magnitude, even, than the incredibly wide-ranging world once encompassing the Ottoman Empire.

This was the discovery of a socialist world. Rooted in violence, the Soviet encounter with Eastern Europe was not one-sided, despite Moscow's assumed and asserted superiority. Soviet soldiers and operatives also came to know the world they tried to conquer and manage. In wartime Europe, writes Vladislav Zubok, Soviet officers often "turned into marauding beasts" having witnessed riches they could not obtain at home. They pillaged accordingly, amassing "war booty, from silk stockings and wrist-watches to tapestries, bicycles, and pianos." The more educated ones "brought home books—literature and philosophy—and precious vinyl records of classical music." Among them, a young Boris Slutsky discovered in Prague and Belgrade "the richness of Russian heritage preserved there in libraries, numerous journals, and Russian churches."[1]

The establishment of Communist regimes in Eastern Europe is often written as a story of struggle. Soviet advisers sought to implement a distinct set of policies—in government affairs, in universities, inside factories—which provoked resistance and backlash.[2] When we step back, however, and take stock of the scale of Soviet international engagement after 1945, it is not the failures that seem surprising. Given the scope of that engagement, how could there have been no failures? The picture that emerges, in fact, is one of Soviet planners caught unprepared by the demands of a new "civilizing mission" in Europe and Asia. It was not written anywhere that the adoption of a Soviet model would have to be total. Even if there had been a master plan for spreading Soviet-type institutions across Eurasia, there was no blueprint to adjudicate all the possible problems of implementation across such a vast geography. If during the early Cold War, Western observers obsessed over the captivity of East Europeans, it seems that more recently, after the opening of archives, we have become fixated on Soviet failures. But it was also possible to look at the Soviet model (party rule plus central planning) and find it by turns repressive, frightening, suffocating, promising, inspiring, and—in the context of a volatile setting in the war-torn Balkans—inevitable.

In a now-classic account of Soviet power in East Germany, Norman Naimark has recounted the myriad obstacles Soviet operatives faced there, including the embarrassing realization that many Germans deemed Soviet culture inferior and that the Soviet cultural organizations tasked with targeting the Germans were sluggish and ineffective. The Soviets Bolshevized the zone, he writes, "not because there was a plan to do so, but because that was the only way they knew how to organize society." They came to Germany "with commonly shared historical experiences and social instincts that influenced the development of occupation policy as much if not more than articulated principles of ideology."[3] Elsewhere, encounters might unfold differently because the challenges were different.[4] But the Soviets brought their history, their instincts, and their experience with the workings of a dual party-state everywhere they went. The scale of Soviet engagement is best understood at both the local and transnational levels since, over time, developments in some parts of the socialist world affected other parts.

In Albania, where the Soviet Union came to be known not as a constant military presence but as a distant mighty patron, local inhabitants also came to view themselves through a new perspective. Rather than asking whether Sovietization succeeded or failed, it is possible to approach the encounter with Soviet ways and means as a kind of opening, as a field of interaction. This shifts the emphasis to the way in which the adoption of Soviet references coincided with the discovery of socialism as a world and how this exposure enabled individuals to make claims—about themselves, society, and the world. A country like Albania was of limited strategic value compared with, say, Germany or Poland. But it did acquire a certain value within the geography of postwar socialism. It becomes necessary, therefore, to think of strategies of discovery, with their intended and unintended outcomes, and how beliefs were tested by transnational encounters. A new socialist world came about not because the imposition of Soviet policy succeeded everywhere, or because it succeeded on its own terms. Rather, a new socialist world emerged because it became possible to see oneself through a socialist lens.

Mental Map

Albanian visitors were struck by what they encountered in the Soviet Union: the grand architecture, vast open construction sites, people on the move, and, inevitably, the awe-provoking descent into Moscow's metro. High-level functionaries appeared dazzled by the glistening marble of the underground stations, covered floor to ceiling in socialist tableaus.[5] One such affected observer was Koço Tashko, the Harvard-educated activist mobilized by the Comintern in the 1930s to help organize an Albanian Communist Party. In an account of an earlier stay, Tashko recalled Moscow as a magical place. "The metro stations," he wrote, were "truly palaces, both in their architecture and quality of construction." He had gone from Paris, "where one would almost faint from lack of fresh air while waiting for the metro at rush hour," a city that had struck him as "dark, bare concrete, filthy all over, poorly lit." Since wealthy Parisians owned cars, Tashko reasoned, authorities did not care to keep the city clean. Moscow was different. "When it is not possible to give everyone a palace," he offered, "then, as a start, people are given collective palaces. Theaters, department stores, schools, hospitals, and the metro are all built like palaces and not merely as tools for profit."[6]

Along with the intellectuals, Albanian peasants also made the journey east and described a modern, well-ordered society. "If I were literate," one such peasant by the name of Ali Kuka told a journalist in 1950, "I would surely need to write a big book to describe all that I saw in the Soviet Union." As reported, other villagers had been so taken with Ali's colorful Soviet stories that they had volunteered to join the collective farm. "We are blessed to have such a great and powerful friend!" one peasant sporting a moustache and a white fez was said to have declared. "May Allah grant a long life to the party and Enver."[7] The reference to Allah may seem surprising, but it should not; in the early 1950s, Albanian Muslim clerics also traveled to the "homeland of socialism," where they visited Moscow (Lenin's mausoleum), Tashkent, and Samarkand. "From all that we saw and experienced firsthand," wrote one Bektashi cleric, "we saw the truth on the issue of religion and the mosque in the Soviet Union, the truth on the moral and political unity of believers in the Soviet Union, the truth on the fraternal Soviet peoples."[8]

Most Albanians could not make the trip, but they also came to know the Soviet Union. Increasingly, in the 1950s, a flood of Soviet cultural figures descended upon the country: Stalin Prize laureates, famed pianists, violin virtuosos, opera singers, *tsirk* performers, ballerinas, and orchestras from the republics. What started out as intermittent exchange soon turned into state-enforced routine. By the middle of the decade, officials would sometimes ask for Soviet artists by name (though this did not mean that their wishes were always granted). In turn, when arranging these delegations, Soviet authorities made sure to mix highbrow cultural elements (classical music) with folk numbers and mass entertainment. They also took care to combine representatives from various republics and ethnic backgrounds—mimicking, in fact, the Soviet Union itself. In a given delegation there might be, say, Russian artists, Georgian dancers, a Ukrainian performer, or a record-breaking laborer from Central Asia.

Thus the Soviet national arts came to this corner of the Balkans. Il'ia Ehren-burg, the celebrated novelist and war journalist, had been among the first of the visitors. He found a country both mysterious and memorable, casting it, as count-less other foreigners had done, as a Roman-Oriental meeting ground: "Here is a truly magnificent landscape—mountains, deep, quiet lakes, valleys covered with flowers and grapes, olive trees, fig trees, the gentle coast of the Adriatic. Here many peoples and cultures have intermingled, uniting the marble of ancient Rome with the cupolas of Byzantium and the flamboyant architecture of Islam."[9] Ehrenburg, who became a patron to aspiring Albanian authors in Moscow, was followed by other Soviet visitors such as Aleksandr Tvardovsky, the renowned Soviet poet who recited *The Land of Muravia* to packed halls; the soprano Valeria Barsova; and Ol'ga Lepeshinskaia, the Bolshoi ballerina rumored to have been Stalin's favorite. Readings and concerts were held in the capital's movie theaters and clubs, but Soviet delegations also toured smaller cities. Often they performed out in the open, weather permitting, since adequate venues were limited.

These visitors, too, understood Albania on their own (Soviet) terms. When describing what they saw, they referred to places back in the Soviet Union, to familiar historical processes from *their own* experience of building socialism. When a group of Soviet visitors traveled to the oil fields of Kuçovë (renamed Qyteti Stalin, or Stalin City, in 1950), the town struck them as an "Albanian Baku." Some locals seemed receptive to the analogy. "They understand us," one Albanian author wrote in reference to the visitors, "because many years ago they themselves went through a period like this."[10] And while some may have found the analogy far-fetched, the growing presence of the Soviet Union in the late 1940s and early 1950s, particularly in a place like Stalin City (depicted in fig-ure 8), became hard to miss.

Local authorities were eager to embrace the analogy to the Soviet past. For one thing, it made perceived backwardness—material and social—seem like a temporary condition on a path to progress. Ehrenburg wrote that everywhere he had traveled in the country, he had heard of firsts: the first pedagogical institute, the first textile mill, the first railroad, the first generation of artists to take the stage. "Albania's star," he declared, "is only just beginning to rise." He had been moved: "Is this not something of a miracle? The same war that turned to ashes the empire of the 'superman' has given birth to a brand-new state in a remote

FIGURE 8. Meeting of the staff of a "high-quality brigade," Qyteti Stalin (Stalin City), March 1952. The banner hanging above Lenin's portrait reads, "Long Live the Mother Bolshevik Party!" ATSH.

corner of Europe."[11] Socialism would make Albania less remote. Elsewhere in ravaged Eastern Europe, hopes of national paths to Communism would inspire generations of reformers wrestling with the arrogant Soviet example. But in this corner, where territorial integrity had never before been guaranteed, Soviet power carried obvious appeal.

The encounter with the Soviet Union could also be unsettling. For one thing, getting to know Soviet achievements brought into sharp relief that Albania lagged far behind. But if Moscow seemed daunting, it was possible to discover more familiar ground farther away—in the Georgian countryside, in Azerbaijan, or the kolkhozes of Dagestan.[12] Albanians came to know these places because their Moscow hosts sent them there, assuming that Albania, with its peasant

population and "backwardness," had much in common with the Caucasus or
Central Asian republics. When the writer Shevqet Musaraj visited the Soviet
Union in 1949 ("the country I have dreamed of for years, the glorious country
of Lenin and Stalin, the hope and joy of all people"), the hosts suggested that he
travel to Georgia. He was told that the republic had problems similar to Albania's.[13] In subsequent years, Soviet authorities would routinely compare Albania's
development path with that of their own republics. One party delegation sought
organizational experience in Azerbaijan, where it interviewed local officials, and
issued recommendations back at home.[14] In 1953 a friendship delegation visited
Moscow and Leningrad but also stopped by a tractor factory in Minsk and a

FIGURE 9.   Gathering in honor of the Nineteenth Congress of the CPSU, Tirana,
5 October 1952. The prewar municipality building, later demolished, is adorned
with portraits of Hoxha and Stalin. ATSH.

textile combine in Tashkent. The visit to Uzbekistan, they reported, had been particularly enlightening, given common interest in cotton production.[15]

Whence such associations between the Albanian and Soviet republics? Those who articulated them pointed to such objective features as a rural economy, industrial aspirations, and lingering social conservatism. The populations of Albania and certain Soviet republics apparently shared similar customs, religion (Islam), and a way of life. All of this was undoubtedly vague. But what made such comparisons compelling was the emancipation inherent in a narrative of former imperial backwaters turned into flourishing socialist republics. That the comparison between Albania and Azerbaijan might be deeply flawed did not fundamentally make that narrative less powerful. If illiteracy had disappeared in the Soviet Union, and socially conservative individuals had openly embraced the building of socialism, why not in Albania? Not everyone, as we will see, readily embraced this point of view. Along the borderlands, some Albanians felt closer to Greece or Italy. European powers had long been involved in the Balkans, and a handful of intellectuals had long insisted on the country's Western orientation. But after the calamity of the Second World War, Albania's western and southern neighbors were in chaos. Party propaganda did not magically make people sympathetic to the Soviet Union. One only needed to look around to appreciate the circumstances.

There were, then, two processes occurring simultaneously. On the one hand, Soviet officials explained Albania's place in the world using their own terms. During meetings with the Albanian party chief in 1949, Stalin asked about Albania's ethnic makeup, the origins of its language, and whether Hoxha, a Muslim, ate pork.[16] The incidental Balkan ally had to be placed somewhere on the map of Soviet world relations. The Soviet higher-ups behaved imperially in such meetings, but in the case of Albania the arrogance also came with a sense of celebration. Little-known Albania had liberated itself from the Nazis and successfully established Communist power. Still, the country desperately needed to catch up with the industrialized world. It had several advantages. First of all, it was small (roughly the size of Armenia, the smallest of the Soviet republics). And since the Soviet Union had decades of experience, this meant that it would be possible to overcome backwardness in even less time. To the extent that Soviet officials genuinely tried to get to know their Albanian counterparts, such knowledge was merely meant to confirm something they already knew: where the country was headed and how it was supposed to get there.

On the other hand, a range of Albanians explained the Soviet Union in terms that made sense to them. Logically, some associated Moscow with money and technical aid, both of which were vital for lifting the country from poverty. For high-level party officials, the Soviet Union presented a security guarantee.

(Hence, making the Soviets familiar with Albania could be construed as a national security concern.) Moreover, the Albanian state lacked the means to promote its interests abroad. The Soviet Union might serve as a giant amplifier of those interests.[17] If Yugoslavia had tried to annex Albania, as the party line now put it, Moscow had no such interest. Stalinism was thus the path out of isolation—the formula for articulating Albanian national interests in the language of proletarian internationalism. The Soviet worldview, shaped by ideology and boosted by the world-historic crushing of Fascism, was by necessity far more expansive than the Albanian. But it was possible to see one's aspirations reflected in it. Geographical distance, which allowed the Albanian regime room to breathe, also required constant mapping. Men and women had to be reminded, repeatedly, of their place in the socialist world.

Talk of friendship came with gross exaggerations. But for many, it also came with new personal experiences, opportunities for mobility, and a sense of discovery. The register of socialism, with its ready-made official phrases and assumptions, also had a corresponding geography. The Soviet Union became a lens through which it was possible to see one's aspirations telescoped into the future. The Soviet encounter, in other words, was the promise of integration into international society. This process is best understood, therefore, not along some spectrum of acceptance and rejection or failure and success, which have long been the dominant tropes in the study of Communist rule. More to the point is to show how discovery—invited, expected, celebrated, disappointing, humbling, eye-opening—created a field for interaction and articulation. It meant new possibilities and a set of terms for reasoning about an imperfect socialist reality. Not only that—these were also terms for making sense of developments around the world.

Moscow Days

Of those who came to discover the socialist world, students constituted a large share. The country's need for educated professionals was only too obvious. Illiteracy was rampant, and the regime pursued it aggressively, at first relying on volunteer-led campaigns but then making it mandatory that all adults under forty learn how to read and write. Officially, illiteracy was declared eradicated in the mid-1950s, but in some segments of the population it persisted well into the 1960s.[18] In the meantime, however, there was great need for engineers, doctors, lawyers, teachers, scientists, and translators. Some professions had to be invented because they did not exist at all. As a result, requests went out to Moscow and Eastern bloc governments for scholarships, in addition to specialists.[19] For a poor country, this kind of exposure was more significant than numbers might initially suggest. Those hundreds of educated youths in the 1950s, in fact, would constitute the country's elite for decades to come.

The numbers, which were modest in the beginning, picked up over the years. In 1948, when the Politburo addressed the issue, there were 586 students abroad.[20] A decade later, a total of 1,240 youths had graduated from Soviet and Eastern bloc universities (another 820 were still enrolled that year), excluding military students and short-term trainees.[21] Like virtually everything else, foreign university spots became part of the central plan, which meant that "correct" allocations required, well, a lot of planning. In theory, allocations were meant to reflect actual needs, as indicated by local enterprises and then sent up the chain of command for assessment, all the way to the State Planning Commission. In practice, as with other aspects of early planning more broadly, decisions were haphazard. Planning officials chose the recipients on the basis of personal "characteristics" (karakteristikë) such as social class and family background and then slashed the requests, which were inevitably larger than the available scholarships.

Bureaucratic errors, as a result, were a common occurrence. The need might arise to switch a student's field of study, which had been decided beforehand, midway through the academic year. A student of mathematics, for example, might be reassigned to medicine, or one from literature to engineering. Confusion ensued also on the matter of determining the social origin of students chosen to study abroad. A scholarship to Moscow (or Warsaw, or Prague) was a coveted prize. Planning officials favored party members, partisans, or those stemming from poor peasant stock. Nevertheless, they admitted committing "political errors" when approving applications from youths lacking the "right" credentials.[22] Such bureaucratic choices held important ideological meaning. A socialist planner might be expected to obsess over the preparation of engineers and economists, but the scholarship lists reflect more than industrial concerns. (Officials were careful, for example, to also allocate posts for schoolteachers.) Underscoring the limited number of available scholarships in 1955, the State Planning Commission agreed to only a quarter of the requested scholarships abroad and suggested concentrating on the most important fields. These might include engineering but also philosophy and Marxism.[23]

For those who earned it, the journey east was physically demanding. In these early years, youths sent to the Soviet Union would have to travel for a week or more to reach their final destination. They would board a ship to Odessa (a trip that might take six days, depending on available connections), and from there they would continue by train for an additional day or two. Upon arrival, they would have to quickly learn to negotiate in a foreign language and through unfamiliar university practices. During their summer breaks back home, they sometimes also served as "ambassadors," as party officials sent them on tours across the country to popularize the Soviet Union or whatever socialist country happened to host them. Officials were suspicious of older prewar intellectuals, including many Catholic men of letters, who had the ability to translate from foreign languages. So they asked some of these students to translate from Russian—books, articles, pamphlets, movies, construction manuals, or technical specifications for industrial machines. Students were caught between two realities: their Albanian past and the Soviet present.

Gani Strazimiri was one such individual. Born in 1917 into a peasant family of means, he had studied painting at Tirana's lycée but held aspirations of becoming an architect. He enrolled in the architecture program in Turin, Italy, but abandoned his studies and joined the partisans back home. Strazimiri's father, a well-known northern fighter, opened his home to the partisans and died during the war. Shortly thereafter, Gani earned a scholarship to study architecture in Moscow, "in the country he came to love profoundly," as one 1953 celebratory article put it, "the great homeland of Socialism."[24] His story followed familiar themes: early aspirations put on hold by the patriotic duty to combat Fascism, sacrifice, and ultimately great reward. But the story was actually more complicated than suggested in the Albanian-Soviet friendship journal. Gani's personnel file mentions all these details but also lingers on the fact that his brother had been accused of showing "sympathy for the Germans."[25] Strazimiri belonged to a generation that sought, in the late 1940s and early 1950s, to make up for lost wartime years. More than a systemic imperative or economic rallying cry, "catching up" could also become a personal mission.

For his thesis, Strazimiri decided to draft an urban plan for the Albanian capital. In handwritten correspondence with officials back home, he expressed the wish that the plan be executed following his graduation. From the deputy minister of construction, he asked to receive the drawings, plans, and studies left by Italian planners, as well as photographs of the capital and an overview of recent construction work. "You know very well in what conditions I will be working tomorrow in Tirana," he wrote in a 1949 letter, "where I will be laboring almost completely on my own in a field where it is difficult to work without solid foundations." Strazimiri also asked for money to buy books, without which, he noted, it would be impossible to write a thesis or do anything meaningful for the city's planning.[26] It is unclear whether Strazimiri received the money, but the Italian-drafted urban plans were shipped a couple of months later, in November, including street plans, studies on mountain terraces, maps, and building prototype designs.[27]

This high-level commitment to one student's thesis, and the urgency evident in the correspondence, is explained by the fact that Tirana lacked a socialist urban plan. Strazimiri received direct guidance from Spiro Koleka, the deputy prime minister and an Italy-trained civil engineer who went on to have a long party career. The young architect proposed a plan for a city of around two hundred thousand, a system of transportation composed of bus lines (though, in the future, workers would use trams to reach the city's industrial sectors). Residential buildings would be limited to five or six stories.[28] Compared with the Italian designs that had preceded it, Strazimiri's plan was different in conception but showed similar ambition. The draft correspondence sent to the prime minister for approval observed that Strazimiri had rejected prior Italian urban planning schemes as "inappropriate for a social system that progresses toward socialism."[29] In fact, the proposal accepted some key choices made by the Italians, including the north-south axis and the two main "rings" around the central urban area.

The city center, on the other hand, proved difficult to solve. Strazimiri's plan called for monumental government edifices similar to the ones that dotted Moscow. The government was to be housed in a palace facing the main city square, as shown in figure 10, raised on a granite platform and endowed with a permanent tribune to accommodate party leaders during mass parades. A statue of Stalin would rise on a platform in front of the façade. On the other side, there would be a similarly grand people's theater. These were choices shaped by Soviet architectural training, of course, but they also reflected aspirations at home. "What is concerning for Tirana," the ministry memo in support of Strazimiri's plan explained, "is the fact that even if the Italian plan were to be executed, there would be no possibility for the kinds of demonstrations, parades, and gatherings that we organize now and that we will always organize in the future."[30]

More daringly, Strazimiri's plan called for the destruction of several Italian-designed buildings, including the national bank, the Defense Ministry, and the city hall. This would have concerned budget-conscious bureaucrats, so the ministry argued that it was a necessary step. The Fascist-inspired façades of these structures "may not seem like a problem today," it argued, "but they will in the future." Once new socialist structures were completed, it would no longer be acceptable to keep Fascist façades. To further bolster this argument, the ministry underscored the fact that the new plan was based on "the new socialist basis in urban planning and the way in which construction is done in the Soviet Union."[31] Not all presocialist structures would be demolished, however. The Et'hem Bey mosque and the nearby clock tower would stay, preserved as examples of "structures built by the people." The Fascist urban plan, which resembled a *fascio littorio* from up high, however, had to be broken. Accordingly, the plan shifted the city's ring to disturb the visual character of the *littorio*, and it also suggested removing—at some unspecified date—the former Casa del Fascio building altogether, suggesting instead a memorial complex to the Second World War perched on the Shën Prokopi hill.

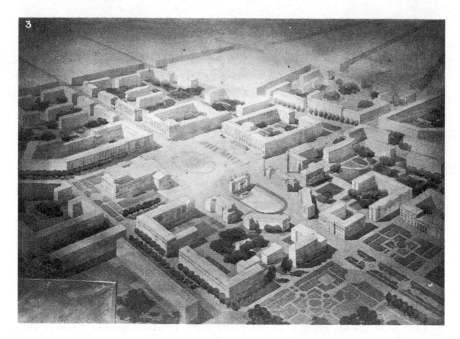

FIGURE 10.   A socialist capital: Gani Strazimiri's study for Tirana, conceived at the Architectural Institute in Moscow, December 1950. AQSH.

None of this mattered, because party higher-ups did not ultimately adopt Strazimiri's plan. When discussing it in 1952, Politburo members were reluctant to use a student thesis as a city master plan. Instead, they invited Soviet architects to carry out the task.[32] Neither did the Italian-designed buildings, with few notable exceptions, face demolition. It is likely that the costs of replacing them were too great.[33] Other projects took precedence in the allocation of money and labor, especially industrial ones. The only idea that became a reality was the statue of Stalin, cast in bronze in the Soviet Union, based on a design by Nikolai Tomsky, who specialized in the genre. His hand tucked under his jacket, Stalin rose south of the city's main square. Even that transaction was not without embarrassment. A while back, Albanian apparatchiks had apparently assumed that the Soviets would present the statue as a gift. But then cost estimates came along (140,000 rubles), while Albanian officials pleaded with the Soviets for the statue's measurements so that a proper base could be manufactured.[34] Just getting Stalin on a pedestal on time (which did not happen until November 1951) turned into an ordeal; building a whole city based on Soviet blueprints was a different matter entirely.

Soviet credentials helped build careers, and Strazimiri quickly established himself in the country's first urban planning office. He designed residential buildings in Tirana's Kongresi i Përmetit Street, in the Shallvare area, and along the city's canal (depicted in figure 11). Arranged according to the Soviet *kvartaly* system of blocks, the structures look similar to Soviet buildings in Rostov-on-Don or Novosibirsk's Kirov district.[35] They featured tall arches, columns, bay windows, and arched balustrades—notable façades in a city that still largely resembled a large village with a smattering of Fascist-era administrative buildings. Without a whole master plan to go with them, Strazimiri's structures seemed impressive but also out of context. The palaces had no larger district to go with them. Some of those who, like Strazimiri, discovered the Soviet Union in the 1950s, might have felt similarly out of context upon their return to Albania. They came equipped with the right credentials. They received desirable jobs. But their superiors were typically less educated than they were. Party officials incessantly spoke of being close to the Soviet Union, but intimate familiarity with the Soviet Union also made Albania seem remote.

FIGURE 11.   Soviet-inspired residential building in the Shallvare area, Tirana, late 1950s. ATSH.

Forging a Friendship

Press accounts and official textbooks claimed that Albanians had been historically bound to the Soviet Union. This was a bold claim. To back it up, authors and apparatchiks pored over old newspapers, delved into personal records, and painstakingly sought to piece together a narrative of centuries-old friendship between Albanians and Russians. They did so in part because of the greater effort, overseen by the party apparatus, to integrate the Party of Labor into a longer history of struggle against Ottoman rule, foreign occupation, and nascent class consciousness. They also did so because the period immediately following the dangerous schism with Belgrade was one of profound insecurity. Before Albania became a founding member of the Warsaw Pact in 1955, such a security guarantee could not be taken for granted.[36] Soviet leaders may have treated Albania, at most, as an afterthought. But a peripheral regime's devotion also reflected deep-running paranoia about its enemies.

It was one thing to affirm the Albanian party as the culmination of a historic struggle and long-held aspirations for freedom—a progressive vision of history crowned by the epoch-defining defeat of Fascism. It was another to try to integrate Albania into the history of the Soviet-led Communist international struggle. Other East European regimes could point to prewar political movements, labor-based organization, and direct contacts with Moscow. There was also a history of pan-Slavism. In Hungary, under Béla Kun, there had even been a short-lived Communist state after the First World War. In Albania, a legacy of international Communism had to be brought into being. Therefore, party operatives developed a genealogy of sorts: the story of an old dream having come alive amid the ravages of war. They did so for self-serving reasons, of course. A genealogy of Albanian-Soviet contacts helped make the possibilities of the future seem all the more plausible.

Agitprop officials, writers, lecturers, and hired researchers combed through documents and old newspapers to locate references to the Soviet Union, Lenin, or the Bolsheviks. They emphasized, for example, that on 4 February 1924, Avni Rustemi, at that point a member of parliament, had demanded that his colleagues observe a minute of silence in honor of Lenin. Rustemi, who later became celebrated as a "revolutionary democrat," was shot within months of that February meeting, lending a mythic air to the episode. Three decades later, this event came to signify some preexisting history behind the Soviet-Albanian bond. Newspapers wrote about other Albanian patriots who had been infatuated with the Bolshevik experiment. They carried stories about marching local partisans singing Red Army songs or Albanian mothers sending their sons off to war with a picture of Stalin folded in a pocket. Some of the partisans reportedly had been avid readers of the *History of the Communist Party of the Soviet Union,* or the *Short Course.* Others had reportedly gathered in the heat of battle to commemorate the anniversary of Lenin's death and to extol the victories of the Red Army.

Discovery went beyond textual evidence, turning into a kind of archaeological practice. Visitors at the Tirana war museum encountered a worn-out volume on a display board—Stalin's short biography—said to have belonged to a partisan by the name of Mustafa Asllani. Looking closer, they would have noticed that the book had a hole (the result of a "Fascist bullet"). A bullet had pierced a Soviet book and taken an Albanian life. The book then reportedly traveled, from partisan to partisan, from Vlorë to Shkodër, zigzagging the country, all the way to Yugoslavia, where "it helped spread the truth of Marxism-Leninism."[37] Another discovery took place in Shkodër, the bastion of Albanian Catholicism. In a wooden case buried under a building, close to a cattle shed, city officials found rifles, dynamite, propaganda leaflets, and books (Gorky's "In the Steppe," Dostoyevsky's *Demons,* Tolstoy's nonfiction), in addition to a Russian language teaching method written in Serbian, which included texts from Lenin and Stalin. "These documents show," one author explained, "that Albanian Communists and partisans illegally learned Russian, the language of the great Lenin, because it would enable them to learn the science of Marxism- Leninism that would guide them in liberating the country from oppressors and in building a new life in Albania."[38]

When the Politburo discussed a draft of the first history of the party in 1950, it ordered that the Russian revolution be used as a template for casting the Albanian party's own history.[39] Three years later, officials from the Central Committee agitprop department screened school textbooks for "political errors," singling out "non-Marxist-Leninist" explanations and "petit bourgeois" traces. They found that first-, second-, and third-graders were not reading enough about the Soviet Union. (The suggestion was to add more Soviet poems.) Moreover, school children learned nothing at all about the "miserable life of children under the yoke of capitalism." High school textbooks, similarly, were due for revision in accordance with the latest Soviet theories on pedagogy and linguistics.[40]

Then, in the summer of 1958, a team of authors traveled to Moscow to discuss a textbook draft of the country's history going back to ancient times. Suggestions from the Institute of History of the Soviet Academy of Sciences included making 1912 (Albania's year of independence) "the beginning of the modern period, but by connecting it to the broader crisis of the capitalist system and the Great October Socialist Revolution."[41] Similarly, accounts could make the connection by emphasizing the Russo-Turkish War (1768–74) and the participation of Albanian-speaking warriors. "Turkish barbarism" was said to have produced a small Albanian diaspora in Ukraine, where the descendants of the Albanians had created kolkhozes and lived happy "within the big Soviet family." The narrative then typically moved to Lenin's defense of Albania's independence (against the imperialism of Italy and Austria-Hungary). Finally, and triumphantly, Albania had emerged in the same camp as the Soviet Union, through its heroic anti-Fascist struggle. Such an account was not limited to children's textbooks; it could also be found in diplomatic memos.[42]

The Albanians were newcomers to "socialist friendship," which might also explain the zeal. In fact, Soviet authorities had cultivated "friendship" long before Albania even had a party. Founded in 1925, the Vsesoiuznoe obshchestvo kul'turnykh sviazei s zagranitsei (VOKS, the All-Union Society for Cultural Ties Abroad) served a dual role: assisting pro-Soviet "friendship circles" abroad and hosting foreign intellectuals and sympathetic fellow travelers in the Soviet Union. In the interwar period, Soviet cultural diplomacy mirrored the regime's obsession with the West. The pattern set was one of both rejection and imitation, as Michael David-Fox has outlined it in the best study on the topic.[43] This meant rejecting capitalist society, with its cruel markets and human exploitation, but also achieving and overcoming capitalism's standing in the world economy. Well before the 1940s, then, this combined pattern of superiority and inferiority had acquired an institutional form in Moscow. Ironically, the Stalinist terror and the all-consuming war had the consequence of leaving in place a form of cultural diplomacy that had all the ambitions but none of the capacity to effectively satisfy demand in a newly acquired sphere in Europe.

Czechs, Poles, Hungarians, and Germans became implicated in friendship work. Typically, friendship societies started out as "cultural" initiatives but then grew into mass organizations. By 1956, for instance, the League of Polish-Soviet Friendship counted 7.5 million members. Its Romanian equivalent had 6 million by the following year.[44] In China, the Sino-Soviet Friendship Association reached more than 68 million members within three years of its establishment (though the number included the People's Liberation Army).[45] It is difficult to say how much of this membership was merely formal. But even accounting for vast exaggeration, it is clear that friendship societies served as levers of mobilization. Formally, the organizations appeared independent from the party. In practice, however, they sought to mobilize people in much the same way as party operatives would do but without the expectation that members would formally join the party. This was important because party membership was not available to all.

From Germany to China, friendship organizations oversaw personnel, buildings, clubs, movie theaters, libraries, and occasionally printing presses. They set up Russian language courses, which by the late 1950s enrolled tens of thousands of individuals. They typically oversaw a network of regional offices, and they published in magazines carrying titles such as *Shqipëri-B.R.S.S.* and *Miqësija*

(Albania), *Ország-Világ* (Hungary), *and Freie Welt* (East Germany), *Veac Nou* and *U.R.S.S. azi* (Romania), *Przyjaźń* (Poland), *Svět sovětů* and *Praha-Moskva* (Czechoslovakia), as well as others in Austria, Bulgaria, and North Korea.[46] Local propagandists depended on VOKS for materials and guidance, but even if that institution had had the capacity or wish to command this kind of activity across a sixth of the earth, it would have been impossible. Inevitably, friendship work involved improvisation and learning on both sides. Soviet officials had to learn how to behave like a Communist force on a civilizing mission—but in an internationalist spirit.

Far from disappearing, that challenge became more pronounced after Stalin's death in 1953. In 1958, a new organization replaced VOKS, now associated with the Stalin era. This was the Soiuz sovetskikh obshchestv druzhby i kul'turnoi sviazi s zarubezhnymi stranami (SSOD, the Union of Soviet Societies of Friendship and Cultural Ties with Foreign Countries), which was divided into sections covering different world regions. Up until then, for the most part, Soviet friendship had been something that projected *toward* Moscow. But in the late 1950s on a so- called public initiative, which in fact was internal criticism that the Soviet Union practiced one-sided cultural diplomacy, friendship societies were also established in Moscow. This was supposed to correct the one-sided relations under Stalin and helps explain the effort that went into making Soviet influence seem less direct in places like Albania.[47] (Inadvertently, it also created tensions with the Albanian leadership, which sought more involvement, not less.) Previously, other countries had dutifully celebrated Soviet holidays. Now, Albania's liberation would also be celebrated in Armenia and Kazakhstan.[48]

Cultural diplomacy was not a Soviet invention, and socialist states were not the only ones to establish such contacts. In the 1950s, the United States increasingly propagated capitalism as a superior economic model and way of life in the countries of Western Europe, along with specific cultural models (art, architecture, literature) that were said to be associated with freedom and individualism.[49] On the ruins of Nazism, these competing socioeconomic visions created battleground areas. Germany is an obvious example. But think also of Japan, Greece, Indonesia, and Yugoslavia. "The Soviets aspired," writes Michael David-Fox, "to alter not merely the views but also the world views of visitors."[50] Soviet cultural diplomacy also came with specific assumptions, expectations, and institutions.

Mechanisms of Discovery

Established on 5 November 1945, the League of Albanian-Soviet Cultural Ties was at first a modest affair. In anticipation of the anniversary of the October

Revolution, a telegram informed Moscow that the league had been presented at a mass rally composed of "workers and friends of Albanian Culture."[51] The gathering comprised around four hundred cultural figures and elected a board, which included well-known writers and high-level party functionaries. The league also received an elegant villa.[52] Its headquarters were equipped with a conference room, a movie theater, and a cafeteria. The library consisted of a collection of some five thousand titles, including seventeen volumes of Lenin's works, Russian-language editions of Stalin's, Marx and Engels (in Italian), and also Fadeev, Grossman, Lermontov, Tolstoy, and Turgenev (mostly in French). Grounds around the villa also hosted a volleyball court and a ping-pong area—all privileges accorded to league members.[53]

Like similar organizations in Eastern Europe, the league initially called itself a "cultural" initiative and opened exhibits promoting the Soviet Union, held public lectures, and screened films. In August 1947, it began publishing a journal titled *Shqipëri B.R.S.S.* (*Albania USSR*). The league also produced a radio program ("Getting to Know the Soviet Union"), familiarizing listeners, as the name implies, with Soviet achievements. It led the commemoration of Soviet holidays: the October Revolution, Red Army Day, Lenin's birthday.[54] In 1949, for example, the celebration of Stalin's birthday spanned twenty days and included lectures, concerts, and a street-naming ceremony.[55] To draw in youths, the organization hosted "cultural evenings" featuring Soviet music.[56] Local branches opened in other Albanian districts (*rreth*), initially in Korçë, Gjirokastër, Vlorë, Durrës, Elbasan, Shkodër, Kukës, and Peshkopi. These entities similarly administered buildings and small libraries, and they held evening classes.

Under Yugoslav tutelage, between 1944 and 1948, vigorous promotion of the Soviet Union had carried some risk. When the league's president, the state planning chief Nako Spiru, had visited Moscow in April 1947, for example, Yugoslav officials had fretted that the "cultural delegation" in fact concealed a political motive. Were the Albanians seeking to bypass Belgrade? After visiting Moscow schools, Tbilisi's university, and the Armenian Academy of Sciences, the delegation then had gone on a tour in Albania, lecturing on the wonders they had encountered in the Soviet Union.[57] Friendship societies in 1948 were limited to Yugoslavia, Bulgaria, and the Soviet Union, and though Yugoslavia had a privileged position in propaganda, party authorities also expressed sympathy for the Soviet Union. When developing school textbooks, for example, they recommended following Soviet examples in addition to Yugoslav ones.

The schism with Belgrade, however, as we have seen, required revision: the security police had to be reined in, the history of Yugoslav involvement rewritten. It also became necessary to reconfigure friendship propaganda. But unlike the Yugoslavs, Soviet authorities seemed reluctant to dictate how to do this. There was the question of the league. Should it be folded under the party apparatus? Who would run it? And who would appoint those running it? How was the party apparatus supposed to balance domestic propaganda with propaganda abroad? Politburo members understood that a central apparatus was necessary to oversee the league. But the dual nature of the party-state, which was at the core of Communist power, also raised organizational and oversight questions with no obvious solution. Some thought that the Central Committee's agitprop department ought to direct every kind of propaganda. But would that not result in the league's simply being a replica of the agitprop department?

Functionaries sought the answers from the Soviet representative in Tirana. He recommended, contrary to what the Yugoslavs had done, opening the league to nonparty members and nonintellectuals. For guidance, officials also looked to the other "people's democracies." At the Politburo, they used phrases like "this is how they have solved this problem in Bulgaria" or "the Soviets do it this way" to bolster their arguments.[58] Soviet directives were important if they were available, but day-to-day league activities and rules, like those of other mass organizations overseeing youth and women, necessarily involved a good deal of guessing. In 1950, references to cultural ties disappeared altogether. The organization's Second Congress in October changed its name to the Society of Albanian-Soviet Friendship. The central administration split into two main sectors (organization and propaganda), and a couple of years later, the journal also took on the title *Miqësija* (*The Friendship*).[59] Implicit in these changes was the move from *learning* about Soviet precedents to *emulating* them. The society made it clear that it now oversaw "the application of advanced Soviet methods in our economy and cultural affairs."[60]

Desperate for grain, tractors, and loans, the Albanian regime also needed the more ordinary things required for propaganda. Party membership cards, for example, struck Soviet officials as cheap and amateurish in design. (They had to appear imposing, the Soviets explained, and be printed on high-quality paper.) The Soviets were consulted on many things, from how to properly translate the name of the party into Russian to how to deal with the letter *ë*, which needed to be manufactured for the Albanian-language materials.[61] On the party's tenth anniversary, Albanian officials initially planned on importing ten-foot portraits of Marx, Engels, Lenin, and Stalin; 250 Soviet flags; cloth portraits of Albanian Politburo members; neon lamps, dyes, paint, and printed brochures. Materials would be designed in Albania, printed in the Soviet Union, shipped back, and then mailed to Poland for local propaganda there.[62] And if the Soviets had a hard time supplying a sixth of the globe with materials, perhaps they could be embarrassed by suggestions, like the one made by an Albanian official in 1954 that lately, China was sending more propaganda materials than Moscow.[63]

They never disguised their authority, but officials in Moscow also obsessed over *not appearing* to run affairs in Albania—this before the post-Stalinist turn in foreign relations in the mid-1950s. In 1949, Soviet cultural advisers criticized an Albanian exhibition commemorating the National Liberation War for not emphasizing enough the Red Army's role. "We were not lucky enough to have the Red Army come to our country," the Albanian representative retorted defensively, "so it is difficult to include images of the Red Army liberating our country in this exhibition." But they also added the politically judicious clarification: "though in effect our country's liberation was enabled by the Red Army."[64] Then, three years later, Soviet officials took issue with another exhibition ("New Albania on the Road to Socialism") for emphasizing Soviet involvement *too much*. Accordingly, the Soviet hosts rearranged some displays, edited some captions, and removed an image showing a military parade in Tirana. Responding to "comments made by foreign visitors," they also removed references to direct Soviet presence in the country.[65]

Soviet cultural authorities thus served as suppliers of materials, but they also played the critical role of editors. One photograph on display, which appeared doctored, might "encourage rumors," so the hosts removed it. Moreover, the text accompanying the images, which the Albanian team had translated into Russian, had to go through another round of translation—from Albanian to Russian the first time and then into the "Soviet language" required of exhibitions of the sort. Acting like editors in charge, Soviet authorities nevertheless insisted that the Albanians appeared to be in control. Two years earlier, the VOKS chief in Moscow had warned the Soviet embassy in Tirana that the Albanian comrades at the Friendship Society ought to reach their own decisions without too much interference from the Soviet cultural representative. The ambassador in turn listed the various shortcomings of the society and how they could be improved. But Moscow would not have it. Officials insisted that society activity was not to be dictated or controlled.[66] It is not difficult to see how contradictory signals such as these might have produced confusion in Tirana.

Within a matter of years, society membership ballooned. During the league's first year, the number of members stood at 1,200, but by 1947 it had shot up to 24,000. After party-led membership drives, the number doubled in 1948. Party envoys organized sign-up campaigns in towns and villages, getting local chiefs, peasants, administrators, and workers to commit. In 1950, membership stood at 114,000, and it doubled again by the middle of the decade. In the late 1950s, finally, the society claimed 320,000 members, or nearly one in four adults in the whole country. In addition to expanding membership, society employees boosted forms of organization. Within the first half of 1949, the organization had established some 450 friendship circles across the country. The following year, there were 1,007 of them. By 1955, there reportedly were 3,550 such smaller groups. In some cities, friendship circles were attached not only to factories and schools but also to specific residential neighborhoods. (One circle in the southern city Korçë, for example, had an Orthodox priest as its leader.)[67]

What made this kind of mobilization possible? Though not a party organ, the Friendship Society used the language and practices of the party. First of all, decision making was centralized in the capital (with regular congresses, a general council, and a presidium) and then along a network of regional offices (twenty-seven by 1950, fluctuating over the years), which were expected to coordinate among themselves. Separate sectors covered propaganda, economic affairs, and culture. On the ground, friendship circles loosely corresponded to party cells. Elected officials within a given factory or enterprise oversaw activity. These units varied in size, from a handful of members to the labor force of a whole factory. Groups met regularly—some every two weeks, others monthly. They devised monthly plans of "friendship activities" and criticized members who lagged behind in productivity or, if based at a school, those members who received poor grades or had fallen short in discipline.

Like party operatives, friendship agitators exploited existing social bonds in their work, all the while challenging preexisting mores. And like party propagandists, they fixated on women and the youth. In 1948, the government took up issues of workplace equality between men and women, marriage, divorce, adoption laws, and spousal conflict resolution.[68] When society agitators traveled to isolated villages, they forcefully advocated for women's emancipation and denounced social conservatism. As they set up regional committees, these officials would, for example, place an older woman next to a younger one. Folk costumes characteristic of the north of the country would mix with typical southern ones. This created an image of countrywide support for the socialist crusade, in addition to addressing the vexing problem of persistent social taboos. It was not a coincidence that Il'ia Kopalin, the Soviet film director, adopted the same approach when shooting his documentary on the birth of socialist Albania.

It is not always possible to distinguish work conducted in the name of the Friendship Society from work carried out in the name of the party. The archives of these organizations overlap. This reflects the condition that developed on the ground, whereby claims about the party's authority fused with claims about Stalin's. Party teams traveled to remote corners of the republic, speaking to families living in primitive huts with thatched roofs. Tuberculosis was rampant. In these impoverished communities, some families lived in the same quarters with their cattle. But the teams also reportedly found pictures of Stalin hanging on the walls of the huts. Local women, they insisted, knew the Soviet leader by name.[69] Perhaps they did. Or perhaps the activists brought the pictures with them or came up with the imagery, echoing what Ehrenburg had written in 1945. The point is, however, that the mechanisms of the party enabled Soviet propaganda efforts, and Soviet imagery in turn could help boost the party's claims. Nexhmije, Enver's seemingly unassuming but ruthlessly driven wife, served as both agitprop chief at the Central Committee and liaison for the society, in addition to chairing the Women's Union. On paper, then, as the Soviets had instructed, the society and the party were separate entities. In reality, lines were blurred.

I have repeatedly referred to agitators, propagandists, and apparatchiks. Who were these people? For the most part, they were peasant males with an elementary education, if they had any at all. This was true at the lower party level, but even at the Central Committee the education level was low.

About half of personnel there in 1952, for example, had some primary schooling. The propaganda sector had the second-lowest rate of employees with higher education (two people).[70] The card-carrying champions of Soviet-style enlightenment, in other words, needed to go back to school. Seeing a serious problem with this state of affairs, the party secretariat considered the solutions. Should they promote younger cadres fresh out of Soviet and Eastern bloc universities? Or should they ship off the party's existing cadres to evening courses? Doing the former, as we will see, ended up posing ideological problems, since foreign influences were hard to control. Doing the latter also posed difficulties. Year after year, provincial cadres attending such courses part-time failed to pass.

TABLE 1.   Party Central Committee membership, 1952

DEPARTMENT	STAFF	WOMEN (%)	WORKERS (%)	POOR PEASANTS (%)	ELEMENTARY ED. (%)	HIGHER ED. (%)
Organization	503	18	13	28	70	1.3
Propaganda	35	5	9	14	11	8
Educ./culture	32	6	—	9	—	50
Administrative	196	6	9	27	50	17
Industries	106	1	13	16	35	19
Agriculture	44	6	16	11	27	27
Trade	108	2	6	18	28	20
Total	**1,024**	**11**	**11.3**	**23**	**52**	**11**

Source: AQSH, f. 14/AP OU, v. 1953, dos. 47, fl. 8.

TABLE 2.   The social background of admitted party members and candidates, January–June 1953

WORKERS	PEASANTS	CIVIL SERVANTS	OTHER	TOTAL
364	751	823	139	2,077

Source: "Informacion," dated by hand 7 August 1953, AQSH, f. 14/AP OU, v. 1953, dos. 62, fl. 5.

Here was a party that spoke in the name of the proletariat but whose ranks had a tiny minority of workers. Top to bottom, it was a party of peasants. By mid-decade, workers constituted less than a fifth of the whole party membership.[71] This state of affairs encouraged ritual campaigns of "cleansing" party ranks from "ideologically illiterate" elements.[72] It was necessary to fill the workers' party with workers, but of course letting in too many people—without proper screening and evaluation of personal history—would create problems and bottlenecks further down the line. It took years to raise the share of workers in the party membership (only in the 1960s did workers constitute more than a third), just as it took years to increase the level of education within the Central Committee and among provincial instructors and party chiefs.[73]

What does this say about the state-backed promotion of the Soviet Union in the 1950s? The Soviet Union's presence in Albania came *after* the fact of the attainment of Communist power. So did all the party structures with their foreign-sounding names filling the workplaces, the airwaves, and the city papers: *aktiv* (broad-based meetings), *organizata bazë* (party cells), the various party branches and subbranches, the circles, and the people's councils. Thus it is possible to interpret this intensity of friendship propaganda also as a reflection of the instinct to correct this historical error—the glaring absence of a proletariat under a regime ruling in the name of the proletariat. This might seem to contradict readings of Marx, but there was precedent for it. After all, was the Soviet party not precisely an example of overcoming the demographic problem of a peasant society?

Party membership, moreover, was not available to all. It was possible to display loyalty without formally joining the party—for example, by joining the Friendship Society. Other reasons for joining included some privileges. There were material rewards for those who signed the most new members, including radios, record players, and cash prizes. Membership also provided access to books and films in addition to opportunities for socialization. Some came for the dances but sat through the long, dreary speeches beforehand. Society organizers ensured that entertainment came with some "educational" content, so films and soccer matches (the latter brought out male audiences in droves) were often preceded by discussions. Participation, finally, can be explained by the fact that Albanian towns, to say nothing of villages, offered few alternatives (if anything at all). Aware of this, agitators set up "cultural brigades" that brought books, music, and films to the provinces. They performed skits, played music, and entertained the children with tricks. To make sure they would not go ignored, they also brought along doctors, dentists, and midwives, who were hard to come by in remote areas.

During one such trip to a province in the country's north, which the regime increasingly targeted, a propaganda crew brought along a movie projector, magazines, and portraits of Marx, Engels, and Hoxha. They also brought pictures of Soviet cities and heroes, which they carefully arranged on the walls of the local school building. Then, at seven in the evening, when it had turned dark, the team gathered all the peasants outside the school for a showing of *The Battle of Stalingrad*. Since the structure stood on the Albanian-Yugoslav border, less than a hundred feet inland, the projector's curtain ended up facing the guarded border, which meant that the Yugoslav side could watch the Soviet epic too. Thus, the awe-struck highlanders sat on their stools, sandwiched between the black-and-white scenes of total war in front of them and Tito's Yugoslavia in the back, erupting in wild cheers every time Stalin's silhouette appeared on the stretched curtain. "On my word of honor, I am seventy years old but I had never watched a movie in my life before," a man by the name of Fran was quoted. "This regime is opening our eyes." During the most violent battle scenes, we are told, the crowd

FIGURE 12. *Auto-propagandë*: A mobile film projector donated by VOKS to the Society for Albanian-Soviet Friendship, 1953. ATSH.

"sometimes forgot that the events were taking place on a piece of cloth," roaring "Hit them! Hit them!" each time Red Army troops were on the offensive.[74]

In 1951, VOKS shipped to Albania a *peredvizhok*, a recent Soviet-manufactured minibus equipped with a movie projector, shown in figure 12. The Albanian word for it, however, conveys the function more effectively: *auto-propagandë*. The vehicle had a radio, a gramophone, and shelves tucked under the equipment for brochures and books. There was seating for ten people.[75] When the minibus broke down, screenings were delayed because local operators depended on Soviet suppliers for spare parts. The cinema-on-wheels crisscrossed the country beaming war films, comedies, and documentaries. Peasants in Korçë, for example, were amazed to discover India in 1956 through footage of Nikita Khrushchev's trip there.[76] Upon the vehicle's arrival for a showing, Soviet music would be blasting from the loudspeakers. The vehicle's exterior carried colorful film posters in Cyrillic. Often, films were shown in Russian, but society propagandists distributed leaflets summarizing the plot. They also stuck around to answer questions after each screening and made sure the film had been "properly understood." By 1960, the society had twenty-five such vehicles. Indeed, Soviet-produced propaganda vehicles outlasted the friendship with the Soviet Union itself.[77]

Months, Weeks, Days, Hours

Propaganda for the Soviet Union peaked during the Month of Friendship, first adopted in 1949. Months of friendship with the Soviet Union also became a staple in East Germany, Poland, Czechoslovakia, China, and North Korea. Every September (with the exception of 1950 and 1954, when October and November were chosen), the society organized special meetings and rallies. Already in 1951, the party daily declared that the Friendship Month had become "a tradition." The editorial hailed the Soviet Union as the country's "savior" and Moscow as the vanguard of progressive peace-loving people: "At a time when American imperialists and others increase armaments, commit to pacts of aggression, spill rivers of blood in Korea, Vietnam, Malaysia and elsewhere, the government and people of the Soviet Union, under the leadership of the Bolshevik party and comrade Stalin, turn deserts into fertile soil, open gigantic canals which will water millions of hectares of land, and build universities and palaces of culture where hundreds will study."[78] Typically, on the eve of the Month of Friendship, VOKS would send a special delegation. Movie theaters screened Soviet-themed documentaries. Society-planned exhibitions featured large-scale displays of Soviet building projects, and smaller-scale displays popped up in factory "red corners." Themes varied from year to year: mass housing built for the Soviet people, provisions for women and children in the Soviet Union, Soviet sport, advances in technology and science. Some factories had their own "Soviet corners," and directors rushed to fulfill society membership quotas. Some enterprises also set up "Stalin corners" entirely devoted to the *vozhd*. Others announced "friendship brigades" and "friendship sectors," which incorporated the most productive laborers vying for "friendship flags." The designation "Soviet" became something to be earned. Labor brigades took their oaths to surpass norms "in the name of Friendship."

Party officials symbolically mapped the geopolitical order of the Cold War over the calendar, allocating months, weeks, days, and hours according to the strategic significance of those honored. Besides the month, there were "friendship weeks," "friendship days," and "friendship evenings." Special weeks were set aside for Azerbaijan or Ukraine.[79] This kind of socialist marking of time was a known feature around the socialist world. In Rudolstadt, near Jena, East Germany, the 1951 Soviet Friendship Month ran from 7 November to 5 December, using the October Revolution anniversary to mark the beginning.[80] In addition to the ubiquitous "solidarity weeks" with Korea, Albanian calendars would be marked for particular themes: the week of kolkhozes, public health, or the week devoted to the construction industry.[81] Friendship days, typically held in schools or houses of culture, consisted of lectures and meetings with writers, engineers, or architects trained in the country being celebrated. Some high schools organized "friendship evenings," which were hour-long student-led variety shows composed of country-specific poetry readings and music.

Throughout this offensive, radio played an important role. Broadcasting was still new; the country's first transmitter dated from the 1930s. A radio corporation had come into being under Italian sponsorship. In 1944, there was still only that one radio transmitter, but by 1952 there were nine (half of them located in the capital). Broadcasting in medium waves, Radio Tirana already covered most cities, but a new Soviet-produced transmitter strengthened the signal considerably in 1952, stretching it beyond the country's borders and consequently pushing officials to produce programs in foreign languages.[82] The state radio agency (Radio-Difuzioni) included, besides announcers and journalists, editors of Soviet and Balkan music, specialists on the people's democracies, and, of course, translators.[83] The agency devised bilateral agreements with its Eastern bloc counterparts, each side agreeing to reserve blocks of time for special programs devoted to the other country.[84] Since home receivers were not as commonplace as in other socialist countries, Albanian government authorities installed loudspeakers in public places.

Programming on the Soviet Union and the people's democracies was common all year round, but there was a marked increase during the Friendship Month.

Consider one day in September 1951. The typical program would include a morning session, commencing around 5:00 a.m., with gymnastics, Soviet music (Russian polka, Azerbaijani folk), and the reading of the lead article of *Zëri i Popullit* (which, as a rule, that month was about friendship with the Soviet Union). The midday session (starting at 1:00 p.m.) would include Russian dances, selections from the bass Mark Reizen, short pieces by Albanian musicians directed by Soviet conductors, Tchaikovsky, Ukrainian music, stories read by Soviet pioneers, lectures, and Soviet *estrada* (variety show) numbers. The Friendship Society-sponsored session ("Getting to Know the Soviet Union") was scheduled for Saturday afternoon. The evening session, finally, which started at 5:30 p.m. and concluded at 11:00 p.m., would consist of the Albanian-language edition of Radio Moscow, traditional Albanian folk dances, songs devoted to Stalin, medical curiosities, Rachmaninoff, Prokofiev, Bulgarian waltzes, poetry, and partisan songs.[85]

The schedule for September of the following year was almost identical in scope, except that there were more special programs targeting youth, peasants, and those trying to learn Russian. Soviet music, plays, and folk dances remained a key feature throughout the decade. The mid-1950s did mark a shift, as local news and reporting constituted the bulk of programming. By then, of course, there *was* local programming to be had, and the agency had enough specialized staff to produce it. As a result, broadcasts of local orchestras, choirs, and amateur groups expanded. Nevertheless, propaganda for the Soviet Union and the Eastern bloc did not disappear. In fact, programming chiefs added Korean and Chinese music to the mix while continuing to censor Western music. Back in 1950, when one local radio chief in Shkodër had inserted some Western music into the program, party functionaries had promptly reprimanded him.[86] As radio receivers became more commonplace, this battle expanded over the airwaves. Albania's geography, in addition to its technological backwardness, made it highly receptive to "dangerous" signals (the BBC, Voice of America, Athens, Rome, the Vatican, and Yugoslav stations), a fact acknowledged—for opposing reasons—by both the authorities and the CIA.[87]

Petraq Kolevica, at the time an aspiring young architect, later recalled this flooding of the airwaves with Soviet sounds: "The radio never stopped informing us about the Soviet Union and broadcasting Russian songs." Referring to the traditional Russian and Albanian string instruments, he wrote that the balalaika "overwhelmed the *çifteli*."[88] Architecture was not yet a separate field of study, so Kolevica enrolled in engineering between 1952 and 1957. He drafted his thesis under Strazimiri, the Moscow-trained architect who had drafted a thesis for a socialist capital city. Unsurprisingly, Strazimiri urged the student to copy Soviet urban plans. Kolevica would later write in his memoir that the Soviet ready-made blueprints seemed foreign. So did Russian music and literature. He was accustomed to Italian *canzonette* and found it difficult to connect to the singing of Feodor Chaliapin or Mark Reizen. The fact that Kolevica became a celebrated translator of Russian poetry is, in retrospect, an apt illustration of how cultural reception works. The introduction to Soviet culture, the architect/translator later admitted, was "a painful phenomenon, love mixed with hatred."[89] Constant propaganda about Soviet culture was staggering, but it was possible to admire Soviet culture *in spite of* it.

Like Ehrenburg, Soviet diplomats gushed about how Albania's encounter with the Soviet Union had produced many firsts: among the first professional ballet and opera performances, carried out with the help of Soviet directors and choreographers, were said to be Boris Asaf'ev's *The Fountain of Bakhchisarai* and Aleksandr Dargomyzhsky's *Rusalka*.[90] The director of the Leningrad Palace of Pioneers came to help with the first youth palace. Finally, the country's first comprehensive state university (inaugurated 16 September 1957) was established under Soviet guidance by joining existing higher learning institutes (pedagogy, economics, medicine, law, polytechnic).[91] But Kolevica's memoir also shows how the flooding of stages and airwaves with Soviet firsts and the incessant claims to invention and socialist genius also brought on exhaustion and encouraged ridicule. Some Albanian youths laughed at the aggrandizement. They declared, in jest, that Russia had invented everything worthwhile in the world. "Russia: native home of the elephant!" the quip went. The joke about Soviet civilization itself turned into an expression of a kind of reverse internationalism: it makes an appearance in both Shostakovich's memoirs and Kolevica's later recollections.[92]

Mobilization, then, was largely enabled by mechanisms set in motion by the party. Bosses harassed, agitators coerced, factory chiefs held out prizes and material rewards. Mobilization took place in an atmosphere saturated with calls to action, emotional appeals, promises of social liberation, Soviet sounds blasting from the radio, and expanding ethnographic knowledge about distant republics similarly striving for socialism. In the end, society membership increased because it had to increase. Just like textiles and steel, membership drives, subscriptions, and book sales had to reach centrally devised targets. This did not guarantee plan fulfillment, though the plan might appear fulfilled on paper. As in other area of planning, numbers were tools of negotiation. But by contrast with industrial output, the outcomes of socialist propaganda posed the additional challenge of not being easily measurable. How many Soviet films were enough? How many speeches? Could friendship be measured? Could love for the Soviet Union? Above all, what use were films and books if Albanians spoke or read no Russian?

The Language of Lenin

In the 1940s, Serbo-Croatian had become common in Albanian schools. Russian, however, was not. Those relatively few party members who spoke foreign languages at all were most likely to speak Italian, Turkish, French, or English, in addition to Serbo-Croatian.[93] For years, party higher-ups wrote their correspondence to Soviet counterparts in French. When Hoxha asked Stalin for instructors and personnel in 1951, the Soviet leader shrugged: What good would they be if Albanians could not understand the language?[94] Learning "the language of the great Lenin"—an early phrase that, incidentally, proved effective even after the assault on Stalin in the Soviet Union—meant learning the language of the most powerful socialist country on earth. It would permit intellectuals to read their works in the original. But workers too would need to understand the instructions of Soviet advisers. The language might appear daunting, so society agitators cast it as the enlightened language of poets and progress. They explained how the partisans had avidly studied Russian texts in the heat of anti-Nazi battles, how they had bled for Lenin. If one was to fulfill a patriotic duty and take full advantage of Soviet expertise, it was imperative to learn Russian.

In the early 1950s, Russian language courses expanded across Eastern Europe, and VOKS officials in Moscow took count of the number of active courses, the annual enrollment, and the textbooks used. All this activity obviously required large numbers of teachers, which meant that certification as a teacher often took merely months. Moscow might provide language methods and an *uchebnyi plan*—a standard teaching plan for teaching Russian across the whole country—or local authorities might come with their materials. In Albania's case, the Soviet specialist Nina Potapova prepared a method (*The Russian Language for Albanians*), and two youths studying in Moscow translated the book into Albanian. The volume was basic but amply illustrated, with an introduction hailing Russian as the language of "the immortal geniuses of humanity—Lenin and Stalin."[95]

The country's first Russian language classes enrolled party operatives, government personnel, and a handful of intellectuals. By 1950, the Friendship Society had set up forty such courses, reportedly attended by some 850 individuals.[96] In addition to apparatchiks and intellectuals, the society specifically targeted workers. By 1953, language courses had spread to Shkodër and Korçë, where 674 students passed language exams that year.[97] Two years later, there were seven two-year evening language schools, enrolling 336 individuals, in addition to forty-six courses with another 728 attendees.[98] The language schools offered classes that met twice a week for a period of two to three years, leading to a certificate. In comparison, the ordinary courses were, as a rule, less time-consuming because the commitment was also smaller. Still, attending language classes was inevitably an additional demand on a factory worker's already packed day.

When it comes to enrollment figures, it is important to keep in mind that officials collected these at the beginning of a given semester. Reports show that some enrolled students eventually dropped out, burdened, as seems entirely likely, with the constant pressure of work and family life. Some stayed in class but skipped the exams. In some cases, upwards of a third of all those enrolled in the course gave up. In 1956, for example, only about 70 percent of those registered in the language schools (1,331 individuals) actually attended courses regularly.[99] The society tackled the problem by tailoring language courses according to working schedules and by admitting only individuals who could complete the full course of study. But these measures did not solve the problem of "hypermobilization," as the following chapter will show. After grueling shifts, party-related meetings, study circles, mandatory factory gatherings, trade union sessions, and, as the case might be, political rallies and women's group meetings, it would have been surprising if these people were not utterly exhausted.[100]

Working with adults was not easy. Soviet recommendations had informed the school reform back in the 1940s, and the Soviets also provided some instructors. But a shortage of teachers persisted for years.[101] A Russian language department opened in Tirana's pedagogical institute in January 1949. Russian language instructors came for periods ranging from two to three years. (Invariably, hosts pleaded with Moscow for contract extensions.) In 1952, more than forty such instructors were in the country, contracted by the Ministry of Education.[102] The following year, the government established a special program designed to prepare Russian teachers. Russian language study had already been part of the high school curriculum since 1950. But by 1953 it had also entered primary schools.[103]

That Russian language classes became common does not mean that those who enrolled in them became proficient. Even if a qualified teacher might be available, the study materials might be inadequate. In some cases, adult learners enrolled in evening language courses used the same textbook as the primary schools did. Some did not have textbooks at all. Resources gradually improved over the first half of the 1950s. Still, in 1955, the Friendship Society estimated that, despite long hours of study, adult learners could not independently use Russian-language texts.[104] Its journal shamed local friendship chapters that had fallen behind and those reputed to lead poor classes. It also published how-to guides specifying how much time should be spent on vocabulary, how much on grammar, and which examples of Soviet literature were appropriate for translation at various levels of competency. Along with the shaming, the journal also showcased success stories. It featured young workers who could now translate directly from Soviet magazines or promising high school students who wrote letters to their Soviet pen pals.[105]

Above all, learning Russian was a political problem. How could apparatchiks convince workers and young people to study Russian when Politburo members did not speak a word of it? "Only three out of the ten members and candidates of the Politburo know Russian," wrote the Soviet ambassador to the Foreign Ministry in Moscow in 1954, "only one of the four secretaries of the Central Committee and only three out of sixteen members of the government."[106] According to Soviet details, only four high-level officials received *Pravda* and *Kommunist*. Albania was not only geographically cut off from the rest of the bloc; it was temporally cut off, too, as news from the Soviet Union arrived late and then had to go through time-consuming translation. A Politburo decree in 1955 underscored the ideological implications of this problem. Party and state functionaries, it warned, "would not be able to successfully conduct their work without absorbing Soviet experience and they cannot absorb Soviet experience without knowing the Russian language."[107]

Just as Communist power in Albania preceded the arrival of Soviet machines, so the arrival of Marxism-Leninism preceded the printing of the complete works of Marx and Lenin. It didn't help that the classics had written so much—it was not easy printing it all. On top of that, there were Stalin's works too.[108] In 1956, party officials sought to publish a two-volume set of writings from Marx and Lenin, translated from Russian. They turned to East Germany, asking for a print run of ten thousand and specifying that the volumes were to "look like the Russian edition."[109] The Germans considered doing the job but on condition of payment. The Albanian side had hoped for a gift. If they were to publish these lengthy texts themselves, they reasoned, it would take up 80 percent of the whole annual publishing plan. Thus the complete works of Lenin, Marx, and Engels waited to be published, year after year. In the meantime, propaganda officials published key texts, excerpts, and small volumes, which were cheaper to print and easier to distribute.[110]

For a high-level party functionary, it was not necessary to speak Russian in order to demand it from others. Neither was a complete run of Marx and Lenin necessary to make Marxism-Leninism operative. It turned out, in fact, that it was not even necessary to have read these texts to appreciate that they carried political significance. Learning the language of Lenin was about more than comprehending Russian. It was a form of exercising discipline and asserting authority. Similarly, state budgets were instruments of enforcement and exclusion: this trip would go unfunded, that book would not be translated. Apparatchiks diligently scrutinized lists—from Tchaikovsky to Stalin—each title assessed for its "ideological value." Just as they negotiated the shipments of tractors or the tons of cotton, officials pondered, for example, the socialist value of Balzac. (Between 1949 and 1953, Western titles slated for translation were limited to *Eugénie Grandet* and Sophocles's *Electra*.) Hoxha, who fashioned himself a Francophone, suggested skipping Balzac after all. Readers "would not understand it."[111] As with learning Russian, texts were understood as instruments of power. The regime may have been largely uneducated, but it was nevertheless attuned to the power of the written word. Language opened borders. There was apprehension in that too. Opened borders required policing.

The Price of Discovery

Enabled by radical centralization, the promotion of the Soviet Union in the 1950s was also constrained by it. After the first Five Year Plan (1950–55), the Friendship Society surrendered parts of its real estate and also lost some of the personnel. At first glance, this might seem in line with waning propaganda for the Soviet Union elsewhere in the bloc. But material constraints do not necessarily reflect a lack of will. Precisely because socialist planning was pervasive, it required cutting costs or shuffling around resources. Between September and December 1955, authorities expected 175 foreigners to visit the country. These included Chinese singers, a Polish study group, Bulgarian writers, a Romanian painter, Soviet teachers and dancers, women's delegations, German scholars of folklore, and a Czechoslovak cultural team. The Ministry of Interior, however, had only three cars available for foreign guests (a Polish Warszawa and two ZIS vehicles). Officials rushed to line up more vehicles, but in the end, the Bulgarian writers and the Romanian painter had to go on foot.[112]

Cultural diplomacy with a sixth of the earth required more than solidarity and goodwill. Discovery assumed that at least some means to sustain international contact existed already. At an April 1955 party plenum on ideology, the Politburo assessed the work of the Friendship Society and found it lacking. The party chief ordered another reorganization, including the removal of the society's president, Bedri Spahiu. The long-standing Central Committee secretary Hysni Kapo took over the society.[113] A separate report prepared by society officials complained that Soviet propaganda in the country peaked during the Friendship Month but plummeted afterward. Many of the friendship circles, it pointed out, existed only formally. Worse, some were led by "illiterates or half-illiterates." With slashed budgets, propaganda in villages also fared poorly. In some locales, movie projectors had to be hauled by mules because vehicles were broken or there were none. Some society functionaries appeared more concerned with "collecting statistics" than with "actual work and its impact on the masses."[114]

The highly critical report on the promotion of the Soviet Union was thoroughly Soviet in tone. It lingered on shortcomings and demanded vigilance. Fault finding, in fact, was a structural need; it served to keep apparatchiks busy in addition to enabling them to justify their ongoing work. Proper identification of problems, especially in matters of ideology, constituted an important factor in eventual decisions over budget and personnel allocations. This is not to say that this particular report, like many others, did not contain truths but that it was difficult for officials then, as it is for us today, to precisely determine the motivation behind each instance of criticism. Occasionally, criticism launched against a specific agency served far more mundane objectives. The party-led criticism leveled at the Friendship Society, for example, while cast in ideological terms, came at a time when the presidium of the People's Assembly had an eye on the society's elegant building.[115]

To justify themselves, friendship officials pointed to "objective" problems. One obvious, and embarrassing, realization was that every Friendship Society president up until the mid-1950s had turned out to be "a party enemy." There was Nako Spiru, in charge in the 1940s, who had committed suicide on the eve of the Albanian-Yugoslav conflict. After that, there had been Koçi Xoxe, the former security police chief who had ended up in front of a firing squad. Finally, the long-standing party members Tuk Jakova and Bedri Spahiu both had served at the society's helm—and both were expelled from the party in 1955 for deviation.[116] Enver's wife, who had overseen agitprop, also came in for criticism for not having properly distinguished between party propaganda and Soviet propaganda (unclear as that distinction still was). Rumors of corruption added to the embarrassment. One colleague accused a society secretary of using VOKS funds to buy goods at private market prices and of snatching a pair of shoes that a local family had sent as a gift to Stalin. (The secretary was demoted.)[117]

Not enough contacts with the rest of the socialist world or failing to show the proper enthusiasm for them constituted a political problem. More contacts also created more problems. This was especially true after the crises of 1956 in the Eastern bloc. Nikita Khrushchev, who won the succession battle after Stalin's death, lambasted his predecessor during a "secret speech" at the Twentieth Soviet Party Congress in February 1956. He repudiated Stalin's cult of personality, charging him with crimes, lies, and despotism. The speech made for high drama. The Albanian party leadership did not circulate it, but word got out anyway. Some party members hoped that a similar change in course would happen in Albania. Rumors of a disease quickly spread throughout the party ranks. Many had noticed the local symptoms but had not dared speak its name. But then the disease had become public, in Moscow, in Polish cities, along the grand Central European boulevards. Eventually, Albanian peasants also learned to pronounce the diagnosis: the cult of personality.

Khrushchev's diatribe against Stalin emboldened middle-ranking party members in Tirana to ask for reforms, including, in the spirit of the Soviet leader's idea

of peaceful coexistence, improved relations with Yugoslavia.[118] At a party conference in the capital in April 1956, several party members raised these questions.
Hoxha's intervention was quick and severe, accusing the officials of an antiparty
conspiracy. The truth is that they did not seek to depose him, and neither had
they conceived any kind of antiestablishment coup, as was later charged. These
were party men. They watched closely what was happening in Moscow, and—as
had become customary—they wanted to use the Soviet example to soften the
party line at home. Still, the effort provided Hoxha with more ammunition to
declare that Yugoslavia was behind the plot. When Hungarians took to the streets
in rebellion later that year, the Soviet Politburo worried about a domino effect
of counterrevolution in the Eastern bloc. For their part, Albanian functionaries
worried that Albanian youths enrolled in Soviet, Hungarian, and Polish universities might bring back dangerous reformist ideas.[119]

But signs of trouble predated 1956. Well before there had been any Soviet
invasion of Budapest, the Albanian security police had terrorized the populace
in the name of "anti-Soviet activities." Five years earlier, for example, an explo-
sion close to the Soviet embassy in Tirana had inaugurated a wave of repression, leading to numerous arrests of individuals unrelated to the incident and
the subsequent execution of twenty-two of them on fabricated charges of having
mounted a terrorist attack against the Soviets. Since then, charges of anti-Soviet
activity had become something terrifying. The Albanian party apparatus had set
up organizations for students studying abroad in the Soviet Union and the countries of the Eastern bloc. Officials reviewed student grades, upheld morality by
way of policing sexual relations, conducted "political work" with the youths, and
sanctioned offenders. Occasionally, the enforced party discipline failed to correct behavior, with the consequence that students were ordered back to Albania,
stripped of their coveted scholarships.[120]

Month after month, the security police kept a watchful eye on letters from
abroad, inspecting them for signs of subversion and thought offenses. In one such
letter from 1953, one Albanian youth studying in the Soviet Union explained to
a relative that cuts to his scholarship (from eight hundred to six hundred rubles)
had hit him hard. "I do not usually eat at the restaurant," he added, "and we only
have a teapot in our room, which we use to make tea for breakfast and lunch."[121]
Another fellow in Hungary complained that he was forced to work, in addition
to taking classes, so as to make ends meet.[122] Other youths faced accusations of
speaking against the Soviet Union to foreign girls. Some were found suspicious
for having expressed amazement that it was possible to buy Soviet magazines in
the United States but that American magazines were unavailable in the Soviet
Union. Finally, some letters intercepted by the security police, including the correspondence of Albanian inhabitants to relatives abroad, discussed the standard

of living in the capitalist West and wondered why it was better than in the social-ist East.[123]

In the history of Stalinism, Stalin's life has served as a kind of template: the years 1953 (his physical death) and 1956 (symbolic death) loom large. Histori-ans of the Soviet Union have focused on the domestic aftershocks of so-called de-Stalinization. Cold War scholars in turn have carefully traced the high-level deliberations leading to the Soviet invasion of Budapest. This has tended to lend the impression of inevitability to the turmoil of 1956. But there was nothing inevitable in an "opening" of the Soviet Union to the West. Not everyone went along with de-Stalinization. Albanian party officials, for example, worried about the possibility of importing counterrevolution. Education chiefs took note of the fact that students in the Eastern bloc had embraced Western popular music and fashion. They were not alone in doing so. Soviet students in East Germany also came under accusations of nonsocialist behavior such as romantic getaways, wasting time at restaurants, and drinking sprees.[124]

In the early 1950s, socialist discovery had been a patriotic duty. Now the Albanian Central Committee warned that Hungary and Poland were dangerous ground.[125] Party higher-ups concluded that Albanian students in these countries, plus East Germany, had succumbed to local anti-Soviet influences. Some youths lost their scholarships as a result of political mistakes—including voicing sup-port for Tito's Yugoslavia, gossiping about party leaders and their privileges, and professing a desire for American consumer goods (glossy magazines, records, clothes)—or for succumbing to the terrible addiction of rock 'n' roll. Others called Khrushchev *kukuruzo*, ridiculing his obsession with corn. Some young men sported long hair; others wore their pants shamelessly short. When con-fronted about the supposed transgressions, the youths retorted that they were mature enough to distinguish right from wrong. Party apparatchiks in Tirana, however, were not convinced. "We have indications," they fretted, "that the enemy exploits the weakness [of our young men] regarding women."[126]

What to do? At a meeting in August 1958, Central Committee secretariat offi-cials admitted that it was impossible to control Albanian youths abroad. The party could not prohibit male students from pursuing women, the forty-three-year-old party secretary Hysni Kapo told his colleagues, "but they should pursue one girl, and not one hundred at once." Desire for Western fashion was similarly hard to curb. Security operatives were quick to condemn Albanian youths for wearing shorts (a symptom of American influence), but how could one fault them if Czech youths wore them all the time?[127] Directives sought to limit the number of Albanian students sent to East Germany and Poland specifically, since these countries were now apparently corrupted by Western influences. But the party elite were themselves consumed with material desires. During a visit to

Leipzig in 1959, the wives of Enver Hoxha and Mehmet Shehu were treated to a fashion show. The trends on display—miniskirts, tight shorts—apparently scandalized them, so the visitors asked that photographs showing them in the audience not be published. Nevertheless, after the show, the two women asked to do some shopping around town.[128]

A few Albanian youths, in fact, did whatever they could *not* to return to Albania. Some fled to West Germany. In December 1958, Greek newspapers reported that a male student of medicine returning by ship from the Soviet Union daringly fooled his friends and the Soviet soldiers and made "a leap for freedom"— jumping onto the dock and then promptly asking for political asylum.[129] There was great risk in doing this, and the majority of Albanian students did not take it. Socialist exchanges of people and ideas, which occurred with the full backing of the party-state, forced the party-state to become even more involved when dealing with the resulting complications.

Gorky's Shadow

Born in 1936, in Gjirokastër, not far from the Albanian-Greek border, Ismail Kadare published his first poems at seventeen. He was clearly talented, so a few years later he obtained a scholarship to study at the Gorky Institute for World Literature in Moscow, close to Pushkin Square. "I was sent to the Gorky Institute to become an official writer of the regime," he would later explain, recalling the institute as "a factory for fabricating dogmatic hacks of the socialist-realism school."[130] Gani Strazimiri, the architect, had been in Moscow in his thirties. Kadare belonged to a younger generation, coming of age after the country's liberation, immersed in the zeitgeist of the headlong building of socialism. Strazimiri had experienced Moscow under Stalin. Kadare arrived in a post-Stalin Soviet Union.

One of his early poems formed the basis for a later novel, *Muzgu i perëndive të stepës* (*Twilight of the Eastern Gods*), which re-creates the author's student days in the Soviet capital.[131] It would be naive to approach *Twilight* as strictly autobiographical, despite the fact that the author has acknowledged basing it on his experience.[132] David Bellos, thanks to whom much of the English-speaking world gets to read Kadare, rightly reminds us that the narrator "is a young man very much like Kadare" but that "he is nonetheless someone else."[133] Like Kadare, the novel's protagonist discovers Moscow's literary world and, through it, the world of socialism, from the parks and libraries to the special resorts for writers along the Baltic coast and the Black Sea. Years later, Kadare would recall meeting fellow authors such as Bella Akhmadulina and Yevgeny Yevtushenko, also alums of the institute, and Konstantin Paustovsky, encountered in Yalta.[134] Indeed, in the novel Kadare used the real names of former teachers and colleagues. But he has also insisted, often and vigorously, that literature and life are two separate spheres, guided by distinct rules. Is it misguided to approach the novel for clues on socialist relations?

On the contrary: the very existence of the book is a testament to the paradoxes of socialism. *Twilight of the Eastern Gods* went through numerous versions over the years. Kadare began writing it in 1962, publishing some parts in an Albanian literary journal ten years later and then as a condensed version in 1978. The novel appeared in French in 1981, with "smuggled" romantic scenes that the author had not published in the Albanian version. A full and *revised* Albanian version appeared in 2006.[135] The novel's life thus resembles a kind of journey over decades: a drawn-out and ever-changing re-creation of the author's part fictional and part biographical encounter with literary Moscow. Precisely as a product of negotiation and strategic deployment, of memory and invention, it is telling. It shows how sudden and surprising geopolitical changes transformed possibilities for expression. In the 1950s, Albanian writers had been expected to categorically embrace Soviet culture. In the early 1960s, as we will see, Albanian-Soviet relations collapsed. This allowed Kadare to write critically of the Khrushchev era—something previously unthinkable.

Twilight of the Eastern Gods centers on the romance between the protagonist (an Albanian student) and a local girl named Lida Snegina. The background, however, consists of snapshots of the Soviet literary world, entangled with the political establishment, and the numerous time zones comprising the vast Soviet empire.[136] The first half of the novel describes the return of students to the institute's dormitory, presumably from vacation. The hallways are filled with aspiring writers from across the socialist world: Russians, Ukrainians, Latvians, Lithuanians, Armenians, two Georgians—"both called Shota (one was a Stalinist, the other anti")—Jews, Muslims, a Greek named Antaeus, and a mysterious fellow from the Siberian tundra.[137] Students devise nicknames for each other according to nationality or ethnic stereotypes, betraying the proper façade of the institution. Central Asian students, for example, are known as the "the Karakum gang." Males refer to some of their female colleagues as "the Belorussian virgins" for no discernible reason. A Chinese colleague has received the nickname "Hundred Flower Bloom."

At the institute, the narrator encounters friendship and jealousy, iron party discipline, and also ruthless ambition, internationalism, and anti-Semitism. The socialist world is composed of ideals and banalities: long dull meetings, standard verbal phrases, predictably "realist" story lines. Students crack political jokes, flirt, drink heavily during long winter months, and dream of magnificent literary careers. The dormitory's long hallways make the narrator feel "a quiver of the kind usually set off by a combination of good and bad memories."[138] The French author Éric Faye has interpreted Kadare's dormitory for the future writers of the Communist world as a kind of Dante's inferno, containing circles (floors) where aspiring minds silently suffer, conspire, and are carefully divided according to political obedience and ability (but also willingness) to tailor their texts according to the tenets of socialist realism.[139]

Like the system sustaining it, socialist realism comes with personal and literary habits. It is here that Kadare's own experiences in Moscow in the late 1950s blur into his fiction, to the point that it becomes impossible to distinguish between them. In interviews, he has admitted that intellectual life in Moscow was full of boredom, self-induced pressures, and the kinds of intrigues that permeate *Twilight*. The politics disgusted him, not because he rejected the ideology ("I had already made my choice") but for reasons of vanity: "The Soviet writers, for the most part, resembled the leaders, the party secretaries."[140] His young but power-hungry colleagues, including those that held some interest in romance, lacked eroticism—something that the youthful character in *Twilight*, like Kadare at the time, seems eager to explore. Rejection of official socialism did not have to be an intellectual exercise. The Polish poet Czesław Miłosz once explained his break with the Eastern bloc as a decision stemming not "from the functioning mind, but from a revolt of the stomach."[141]

In conversation, Kadare told me that he had grown aware, early on, that Albania's peripheral position offered a unique window into the socialist world.[142] In his texts and memories, Moscow appears contradictory. On the one hand, it seems to dull the senses with the endless lectures and the rituals of self-criticism. On the other, it was in Moscow that Kadare discovered Kafka and Joyce.[143] The socialist homeland could be a conduit to the forbidden as well as the formulaic. An important episode in *Twilight* highlights the stakes of this kind of discovery. Wandering into a deserted apartment one day, the protagonist stumbles upon a manuscript. The incomplete pages describe a certain Doctor Zhivago. Sometime afterward, the narrator discovers that the novel's author, Boris Pasternak, has received the Nobel Prize for Literature. A collective backlash against Pasternak erupts within Moscow's literary world. Soviet apparatchiks thunder at the Western "provocation," demanding the author's removal from the Soviet Union. As Pasternak is forced to turn down the prize, the Albanian narrator despairs. Opportunistic colleagues join the condemning chorus. As relations with Albania deteriorate further, his friends begin to shun him. Soviet-Albanian friendship suddenly feels like a trap.

Kadare's fictional Moscow is gloomy, oppressive, flooded in hypocrisy. When we look deeper, however, a more complicated history of discovery emerges. The Soviet capital is also a site of intellectual, emotional, and sexual discovery. Kadare has admitted that he very much missed the Soviet metropolis upon his return to Albania.[144] Compared with Tirana, Moscow seemed vast and metropolitan. Suffocating as it had been, it had also offered him a degree of freedom. "In Moscow, you are abroad, you are a student, you are free, you don't know anyone, and you can do anything," he recalled decades later. "I felt completely free in a capital of eight million."[145] Back home, it seemed like everyone knew everyone. Intellectual life was limited. The guardians of cultural affairs in Tirana were small-minded. Somewhere between the fiction and the recollection, then, multiple versions of Moscow emerge. There is the Moscow a twenty-something Ismail discovered in the 1950s. Then there is the fictional Moscow he put together in the 1960s and 1970s, under shifting geopolitical circumstances in the socialist world. Finally, there is the Moscow reinvented—with echoes of nostalgia—once Communism had become history.

The discovery of socialism became a narrative to be revised again and again, and it also constituted changing forms of intellectual capital. In a context like Albania's, Soviet university diplomas carried weight. A twenty-four-year-old with the right Soviet credentials could quickly shoot up the hierarchy. But access to the Soviet Union, with all its unpredictable turns, could also serve as a reference point despite all the official propaganda. Kadare has insisted that Moscow also made it possible to learn by negative example—striving, for example, *not* to write like his colleagues at the Gorky Institute. (His form of inoculation to socialist realism, he has maintained, was to read Shakespeare and the Greek classics.) And because he had intimately gotten to know the center of the socialist world, the author could mine the experience for his own purposes, beginning to put together an alternative literary universe.

Not everyone got to straddle these spheres so intimately. But whether in person or by way of fiction, the country's nascent elite came to discover some facet of the socialist world. Exposure could be eye-opening and liberating, but it could also be alienating and risky. For different generations, Soviet experience defined professional paths. It allowed an aspiring architect like Gani Strazimiri to project a bold architectural vision, just as it allowed hundreds of other youths to arm themselves with "red expertise." Discovery meant possibilities, but the possibilities were not endless. There were specific hazards, including ideological errors to be identified, acts to be submitted to criticism, offenders to be punished. The Albanian establishment was thus confronted with the problem of contamination. The Eastern bloc crises of 1956 did not introduce this problem, but they heightened the urgency. It turned out that there was an unforeseen problem with socialist internationalism: it could actually work. Internationalism could promote learning and solidarity across national borders, sometimes despite all the official hand-wringing. This raised the question, How could one import only some parts of socialism but not the others?

THE METHODS OF SOCIALISM

And then revolution dragged the veil from the faces of our women. We rejected the false idea that civilization would do harm to our mountain life. We had shut ourselves up in the mountains and let progress pass us by. We had remained motionless in one spot for thousands of years. Now we have to make up for all that lost time, but now, too, no power can hinder the onset of progress amongst us.

A schoolteacher (1951)

What we know about the man who spoke these words is what Slovak journalist Ladislav Mňačko wrote about him: He was young, a teacher, and "a Communist who entered the Party during the fighting." The two met "on the crossroads from Tirana to Scutari." But not too many more details were necessary because the teacher's words encapsulated all the essential elements of the official story of Communist power: centuries of darkness, tribal mores that had to be broken, the folly of Islam, the sweeping rush of revolution, the inevitable onset of modernity. The teacher worked in a shabby school building, but the visitor noted that it would soon be torn down and "a new uniform type of school will take its place." Inside one of those classrooms, Mňačko encountered an eight-year-old girl named Liri (Freedom). In older times, he wrote, she would have grown up to become a drudge in some household, an ignorant victim to a husband's will, a slave to arbitrary custom and the "absurdly strict bonds of religion." Not anymore. This was socialism now.[1]

Mňačko recognized that Albania was not exactly well located for the socialist project. In the past, he wrote, Albanians had fought "for their very existence against pitiless invaders." Now they were encircled by Tito's Yugoslavia and a hostile regime in Greece. But this also made it, in his view, an example of how a small state could overcome adversity against all odds. Doing so required willpower but also money and machines, which made Albania dependent on Soviet patronage. During his five meetings with Stalin between 1947 and 1951, the Albanian party chief asked for loans, weapons, and personnel. The Soviet leader, as we have seen, recommended caution in nationalizing businesses and in proceeding with collectivization. Albania was not supposed to mindlessly mimic the Soviet Union. The country, Stalin warned, ought to learn to stand on its own.[2]

But Albanian officials kept coming back to Moscow to plead for more relief. Later that year, the two party chiefs met again in Sukhumi, on the Black Sea coast, and Hoxha gushed about Stalin's hospitality, the cheerful dinner, and the jokes with the generals. He was impressed to see that the leader of the powerful Soviet Union had no waiters; he sliced his own meat from a tray. Stalin handed his Albanian guests four sacks of Georgian corn to grow. ("Wonderful corn," Hoxha gushed.) Along with the seeds, Stalin dispensed advice on the Greek civil war, on handling Yugoslav provocations, on combating malaria, on land cultivation, on organizing the police, on dealing with clerics, and on matters of history. "The great Stalin is extraordinarily simple," Enver boasted. "I will never forget that evening for the rest of my life."[3]

In fact, "the great Stalin" was repeatedly critical of Albanian missteps. In 1951 he chided Hoxha for requesting another round of industrial aid while ignoring agriculture. "Did you plant the corn I gave you?" he asked the visitor, "or did you throw it out the window?"[4] During the conversation, Hoxha obsessed over the possibility of a Yugoslav military attack. Stalin worried about the economy. He agreed to provide more aid but was reluctant to encourage economic dependency. He clarified that the Soviet Union would not establish joint companies, as the Yugoslavs had done, since Albania was neither a Soviet satellite nor a wartime collaborator. During another meeting, the Soviet Politburo member Anastas Mikoyan agreed that building factories—establishing a working class—was an important task. But he also complained that the brand-new Soviet factories lay empty. Whatever they managed to manufacture was of poor quality. "You have a lot of plans," Mikoyan added, "but you don't execute them."[5] This would backfire, he warned, as people would eventually begin to grumble, "Why did they get all these shiny Soviet factories that produce nothing?" Like Stalin, Mikoyan insisted that Albanian functionaries think about growing grains, lemons, olives, and oranges.

Then, after Stalin's death in 1953, Hoxha was back in Moscow, where Georgy Malenkov, Lavrenti Beria, and other Soviet officials duly warned him that Albania's situation was extremely serious. The country's economic prospects were bleak. The peasants were being squeezed to the bone. Workers could not afford basic necessities. The state administration was bloated. ("Not even a Rockefeller or a Morgan could afford to maintain such a bureaucracy, feeding off the back of the peasantry," Beria thundered.) The criticism this time around was far more severe than in the past.[6] A short time later, Beria was arrested. "Now that Beria has bid us goodbye," said one individual under surveillance, as reported by the Ministry of Interior, "and they're snapping each other's heads off, let's see if this one here [Mehmet Shehu] will also get booted—after all, they must follow the Soviet example."[7] Gruesome irony: to expect the imitation of Soviet examples in purges too.

Despite the rebukes in Moscow, the regime did not fundamentally change course. The country lacked a proletarian base; hence industry remained a priority. Basic goods continued to be scarce, distributed according to a dual-pricing scheme based on *triska* (ration cards).[8] The Soviet Union, in turn, could be counted on to provide a cushion when central planning went wrong. Economic decision making continued to be highly centralized, and prices and wages fixed. The government abolished food rationing in 1957, but scarcity endured. For years, the country churned out crude oil but was forced to import petroleum products because it lacked refineries. The chemical industry was tiny. Albania exported chrome ore and bitumen, but the need for grains and consumer goods was great. Cornered, party officials asked their Soviet counterparts to delay loan payments (or better yet, convert them into grants) and issue new ones, while interest accrued.[9]

Such was the socialist dynamic: Albanian self-proclaimed Stalinists using Soviet means to achieve socialist planning goals while Soviet officials berated them for doing so. Immediately after the Second World War, the Soviet regime had obsessed over security. Yet it did not cease to be, as far as the Albanian party was concerned, also a model of revolution. This helps explain the pursuit of Stalinism despite Stalin's periodic pronouncements. Both sides spoke the same language in matters domestic and foreign, even as they looked at the world from different vantage points. These differences and the substantial domestic obstacles notwithstanding, socialism persisted in the Soviet Union, as it did in Albania.

Soviet Labor, Albanian Lives

Almost all accounts of Stalinism stem from the Soviet Union or the territories occupied by Soviet troops after the Second World War. This has produced questions of legitimacy and resistance, mirroring, to an extent, the obsession of East European exiles with these regimes' "illegitimate" origins. A view of Stalinism from the Albanian periphery invites a different perspective. Since there was no military occupation, the imposition of Soviet practices unfolded in less direct ways. This shifts the discussion from Stalin's plans and the Soviet domination of East Europeans, to how Stalinism could take on meaning that was ultimately beyond Soviet reach. The incorporation of preindustrial Albania into the socialist world was bound to be a long shot. I depart, therefore, from the assumption of failure. But it is important to analyze how failures could be instrumental. It becomes necessary to consider how geopolitics meshed with an ambitious socialist project, endowing Soviet examples with local meaning along the Mediterranean.

With a groundbreaking study of a single industrial Soviet city in the 1930s, Stephen Kotkin conceived of Stalin-era socialism as a new social identity that became unavoidable, entailing a "participation of the masses in the socialist system, on negotiated terms, that helped account for that system's stability."[10] The goals of the planning authorities were important, but the argument rested on how Soviet workers made sense of the larger socialist mission. Soviet men and women learned "to speak Bolshevik"—a catchy turn of phrase that has taken on a life of its own in hundreds of footnotes, including in critiques of Kotkin, which have helped define his analysis as a transformative point in the study of Stalinism. The turn to self-fashioning and social identification has inspired a fascinating literature on Soviet subjectivity.[11] But it has also had the peculiar outcome of obscuring how the associated practices and institutions created by the Soviets did not have to stay with the Soviets. Precisely the fact that socialism was a form of subject making that the Soviets could not control caused much frustration in Moscow.

Is it obvious at all that an analysis of 1930s Soviet society should be applicable to 1950s Albania? Stalin did not think so. He warned the senior Albanian party officials that it would be foolish to pretend that their challenges were similar to what the Soviet Union had faced. Nevertheless, imitation happened, and this requires explanation. An obvious one is that the party establishment came to expect it. Socialism became synonymous in Albania with the momentous and bewildering construction of a modern state. Zog's modernization efforts pale by comparison. For long hard years, the Soviets had toiled and bled to jump-start a noncapitalist modernity. They had borrowed from the West in the name of overcoming the West. This ethos had produced brand-new cities, factories, and a historic military victory. And now? The party men in Moscow told the party men of Albania—who had led *their own* anti-Fascist struggle and had done everything necessary to secure Communist rule, including murdering rivals and imagined enemies—that the Albanian regime had to exercise caution. It would be foolish to rush. A small, isolated, and desperately poor country could not fast-forward to socialist modernity after all.

These warnings notwithstanding, signs of Soviet modernity became conspicuous. Between 1948 and 1955, Moscow provided a cement factory (in Vlorë), a sugar-processing factory (in Maliq), and an oil refinery (in Cërrik), among other projects. One of the biggest prizes of all, however, was the Stalin textile complex outside the capital. This was the regime's showpiece: Soviet in design but deeply embedded in Albania by way of its workforce. Kombinat, as it became known, was a kind of microcosm of the country during these heady years. Symbolically, it was also a construction site of human capital. In addition to churning out textiles, the mills would make conscious workers out of illiterate peasants. "Some very modern new factories have popped up," observed one East German diplomat in 1952, "but these are staffed by people who, until a short while ago, were shopkeepers, farmers, and illiterates."[12] The Stalin mills became a training ground for introducing "Soviet methods" (*metoda sovjetike*) into the everyday life of such individuals.

One way of making sense of socialist labor campaigns is to view them as exercises in domestic politics. And it is true that the back-and-forth over the definition of Soviet methods in the 1950s reveals a great deal about the logic of a party-directed push to build a workers' state in an agrarian country. But the campaign was crucially also about mapping Albanian national ambitions on an international stage.

Kombinat

Albanian officials invited Yugoslav industry experts in 1947 to help build a textile factory. But the project was marred by delays and disarray, a fact that party propagandists later attributed to Yugoslavia's "Trotskyite" efforts to sabotage Albania's rebirth after the war.[13] Tirana turned to Moscow next. The contracts signed with the Soviet Union called for the construction of a textile complex (depicted in figure 13) on the basis of Russian designs and machines, as well as the labor of Soviet personnel responsible for providing assembly assistance and training.[14] The Soviet-drafted blueprints also highlighted provisions for workers like housing blocks, clubs, cafeterias, and recreation areas.

The weaving mills would churn out desperately needed linens, coats, and uniforms. But the project stood for something bigger than textiles. This was a campaign against something systemic: party authorities depicted it as a battle against long-standing backwardness, delivering precious Soviet machines where previously there had been only mud and misery. The construction of socialism required the taming of the landscape—digging trenches, draining infested marshes, clearing the land. Along with the construction of the country's first railroad, the land reclamation projects of the late 1940s stood as the cornerstone of the party-state's ambitious modernizing plan.[15] Former swamps gave way to factories thanks to the power of the people's will and Soviet machines. "The swamp is now in bloom!" the Albanian-Soviet Friendship Society's journal would declare at the closing of the decade. "The seeds of happiness" were sown thanks to Soviet tractors.[16]

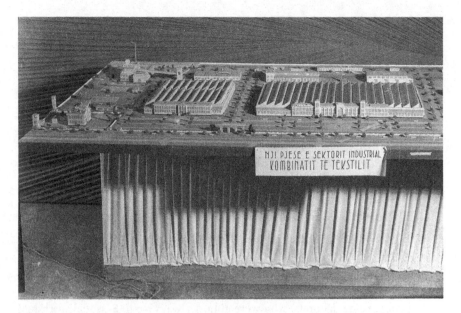

FIGURE 13. Kombinat: Architectural model of the Stalin textile complex, February 1951. ATSH.

The location of the textile complex outside the capital was also noteworthy. The area was less than three miles away from the city. The nearby village, Yzberish, consisted of scattered houses and small parcels of land. These were flanked by marshes that regularly swallowed the nearby fields in late fall until early spring. The wetland, which workers eradicated by digging ditches and draining the soil, spanned an area of 350 acres. There, along the foothills, the mills began to rise in the late 1940s, giving shape to a strange and remarkable panorama: massive shiny structures popping out of the bare, muddy landscape. The location—a bumpy bus ride away from Tirana—made Yzberish seem like something less than a town but more than a village. A handful of two-story housing units rose south of the mills and then a club, a school, a kindergarten. The main road was eventually paved. But this place never even got a proper name; it simply became known as Kombinat. Over the years, its inhabitants also became informally known as *kombinats*. People and territory became inextricably identified with the Soviet machines.

Rural but striving for urbanity, Yzberish became a kind of microcosm of the country during the first decade of socialism. Kombinat was the first big industrial project to be built from scratch. The assembly, let alone the operation, of the different sectors—spinning, weaving, dyeing, and finishing departments in addition to repair sectors and attendant shops—was unprecedented. The complex was not only the embodiment of "selfless Soviet aid." Party propagandists claimed that this was a factory for *making workers*. Along with streamlining textile production, in a country where men and women still wore old-fashioned handmade garments, the mills would be converting unskilled peasants into conscious workers. "There," noted one celebratory article, "our working class will grow up and mature."[17] Another author agreed that the mills constituted "a great school."[18] Peasant boys and men and, significantly, hundreds of young peasant women handling the weaving machines would receive training from Soviet specialists. They would move into new apartments. They would assume a new identity.

Such talk of Kombinat serving as a school was more than mindlessly rehearsed propaganda. Party functionaries worried about the lack of a working class in a workers' state. Even those workers who could loosely be defined as such were overwhelmingly unskilled, so the problem was technical and also ideological. Consider the numbers: by 1954, national construction enterprises counted 9,600 workers, about a third of whom qualified as "specialists" (400 of the workers were women). Only half of the ordinary workers, however, were permanent.[19] Enterprises relied heavily on seasonal laborers, who were almost always rural. Seasonal work had a tendency to hinder training, consistent plan fulfillment, and professionalization. Then there were the waves of party-mandated purges of the workforce from "antiparty elements," former landowners, alleged collaborators, real and imagined criminals, and other assorted suspicious persons. Antikulak campaigns further exacerbated the problem. As practiced in the 1950s, socialism both obsessively required and inadvertently undermined the creation of a working class.

Stalin had worried that the Albanian regime might alienate the peasants. In the early 1950s, in fact, collectivization faced backlash. It went into high gear only during the second half of the decade, expanding the socialist sector to over 80 percent of the available agricultural land. One Soviet report admitted that Albanian authorities had "erroneously" labeled some poor and middle peasants as kulaks.[20] To make up for shortages, government authorities used prison laborers extensively in construction. But they still struggled with the labor force and spent considerable time discussing how to enlist youths in construction.[21] Even if they managed to get more peasants to work in industry, or more young people to "volunteer," the problem of political reliability only became more pronounced. In 1953, the interior minister warned that there were more Communists "sitting in offices than in production." Potential party enemies, in other words, stood where they could do the most damage, while Communists filed report after report behind a desk. He urged his colleagues that "our machines need to be taken over by Communists."[22]

The urgency of the early 1950s was a function of necessity just as much as ideological fervor. It also helps explain why the Stalin textile complex entered the

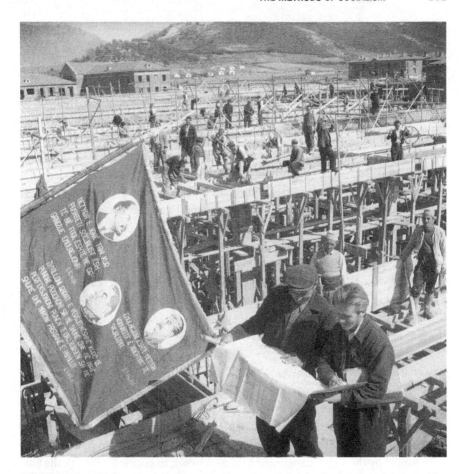

FIGURE 14.   Workers at the construction site of the Stalin textile complex with a flag adorned with pictures and quotations from Lenin, Stalin, and Hoxha, early 1951. ATSH.

official history of Albanian socialism as a colossal victory achieved within two years. Unsurprisingly, a different picture emerged on the ground. Construction began on 31 July 1949, with Enver Hoxha ceremoniously laying the first stone. Officially, the complex began work in November 1951.[23] Yet construction of some parts proceeded long after the finishing date. The inauguration also proved immature when the mills suspended work altogether in early 1952 for lack of raw materials.[24] Before the inauguration, one local farmer had urged his colleagues to cultivate industrial plants because "like people who are born, grow up, and need to eat, so the rising Combine is about to be finished and will soon need cotton."[25] The complex was finished, there was no cotton, and without it, the brand-new mills stood in silence. When work picked up again, it dragged on for months at a time. By the end of 1952, most of the industrial sectors were ready. Then a mill for woolens was added to the original project, so construction resumed. Some 1,141 workers received medals and honors of some sort for their work. But bottlenecks, long delays, errors, finger pointing, and shortages persisted for years.[26]

From the early stages of construction, it became clear that the transfer of Soviet blueprints was not a simple matter. Physically getting the materials to Albania was an ordeal. There were limited options: by the diplomatic courier service of the Soviet embassy in Tirana (obviously dependent on the willingness and availability of Soviet diplomats); by cargo ships (Odessa to Durrës), a long and infrequent journey considered difficult and requiring "trustworthy" couriers; or, finally, by diplomatic mail to Albanian embassies in Eastern Europe and then by hand delivery the rest of the way to Tirana. Frequently, blueprints traveled on commercial vessels or by hand when delegations happened to make the journey. Long vessel journeys and altered schedules of informal couriers inevitably caused delays. The general construction plan, for example, crucial as it was, arrived weeks later than the scheduled date. Inspections carried out with the Soviet construction adviser and a Soviet chief engineer determined that up until the end of June 1950 only 39 percent of all planned work had been carried out.[27]

When some Soviet blueprints arrived, other materials, like specifications for a power station, were still missing. When shop floor plans were all accounted for, construction could not move ahead because of delays with hydraulics. Similarly, construction of workers' housing stalled because technical details of the sewage system were not yet available.[28] There was an inflexible logic to the order of construction, impervious to the constant pressure from above to have the mills operational by the strict inauguration date—chosen to symbolically link the Stalin complex to the anniversaries of the Russian Revolution and the founding of the Party of Labor. Frustrated, government higher-ups pushed hard.[29] There were instances when blueprints traveled from Moscow by different channels, arriving at different, unpredictable times.[30] Shipment of heavy machines was an ordeal of a completely different magnitude. The equipment for the textile mills might survive the long journey at sea to Durrës, only to suffer damage during the short but rough ride from the port to the construction site outside Tirana. Was it perhaps because local workers did not understand the Russian-language handling instructions? Or could it be, as the Soviet furnishers suggested, a case of "enemy work"?[31] No aspect of technology transfer could be taken for granted.

These hurdles were part of the reason why the industrial complex that emerged in Yzberish could seem all the more impressive. Coming from Tirana, visitors were suddenly faced with an ornate arched entrance flanked by two towers designed to resemble vernacular structures. The massive doors on the first floor were crowned with stucco arches. Above, an elaborate cornice fixed Stalin's name and the dates of construction on the façade. The winding gallery, which encircled the northwestern edges of the complex's main square, sustained a typical roof made of mud bricks. Behind it, in a linear procession, lay the mills and the shops. In front of the entrance, facing south, an enormous statue of Stalin with an outstretched arm stood on a plinth. There was a workers' club named, appropriately, "May 1." Black-and-white photographs from the time, like figure 15, show that it was modestly appointed inside. But it was new, and it held the promise of some social life.

Unfinished and cluttered, the textile complex became a backdrop to choreographed meetings with famous Soviet visitors who inevitably made a stop during their official Albanian trips. The screenwriter Arkadi Perventsev wrote of young

FIGURE 15. Game room at the construction workers' club, February 1951. The sign on the wall reads, "Glory to the Bolshevik Party!" A display of photographs depicts local Stakhanovites and their work routines. ATSH.

peasants knee-deep in construction "eagerly drinking in the stories about the Soviet textile mills."[32] When we look at the emerging geography of the socialist world, the Albanian textile works seem recognizably Soviet. Plenty of other industrial towns, a large number of them also named after Stalin, dotted the Eastern bloc of the early 1950s. For example, there was the Stalin chemicals complex in Dimitrovgrad, Bulgaria, which featured a similarly grand entrance, along with the city's Stalin Boulevard, Museum of Socialist Construction, and Park of Leisure and Culture.[33] But it was precisely this indistinct Sovietness that served to mark unknown Albania on the international map of Stalinism.

The workers' district, which emerged on one side of the road leading to Tirana, was at first no district at all. A couple of two-story units emerged, arranged in the Soviet block (*kvartaly*) system. Over time, this arrangement proved too elaborate, the Soviet architectural blueprints too costly. Out of necessity, the total Soviet design became approximated into a local hybrid. The originally planned structures housed the local party chiefs, the top managers, and the administrators. These were numbered buildings, but many locals referred to them simply as "the Soviet buildings." Projections for 1953 called for 3,500 workers, employees, and trainees living near the complex. Fewer than half of them could be housed on site, which meant that some 1,000 individuals would have to stay in Tirana and the rest required new housing.[34] As the workforce expanded, the contours of the residential area grew. By the end of the decade, this emerging settlement would house close to 14,000 people. Most were workers in the mills, joined by their families, who relocated from around the country.

When it came to building additional housing, the dilemma was this: Soviet designs, spatially more generous, were preferable but cost more. The alternative was stripped-down one-story prototypes that could be replicated easily. Government officials were thus faced with the dilemma of sticking to the Soviet blueprints or downgrading them. Some officials proposed using mud bricks to keep costs low. Others insisted on using better materials. Such deliberations exuded frustration with the realization that construction in Yzberish, highly touted as the symbol of nascent socialist industry, had to diverge from the Soviet scheme.[35] Two architects surveying construction results in the spring of 1954 noted that the local building enterprise, apparently faced with a shortage of materials, had combined bricks with concrete slabs when finishing interiors and surfaces. Soviet blueprints had not simply been downgraded; some of the built elements seemed to bear no resemblance to those in the original plans. Walls were crooked and door frames asymmetrical. There were odd nooks and corners resulting from sudden changes in the thickness of the walls.[36]

Living conditions around the mills were poor, mirroring conditions in much of the country. Construction workers lived in structures that were, like the workforce itself, temporary (but which became permanent as money dried up). One early newspaper report of the construction campaign described workers as living in twenty long barracks, each divided into three rooms. Inside, some thirty workers slept wherever they could. "[37] (Photographs from the time show some barracks containing at least fifteen beds each.) Twice weekly there was the possibility to shower, though it is unclear if showers operated regularly. Distinguished workers enjoyed a special barrack and were entitled to better meals—in theory. But even the more enthusiastic reports did not conceal the fact that workers lived in ramshackle huts, slept in bunker beds stacked with little or no space between them, and enjoyed few, if any, provisions, such as a stove. Winters were harsh. Windows more often than not failed to keep the wind out. One in five working days could be lost as a result of illness. Working day or not, workers still had to be fed. Government rules called for every worker to be provided with bed sheets, a cover, and a dresser. But linens were few, and there were no dressers to be had.[38]

What was the daily routine of a worker at the Stalin textile factories? The best on-the-ground view emerges not from Albanian sources but from the CIA. In 1954, American intelligence operatives filed a report describing a typical worker's day. They took the example of a married couple with two children, a family living in a one-room apartment with a kitchen but no bathroom. The husband would begin his day at 5:00 a.m. Yzberish was too far to walk, so the man would catch the bus (a fleet made of old Italian Fiat vehicles; in fact, Tirana's inhabitants kept calling the transportation authority S.A.T.A., after the Fascist-era entity). At the entrance, the worker would hand in a document (*fletë-hyrje*), which he would get back at the end of the shift. There were two eight-hour shifts: 6:00 a.m. to 2:00 p.m. and 2:00 p.m. to 10:00 p.m. At the end of his, the worker would complete a form specifying working hours and norms achieved. This was important because those scribbled numbers would determine wages earned.

The end of the shift did not mean the end of a working day, however. There were endless meetings to attend. A worker would typically participate in a political education session, a meeting on plan fulfillment, and another meeting called by the trade union. Additionally, there would be special sessions on international affairs or events organized by the Soviet-Albanian Friendship Society (recitals, press readings, occasionally dances). If the worker happened to be a party member, he would have more meetings still; the CIA memo estimated that in fact a party member might spend more hours per month (220 vs. 208) in these kinds of meetings than actually on the shop floor. Sunday was typically occupied with "volunteering." ("Subject worker has only one Sunday a month to call his own.") His wife's responsibilities, in addition, would also involve meetings of the Women's Union.[39]

This overall picture would have been familiar to many other industry workers. For example, an inspection among workers of artisanal and textile cooperatives in the capital a few years later revealed that more than a hundred workers relied on a single public bathroom in cramped quarters. The facilities were not cleaned as frequently as required by established public hygiene guidelines, so even in those units boasting more than one bathroom, half or more were constantly clogged. Basements, hallways, courtyards, and workers' clubs were filthy, unkempt, and packed with litter. Clean drinking water was frequently unavailable. Workers lacked first aid kits and proper uniforms.[40] (Administrators waited for the Stalin textile mills to produce the first cotton garments in order to clothe workers.) Add to these conditions the dangers inherent in the construction industry, where on-site injuries, including deadly ones, happened frequently.

Beyond matters of shelter, hygiene, and safety, there was the problem of feeding the workforce. In cafeterias, pasta was a daily staple. Even if one could afford to pay more (for having attained higher production targets), there was not much to obtain. Depending on luck and on whether foodstuffs came from the executive committee (local authorities) or directly from the consumer enterprise, deliveries might include wheat bread, which was popular, or the more common and disdained variety made of corn.[41] Meat and eggs were hard to come by, and the distribution of vegetables was also irregular. In 1955, some construction workers reportedly went without food deliveries for several days. A few construction sites had their own retail network of small stores (food, clothes, cafés) attached to them, but others were completely dependent on outside deliveries. Trade officials, viewing such retail stores as unprofitable, seemed reluctant to expand their network.[42] When one reads the endless litany of shortcomings, it can be easy to miss how movement to a place like Yzberish could constitute a form of social advancement. Those who relocated there, and especially the women, were eager to assume a new identity—as workers—and adopt a way of life that was very different from the rural one.

Two such workers, named Ollga and Afroviti, put it this way, years later, in 1959: "When we first got here, we found only two ramshackle, filthy barracks blackened by smoke." Where the Stalin mills stood now there had been only mud and mire. "We had just arrived from the village," they recalled, "and we did not even own a pair of sandals. We had no shoes. We could only dream about boots." The article, marking Khrushchev's historic visit to the Stalin mills that year, described these women as having abandoned their heavy rural garb to work in factories that would produce fashionable dresses made of light, colorful fabric. "One's soul is joyful," the author added, "when seeing girls who yesterday were herding goats now seeking out fashion, sandals and rose-colored sweaters; yesterday's peasant boys now seeking knowledge; and the old folk enjoy the shades

FIGURE 16. A female worker in the dye sector at the Stalin textile complex, February 1953. The small banner reads "Most distinguished in working for peace." ATSH.

in the parks of this newly erected town."[43] Everything in this place was less than a decade old—the buildings, the trees, the six bustling kindergartens. So were Ollga's and Afroviti's children (Gjergji, Vasili, Vjollca), who were born in this new place.

This was a common theme in press reports, which lingered on the bleak past lives of formerly "locked up" women. Anti-Fascist liberation had thus morphed into personal liberation. Some women, reporters were careful to point out, had studied or visited the Soviet Union. Others had enrolled in local courses. They had become skilled weavers, machine operators, shop managers.[44] The tone was similar to that of Mňačko, the Slovak journalist, who wrote that Albanian women used to be "enslaved" by religion. In the Albania of old days, he explained, sometimes "an animal had a greater value than a woman, and the value of a woman used to be quoted in terms of money." The anti-Fascist struggle had mobilized the younger women, and now they worked in government, hospitals, or "behind the wheel of a car." A recent outcome of the party-led battle against the Muslim veil was that whenever a women's group now entered a village, "men tremble."[45]

The visitor relished the novelty of all this. But the battle over women's veils predated the Communist regime. Lev Sukacev, the commander of the Albanian Royal Guards under Zog, recalled how the king had outlawed the harems, forcing his nobles to bring only one wife—unveiled—to formal receptions. "How different was the lot of these silent sufferers," he later gushed in his memoir, "after they were given a freedom they had not even petitioned for! They were not 'allowed' to remove their veils—they were *required* to do so. And to wear European dress as well."[46] There was precedent, then, for the state to intervene in women's lives and to do so by way of disciplining the women's husbands and brothers. An important difference was that the 1950s campaigns were not limited to the country's elites, and they came with promises of economic self-reliance and new labor relations, as well as new family laws, including provisions for divorce. The Abkhazian writer Georgy Gulia, who visited the country during the 1952 Friendship Month, announced that the veil was "gone for good." A few years earlier, girls used to be betrothed to strangers when they were still children. Now they were speaking up against their parents and yearning to surpass production quotas.[47]

The faces of unveiled women stood as a testament to the power of socialism and modern technology. They were also a reminder of the unfinished business with religion. In 1949, the party boss admitted to the Soviet ambassador that religious practices and bonds were hard to break. One way the party could do this, he thought, would be by controlling the finances of the religious communities.[48] If churches and mosques followed the party directives, they would keep receiving funds. Those deemed anti-Communist, however, like the northern Catholic community, could be starved. A special office within the government had jurisdiction over the clergy. Under pressure, many religious leaders submitted. A 1952 gathering of Catholic, Orthodox, Muslim, and Bektashi (a dervish order with an important presence in Albania) clergy championed the international efforts for peace and praised the regime's treatment of believers.[49] When the Sudanese ambassador to Rome visited Albania, he appeared shocked at the clerics' touting of the party line. The local mufti, he reported, was "a different kind of Moslem than I." While perfectly orthodox in his adherence to Islam, the Albanian cleric apparently turned the conversation—repeatedly—to the superiority of Communism. Stalin's statue, the visitor took note, "was even taller than the mosque."[50]

In this ongoing effort to exploit existing social bonds and forge new ones, factories became places where workers were agents and subjects of social transformation. There was pride in working in a brand-new factory. There was also pride in its Soviet origins—this foreignness did not necessarily make the structures seem alien because they quickly became part of a local story of overcoming the past. The Stalin mills stood for the idea of Albania's catching up, which explains the urgency of declaring them a success even as the machines kept breaking down. Then, in 1952, the first cotton garments came out—hefty, ill fitting, but *Albanian*. It is in this regard that the Stalin textile complex became a kind of microcosm of the country: the boastful party rhetoric, the conspicuous Soviet engineers, the peasant women operating machines, the shoddy sleeping quarters, the inevitable pasta in the crowded cafeteria.

Authorities intended the Stalin mills to become a symbol, and unintentionally the mills became a symbol: of the confusion of forced industrialization in an agrarian setting, the misery of breakneck labor, of distress and disease, and also of all-consuming aspirations for a better life. The mills also became a training ground for Soviet methods—metaphorically, in terms of how one was supposed to engage with the project of building socialism, but also literally, as physical acts. Against the barren landscape, this industrial growth outside the capital looked foreign. The strange thing was how quickly it became familiar.

Stakhanov Travels to the Balkans

A Soviet campaign designed around the feats of the Donbas miner Aleksei Stakhanov in 1935, Stakhanovism pushed workers to surpass production norms and break existing records. In the early 1950s, the movement spread across the Eastern bloc. East Germany had Adolf Hennecke, a coal miner from Saxony, whom the local party apparatus turned into a model laborer. Poland had Wincenty Pstrowski, also a coal miner, and the hero bricklayer Piotr Ożański. The Hungarians had their local example in Ignác Pióker. Bulgaria had talented weavers, front-rankers, and Stakhanovites modeled on Soviet examples. Andrzej Wajda's classic *Man of Marble* immortalized this history in the figure of Mateusz Birkut, a Polish Stakhanovite of peasant stock, who was able to lay bricks at record speed in the steelworks of Nowa Huta. With its enforced enthusiasm and forced routines, Stakhanovism invited backlash and ridicule, not to mention the ire of workers compelled to do more with less.[51]

Albania declared its first Stakhanovites in 1952. The government enacted rules for promoting shock workers (*sulmues*, literally, attackers), drawn from Soviet examples. It established special elite worker courses and a system of rewards for the highest achievers. The party newspaper extolled the latter repeatedly, singing the praises of advanced Soviet industrial knowledge. Examples included individuals like Enver Hoti, a worker at the Shkodër cement works, who pledged to work an equivalent of five times the daily quotas (*norma*) and who reportedly christened this achievement a "peace norm," a gesture meant to embrace the two rallying cries of the day—breakneck work in the factory and peace across the globe.[52]

Given a context in which labor was seasonal and the workforce unskilled, reports of sudden record-breaking productivity bursts understandably invite suspicion. Indeed, according to government regulations, enterprises were themselves responsible for drawing up lists of their overachieving workers. Local party and government bosses reviewed these before forwarding them up the government chain.[53] This bureaucratic process, cumbersome as it was for managers working under the pressure of the plan, hinged on careful record keeping, precise estimates of working hours, and output per individual worker. It is impossible to assess how much of this record keeping was factual and how much was aspirational. Correspondence between branch ministries and local enterprises suggests that there was quite a bit of embellishment.[54] But exaggeration was the point: once some physical barrier had been reportedly broken, nearly everything might seem possible. The Soviet example appeared more attainable. Albanian planners vigorously embraced Stakhanovism, which, they asserted, was not merely a sustained effort to break production quotas but a lifestyle that extended beyond the factory.

That kind of rhetoric notwithstanding, government authorities relaxed the requirements for earning the Stakhanovite title, a reflection of the fact that laborers were overwhelmingly unskilled. According to 1952 rules, workers could earn the title if they adopted techniques and methods from well-known Soviet Stakhanovites. Less frequently, at least in the early 1950s, workers might come up with their own innovations (*inovatorë*), resulting in surpassed norms, improved efficiency, and lower production costs.[55] Elections of Stakhanovites took place at the beginning of every month, with each enterprise charged with the task of choosing them. In Stalin City, for example, twenty-six workers received the title in the summer of 1952. Their portraits appeared in the party newspaper under the headline "The Glory of Our Working Class." Shock workers and innovators were eligible for better housing, and they topped the lists for bonuses, scholarships, or a cabin in the workers' seaside holiday camp.[56] Beyond praise, then, material privileges were important because, as an earlier government memo had put it, "this assistance that these workers get ought to have an impact" on the rest of the working collective (*masat punonjëse*).[57]

Stakhanovism came with the ubiquitous *norma*, chief weapons, as one historian of Soviet labor has referred to them, "which the regime employed to try to force workers to conform to its desires and demands."[58] Instead of daily quotas, *puna me akord* entailed a certain amount of work or output supposed to be achieved within a month or longer. Higher intensity of labor could be attained through regular raises of work targets and changes in the categorization of skills, which were tied to wages. But the movement also came with a distinct material culture. Visual propaganda included conspicuous boards specifying daily activity and plan fulfillment, placards showing individual and collective pledges (sometimes addressed directly to Hoxha as *Komandant*), and places of honor reserved for displaying the photographs and names of members of the top-performing brigades, like those shown in figure 17. There were flags for which brigades competed with one another every month. Those lagging behind, on the other hand, could similarly end up being taken to task in this public fashion.

FIGURE 17. The language of speed: workers' emulation board at the Stalin textile complex, February 1951. The box on the right lists the eighteen highest-achieving workers at the site, headed by the local mason Negri Nikolla. On the left, illustrations depict the best and the worst: the most efficient sectors are represented by an airplane, the slower ones by a bike and a carriage, the least efficient by a turtle. ATSH.

The other crucial element was the presence of individuals who lent a face to the movement. Halil Kraja, a lathe operator at the Enver Machine Works in Tirana (figure 18), was among the more prominent.[59] Kraja was the first in the country to adopt the working methods of the Urals Stakhanovite Pavel Bykov, under the guidance of a local Soviet engineer.[60] Government officials showcased Kraja as Bykov's faraway pupil, sending him on a tour around the country to popularize the methods. During such meetings, Kraja swore that Soviet innovations had enabled him to cut metal much faster. "At first I worked alone," he wrote in an article in the Friendship Society's journal, "but over time my friends trusted me and followed along.[61] Kraja proudly reported that his colleagues had sometimes been able to implement the method on the spot. Indeed, such was the intensity of the propaganda around Kraja that word of his feats traveled across the Atlantic, reaching the American intelligence agency, which described him as "a Moslem aged 26 from Shkodër, a fanatical Communist."[62]

Kraja's example shows that the adoption of Soviet models relied on face-to-face encounters, especially since many of his coworkers were not party members (and some not even Albanian).[63] The plant got its bolts, aluminum, bronze, cast iron, and carbon steel from the Soviet Union. Then, during the 1952 Friendship Month, it also received the Soviet Stalin Prize laureate Mukhanov. The so-called Levchenko-Mukhanov method, named in his honor, was meant to increase

FIGURE 18. Exemplary body: Halil Kraja, a worker at the Enver Hoxha Auto and Tractor Plant, toured various cities to promote Soviet methods, 1950. ATSH.

productivity by cutting down production time and limiting the use of raw materials. Photographs from the time (see figure 19) depicted the visitor speaking with his Albanian counterparts, an encounter that presented the local Albanian innovators as heirs to Soviet technique.[64] The following year, *Pravda* published an article quoting another distinguished worker named Shaban, who had this to say about the Soviet technical experience: "Six seas separate us from the Soviet Union. But there is no friend nearer and dearer to our people than the Soviet people. Every day, when I place my hands on the cutting machine, made in the Soviet Union, it seems to me like I am shaking the hands of the Soviet friends who set my motherland free."[65]

FIGURE 19.   Stakhanovism as a meeting ground: Soviet Stakhanovite Grigory Mukhanov speaks with Albanian counterparts during a visit to the Enver Hoxha Auto and Tractor Plant, September 1952. ATSH.

Shaban did not mean an actual military liberation by Soviet hands. But the arrival of industrial machines might be seen as offering a kind of liberation too—from the drudgery of old ways—and as a kind of substitute for the Red Army's actual liberation of Albania. Other workers echoed similar narratives of salvation. Servete, a worker at the Tirana woodworking plant, credited the party with saving her from "the abyss of fanaticism" and leading her into a new, revolutionary life. She had started work in 1947 and had quickly learned the skills of the trade, taking the initiative to be among the first to adopt Soviet methods in her plant. This had made her an example for the other workers. Not long after, she had mastered two separate skills, as both a carpentry mechanic working at the sawmills and in polishing the furniture. The effort seemed to have paid off: she earned praise and higher wages, and she became a Stakhanovite.[66]

Figures from 1953 put the number of workers engaged in some type of "socialist emulation" at 48,141. Of those, Stakhanovites numbered 5,200.[67] Authorities convened a special conference, modeled after a similar event held in Bulgaria, but it did not go well. Some ministers apparently skipped the proceedings, inviting the wrath of Mehmet Shehu. Soviet methods were an important party matter, he thundered at them, but they had instead perhaps chosen "to go to the stadium to catch a game."[68] Ignorance of Soviet methods, officials kept warning, would no longer be tolerated.[69] Some of the hurdles were obvious. Russian-language instructions required translation, and the obscure texts made references to things like mysterious machines, soil types, and ventilation systems. To do the job, government officials turned to students who had recently graduated in the Soviet Union. In this translation frenzy, some managers simply copied Soviet quotas, as one memo put it, "straight from Soviet books, decreased by a small factor, but without measuring them against our building conditions, the capacity of our workers, and the tools available to us."[70]

Metoda sovjetike entailed distinct ways of doing things. However, in practice, a Soviet method initially stood for anything that maximized efficiency and lowered production costs. This ambiguity allowed managers to report higher instances of Soviet borrowings and also raise labor expectations. What qualified as a Soviet method, say, in early 1952 might be insufficient the following year. Yet this ambiguity of definition also posed a problem in measuring the success of Soviet borrowing. If virtually everything (blueprints, machines, manuals) came from the Soviet Union, was it not the case that all production at the Stalin textile complex, as an example, resulted from employing Soviet methods? Since they were about worker education, it became necessary to identify Soviet methods more explicitly, count them, and report them as discrete acts. The term came to refer to specific techniques that Stakhanovites or shock workers could champion and popularize. In 1954 alone, the Albanian-Soviet Friendship Society organized over six hundred meetings to "spread Soviet experience" in factory work. One thousand other meetings focused on Soviet methods in agriculture.

There were Soviet methods in mining and in driving, for gathering cotton, for classifying soil and for painting walls, for repairing tools and for cutting metal.[71] Farmers could plough the earth according to published Soviet techniques ("the fish backbone method"). There were reports that cows produced more milk if one employed Soviet methods in feeding them. Truck drivers could record their trips using a Soviet-style chart.[72] Workers in the oil industry could adopt the "Kafarov method."[73] Doctors might learn from the teachings of Ivan Pavlov, the well-known Russian physiologist.[74] Such Soviet methods became so prominent because the party vigorously championed industrialization, but Soviet methods also existed in many other areas of governance. How should the state deal with hooligans? "Refer to the Soviet materials we have obtained," Politburo member Hysni Kapo instructed the minister of health.[75] On some issues, officials referred to the Soviet materials but did not find the answers. How should the government handle prostitution? (Albanian bureaucrats proposed withholding medication as a form of discipline.) What about adulterers? The Soviet manuals did not say. Instead, officials looked to regulations in the "people's democracies."[76]

In 1951, the party's agitprop department declared that Albanians apparently had trouble making sense of foreign words. Therefore, it recommended rendering foreign words phonetically into Albanian, despite the fact that the Albanian language, unlike Russian, uses a Latin script. "We should add that in the Soviet Union foreign words are also written phonetically," added the memo signed by Nexhmije Hoxha.[77] Such references to Soviet authority served to make linguistic choices seem far more obvious than they were. Appropriate films for viewing, similarly, conformed to lists drawn from the Soviet distribution representative. Albanian theater conformed to the "Stanislavski system," thanks to the efforts of a Soviet director dispatched to the country. "Our theater does not depend any longer on the whims of this or that person," one survey of cultural affairs explained, "but it is rooted and supported by well-known Soviet theory."[78] Soviet pedagogical models entered Albanian schools thanks to Soviet-trained administrators. In some of these areas, Soviet methods consisted of ready-made blueprints. But Albanian bureaucrats could also guess what the right path might be simply by referring to Soviet literature on a given subject.

Imparting Soviet expertise required a constant supply of Soviet personnel. At this stage of the Cold War, foreign observers, including Western intelligence operatives, greatly exaggerated the number of such advisers. Still, in a small and isolated country, even small numbers of foreigners drew attention. Uniformed military advisers were the most conspicuous, but Soviet personnel could be found across civilian ranks too. Some high-level advisers sat in on government meetings despite being limited, on paper, to a "consultative" role.[79] These relations required

defining roles, expectations, and duties, which were not obvious. Talk of friendship and brotherly assistance notwithstanding, Soviet-Albanian encounters during these years were as much about creating distance as they were about speaking
the same language of progress and achieving approved industrial goals.

Take the example of Maliq, where the much-touted construction of a
Soviet-designed sugar-processing plant was under way. The Soviet assembly workers impressed the locals, according to one report, "with their experience and great
Stakhanovite skills." The Soviet guests had beds, mattresses, and sheets. They had
access to a radio and board games (but there was no vodka left in the local market).
But they also lived separately from the local workforce, their living quarters secured
by guards, and they ate in a special cafeteria—their meals prepared by Albanian
personnel screened for "good political standing."[80] In Stalin City, Soviet oil technicians similarly complained about having to walk eight kilometers to work (there
were no cars) and about fruits and vegetables being unavailable in the local market. (One specialist complained that fish had been served only once.) The ration
cards were useless because local stores lacked supplies.[81] Conditions in the capital would have been somewhat better. There too, however, there were complaints
about missing heat during winter. A strongly worded government memo warned
that unheated interiors produced bouts of flu and bronchitis.[82]

Faced with Soviet complaints, in 1951 the government established an office
dedicated to handling the socialist visitors. Authorities kept the Soviet personnel
separate, in part to provide them with better living conditions than the locals,
who had to get by on less. But the enforced distance, which could be construed as
a sign of respect and a form of insurance against political problems, contradicted
the whole Soviet mission: How could one impart Soviet methods if physical contact was limited? But then, when there was contact and interaction, disagreements
ensued. In Stalin City, Soviet engineers and their Albanian counterparts found
themselves locked in a conflict at the end of 1952. Since this involved Soviet specialists, personality clashes turned into a political embarrassment, involving the
Soviet ambassador and the Albanian Politburo.[83] These were the initial indications. A local director had reportedly ignored the technical advice provided by
Soviet engineers attached to the project. Disagreements had turned into angry
arguments, which eventually turned into daily abuse. An investigation ensued.

Investigators interviewed the local party boss, the Soviet team of engineers and
experts, and a number of security police informants. The Soviets deemed the local
director abrasive. One rig specialist complained that Albanian workers labored
efficiently, in line with Soviet recommendations, when he was on site but that they
slacked off as soon as he left. The local personnel complied, he said, "only because
they are afraid of controls."[84] If Soviet technical recommendations (he referred
to them as "our Soviet experience") could be so readily ignored, what were they
doing in Albania in the first place? Albanian managers, for their part, complained

that it was a daunting task to get unskilled workers to comply with Soviet expectations. Moreover, the local party boss pointed out that the Soviet engineers had not always been in agreement on certain technical matters. On occasion, they had issued contradictory advice. Sometimes they had been wrong. (By way of his party position, this official was in a unique position to admit this so directly.)

Back in 1949, the Soviet ambassador had passed on the observation that Albanian workers accepted Soviet recommendations "unconditionally" but failed to put them into practice.[85] The conflict in Stalin City a few years later shows that Soviet recommendations might involve conflicting ideas. And because it was risky to deny the applicability of Soviet experience, it became tricky to address technical problems directly.[86] The upshot was that Soviet experience continued to serve as a powerful but nebulous reference. Around the country, then, managers sought to make Soviet methods more explicit: a way of building a wall, a way of cutting metal, a way of organizing theater. But workplace relations reflected unsettled questions about power dynamics that went well beyond the confines of a textile mill somewhere on the fringes of an Albanian city. Were the Soviets actually in charge here or not? They were not, in any formal sense, although Hoxha brought up the issue with the Soviet embassy in Tirana, advocating for more involvement of Soviet chief engineers in the name of efficiency.[87]

But Soviet engineers were not subordinate to their Albanian counterparts either. The place they occupied in the country's enterprises was ambiguous: They were special *guests*. Some locals felt intimidated by them, but others felt emboldened, like the Stalin City manager who retorted to a frustrated Soviet expert, who had threatened to leave for the Soviet Union, that there was no reason for him to leave because "Stalin sent you here to help us." Investigations into the affair were thorough because of the political implications involved. Mehmet Shehu, deputy premier at the time, held special meetings with all officials involved. It became clear that Albanian managers could not hold Soviet specialists accountable in the same manner as they could ordinary personnel. In drawing these lines, state authorities combined expectations of cultural authority (hospitality accorded to the foreign guests) with ideological reasoning (the value of Soviet expertise). Disrespecting the Soviets could be doubly problematic—a social as well as a political problem. When speaking to these guests from the homeland of socialism, then, locals were to speak *in a socialist manner*.[88]

Exemplary Bodies

Nowhere was the introduction of Soviet methods more conspicuous than in construction, which carried symbolic significance for the party-led crusade to make the country modern. Albania's construction industry consisted of ten national and local enterprises, including special entities devoted to roads, bridges, railways, and housing. Ministry officials vigorously promoted "rational" Soviet industrial methods among workers, allocating special funds and perks to those who employed them. The highest achievers had their pictures published in the party paper, their feats publicly celebrated on bulletin boards.[89]

One such method, especially popular during the early stages of construction, bore the name of Andrei Kulikov. A Soviet mason, Kulikov had figured out a way to lay a brick in two seconds. This Leningrad builder had become something of a celebrity among fellow workers in the Soviet Union, but his name also circulated in 1950s Albania.[90] The Kulikov method involved a few simple but important steps: strategically organizing the work site before the shift and minimizing body movements. Workers also made use of a special shovel to lay the mortar. In May 1950, the Friendship Society called a special national conference in Yzberish to popularize the method. Instead of the usual speeches, the meeting took the form of a mass competition between construction workers in Yzberish and Maliq—the two showcase projects of the decade. The Yzberish team won the Friendship Society's cash prize.

The Kulikov method also got an Albanian face: a mason named Negri Nikolla, who worked on the construction of the Stalin textile works. Nikolla began applying the Kulikov method in 1949. It remains unclear who picked him for the task (in all likelihood, it was the local party organization or the Friendship Society). In a newspaper article entitled "23 cubic meters in 8 hours," Nikolla admitted that Soviet methods had at first struck him as extremely taxing. He had overcome the difficulties, however, by carefully listening to his Soviet supervisors and by committing fully to the tasks. The effort, he reassured readers, had brought rewards: "With this new Stakhanovite method, I have managed to earn 800 lekë in one day whereas with the older ones only 200 lekë. My work has been widely praised but I have also gotten paid."[91]

Like the Stakhanovite Halil Kraja, Nikolla toured the country to promote "his" Soviet method. "These are new times, my brothers," he reportedly told other masons during a meeting. "Here is what I mean, comrades. Instead of thirty different movements I used to make when laying bricks before, now thanks to the Kulikov method I only make three." Nikolla urged his fellow workers to go even further: "Comrade Kulikov lays thirty to forty bricks per minute. We too must make more rational use of our time, as he does. Each new day will bring us better results."[92] At the end of the meeting, Nikolla reportedly rolled up his sleeves and demonstrated the Kulikov method. A reporter described the scene. The process "was peculiarly speedy." In forty minutes, the team working with Nikolla managed to build a wall with a perimeter of fifteen meters. Another team, which had been laying bricks parallel to Nikolla's group but by employing "old methods,"

FIGURE 20. The new ways: on-site demonstration of Soviet methods in construction, February 1951. ATSH.

barely finished a meager three rows along a perimeter of four meters. The superiority of Soviet body movements was plain to see. "Even if one were a machine," a bricklayer who witnessed the demonstration observed, "it would be impossible to build faster than this."[93]

Such reports about the miracle mason were grandiose in tone, but they were also riddled with folksy idioms. Unlike the Soviet advisers, whose authority might seem daunting, Nikolla was a common man in appearance and speech. The scraps of evidence that have survived show that he could be skilled in exercising the official rhetoric ("the new times" of socialism, "plan overfulfillment," exertion in the name of a higher goal), but he also resorted to colloquialisms. This is not surprising; his speeches were supposed to convince other uneducated peers. Nikolla appeared at once as an unpolished common worker and as a highly conscious Sovietized subject. Whether he actually spoke in the exact words that newspapers attributed to him is hard to say. His speeches were often cast in a peasant patois, which helped make the Soviet practices more intelligible. The message was simple: It was possible to *become someone* through the Soviet example. By all accounts, Nikolla appeared proud of his work. When colleagues witnessed the result of his fast-paced body movements, he explained, "They started admiring me for my success."

Accounts of these labor campaigns in Eastern Europe have sharply focused on what they say about working-class identity and domestic power dynamics in each country. But there is also something to be said about the international quality of this moment. It meant something that an anonymous Albanian bricklayer, hailing from some obscure town, earned some recognition halfway across the world. Nikolla's name, for example, came up in Perventsev's English- language account of Albanian socialism.[94] On the occasion of May 1, a piece in the bulletin of the Soviet embassy in Washington presented him as an example of the battle for a new socialist international order. The author, Soviet playwright Nikolai Pogodin, wrote that Nikolla spoke "like the master of his country, like the son of a people who have power."[95] Another account highlighted the fact that Nikolla kept a small placard depicting a white dove in flight, the symbol of the postwar Peace Movement, by his side, at his workstation, in order to give him "more strength."[96] The personal story highlighted a country's stormy integration into an emerging socialist world—Soviet, Polish, Hungarian, Bulgarian, and Albanian exemplary bodies executing common tasks, seemingly unified in a mutually shared social mission.

To appreciate the local reception accorded to someone like Nikolla, it is necessary to recall that an average 1950s Albanian factory worker would have been inundated with the names of Soviet hero laborers: Orlov, Malev, Shirkov, Maksimenko, Shavliugin, Kulikov, Rahmanin, Levchenko, Mukhanov. Then there were new phrases describing the techniques: the "chain method" (workers operating as a chain); "fast transport"; the Kovalev bricklaying method (pioneered in Ukraine in the early 1950s); Duvanov (brick burning); and many others.[97] Site managers and pamphlets bombarded workers with calls to reorganize construction sites, to rearrange their bodies in a more "rational" manner, to streamline their movements, to bring production costs down.[98] Nikolla's urging that his peers use their bodies like machines, that they turn the construction process "semiautomatic," was part of this larger, sustained, aggressive, and exhausting verbal campaign.

Some of the Soviet terms were approximated into Albanian; the new language denoted something of the novelty of socialist planning. Most Soviet methods came to be known by their respective Soviet authors, but some names were straightforward. In masonry, for example, there were the "double" (*dyshe*), "triple" (*treshe*), and "quintuple" (*pesëshe*) methods, simply indicating the number of workers involved. Thus, the double (two-person) method consisted of a skilled mason and his apprentice. The lead mason would start out by laying bricks on the exterior side of the foundation, completing the first row along the whole perimeter of the building. His assistant would hand him the bricks and lay the mortar. The mason would then switch to the internal walls of the structure; both would complete the fill-in work. Everything was geared at minimizing movements. Another worker could be added—making it a *treshe* method—enabling two assistants to lay the bricks on the interior walls. A combination of five persons was also possible: two master masons and three assistants working as a human chain. It was not easy visualizing this. So the Friendship Society issued drawings, in addition to coming up with the requisite translations.

The Friendship Society was the main vehicle for popularizing Soviet construction techniques. It did so by way of special publications such as a bulletin called *Punëtori Sovjetik* (*The Soviet Worker*), which drew from Soviet titles such as *Komsomolskaia Pravda* and *Rabotnitsa*. It also furnished blueprints directly to local enterprises, along with pictures and short biographies of Soviet Stakhanovites. In 1949, a party memo had been critical of formal efforts: "Until today, we have applied these methods only through hearsay," it admitted, "and we have claimed that we employ Soviet methods."[99] Instead, the Friendship Society dispatched Soviet engineers to construction sites to demonstrate the methods in person.[100] The local Soviet head engineer in Maliq reportedly supervised the application of Soviet methods himself, ensuring that compliant workers received raises. Typically, however, activists designated a local worker—someone like Negri Nikolla—to become the champion of the Soviet work ethic.[101]

Published accounts of workers who had successfully applied Soviet methods and thus had saved time and money usually appeared in the Friendship Society's journal under the heading "We apply Soviet experience!" The first-person accounts and the photographs that accompanied them provided a glimpse of the heroes' humble origins. Here they were: bricklayers, shoemakers, machinists, and lathe operators sharing in the glory of Soviet methods, firing off percentages and hard numbers specifying how much money they had saved, how many limits they had transcended. The practice was not limited to the society's journal. The party newspaper also printed surveys of the application of Soviet methods. In July 1952, for example, it ran an article on a worker who employed three Soviet methods at the same time.[102] The adoption of advanced Soviet techniques, the article pointed out, ought to be carried out through "an aggressive war." These working bodies were fighting bodies: "Old ways reluctantly give way to new ones, and behind this there is also the work of enemies." Soviet methods, then, required "initiative and courage" but also constant vigilance against hostile elements "who will say anything to discredit the Soviet experience."[103]

Adopting Soviet experience was thus a form of duty and patriotism. However, party officials did not shy away from appealing to self-interest. In interviews, Nikolla emphasized the higher wages that Soviet techniques had earned him. In 1953 he also reported receiving a gramophone and thirty Soviet records as rewards. Kadri Abazi, who had been among the first workers in the country to employ the Levchenko-Mukhanov method, received a radio. Nasho Badjavaja, a driver who rode his ZIS truck for 119 kilometers without incurring major repairs, received a camera and a desk lamp. Others received books, newspaper subscriptions, corn, cotton, grain, plows, and beehives.[104]

Neither the incessant propaganda nor the perks would have been effective without enforcement on the ground. In fact, it was a kind of double enforcement—both through the party channels (including the Friendship Society) and the government chain of command. A government office might arbitrarily decide, for example, that Soviet methods were to be applied at no fewer than 60 percent of all construction sites.[105] Construction officials would then send the orders to special work brigades, which would then manage the tasks and keep tabs on factory workers. Officials with the trade union mobilized in the effort too, arranging meetings and competitions among workers. This constituted a kind of cycle: whenever the party apparatus looked into the matter of Soviet methods, it found the effort lacking, and so propaganda and pressure went into high gear. A year or two later, there might be complaints of work that was still insufficiently Soviet in style. The chain of command would mobilize again, launching more investigations. Inevitably, there was much overlap in all this party, government, and Friendship Society agitation.

Numbers were part of this state-enforced cycle. Reported percentages might seem impressive, even allowing for exaggeration, but the point is that no number would have been enough anyway. Asking for more Soviet-type practices, after all, was the Friendship Society's reason for existing. If everyone already seemingly agreed that Soviet achievements were desirable, whom exactly was this organization trying to convince? This partly explains why reported numbers oscillate, depending on the source and the intentions of those deploying the numbers, between impressive highs and alarming lows. In early 1953 the state-run construction enterprises and large-scale industrial projects employed more than 16,600 people (including 1,610 women). At the end of the first quarter, there were 679 Stakhanovites (7 were women). The number of shock workers stood at 5,604, including 352 women. Over 4,000 workers, moreover, were said to be employing some type of Soviet method in their work.[106]

In coming up with numbers that showed progress, local managers could use a range of tricks. For example, they might report success with the Soviet practice of issuing work orders (*urdhri i punës*) even if they had issued these only formally at the end of the workday. Or they might report the total number of workers involved without specifying which Soviet methods had been employed, which was important because some methods were less labor-intensive than others. Alternatively, they could make up the numbers altogether. Some enterprises employed Soviet methods temporarily. Workers might use a Soviet method for a few hours and then go back to old methods (but still report the whole week as a "Soviet week"). Designed to rationalize labor and come to the rescue of workers, Soviet methods made working days more complicated for an already burdened and largely unskilled labor force. In addition to dealing with shortages and quotas, workers also had to somehow Sovietize the whole ordeal at the end of the shift.[107]

Designed to overcome backward ways, Soviet methods ironically served to expose and magnify the persistence of those old ways. Authorities obsessed over workers' lack of skill or enemy work, but there were clearly also material impediments in place. Soviet guidelines specified machinery that local enterprises often lacked. Other times, machines might correspond in type but vary in capacity and endurance. Therefore, it became necessary to translate Soviet methods not only in terms of language but also in terms of technical expectation. The widely touted Kulikov method, for example, required special shovels that local workers did not have. Instead, they kept using ordinary shovels. (Did that still qualify as a Soviet method?) Shabby local machines and unskilled workers joined with high-minded Soviet technical formulas and ideas about social engineering. Success, as defined by planning targets, required ever-greater physical exertion, even as machines broke down and managers scrambled to make up "Soviet hours" of labor.

Given labor shortages, skilled workers were in high demand, and they were shuffled from construction site to construction site. This exacerbated the problem, since spreading Soviet methods depended on the more skilled. Expectations of increased efficiency did not necessarily mean better machines and more supplies. It was not surprising, then, that factory workers kept going back to old methods after performing the expected rounds of Soviet methods. Some acknowledged the benefits of the Soviet examples but also pointed to objective impediments to their adoption. For party and government officials, however, this reversion to the old ways symbolized the stubborn persistence of the old world—lingering backwardness, which was not merely an economic state but a moral stance, a mentality, a way of being.

Party apparatchiks had a solution to the problem: more involvement of the party. "Success or failure in the adoption of Soviet experience," observed a May 1956 article in the Friendship Society's journal, "has typically depended on the work of the party organization in the respective enterprise."[108] It singled out the Enver Machine Works in the capital as a success story. Key to that success had been the factory's party organization, which had diligently taken up the task. The society had provided the necessary Soviet literature and the party organization had then selected Kraja, the lathe operator, to be the campaign's representative. As had happened elsewhere, workers initially feared that the machines would break down from the overexertion required by the Soviet routines (Soviet workers had voiced the same fears in the 1930s). But the managers had pushed along. More than 89 percent of all workers were now reported to employ some Soviet technique. Some resistance lingered, but in such cases the party organization called meetings and criticized the individuals at fault.[109]

Beyond local party organization, the other key factor was direct Soviet involvement. In the summer of 1954, Peter Epifanovich Solov'ev came to Albania to help spread Soviet methods in the construction industry. A Stakhanovite and master mason, Solov'ev demonstrated the methods in person (internal reports dubbed them "the Solov'ev methods"). As with Nikolla's public performances of the Kulikov method or Kraja's invocations of Mukhanov, Solov'ev demonstrated the new methods alongside the old so that everyone could *see* the superiority of Soviet expertise.[110] Internal correspondence, however, indicates that Solov'ev was initially exasperated by the local reception. Construction enterprises, he came to find out, were in such chaos that they did not even know where to assign him at first. Upon his arrival in Tirana, the Soviet visitor was forced to stay in a hotel since no provision had been made for a translator.[111]

One note boasted that a Soviet chief engineer had saved the state between 10 and 20 million lekë within a period of six months.[112] The wide gap in the estimate illustrates the kinds of wildly varying numbers, and exaggerations, that populate the archive of postwar socialism. The savings cannot be verified. What we do know is that Soviet advisers played an important role indeed, because they routinely took their Albanian counterparts to task. One Soviet construction adviser, for example, criticized officials for botching Solov'ev's visit. Local managers, he complained, appeared unprepared to draw from Soviet expertise. They were keen on mechanically copying Soviet *tipovye proekty*—standard, stripped-down prototypes that could be replicated easily—but they mindlessly scattered these around the country without regard to climate and local conditions. Soviet expertise, in other words, encouraged imitation, including mechanical imitation of body movements. Yet mechanical copying of blueprints was also apparently undesirable. This adviser did not specify how it was possible to assess correctly what to copy and what not to copy. Faced with the criticism, local officials admitted to having committed errors.[113]

If there were no Soviet advisers to consult, it became imperative to expand press coverage of Soviet methods.[114] The Friendship Society pushed workers to write directly to their Soviet counterparts. Letter-writing campaigns peaked in September and October, during the Friendship Month. An elected commission within a given enterprise or factory drafted the letter to a particular Soviet factory. This group would ordinarily be composed of managers, the local party secretary, and distinguished workers. Upon producing a draft, the commission would then take it to "the collective," where it almost certainly would be resoundingly approved. With Soviet party leaders reluctant to keep sending personnel to Albania in the second half of the 1950s, Albanian managers galvanized workers to write directly to Soviet agencies. In 1955, for example, some 1,200 pieces of mail went out to the Soviet Union. Factory workers, farmers, and schoolchildren wrote to fellow workers and pupils in Moscow, Stalingrad, Voronezh, Tbilisi, Riga, or Baku and then read aloud, in school or at work, the responses they received.

A socialist tone permeated these letters, which often took the form of requests for technical solutions. A local mason in Stalin City named Pando Mihali, for example, wrote in 1956 to a Soviet mason employed by a construction trust in Dzerzhinsky, in the Moscow oblast. In response, Mihali received a detailed description of the organization of labor in the Soviet enterprise. The Soviet worker explained that his fifteen-person brigade worked as a mechanized lot—a variation on the human chain theme so widely publicized among Albanian workers.[115] In another example, construction officials came across an article on wall plastering techniques in the Soviet press. Through the Friendship Society, they contacted the newspaper and asked for instructions. A few months later, the paper published a longer article on the technique. Back in Tirana, a decree ordered its application.[116] Even when written by one individual, such letters became collective events through discussion and dissemination in the factory or publication in the newspaper. Cast in the language of technical problems, they were also exercises in narrating Albania's path to socialism.

Staging

What exactly was *Soviet* about Soviet methods? Countless individuals became involved in the process of defining these practices—speaking about them, writing about them, counting and recounting them. This involved workers like Negri Nikolla and Halil Kraja, uneducated as they were, and the peasant women operating the spinning machines at the Stalin textile mills, who came to identify with this Sovietness. But does it make sense to think of these acts as Soviet because contemporaries did? Were they not, very often, simply more efficient modes of organizing labor? After all, pre-Second World War Soviet planning had liberally borrowed from Western industrial techniques in an effort to propel the country forward through mechanized production and unified standards. In retrospect, the Soviet methods of the 1950s seem like a reenactment of the efficiency studies that industrialized states had championed decades earlier. What was socialist about them?

An obvious answer would be that the term "Soviet" simply referred to their foreign origin. This is important because modernity had long been associated with foreign planning, with the crucial difference that recent models for Albania had been predominantly Western. At least since the 1920s, "Italian" had served that function, as illustrated in the capital's urban planning. To a much lesser extent, Yugoslav planners had also sought to modernize the country in the 1940s, but the relations between the parties had been complicated and Yugoslav presence short-lived. Of course, there were essential differences between, say, the Italian Fascist planning model and what was on offer with Moscow. But many 1950s working-age men and women would certainly have remembered the Italian engineers and technicians who had brought along their blueprints in the 1920s and 1930s. Enforcement of Soviet practices crucially depended on coercion and disciplining. But it was also made operative by this preexisting experience with foreigners and their plans.

In addition to serving as a geographical marker, the term "Soviet" came to mean something recognizable across a larger landmass: a centralized economy, one-party rule, a pervasive push to build industries. This connected the Soviet past to Albania's present. Some were captivated by Soviet techniques because they believed in the moral superiority of socialism. Others may have looked down on the Soviet Union, ridiculing the endless parroting happening at all levels of society. But they could just as easily have recognized that Albania was weak, poor, and isolated. (Would it have been surprising if these same individuals had embraced the Fascist planning of the 1930s, with its promises of integrating a small country within a Rome-centered empire?) This did not necessarily imply a slavish desire for a mighty patron. It was possible to recognize the value of foreign tractors, machines, and textile mills and *also* Albania's independence. Viewing the exercise of Soviet power in terms of captivity overlooks these possibilities.

Soviet was about style, but it was about more than aesthetics. Soviet architectural elements became conspicuous across the Albanian landscape: the gates of the Stalin mills; the colonnaded workers' club in Maliq (indistinguishable from, say, worker clubs in Soviet Central Asian republics); the ornate façades and gleaming interiors of the film studio in the capital (named New Albania). The Soviet Union as a model encompassed all of this but also techniques of organization, modes of speech, and ways of reasoning. Formerly unknown factory workers like Nikolla invoked the Soviet Union to make claims of their own. Party functionaries invoked the Soviet Union as a form of authority for their own purposes. In an early example, the finance minister had explained that wage categories, which had recently come under fire, corresponded to Soviet examples. He was using the invocation as a kind of shield, but in this case it backfired. "You may have worked according to Soviet experience," thundered the party chief in response, "but you have not applied it well."[117]

Workers learned to recount Soviet techniques as discrete acts because it became imperative to do so, exaggerating the feats and inventing explanations for their failures. In so doing, they socialized—as part of factory brigades, the party organization, study groups, or letter-writing campaigns. The form of these "Soviet acts" carried significance, as did their proper verbal identification. Soviet methods always entailed more than, say, Nikolla's choreographed body movements. They were also about the expectations that went along with the practices, calculations of savings and profit, unspoken reporting tricks, and modes of appropriate speech. Surely, Soviet methods were about efficiency and piece rates, but they were also about these other terms that required learning. Like the order of bricks to be laid at the construction site of the Stalin textile mills, Soviet methods signaled a kind of social order. They were about *staging*.

Naming was part of this larger effort to rehearse socialism. Small acts—building a wall, cutting metal—became emblematic of something greater. Inherent in all of this were techniques of control. Technique refers to an art of doing something that requires special knowledge or skill, but crucial to the definition of what constituted a Soviet technique was also the naming of its opposite. Party apparatchiks blasted "backward ways" as *shfaqje anti-sovjetike*. *Shfaqje* refers to a performance, an act of showing (a circus number, or a puppet show, might constitute *shfaqje*). Recall that in 1956, as mentioned in the previous chapter, authorities would accuse Albanian students in Hungary, Poland, and East Germany of having fallen prey to foreign influences (*shfaqje të huaja*) abroad.

In the language of the party apparatus, such influences took on the qualities of a deformity or disease (*shfaqje të shtrembëra* and *shfaqje të sëmura* were other iterations, meaning "deviant" and "sick manifestations"). The performative aspect of compliance was thus reflected in the official manner of speaking about supposed subversion. Authorities sought to stigmatize the possibility that Soviet-style socialism might not be applicable at all. But what was most important about the concept of *shfaqje* was precisely the imprecision. It was flexible enough to allow for the inclusion of a broad and alterable range of undesirable practices—social conservatism, religious rituals, the veil covering a woman's hair. This tells us that Soviet models became closely connected to deep processes of social engineering in the 1950s. Factory superiors demanded repetition and revision—the hallmarks of strategies to sculpt human behavior. The socialist style of doing something, which required ongoing definition, was also somehow supposed to become the only way to do it.

Staging a Soviet method might seem like a farce. In the showcase Soviet city of Magnitogorsk, workers came to recite the tenets of Stalinism *as if* they believed them. "When a compelling revolutionary vision resembling the 'higher truth' of a revealed religion is refracted through patriotic concerns and a real rise in international stature," writes Stephen Kotkin, "we should not underestimate the popular will to believe or, more accurately, the willing suspension of disbelief."[118] In the decade after the October Revolution, speaking the language of socialism had been an act of faith. What about the early 1950s? From a distant vantage point—post-Fascist Albania—the available repertoire of Soviet references seemed vast. This allowed functionaries and managers to assert their authority by pointing to an already established narrative of Soviet progress (while discrediting alternative modes of behavior as backward ways).

It was not necessary to understand all the mechanisms that made up the Soviet Union to speak of Soviet experience as something coherent. After all, there were more than thirty years of concrete Soviet achievements. Merely by existing, the Soviet Union served as an example of a possible future. Was the Soviet Union not superior to Yugoslavia, Albania's former patron? To a Czech or a German, Soviet technology might have seemed inferior. But in Albania this campaign coincided with the establishment of professional ranks, the expansion of literacy, and an ongoing push for women's emancipation. Mimicking the Soviets was not meant to produce an exact replica of Soviet society (though it reproduced a great deal). But through routines, *metoda sovjetike* invited individuals to also refashion themselves as more advanced Albanians.

To stage a Soviet method was to face endless hurdles. Authorities sought to measure the benefits of Soviet techniques, which encouraged the circumvention of rules. In this back-and-forth, party operatives, managers, and workers repeatedly engaged in defining what was proper Soviet technique and how it could be applicable to Albanian conditions. It turned out that the country's underdevelopment, which made advanced Soviet techniques urgent, also hampered their quick adoption. Enacting Soviet industrial techniques required a functioning industry and a robust central authority. From the mundane (incompatible machinery, mistranslation, missing tools) to complicated questions of ensuring compliance, the state kept introducing new problems. Workers and supervisors became complicit in figuring out solutions. Inherent in all of this was the idea that not everyone would immediately believe in the socialist future. Eventually, however, they would.

This also helps explain the contradictory internal assessments of Soviet labor campaigns. Government officials praised them extravagantly only to then detail, with great alarm, myriad flaws and failures. Questioning the applicability of Soviet models, or merely hesitating to adopt them, raised the issue of one's ideological loyalty. When monetary and moral incentives did not yield results, there might be sanctions or threats of sanctions. Those lagging behind could be made an example for others. But reports of shortcomings were also powerful tools, which might explain the practice of writing a critical report first and only later filling in the blanks, as necessary.[119] In other words, one proceeded from the assumption of shortcomings. The state, which aspired to a total plan, also planned its shortcomings. The widely touted Soviet methods always contained within them the expectation of failure. The Soviet ideal appeared foreign but familiar, distant but ever-present, technically attainable yet utopian.

This ambiguity allowed authorities to shift the terms of success as necessary, and it also enabled disciplining. It raised questions too. If the Soviet Union was the future, how long would it take to get there? How long would it take to reap the fruits of socialist labor? It was one thing to ask a poor worker to make sacrifices in 1950. But how many years would she have to keep waiting? Five years—the length of a state plan? Ten years? Elsewhere in the Eastern bloc, frenzied Stakhanovite campaigns backfired, and governments embarked on a new course after 1953. In Albania, however, the state-directed promotion of Soviet models continued into the second half of the decade, as did the obsession with "rationalization."[120] Somewhere between the shabby classroom of the unnamed schoolteacher on the crossroads from Tirana to Scutari in the early 1950s and the women operating the brand-new textile machines at the Stalin complex outside the capital at the end of the decade, a socialist order crystallized. It was recognizably Soviet, just as it was unmistakably Albanian.

SOCIALISM AS EXCHANGE

On the one hand, Communism is open and kind to all; on the other
hand, it is exclusive and intolerant even of its own adherents.

Milovan Djilas, *The New Class* (1957)

I remember the Hungarians with admiration because, rest assured,
they were not the same Communists as our Communists.

Mark Alia, a 1950s trainee, interview (2011)

Wolfgang Hentzschel and his East German colleagues found themselves in something of an ordeal during the summer of 1961. They were stationed in Kurbnesh, an isolated locale in the mountainous area of Mirditë, in northern Albania.
A small village situated close to copper reserves, Kurbnesh was undergoing a
stormy transformation into an industrial town. Albanian authorities had decided
to build a copper enrichment factory. East German engineers and specialists had
agreed to supply their advanced industrial experience. The finished outcome of
Albanian-German cooperation would carry the name of Wilhelm Pieck, East
Germany's first president. Like the Soviets at the Stalin mills outside the capital, Tirana, Eastern bloc specialists came to Albania in the 1950s, bringing along
their plans, machines, and a sense of wonder about a country they knew virtually
nothing about.

In a report to Berlin, however, Hentzschel admitted that his group had
become embroiled in "a war of nerves" in Kurbnesh. The Albanian managers
were stubborn and the engineers poorly trained. "The organizational failures of
the Albanian leadership," he wrote, "can be explained by the historical development and mentality of the Albanian people." He detected excessive ambition and
self-consciousness among the personnel, as well as a "distinct arrogance in technical and economic issues," for which he blamed constant party propaganda. He
pointed out that the local managers heeded German advice only when their own
decisions backfired.[1]

It so happened that a West German journalist with the *Frankfurter Allge-
meine Zeitung* obtained an Albanian visa at this time. This was not something

that happened every day, so he jumped at the opportunity to fly to Tirana. Once there, he tracked the East German engineers from Kurbnesh and spoke to them about the escalating tensions with the locals. "It had not been easy," the journalist reported back, "to accustom the Albanian hands, who had no feeling for exacting technical work, to order and discipline." It was not easy to make technical workers out of former shepherds.[2] Here was the politically divided Germany in some unexpected unity on the issue of Albanian backwardness. They may have come from different sides of the Iron Curtain, but the German visitors crisscrossing Albania also spoke a shared language of development and projected a familiar image on the deficiencies of the natives.

The hosts, however, drew a different picture. The previous summer, Albanian authorities had singled out delays in machine and material shipments from East Germany and criticized the visitors for not working hard enough. The copper enrichment factory was originally supposed to go into operation in April 1960. Instead, it took several more months to get production going, forcing trade officials to revise planned figures for copper exports to the bloc. In a letter directed to the party boss and the head of government, the minister of mines castigated the East German specialists. "I must note," he wrote, "that the comrades in Kurbnesh also told me that some of the German specialists are not very good." Instead of worrying about production, he added, they had had the nerve to ask for a week of vacation on the coast.[3] Testing of a section of the factory had finally commenced later that summer. But then there were complications with the machinery. This required bringing in more specialists from East Germany to solve the new problems.[4]

When one reads these reports from both sides, it seems that the East German transfer of technology to Albania was an utter failure. True, a modern factory did eventually emerge in Kurbnesh, but socialist cooperation seems to have been anything but fraternal. Still, the point is not whether the East German experts exaggerated local conditions or whether the hosts blamed the visitors for their own planning failures and unreasonable expectations. After all, between the summer of 1960 and the summer of 1961, political relations between Tirana and Moscow turned icy; these records reflect straining political relations with Berlin as well.[5] Such tensions between East Germans and Albanians, as we shall see, also had a lot to do with the unintended consequences of transnational socialist contacts. The point, therefore, is to ask how such encounters came about in the first place.

It was not obvious how technical expertise could be transplanted from East Germany to remote Albanian provinces, just as it had not been obvious how Soviet methods could help make conscious workers out of illiterate peasants. At first glance, the numbers of foreigners seem small. By 1960, for example, 114 Soviet, Bulgarian, Hungarian, and East German specialists worked in urban

planning bureaus, factories, nationalized brickworks, and agricultural enterprises alone.[6] But to put that number into context, it should be noted that at the
same time, there were 105 Albanian architects, urban planners, civil engineers,
geometers, and drafters *in the whole country*.[7] Similar contingents of varying sizes
worked in other industrial branches, including mining, manufacturing, planning
agencies, and schools. In addition to the Soviet officers, advisers, and engineers,
East Germans, Czechs, Poles, Hungarians, and Bulgarians descended on Albania to help build socialism. They came to reclaim land, survey forests, design
parks and urban plans, supervise food processing, repair machines, help with oil
extraction, and combat polio, tuberculosis, and scarlet fever. They constituted, in
short, the transnational agents of the Eastern bloc.

Official propaganda exaggerated its cohesion, but the Eastern bloc was real.
It was more than a geopolitical concept or a military alliance. It also came about
through formal and informal interactions, coercive and voluntary transfers and
circulations enabled by Communist parties and centrally planned economies.
In addition to replicating center-periphery dynamics, the Eastern bloc provided functionaries with career opportunities, privileges, and access to other
well-connected agents. This transnational horizon is best captured in the multilateral circulation of people, ideas, and technologies and in day-to-day interactions. The stories of Soviet involvement in Europe and Asia and the involvement
of Eastern bloc planners are typically not told together, but these were not separate spheres: the Soviets launched a wide-ranging integration effort in the socialist world, in which they actively continued to participate but which they could
not ultimately control.[8]

The outward signs of Eastern bloc exchange were hard to miss. There were the
endless exhibitions devoted, in procession, to each of the people's democracies,
the choreographed visits of youth delegations, teams of writers, painters, and
filmmakers. There were the newspaper articles about kolkhozes in Bulgaria and
the radio programs about the reconstruction of Polish cities. In Albania, where
the presence of the Soviet Union had become commonplace by mid-decade,
Eastern bloc commodities and techniques (Czech vehicles, German engineers)
also became synonymous with the promise of socialist modernity. Many authors
have rightly pointed to the fact that economic developments in Western Europe
deeply affected Soviet and East European states. But Albania shows that there
were also comparisons to be made *within* the Eastern bloc. Expanding transnational contacts made these comparisons inevitable—between East and West but
also between Moscow, Berlin, Prague, and Tirana.

The transmission of "socialist experience" is better thought of as an emerging field of interactions—enforced but unpredictable, chaotic but productive—from the formal bureaucracy set in motion with Soviet guidelines

to routine encounters in remote construction sites and industrial towns in the mountains of Albania. Such a perspective brings into focus the peculiarities of socialist exchange. Guided by the logic of central planning, socialist development aid put so-called proletarian solidarity to the test. Encounters between foreigners and locals in Albanian factories and construction sites exposed assumptions about solidarity and cultural dominance, political commonalities and frustrating technical differences. Exchange could foster a sense of belonging, but it was no guarantee for unity and understanding.

Commonwealth of Plans

Socialist functionaries insisted that cooperation among their states was shaped by a sense of proletarian solidarity and internationalism. Relations between them, they were keen to explain, were "relations of a new type."[9] Not so under capitalism, this line of reasoning went, where economic relations were shaped by the rule of dominant and aggressive powers over small and helpless states. But socialist exchange was also clearly informed by geopolitics and economic interests. Take, for example, the Council for Mutual Economic Assistance (CMEA, or Comecon), the international economic organization founded in January 1949. Originally composed of Bulgaria, Czechoslovakia, Hungary, Poland, Romania, and the Soviet Union, it added Albania to its ranks in February of that year and East Germany in 1950. Mongolia, Vietnam, and Cuba gained membership in the 1960s and 1970s, whereas China, North Korea, and Yugoslavia attended meetings as observers.[10]

The Comecon came about at a moment of divergence in the continent. Some authors have argued that it was a response to the Marshall Plan. Established in April 1948, the Organization for European Economic Cooperation administered European reconstruction aid. Championing "productivity," Washington invited French and German managers to study US businesses and see the benefits of free trade. United States technical teams, in turn, traveled to the recipient countries to dispense advice. All of this signaled an enduring approach in the West that considered technology transfer to be a crucial ingredient in "curing" underdevelopment. The 1950s saw the establishment of numerous such technical assistance programs. International scientific cooperation similarly expanded in areas such as the geophysical sciences and urban planning. But there is also some indication that the Comecon served as coordinated economic pressure on Yugoslavia after the vociferous schism of 1948.[11] Whatever the degree of anxiety over the Marshall Plan, it is true that East-West apprehension went both ways.[12]

If there was any longer-term plan for the Comecon, the Albanian leader probably missed it because he appeared utterly confused about the organization's purpose in 1949.[13] Indeed, socialist exchange between 1947 and 1955 consisted mostly of bilateral agreements. There were a number of reasons for this. During Stalin's lifetime, the Comecon was scarcely envisioned as a supranational body ("sovereignty" serving as a guiding maxim to counter the "imperialism" of the United States in Western Europe).[14] The Comecon served to reinforce existing and independently running central plans and sustain the transfer of the Soviet economic management model to the newly acquired bloc. Each member state enacted its own economic plans and established its own research institutions. The organization's early activities were limited to the coordination of a handful of research projects, and it largely remained "an institution for pursuing (or at the very least presenting) national interests" to Moscow.[15]

Efforts to integrate socialist economies intensified in the late 1950s. A meeting of national representatives in Moscow in May 1958 sought to outline a new international socialist division of labor. The Albanian and East German interventions at the meeting give an indication of the challenges facing socialist integration. The Albanian delegation asked for substantial aid, arguing that even in the 1970s the standard of living in Albania would be much lower than elsewhere in the bloc. The East Germans, for their part, also sought to increase *their* standard of living, arguing that neighboring West Germany posed a threatening example of capitalist consumerism. Khrushchev noted that both East Germany and Albania bordered on the capitalist world and thus deserved this kind of assistance. The former, the Soviet leader explained, ought to be a socialist showpiece to counter West Germany, whereas Albania would become an example for the Arab world.[16] Here were two countries, East Germany and Albania, with very different economies and yet facing similar constraints (Western borders).

Khrushchev's attempts to spearhead further integration faced serious obstacles. Even with a charter adopted in 1959 and an executive committee established in 1962, the effort to centralize the Comecon did not suddenly alter its character.[17] Soviet measures designed to establish a common planning structure and economic enterprises across the bloc later met with intense Romanian objections. But significant constraints to socialist integration were also built into the economic infrastructure of member states. Planning centered on physical production targets, a feature that also shaped international trade within the Eastern bloc. Central plans, moreover, required constant tweaks, which further complicated cooperation among member states. One economic historian did not see the problem in the disparity between Comecon members (Western economic organizations had the same). "The difficulty seems rather to lie," he wrote, "in the forms of central planning to be harmonized."[18] Add to this the fact that socialist economies had difficulties with multilateral trade. "As in relations between centrally managed enterprises within each country," observed one economic historian, "money was not allowed any such active role as expressing purchasing power capable of acquiring any product at a posted price."[19]

One result was that multilateral trade acquired barter-type dynamics. Because of the demands of central planning, disparities in pricing among the bloc countries, and the urgency of imports, trade arrangements often started with lists of products to be "adjusted."[20] This setup might have worked for bilateral relations, but it was ill suited for multilateral agreements. Relations among socialist countries, in other words, were shaped by the arrangements of central plans, even as, crucially, relations with capitalist countries demanded the adoption of other terms. Comecon's paradox, one author wrote, was that "under Stalin the USSR had the power, but not the will, to impose any degree of economic unity short of outright annexation; while under Khrushchev it had the will but not the power."[21]

Trade was only one facet of socialist exchange, however, and it would be misleading to think of socialist exchange as limited to it. Socialist states also exchanged technical blueprints, personnel, and innovations. Here, too, officials were keen on emphasizing the distinction from Western technical aid programs. "Even among capitalist countries there is cooperation in the realm of science and technology," admitted one official at the East German State Planning Commission on the occasion of the signing of an exchange agreement with Poland in 1950, "but capitalists view such scientific realms as frivolous, so it happens only infrequently." He went on to argue that capitalist countries were driven by reckless self-interest and that they would use any weapon available to them—espionage, threats, blackmail—to obtain technical supremacy. Political and economic strength, he reasoned, trumped any genuine cooperation in science and technology. As an example he took the fuel used by the US bombers that demolished German cities, which, he explained, had been produced according to IG Farben patents—the ominous result of the convergence of imperialist interests with technical expertise. By contrast, people's democracies based technical transfer on principles of solidarity and friendship.[22]

Governments signed agreements to transfer building plans, patents, technical descriptions, formulas, models, and samples. The documents outlining these terms of exchange themselves exuded uniformity; many of them, in fact, were copies of bilateral agreements between individual countries and the Soviet Union. It is easy to trace this kind of exchange across national archives because it came with its own jargon and bureaucratic practices. The label "technoscientific cooperation" began to permeate the bloc in the 1950s (*nauchno-tekhnicheskoe sotrudnichestvo* in Russian; *technisch-wissenschaftliche Zusammenarbeit* in German; *bashkëpunimi tekniko-shkencor* in Albanian). Within the overlapping webs of socialist international relations, it was not always possible to differentiate technical exchange from government agreements providing for capital assistance, ad hoc training programs, cultural diplomacy, or similar provisions attained through party channels. But there were efforts to harmonize technical borrowing. This search for greater uniformity was an indication of pervasive copying at all administrative levels, of the prevailing ethos of planning, and of the drive to make exchange a routine state matter.

From Poland to Albania, and in between, technoscientific exchange occurred regularly, according to annual bilateral negotiations. Both sides would agree on provisions on payments and costs, typically (but not always) carried by the recipient country. Meetings alternated between the capitals of the countries involved, with each side preparing technical requests in advance. The assumption behind this form of technical transfer was that negotiators directly relied on centrally approved plans. Each side was supposed to predict—at least in theory— short- term needs and allocations in virtually all sectors of the economy. But it was also necessary—again, in theory—to determine the relative strengths of each Eastern bloc partner. Technical transfer thus assumed a certain level of information, or the ability to obtain it, in addition to a robust centralized system.[23]

During the second half of the 1950s, there was a Comecon-wide push to create intergovernmental agencies coordinating this kind of work. In 1956, at a session in Berlin, permanent branch commissions took on the task of harmonizing socialist exchange in specific areas (agriculture, engineering, chemicals, metal, oil and gas). A Berlin-based commission on construction, tackling standardization in building practices and urban planning across socialist space—the subject of the following chapter—set up its headquarters in Berlin. A myriad of other subcommittees and working parties emerged, to the point that those involved had a hard time keeping track. They were each headquartered in a different Eastern European capital, overseen by local staff. On paper, exchange looked harmonious and fine-tuned. Internal correspondence and documents from different countries, however, show that it was frequently the product of improvisation and the seed of contention.[24]

"World History knows of no such examples," boasted one Comecon celebratory piece, "when scientific and technological achievements worth hundreds of millions of rubles were handed over gratis to other countries to help them accelerate their progress."[25] Other Soviet sources reported numbers of technical documents shipped to other socialist countries.[26] Such numbers, needless to say, reflect official Soviet calculations of formalized exchange, and they say nothing about the machines and other industrial resources the Soviets picked up across Eurasia after 1945. Framing it as a kind of "imperial scavenging," Austin Jersild has highlighted this wide-ranging campaign to adopt technical knowledge and innovations. Driven by a sense of competition with the capitalist West, Soviet technical and managerial elites scoured the bloc to appropriate everything they deemed beneficial to their science and technology. This "scavenging" mentality, the author observes, pushed them toward the west (Prague) more than the east (Beijing), with the Chinese increasingly seen in the 1950s as unable to offer much of value to the Soviet technical revolution.[27]

Soviet calculations were an important part of this picture. But they should not obscure how Eastern bloc countries increasingly engaged in exchange with one another too. As "a socialist division of labor" became the new Soviet mantra in the late 1950s, so technical exchange within the Eastern bloc gained urgency. According to one estimate, for example, between 1952 and 1957 Albania received 227 specialists and 1,469 documents as part of such technoscientific agreements. It also sent 392 trainees to other socialist countries.[28] The numbers might seem small, and they do not include special Soviet specialists or ad hoc bilateral arrangements. It is important, moreover, to remember that small numbers could still have a relatively large impact given the country's size, the scale of development, and the level of centralization. Across the Eastern bloc, technoscientific cooperation produced its agencies (at ministerial, government, and international levels) and employed its agents. It allows us not only to peer into the substantial challenges of taking a national central plan beyond a country's borders but also to consider the role and experience of thousands of different actors, including party apparatchiks, bureaucrats, and managerial elites, all the way down to enterprise bosses, supervisors, engineers, and ordinary workers.

Making Up Socialist Experience

It is hard not to think of Albania's economy as an outlier in the Eastern bloc. The country did not have enough trained negotiators, translators, and personnel to attend international meetings, let alone implement complex technical projects or harmonize rules.[29] It was the lowest-income country of the bloc and thus heavily depended on capital assistance and subsidies. It relied almost exclusively on trade with other Comecon countries (the Soviet Union took about two-thirds of its exports).[30] Unable to produce goods that could be sold in the West (in exchange for much-needed foreign currency), it relied on the Soviets to purchase its crude raw materials and substandard products in exchange for consumer goods. Running a trade imbalance of roughly 100 million rubles by 1957, the regime used socialist credits to fill the gap. Structurally, Albania seemed closer to Mongolia than to, say, Czechoslovakia. Soviet officials recognized the fundamental economic challenges (agriculture in particular), in addition to the chronic problem with balance of payments. The upshot was clear: Tirana would keep coming back for more credits and grants.[31]

Imports and trade terms aside, the imparting of socialist experience entailed, above all, the exchange of experts and technology. Albania signed bilateral agreements starting in 1951.[32] Officials often assumed that this technical aid could be had for free, or, at the very least, at deep discounts. In fact, negotiations with Eastern bloc partners proved so difficult that the Albanian side was forced to reconsider its terms by agreeing to pay foreign specialists salaries and hand out bonuses. "The sacrifices that we will make to care for these foreign technicians (including the Soviet ones)," noted one memo, "will be more than worth it." After repeated requests from Tirana between 1949 and 1951, Bulgaria and Romania signed agreements. Even there, the Romanian party official Ana Pauker urged the Albanians to take better care of the Romanian specialists (some had lodged complaints about tough living conditions). Drawing from practices in Czechoslovakia and elsewhere in the bloc, Albanian officials suggested creating a special apparatus to deal with technical transfers from the people's democracies.[33]

When other Eastern bloc countries did take an interest in Albania, they looked into supporting development in areas of economic interest to them. Thus Czechoslovakia took up nickel mining, and Hungary assisted with the food industry. East Germans, in turn, became involved with geological research and copper mining, in addition to building a fish factory in Vlorë. Such were roughly the areas in which Albania could serve Eastern bloc economies: fruits, vegetables, medicinal herbs, chrome and copper products, nickel, bitumen, phosphate, talc, and magnesium. The Albanian government, in turn, was eager to use foreign loans to build chemical plants and mineral processing factories.[34] It is difficult to come up with a definitive number for such payments in the 1950s because different sources provide different figures (depending on whether grants are included). A reliable estimate of socialist loans by mid-decade is something in the range of 900 million to a billion rubles.[35] Military aid was provided gratis by the Soviet Union; the Albanian state paid only for the army's salaries and food and partially for its clothing.

Faced with Albanian pleas, the Soviet Union occasionally converted loans into grants. In 1957, for example, Moscow forgave payment of over 300 million rubles. The East German trade representative in Tirana understood this to mean that the East Europeans would have to follow suit. "The question is," he wrote, "who will be the first to do so."[36] After the Sino-Soviet split and Albania's entanglement in it, these numbers became a bone of contention. Tirana had reason to underestimate previous foreign aid, whereas the Soviets (and, much later, the Chinese) reported higher figures. If we have difficulty with the numbers, then, let us recall that socialist officials faced the same hurdles. Back in 1953, the East German representative in Tirana had been frustrated with the difficulty of obtaining accurate numbers for Albania's industrial output. Local authorities, he surmised, had fed him suspicious figures.[37] As Berlin contemplated converting loans into grants (as Moscow had done), it was also forced to gather reliable figures for what other socialist countries provided to Albania—not as easy a task as it might seem. In short, the protagonists of socialist trade hardly trusted the numbers they handled. In creating and then contesting them, they helped define a space for negotiation.

By mid-decade, Albania had signed technical aid agreements with nine socialist countries, including China and North Korea. Deprived of resources, the government initially did not create a special office for technoscientific exchange, and then, once created, the office was shuffled from ministry to ministry. In the summer of 1953, for example, it fell under the Ministry of Foreign Affairs but lacked personnel. It then moved to the Ministry of Trade, where it was located until 1955. Soon thereafter, however, there was talk of placing it under the State Planning Commission (to imitate, essentially, Poland, Czechoslovakia, and East Germany, where technical transfer was the prerogative of planning commissions). Amid all the confusion, government officials launched periodic investigations, only to discover that the situation was even more confusing.[38] Often, technical exchange ended up in the hands of overworked bureaucrats covering trade. Finally, in 1956, a government provision placed scientific and technical issues under the central apparatus of the Council of Ministers.[39]

This kind of chaos and reshuffling may be explained by personnel shortages and competing priorities. There was an additional problem, however. Technoscientific cooperation was new. Many officials seem not to have understood what it meant. Some thought of it as just an additional burden. To some extent, the presence of Soviet advisers and specialists provided one model of exchange, but relations with other socialist countries required engagement on many fronts. As a result, government memos went out calling for an "intervention from above" to address the shortcomings. The transfer of the main office dealing with technoscientific matters was a response to this kind of pressure. The Council of Ministers' stamp was supposed to grant the agency a degree of authority. Still, meager resources continued to plague the sector, and so the government and the Central Committee kept addressing the issue time and again. With skilled workers and trained personnel in short supply, Albanian officials hailed technical transfer as an important opportunity to catch up to more advanced socialist countries. But it also quickly became clear that the transfer of socialist experience kept complicating things.

How could a small country harmonize borrowing from the socialist world when it had a hard time harmonizing its own enterprises? Just the paperwork to be filed with offices in eight different countries was extensive. It required enterprises, branch ministries, and the country's embassies and trade representatives abroad to be kept up-to-date on exchange terms, responses, confirmations, cancellations, or modifications to existing contracts. As with Soviet methods in construction, moreover, technical documents and licenses required translation. Managers were then expected to supervise adoption, write up the outcomes, and report back through the chain of command. Investigations carried out through-out 1956 revealed that documents, including some classified secret, had gotten lost in the process of circulating from office to office.[40] Among those held in depositories and libraries, numerous items had not been translated at all. In one example, some old patents still lay in the same boxes they had been shipped in.[41]

Occasionally, the Albanian side received partial documentation, which made the adoption of a new industrial technique impossible. Or machines might be found to be incompatible, which would drag work out for lengthy periods of time. Errors or poor planning in one aspect of circulation, in other words, ham-pered efforts further along the line. For example, Bulgaria sent equipment for a glass manufacturing plant in 1955. (State officials increasingly pushed for higher production of standardized mass consumer goods like bottles, lampshades, glasses, jugs, and buttons.) It turned out, however, that the Bulgarian equipment worked only with corresponding glassware models used in Bulgaria. The Bulgar-ian side had provided very few such models. In order to commence production, it was necessary to send the specialist back to his country for one month.[42] On another occasion, the following year, technical documentation obtained from East Germany—also on the production of standardized consumer goods—had arrived without the necessary chemical formulas.[43]

Shortly before the Bulgarian had come to help with lampshades, Hungarian designers arrived to help with a monument for the fifteenth-century national hero Gjergj Kastrioti (Skanderbeg). At first, the Albanian side had to reach an agreement with the Hungarians on the number of specialists required for the task. The hosting enterprise, however, could not put them to work right away, given scarce building materials. So the Hungarians ended up waiting. Eventu-ally they left the country.[44] One summary painted a picture of disarray, which it deemed unacceptable, given indications that "Bulgaria has received a colossal amount of help from Czechoslovakia and the Soviet Union, and so have oth-ers."[45] Other countries, it pointed out, regularly reported benefits from technical exchange to the Comecon. Albania did not, however, because it hardly knew what these were. The foreign trade section of the Albanian embassy in Budapest con-firmed the assessment: "People's democracies have paid considerable attention" to technical exchange, which was, it added, both "economically and politically" a sensitive issue.[46]

The adoption of socialist experience required money and a central plan, but across-the-board planning often translated into slashed budgets. Officials frequently turned down invitations to conferences but urged their bloc partners to send the materials and the notes.[47] Whenever it became necessary to tweak the plan, the centralized system of allocations made it difficult to reassign the specialists attached to a particular project. The plan enabled wide circulation of documents, but it was notoriously inflexible when it came to bottlenecks. When problems arose, government officials had a tendency to ask for more Eastern bloc specialists or to appeal for contract extensions for those already in the country. (Another alternative was to send more trainees to the Eastern bloc.) This became a structural feature of socialist exchange in the Albanian periphery—it was easier to ask for foreign intervention than to address local inefficiencies. Seen from the perspective of an enterprise, more qualified foreign specialists were, at the very least, an additional resource to fulfill the demanding plan. Socialist exchange could, to put it another way, help conceal defects.

After continuous interventions from above, there was an increase in technical exchange during the second half of the 1950s. In 1957, for example, the country received 565 technical documents, which was about a third of the total for the previous five years. During those years, Eastern bloc countries also sent 10,269 new patents.[48] Technoscientific agreements brought some 263 specialists to the country, whereas 392 local workers and specialists went abroad for training.[49] Still, the problems with the proper adoption of socialist technology persisted. The Politburo brought up the topic again in 1958. It ordered all enterprises and state agencies to organize the technical documentation received from socialist countries, in addition to the notes and instructions left by foreign specialists upon their departure. It also suggested expanding the publication of technical literature and called for local party committees to pay more attention to the problem. (It did not allocate more personnel, however.)[50] As with the promotion of Soviet construction techniques, self-criticism served an institutional role, allowing colleagues to take each other to task. The ability to lash out at a minister for failings in this area, in fact, stemmed from the assumed ideological importance of the task at hand, in addition to the supposed economic benefits. One could make an economic argument about why a certain Hungarian or Bulgarian technique was not feasible, but was it possible to challenge the idea itself of borrowing more advanced socialist technical experience? When faced with criticism from above, local managers and chiefs found numerous reasons to explain deficiencies. Nevertheless, they could not deny the *potential* of socialist exchange, even if, say, East German mining practices might seem inapplicable, or a certain technical solution appeared beyond reach.

The language and logic of "fraternal assistance" required learning, although the lesson was not always clear. Of what immediate use was a report on, say, housing design in East Germany or labor norms in Bulgaria? Echoing Soviet leaders in the early 1950s, the prime minister warned that socialist experience ought not to be "mechanically copied" but rather "appropriated to our local conditions."[51] What did that mean exactly? The more officials spoke of socialist experience as something tied to the country's standing in the world, the more it became clear that seemingly technical problems could quickly escalate into questions of political credibility. In the face of uncertainties, government officials, managers, and personnel continued to behave as if the transmission of socialist experience were merely a matter of overcoming objective constraints, of disciplining the workforce, and correctly translating and adopting the right labor practices. Under pressure, some managers made up requests for technical documents and experts, wildly guessing, for instance, what Czechoslovakia and Bulgaria could provide (on the basis of word of mouth). They asked for specialists even when they were not sure they could house them or put them to work.[52] It sometimes happened that different enterprises asked for similar specialists at the same time or requested materials and documents they had already received.

Socialist exchange encouraged expectations of reciprocity. After all, the transmission of socialist experience was not—in theory at least—supposed to go only one way. No matter how backward, Albania was also supposed to contribute to other Eastern bloc partners. In reality, local officials struggled to come up with technical solutions and commodities that the country might offer.[53] Exchange, as a result, served to highlight already existing fault lines of economic and scientific development in the bloc. Still, the *appearance* of mutuality had to be maintained. It did not matter that this was essentially a formal act. Some effort went into importing some Albanian experience abroad, and the practice came to be expected and performed. These procedures—the improvisation of technical needs, the formality of exchange—produced documents that seem surreal. Take, for example, items to be exchanged with Bulgaria in the second half of 1956. Long on Bulgaria's side, the list reflects a wild preoccupation with anything and everything, from irrigation to vegetable seeds, viruses, labor norms, and fashion catalogs:

Technoscientific Agreements between Albania and Bulgaria, 1 August–31 December 1956[54]

Bulgaria agrees to provide:

1. Materials on weights
2. Materials on food products
3. Illustrations of ploughs
4. School lessons for food industry courses
5. Materials on agriculture cooperatives

6. Instructions for cooperatives
7. Materials for exhibitions
8. Instructions on irrigation
9. Material on soil preservation
10. Labor norms in agriculture
11. Technical norms (for state enterprises)
12. Technical norms (on fuel)
13. Labor norms in machine and tractor stations
14. Collection of magazines
15. School program for agrotechnical courses
16. Literature on soil amelioration
17. Programs for agrotechnical schools
18. Textbooks for technical schools
19. Programs for cooperative courses
20. School programs in mechanical agriculture
21. Institute programs
22. Collection of diseased plants
23. Vegetable seeds
24. Accepts one Albanian specialist on the silkworm
25. One Bulgarian specialist on tobacco diseases
26. Financial matters on the payment of expenses for visiting Albanian pupils
27. Blueprints of ships
28. Accepts two Albanian specialists to learn about construction material enterprises
29. Extension of contract for one Bulgarian architect
30. Material on [unclear]
31. Material on rural health services
32. Medical school programs
33. Diphtheria toxin (for filtration)
34. Diphtheria toxin (for immune system testing)
35. Sanitation-themed materials
36. Materials on smallpox vaccine
37. Accepts two Albanian specialists on the processing of mothers' breast milk
38. Sends to Albania three doctors
39. Scientific descriptions related to tobacco, fruticulture, vegetables, and corn
40. Publications on irrigation norms
41. Climate atlases

42. Ethnographic methods
43. Photographs of material culture
44. Materials on the restoration of monuments
45. Accepts one Albanian specialist on animal breeding
46. Fashion catalogs
47. Guidelines for the organization of a fashion institute
48. Materials on labor organization
49. Specifications for a plum dryer
50. Materials on the gathering of eggs
51. Materials on the collection of fruits and vegetables
52. Accepts five Albanian specialists for training in dairy products

Albania agrees to send:

1. Olive seeds (wild and cultivated)
2. Two Albanian specialists to Bulgaria to sign exchange agreements on patents and innovations

Boxes of paperwork traveled from Sofia to Tirana, much of it never translated, let alone put to use in any way. As with Bulgaria, Albanian officials offered to send rare plants, medicinal herbs, decorative materials, and catalogs of traditional clothing and textiles to other partners in the bloc.

Writing the history of modernization as a seemingly global process can obscure how socialist states wielded a specific instrument in pursuing development: Communist parties. In the context of centrally planned economies, party involvement was critical in solving problems, just as it spawned other kinds of unexpected problems. From the earliest years, Albania's party served as a communication channel to the bloc. Back in 1950, for example, one East German official met with Hoxha to discuss the fate of some 150 German prisoners of war. The visitor toured a factory in Tirana, where he saw broken machines. The conversation then turned to the possibility of obtaining some German personnel to fix them.[55] Before diplomatic relations and choreographed technoscientific exchanges, there were parties. It helped that many of the men who made up the government in Tirana also occupied the high offices of the Central Committee. They could informally deal with other party men in the bloc. They may have lacked technical expertise, but they quickly learned how to exploit socialist solidarity. "We are building socialism under very difficult circumstances," Mehmet Shehu told East German premier Otto Grotewohl in November 1954. "Without a doubt we have had successes, but we live within the capitalist orbit and have to overcome extraordinary difficulties."[56]

If Eastern bloc functionaries hesitated to provide experts or favorable terms, the Albanian leaders used party channels to exert additional pressure. They did

FIGURE 21. Socialism as comparison: Politburo member Gogo Nushi inspects East German light bulbs at the Berliner Glühlampenwerk, 14 July 1958. Bundesarchiv (BArch), Bild 183–57000–0527 / Rudolf Hesse.

the same thing when credits dried up or planning targets required hard-to-obtain imports. And if Eastern bloc countries showed no interest in purchasing Albanian exports, party leaders urged their Soviet counterparts to pressure the Eastern Europeans to buy up.[57] The threat of Western standards of living loomed large in framing this kind of "fraternal extortion." Comparisons with the West, encouraged by Khrushchev in the late 1950s, would have far-reaching consequences for the socialist project in Eastern Europe. But Albania had the additional "advantage" of economic backwardness by comparison with other East European states. These comparisons *within* the socialist world could be especially unsettling. Westerners living better than Easterners was an ideological problem. But what about Hungarians living much better than Albanians? Or the Bulgarians? (To say nothing of Yugoslavia across the border, whose leadership spoke of socialism but buttressed standards of living with capitalist money.) Exaggerated and riddled with complications, socialist exchange nevertheless succeeded in creating this comparative field.

The Problem of Comparison

Not all the Eastern bloc specialists who took up jobs in 1950s Albania were experienced; some, in fact, were recent university graduates. A trip to this Balkan country was largely an experiment. It sometimes proved difficult to find specialists who were willing to make the move, as only a few could take their families with them (typically only those staying longer than a year). In the early 1950s, there had been the additional hurdle of having to ensure the political loyalty of the personnel.[58] Some did volunteer for the jobs, driven perhaps by enthusiasm and the professional challenge of building socialism under challenging circumstances. To be sure, there were special salaries to be had, but these did not necessarily contradict a genuine sense of passion in imparting advanced socialist experience to a less advanced country.[59] Ceaselessly repeated, the solidarity among the people's democracies was not entirely spurious. Benefit calculations certainly drove technical exchanges, but professional opportunities, political considerations, and beliefs about the Communist world were not inconsequential.

Solidarity did not guarantee that technical assistance would be free of problems. As was the case with Soviet engineers in the early 1950s, the place occupied by Eastern bloc specialists was ambiguous. They were often more qualified than their local counterparts but were unable to shape outcomes or influence planning. Eastern bloc specialists were involved in decision making, but they were also outsiders, relegated to an advisory position. Their technical skills were in demand, but their authority was difficult to pin down. Nor was it any easier to establish with certainty whether Albanian workers were subordinate to them. Of course, foreign specialists could make use of their contacts at their respective embassies in Tirana—they frequently did when misunderstandings arose. Disagreements could also be resolved through party channels or by going straight to the enterprise director or the minister. But the problem was deeper: exchanges of technical personnel created a vague space of authority within agencies. Higher-ups drew a sharp distinction between "colonialist" Italian engineers in the 1930s and the "scheming" Yugoslavs after 1945, on the one hand, and, on the other, the Soviet and Eastern bloc personnel. Relations between foreigners and locals, however, were fraught with tension.

Nothing exemplified this tension better than questions of pay and privileges. According to a 1949 agreement, Soviet specialists were supposed to earn the same salaries as their Albanian counterparts. Pay was supposed to vary according to professional rank, level of education, and range of experience, as well as the nature of the contract signed. That is to say, those Soviet specialists sent according to special government arrangements received salaries in line with preapproved schedules, which often also included provisions for local travel and vacation. But the Albanian government decided to pay the Soviet personnel more. Payroll records from these early years make it clear that there was a hierarchy comprising government advisers and managers, going all the way down to midranking officials, employees, and technical aides. Soviet academics sent to organize schools were also among the highest earners. Specialists earned an average of 10,000 to 12,000 lekë, and chief engineers earned more. The salaries of Soviet advisers to branch ministries, who were in a special category, were even higher (18,000 lekë).[60] Soviet officials had insisted on equal treatment between their specialists and the Albanian counterparts. The ambassador raised this objection directly with Hoxha.[61]

These numbers tell only part of the story, however. When food rations came up, one Soviet specialist asked not to have rationing applied to his group. This frustrated the Albanian head of government. "Mikoyan told me personally," Hoxha explained in a cabinet meeting, "that the Soviet specialists ought to be paid the same as Albanian specialists." But now the Soviets were asking for an exception. "Their salaries are not smaller than our salaries—and we are ministers and deputy prime ministers," chimed in Mehmet Shehu. Perhaps, they reasoned, it was necessary to inform the Soviet specialist that Albanian ministers and deputy prime ministers were also subject to food rations.[62] To make things more complicated, some Soviet specialists received travel and per diem allowances in Albanian currency. These then had to be converted into rubles back in Russia, and because of different allowance schedules and conversion rates, it effectively meant having to give back money. This, too, prompted the Soviet ambassador to raise the problem of salaries again in 1955.[63]

What about the salaries of non-Soviet specialists? In the late 1940s, the issue had been complicated by the presence of various other foreigners, including Italians, Russians formerly living in Yugoslavia, and a smaller assortment of foreign-born individuals who had moved to Albania between the world wars. In 1949 the government had taken up the "delicate and very important" issue of foreigners' salaries, but it became increasingly important to formally distinguish between these foreigners and the personnel from the "fraternal countries."[64] When the government abrogated an older law regulating salaries of foreign personnel, it also decided to pay foreigners who "had been in the country for a while" as if they were Albanians, thus distinguishing these from newly arrived Soviet and Eastern bloc personnel.[65] Pay, in other words, was a matter of contracts and regulations, but it also served to separate politically useless, or even suspect, foreigners from the politically significant agents of the socialist world.

It sometimes proved difficult for authorities to distinguish between these foreigners. One construction enterprise faced this dilemma when trying to ascribe a nationality to a man by the name of Mikhail. Records showed that he had come to Albania from Yugoslavia, but since he was Russian by nationality and had recently obtained Soviet citizenship, it was unclear how he ought to be treated.[66] For Mikhail, needless to say, it made a whole lot of difference whether authorities decided to treat him as a Yugoslav or as a Soviet citizen. In the aftermath of the Stalin-Tito split, a number of Russians had moved from Yugoslavia to Albania, often taking jobs in construction. Like Mikhail's, their background and political orientation was at best unclear—and possibly suspect.[67] Authorities found it easier to underpay an Italian engineer or a former Yugoslav resident with a suspicious past than the personnel of socialist fraternal states.

Such seemingly technical discussions about pay rates concealed deeper concerns about political loyalty and internal enemies. A 1953 Interior Ministry report to the Politburo identified certain resident foreigners as hostile elements. Chief among them were recent Yugoslav immigrants, who numbered 493 (around 40 had been arrested as alleged spies). Of the other 21,775 foreigners living in Albania, the report noted, it was necessary "to carry out a selection among them and expel undesirables (Lebanese, French, Turks, Jews) as well as repatriate the nationals of friendly countries."[68] Some of the Yugoslavs in construction faced charges of sabotage. Other foreigners were suspected of assisting the American intelligence service. Finally, there was also the Greek minority in the south, which needed to be forcefully told, as Hoxha put it, that "beyond our border is hell and on this side it is heaven."[69] At this point, authorities did not reveal any political suspicion toward Eastern bloc specialists, but in later years it would become clear that not all of those foreigners were trustworthy party members either.

When it came to decisions to pay foreign specialists, the expectation of sustaining standard norms with socialist partners could be self-defeating. The problem of rationing had created some misunderstanding with Soviet specialists. But the phasing out of rationing for some articles (milk, eggs, clothing) also created problems with the Czechs. In 1956, the Czechoslovak embassy explained that specialists would now be required to purchase foodstuffs at market prices, meaning that a new agreement was in order to make up for the additional costs. It turned out that the Czechoslovak request was supported by a clause in a 1955 mutual agreement, which allowed for salary changes in case of new guidelines affecting the standard of living. Yet no similar provision existed with the Soviet Union and other countries. The Albanian side at first demurred, concerned that other countries would follow suit and demand better conditions for their specialists also—a troubling manifestation of imitation within the Eastern bloc.[70] When Albanian authorities tried to remove the clause, the Czechoslovak side refused. Harmonizing payments across the board among Eastern bloc specialists, the Czechoslovak embassy insisted, would mean shortchanging some of its specialists.[71]

Equality among socialist states implied that there ought to be a uniform treatment of advisers as well. But it was written nowhere that, say, Bulgarians and Czechoslovaks employed in local construction sites were supposed to earn the same salaries and receive the same monthly bonus. Here, too, the problem was that bilateral agreements between states prevailed over Comecon-related arrangements, a situation brought into relief by a prevailing expectation of greater uniformity throughout the bloc. The Albanian position was to try to have it both ways. They paid attention to how much Soviet advisers and technical staff earned in other Eastern bloc countries. Internal secret reports translated from Czech into Russian also provided the Albanians with basic data about cooperation between Czechoslovakia and the Soviet Union.[72] When beneficial, authorities used these examples to seek similar concessions from the bloc. When asked for increased contributions, the Albanian side routinely stalled and tried to reap concessions.

The 1956 uprising in Hungary, and especially the Soviet handling of it, raised the urgent problem of redefining relations across the socialist world. Chinese and American scholars have shown how Soviet dominance was reflected in matters of pay (for Soviet experts in China, for example) and the general privileges accorded to Soviet personnel.[73] But Albanian government officials themselves contributed to the establishment of these unequal terms. It took Soviet prodding, in fact, to get the government to normalize Soviet salaries during the first half of the decade. Focused on finding evidence of Soviet domination, existing accounts of socialist relations have also missed how Eastern bloc actors (and later the Chinese) actively pursued hierarchies of their own with underdeveloped countries like Albania. Salary figures from 1956 show that while Soviet advisers were still clearly privileged, Soviet technicians were actually a good bargain for the Albanian government. A Czech engineer earned almost twice as much as a Soviet one.[74] In this context, the achievement of some kind of socialist uniformity seemed against all odds. Officials instead followed a case-by-case approach, stretching budgets as far as possible and relying on political maneuvering—the recital of the tenets of socialist solidarity among fraternal states—when it was financially expedient to do so.

This kind of exchange encouraged endless comparisons: salaries, numbers, percentages, and costs. This did not mean that authorities always abided by examples drawn from the Eastern bloc, but it did mean that this comparative dimension became increasingly unavoidable. Eastern bloc countries engaged in comparisons all the time. Delegations of workers on study trips compared working conditions in their host countries with the ones back at home. Engineers and technicians compared the industrial capacity of their own countries with the terribly modest conditions they found in Albanian construction sites. Comparisons were powerful, and it was not possible to control how individuals employed them. Albanian managers and workers could compare their working conditions with the more advanced countries of the bloc to justify shortcomings. One presumably stood a better chance with superiors if one's reasoning was supported by examples drawn from the people's democracies. The bloc, in other words, became re-created in personal relationships across shop floors and construction sites.

Encounters

Like the Soviet staff accompanying the industrial machines delivered as part of the first Five-Year Plan, Eastern bloc specialists came to interact with Albanian individuals at all levels—government offices, provincial committees, factory shops, and construction sites. The adoption of discrete socialist practices implied an ongoing process of translation and negotiation between foreign examples and local circumstances. Throughout this process, the possibility of misunderstanding loomed large. For a start, there was the distinct possibility of mistranslation. At the Tirana-based Machine Works, for example, East German equipment kept falling in disrepair. The GDR specialist dispatched in 1956 to figure out the problem concluded that the equipment instructions had been poorly translated (this meant another round of translations into Russian).[75] Poor translations had planning implications: machine breakdowns, a shortfall in output, financial loss.

These in turn might invite even more scrutiny and investigation from above, in an effort to investigate whether sabotage might be involved.

Translation was a problem across the socialist world, but Albanian government officials were constantly forced to shuffle a very small number of translators from office to office, construction site to construction site. By the mid-1950s, as we have seen, recent graduates of Soviet and Eastern bloc universities had taken up administrative and technical positions. Nevertheless, their expertise was still no match for planning ambitions. Special funds for translations were hard to come by. As with Soviet films and Russian textbooks, authorities often made use of students, Soviet advisers, or local managers who happened to know Russian. Some of these individuals were eager to obtain the assignments as a way of supplementing their salaries, but the arrangement also meant that translations could take months, even years.

The image of harmony pervaded press accounts of socialist exchanges, but misunderstandings were common and not always a function of language barriers. Conflict between bloc visitors and locals often arose because of living conditions, even though foreigners—as a rule—received better treatment than locals. Still, some foreigners enjoyed better living arrangements than other foreigners, and this also encouraged comparison among specialists from different socialist countries. A Soviet doctor brought in to care for the party leadership, for example, had access to the "leaders' store" (*dyqani i udhëheqjes*), a special retail unit in the capital catering to Politburo and Central Committee bosses.[76] A limited number of high-level government advisers enjoyed the same privilege.[77] Elsewhere, especially outside the capital, provisions were considerably poorer.

Housing was another source of contention, and it remained so throughout the decade. Because of shortages, many Soviet and Eastern bloc specialists slept in hotels. In one instance in 1952, Soviet specialists staying at the Italian-designed Hotel Dajti in Tirana moved out to make room for other delegates visiting the capital. Some of the specialists got their old rooms back, and some did not, with the consequence of getting the government apparatus and the Central Committee involved in the process of hotel room distributions.[78] On another occasion, four East German specialists arrived in Tirana to find out they had no accommodation. (In this instance, the German side was apparently at fault.) The visitors "were very angry," a diplomat informed Berlin, "especially since they had been told in Berlin that everything had been arranged and that they would even be awarded the Stalin Prize here." Instead of the Stalin Prize, they found a fully booked hotel. The visitors threatened to go on strike if they did not get better accommodations than the "very primitive" and bug-infested rooms they reported receiving.[79]

The visitors eventually got their hotel rooms, but the East German representative warned Berlin that specialists traveling to Albania were supposed to have
no illusions about the country's living conditions. A few years later, Bulgarian
urban planners were housed in an apartment reserved for a Soviet agriculture
adviser, who was left without a clear alternative, prompting officials to warn, with
characteristic exaggeration, that the incident was "an embarrassment not only
for our enterprise but for our state itself."[80] Like salaries, housing allocation was
supposed to follow professional status. Chief engineers and other high-ranking
officials were supposed to be allocated two rooms, with lower-ranking engineers,
academics, geologists, and specialists of a similar rank eligible for a single room
and a smaller quantity of furniture. Last on the list were ordinary technical workers, who were supposed to get shared rooms and were eligible for only basic
supplies.[81]

In reality, there was less of everything, and allocations were often arbitrary.
Security police operatives, for their part, kept an eye on how locals treated the
foreign guests. In the secret reports they filed, they noted that Eastern bloc specialists complained of "unequal" treatment. In one example, Czechoslovak specialists had made use of a car—the only one available to the enterprise. Quickly
thereafter, the Hungarians had complained of favoritism: "They take the Czechs
to the beach in Durrës," they reportedly griped, "whereas we cannot even get a
car to get to the hospital."[82] A 1956 assessment warned that "Albania is currently
being discredited among friendly states because of our poor work with foreign
specialists."[83] It was hardly surprising, it added, that some Eastern bloc specialists
apparently refused to come to the country, given prevailing rumors about tough
living conditions.

Housing, food, and transportation were also key themes in the reports of
Hentzschel's engineering team in Kurbnesh. Their housing was more than a kilo-
meter away from the work site and consisted of new one-story buildings composed of two rooms, a hallway, a kitchen, and a bath. While there was adequate
power, water was available only when the supply pipe from a nearby spring did
not freeze or dry up. The group of men had the assistance of two local women,
who cooked and cleaned for them, and an additional male assistant entrusted
with the task of supplying firewood and foodstuffs. (Because of "chronic lazi-
ness," the report pointed out, this man had proved "practically useless.") By local
standards, the East German group appears to have been living well, bearing in
mind that some of the miners and factory construction workers were ravaged by
disease and did not even have a cafeteria.

But the report noted that the provision of foodstuffs was "distinctly bad."
Everything except bread, sugar, and tea had to be brought in by car from Tirana.
On rare occasions, the local market provided meat, fruit, and vegetables. But for

the most part, the report added, "only when German food was delivered was it possible to somewhat adequately feed oneself." Medical services were similarly modest: a young doctor had been stationed in Kurbnesh at some point, but teeth in need of repair required a trip to the polyclinic in Tirana. Regular mail from Kurbnesh to Tirana took three or four days, whereas a letter to Germany took fourteen (packaged goods mailed from Germany took two to four months to arrive). For entertainment, a nearby barrack showed old Soviet films three or four times a week. Trips to other cities required special permission (*autorizim*), which could be obtained only in a town two hours away. That was reason enough, the author of the report concluded, for the team to refuse any extension to their work contract.[84]

Socialist exchange exposed feelings of superiority and inferiority beyond the reality of material hardship within a fraternal state. In 1955, the Interior Ministry chastised a Polish group of visitors for taking pictures of "nonsocialist" scenes around the countryside (destitute children, gypsies, but also "beggars, badly dressed peasants along with their animals, old dirt roads, ruined houses"). One can only speculate about what the Poles were thinking, but the authorities insisted that such scenery "does not correspond to the reality of our country."[85] Inside factories and plants, foreigners took other kinds of snapshots of Albanian backwardness. One Czechoslovak specialist attached to an auto plant between 1957 and 1959 (he had to wait several weeks for a translator) found poor working conditions and unskilled workers. "Workers generally work as they please," he observed, "without any effective guidance or any controls in place. One can hardly speak of discipline under these conditions."[86] He attempted to enact work changes but was forced to intervene directly with the minister to get results. In any case, the plan went unfulfilled during his tenure at the plant. Local managers blamed the scarce resources available; the visitor, however, blamed existing labor practices and poor organization.

Foreign specialists were technically useful and politically significant. But they were also a daunting presence, since they served as a constant reminder of the glaring limitations of Albanian factories and workshops. By merely doing what they were supposed to do, the visitors exposed endless deficiencies. They pointed to problems with personnel and machine capacity.[87] They discovered that much-needed Soviet vehicles lay in storage or that Albanian engineers disassembled expensive instruments out of mere curiosity without being able to then put them back together. One Czech specialist brought up lax safety provisions, thus annoying his Albanian counterpart responsible for workplace safety.[88] Another, working at the porcelain workshop in Tirana, complained that he did not have enough trainees. He also identified errors in the handling of raw materials and the absence of a specialized laboratory for testing. Yet another, a specialist in metals, at one point made twenty different proposals for improving work, but the local supervisors apparently studied none of them.[89]

Breeding workplace frustration, socialist encounters also facilitated discussion—and thus opportunities for misunderstandings—about the different national experiences with central planning. Mark Alia, an Albanian teenager at the time, worked with a Hungarian team sent to assist with land reclamation between 1955 and 1958. On one occasion, the leader of this team, who was a party member, asked Mark, "What does your party newspaper say?" Mark responded that according to the newspaper, people in the United States were starving. By comparison, Albanians had a good life. Upon hearing this, the Hungarian chief reportedly blurted out, "Your party paper is lying!" Such were the unexpected turns of socialist contacts: during the turmoil of 1956 in Budapest, the Hungarian chief was only too happy to be stationed in Albania, fearing that he might be a victim back home.[90] In Albania, in other words, a Hungarian could at the *same time* be appalled at the local unreconstructed Stalinist party, fear the anti-Soviet uprising back in his home country, and become implicated in projects (like irrigation canals) that made use of the forced labor of Albanian political prisoners.

Mark's Hungarian supervisors saw firsthand the miserable living conditions in Albania, and they reportedly despised some of the Soviet advisers, who enjoyed special privileges. Faced with criticism about the handling of foreigners, government ministers pushed back, arguing that not all Eastern bloc specialists behaved properly. "Are we talking about the Hungarians who came to help with food preservation?" asked the minister of industry and mines in a 1957 meeting, adding that those Hungarians had been "evil." What was evil about them? He pointed to the fact that the Hungarians had not properly "instructed our people" and that they had expressed the wish that "there were no Soviets in Hungary."[91] The prime minister also lashed out at Albanian trainees abroad. "We spend millions of rubles. But these people that we send abroad do not even make use of the things they see over there." Still, Shehu also appeared impatient with foreigners' complaints about living and working conditions. "We have created very good conditions for them within our constraints," he explained. "Not even our ministers live as comfortably as the Czech specialists here."[92]

There was tension in this kind of arrangement: Visitors from more advanced socialist countries were supposed to point out problems, but the enumeration of endless problems also served to expose the failures of local officials, managers, and workers. In 1959, East German housing specialists came to experiment with low-cost building materials. Like countless others before, the visitors made note of the unskilled labor force. Eventually it dawned on them that some locals had assumed that the East Germans would be building the cheap housing units by themselves.[93] Another team, sent to help standardize the manufacturing of children's wooden toys, discovered that the local "industry" consisted of two plants, seven smaller shops, and numerous craftsmen who worked with little central supervision. The visitors also toured a shop specializing in wood products, headed by a Soviet technician. It lacked heating, they noted, and the walls were exposed brick erected on a concrete floor and supporting a shoddy ceiling made of clay bricks and cardboard. Some sectors seemed like temporary structures—indeed, the whole building seemed like a series of poorly executed expansions, featuring old equipment and floors covered in dust and chipping.[94]

Some of the visitors may have been keen to emphasize their heroic work in difficult circumstances. For their part, Albanian supervisors might have wanted to defend themselves, tactically admitting to some problems so that they could reject other charges. Records often give us only hints of the underlying tensions and uncertainties. At the center of encounters was the unquestionable enthusiasm about the potential of socialist exchange and the deeply entrenched belief that a developed country like East Germany or Czechoslovakia could effectively impart advanced methods on a less developed country. Relations departed from that assumption—that the transfer of socialist experience was the only logical outcome. In practice, countless technical glitches tested this idea. Conflicts and discontent were the result of different standards in living arrangements and benefits but also of professional misunderstandings and, crucially, unsettled questions of hierarchy. Add to that the tendency, inherent in the process of obsessively trying to reach immediate planning targets, to discourage disruptive changes at the level of a factory or workshop.[95]

In the late 1950s, government authorities fantasized about bringing East German tourists to the Albanian seaside. The Deutsche Reisebüro, however, complained about inadequate hotels and service. Officials in Berlin floated the idea of building a brand-new hotel in Albania to address the problem, and a direct line to Tirana opened in 1960 (figure 22).[96] Shortly after that, however, in light of ongoing Sino-Soviet disputes, political relations between Albania and the rest of the Eastern bloc grew tense. Some of the foreign technical specialists now shouldered the blame for missed deadlines and failed operations.[97] This was the other side of socialist exchange. As they had done in the 1940s, with Italian and Yugoslav personnel, government officials desperately needed the foreign experts but also saw them as easy scapegoats. Still, Albanian managers were anxious to keep the Germans as long as possible. In Kurbnesh, they hoped to keep them around at least until the plant's capacity had increased. They tried hard—in Tirana, and in Berlin—to get contracts extended, but the Germans were unmoved.

Authorities in Berlin at first tried to let the contracts expire.[98] Then they asked their engineers to leave the country altogether, which apparently put some of the East Germans in breach of contract. "As soon as the Albanian

FIGURE 22. Socialism as encounter: the opening of Deutsche Lufthansa's Berlin-Tirana flight route, April 1960. During the stay in the Albanian capital, an East German flight attendant poses with a donkey—a ubiquitous local sight—in a depiction of socialism as modernity expanding. BArch, Bild 183–72291–0002 / Weiss.

Government learned of this," observed the West German journalist witness-
ing these events, "they set every possible wheel in motion to try to prevent
or at least put off the departure of the German experts." What would happen
to the factory? The East German engineers told him that the factory would
have a hard time operating under Albanian leadership. Those Albanian technicians who had traveled to East Germany to learn new techniques had "quickly
reverted to the slap-happy attitudes customary in Albania." The prospects
seemed gloomy: "The Germans who left were certain that a few months under
Albanian direction would suffice to ruin the plant."[99] What was meant to be a
site of socialist collaboration—in the name of Wilhelm Pieck, no less—turned
into a manifestation of discord.[100]

Eastern bloc visitors encountered a country that appeared both familiar and
foreign: distinctly rural and full of nonsocialist scenes but also recognizably red
and collectivist. They encountered a militant country—but also, somehow, a
country that seemed resistant to change. This kind of socialist exchange was paradoxical: both formal and informal, real but exaggerated, subject to ideological
reasoning as well as technical considerations, concerned with seemingly objective criteria of comparative advantages but also thoroughly steeped in spoken
and unspoken expectations of solidarity, equality, and reciprocity. It brought to
the surface cultural prejudice and feelings of technical superiority, which socialism was supposed to eradicate but which were impossible to ignore. Rather than
resolving this paradox, I have attempted to show how it came about.

The factors that helped foster socialist cooperation also limited further integration in the Eastern bloc. Nationalized industries, for example, greatly facilitated exchange among socialist states insofar as they enabled more efficient
controls and transfers of personnel from above. Licenses and patents, similarly,
could be more freely distributed among centrally planned economies, where the
urgency of protecting trade secrets did not exist, as it did in the private sector. Yet centrally planned economies had a tendency to overemphasize vertical
hierarchies to the detriment of horizontal ties between enterprises and agencies.
As with trade, technical cooperation was driven by output considerations, often
turning the process into little more than an artifice of the central plan. It was not
that actual exchange did not occur; rather, it was notoriously difficult to assess
its efficiency or even its overall impact. In short, socialist exchange was enabled
and constrained by radical centralization, output-focused economies, the parallel structure of the party-state, and the formal and informal channels maintained between socialist states. This accounts, in large part, for its contradictory
nature: vast in ambition but inherently self-limiting, planned but also informally
arranged, pervasive but difficult to measure.

Even when it seemed to founder, as East German-Albanian encounters in the early 1960s reveal, exchange exhibited a socialist logic, including the scapegoating of others through ideologically informed reasoning. Before producing the material standards of socialism, the Eastern bloc produced standard expectations. It thus sought to develop integrated terms of comparison. Comparisons could be empowering. But over time they could also become unsettling. Socialism circulated industrial blueprints, machines, and experts, just as it circulated illusions and disillusionment. In the early 1950s, Albanian officials had compared their country's path with the Soviet 1930s crash course on industrialization. Ten years later, comparisons with the rest of the Eastern bloc had also become commonplace. Albania and East Germany were worlds apart in terms of any imaginable industrial indicator. But they came together and attempted to speak in the same terms. *That* was socialism.

MUD AND CONCRETE

Future generations that will come and see the buildings of our time will not be able to believe that they were built by workers who ate bread that tasted like mud, with a tomato or a piece of red *halva*. When I looked at them, as they sat down to eat their lunch, as they opened their pitiful plastic bags, it became clear to me—the misery of the life of our people. I saw those humble women nearly break down from going up and down the scaffolding or walking in the construction mud all day, only to have the supervisor scold them in the staff meeting later that evening for not having fulfilled the plan.

Petraq Kolevica, *Arkitektura dhe diktatura*

Two years after winning a Pulitzer Prize for his *New York Times* reporting from Moscow, Harrison Salisbury arrived in Tirana—the first American to do so in a decade. It was late August. Upon landing in the capital's tiny airport, he thought he had landed "somewhere in the Soviet Union, possibly in the mountains of the Caucasus." The city teemed with soldiers donning ragged Soviet uniforms. "We take a little sightseeing trip. Some nice buildings, fine new stadium, queues at food stores. Soldiers, soldiers. Hotel full of Russians. Waiters speak Russian."[1] Elsewhere in the bloc, Stalin had become something of an embarrassment. But not here. Stalin was all around the Albanian capital: Stalin's words etched on façades, Stalin's portrait hanging inside the city's museum, Stalin's name on people's lips. Soviet presence was so great, Salisbury wrote, "that even the Albanian toothpaste tastes the same as Moscow's."[2] After a week of meetings, he "could not discover one iota of difference between the Albanian state system and that of, say, Kazakhstan or Georgia, in the Soviet Union."[3]

The American visitor had an audience with the prime minister. He took notes. He took pictures: women and men taking a stroll or resting by Stalin's statue, men in traditional felt hats, young mothers, the mostly empty boulevard at daytime. "Note continued absence of traffic," he typed on the back of the photographic strip.[4] In Warsaw and Sofia, Salisbury had come across rock 'n' roll, Western consumer culture, anti-Moscow sentiment, and ripples of revolt. But nothing of the sort could be seen here. Instead, the Soviet-equipped Stalin textile mills kept churning out woolen garments "of poor quality." Government bureaucrats and local party men kept using "standard pre-1953 *Pravda* clichés."[5]

The Albanian regime, to be sure, had attained considerable results. Salisbury spotted shiny new factories and mentioned a population increase, declining disease rates, and healthy-looking children. But the materiality of Albanian socialism was also a peculiar mix: decrepit roads, peasant scenes, "two-tone Volgas" made by the Soviet Gorky auto plant, donkeys more common than jeeps, Czech Škodas and Soviet trucks "laden with chrome ore and supplies," the ubiquitous reeds used to build walls and fences and to make rugs. "Albania," he pronounced, "still living in the age of Stalinism."[6] It was an odd part of the world, Salisbury explained to a US diplomat in Belgrade, and he hoped he would rarely have to go back there. Then, back in the United States, he told the director of the CIA that US propaganda in Albania—if there was any—was not working.[7] Suspicion of the West ran deep there.

In such a rural country, cities and industrial settlements became contradictory displays of socialism. One could see the contradictions, as Salisbury did, as alienating—manifestations of division and divergence in an imperfect socialist reality. But one could also approach the material reality of socialism as something desirable. During a visit to Tirana a year later, a Sudanese diplomat saw Soviet-designed textile mills that, as he put it, he "would love to have," while decrying the sight of "ill-clad, ill-housed, ill-fed" men and women.[8] Tirana featured vernacular houses, unmistakably Ottoman traces, and Italian administrative structures—encircled by expanding construction sites funded with foreign credits and staffed by Soviets, Czechs, and East Germans. Looking deeper, however, one saw similarities with the rest of the socialist world: similar battles over space, a mass movement to build cheap housing, and an ongoing push to give socialism material shape. Socialism was more than party organization, Soviet labor campaigns, and Eastern bloc engineers. It took on recognizable material features across borders and economies.

The inexperienced Albanian authorities might have preferred to raze old structures and build everything anew. But they could do nothing of the sort. For a start, they lacked the people and the means. Italians had introduced some city planning principles, but the government did not begin to take them seriously until the late 1950s. Central planning thus preceded urban planning, which remained an afterthought for many years. Armed with credits and grants, the government pushed industrialization, increasingly directing resources and labor to the provinces. The more haphazard buildings kept popping up, the more they complicated the path toward unified urban plans. Whereas the Stalin mills outside the capital and the Kurbnesh copper factory could become showpieces of state power, cities like Tirana also served as a reminder of the continued presence of the past. Socialist planning, to put it differently, delayed the urban planning of a socialist capital. The absence of trained city planners, labor shortages, and demographic shuffling, combined with systemic and international factors, like the demands and outcomes of the central plan, technological inventions, and imitation of foreign models, shaped ambitions and decisions—and, ultimately, the socialist city.

The Invention of Urban Planning

These were the big socialist projects of the 1950s: the Stalin mills, a hydroelectric power station named after Lenin, a sugar refinery, an oil refinery, a cement factory, and a film studio boasting Soviet equipment, marble panels, and Corinthian columns. In the late 1940s, Albanian party officials could blame delays on the Yugoslavs. "When they were expelled as sworn enemies of the people," one government construction survey put it, "they said that we would never be able to build railroads."[9] The railroad had been built. But it was harder to explain chaotic planning in the cities. By mid-decade, many structures in towns and smaller settlements were still unregistered. With the exception of Tirana, Durrës, and Elbasan, cities had only Italian-designed urban plans and partial studies dating from the prewar years.[10]

The Politburo had addressed the problem of urban planning in early 1948, vowing to transform Tirana into a proletarian city. Party higher-ups had envisioned broad avenues, buzzing houses of culture, leafy leisure spaces for workers, and special residential blocs reserved for Soviet advisers. A special commission on urbanism had been tasked with confronting Tirana's many woes: the filth, the lack of water, poor sanitation, and widespread malaria. At that point, Tirana was still a city of darkness. Lack of artificial lighting was, for the ruling party, a political problem. Good lighting, Hoxha told his colleagues, would influence the mentality of the "peasant living in Tirana and his backward ways."[11] He recommended that architects borrow from "the style" of other socialist states.[12] In short order, Soviet-trained architects such as Gani Strazimiri began designing "people's palaces." Ottoman-era quarters, however, still dominated the landscape.

In the 1950s, the capital was the largest recipient of new construction projects.[13] In response to the housing need, officials disposed of older properties and quickly organized volunteer teams to build cheap housing. Built hastily and in the absence of a master plan, the industrial and the housing structures stood scattered around the city's perimeter. Brand-new low-rise apartment blocks rose next to plain villas and shabby houses with walled courtyards. Over the years, state enterprises occupied some of the empty lots. This meant that structures often came first; only after the fact were officials faced with the problem of extending roads, water pipes, sewage, and electricity. Having failed to quickly impose a total urban plan, government authorities were faced with the task of constantly responding to the haphazard nature of do-it-yourself socialism.

One 1956 report blamed the haphazard construction of individual builders (unable to meet demand, the government allowed "private persons" to build their own homes), noting that cities had "become ugly because of private constructions that do not follow any criteria."[14] Desperate, planning officials asked for partial studies, instructing architects that they could draw "to a certain extent from the Italian studies."[15] Two years later, the government finally adopted a draft urban plan for Tirana. It envisioned Tirana as a future city of 180,000–200,000 inhabitants (from roughly 68,000 inhabitants as of 1945).[16] In line with the guidelines set a decade earlier, the urban plan emphasized "industrial zones" around existing and future factories ("considering analogous cities in the Soviet Union and the people's democracies") as well as a large national park (the Great Park of Culture and Leisure) and a zoo. Still, under central planning, it proved difficult to stick to the master plan, which nevertheless left many issues (like the city center) unresolved. Scattered constructions kept popping up.

What about elsewhere in the country? Reports were similarly critical of construction errors, underscoring the absence of comprehensive plans. One construction chief complained that the schedule for building large objects had changed six times between 1953 and 1954, costing many months of labor and grief.[17] Industrial settlements such as Memaliaj and Bulqizë rose in areas exposed to strong wintertime winds, making the life of workers and their families harder. In Sarandë, someone had somehow decided to build an unsightly mill in the middle of the city. In Pogradec, one of the country's vacation resorts, the city center boasted a prominent SMT (a machine and tractor station, modeled after the Soviet *mashinno-traktornaia stantsiia*). Other cities had similar unsightly warehouses located in their centers. There was a report that a school in Kukës had been built "backwards."[18]

There were many problems in devising a national urban planning program. Elsewhere in the bloc, governments nationalized design enterprises, created state planning bureaus, and made urban planning part of the Five Year Plan. Architecture, which in the past had involved private practice, firmly turned into a state matter.[19] In Albania, however, one had to first invent the practice. A design enterprise (Projekti) came into being in 1947, quickly becoming overburdened. In 1952 the enterprise got a separate urban planning sector. Three years later, there was a proposal to establish another urban planning commission within the Construction Ministry.[20] This overlapping bureaucracy revealed an uncertainty about where urban planning belonged—was it primarily a local matter or a government matter? The ministry held final authority on important matters, but city offices oversaw much of the housing stock, by way of special public works sectors. Referring to this confusing state of affairs, a 1956 ministry memo put it succinctly: "It is clear that it cannot get any less normal than this."[21]

Since there was a marked shortage in qualified experts, the same individuals ended up being shuffled from office to office. In 1955, the urban planning sector of the design enterprise had a staff consisting of two architects and one planner, an economist, and four geometers.[22] It took years to build the ranks of trusted architects, engineers, and urban planners. The older generation had studied in Western or Central Europe and included people such as Vasil Noçka (Stuttgart), Skënder Luarasi (Graz), Anton Lufi (Prague), Kristo Sotiri (Venice), and Gjovalin Gjadri (Vienna). Superiors saw them with suspicion. Instead, in the 1950s, a new crop emerged: Gani Strazimiri, Sokrat Mosko, Besim Daja, Eqerem Dobi, and Koço Miho (all Soviet-trained). Misto Mele, who also studied in the Soviet Union, was among the first to specialize in urban planning. Enver Faja studied in Poland and Valentina Pistoli, one of few female architects at the time, in Bulgaria.

One young student of architecture, Maks Velo, described his professors as "freshly arrived from the Soviet Union."[23] Another observed that this Soviet orientation meant that the Albanian curriculum was heavy on technical subjects but light on the history of planning, the theory of architecture, and aesthetics.[24] For a while, *Arkhitektura SSSR* was the only available architectural journal. Inside the minuscule planning offices, one could thus find designers of different generations and persuasions. The Soviet-trained newcomers enjoyed a good deal of authority, though they were also in competition with one another.[25] The ranks were so small anyway that state enterprises routinely hired engineers and architects for major industrial projects (some also made informal arrangements with private individuals building their homes). The Five Year Plan prioritized industrial projects, and so different enterprises ended up competing over a handful of specialists. Local city authorities (executive committees) complained to the ministry even as they themselves, under planning pressure, kept asking for the skilled staff.

There was scarcity in skill, and there was also scarcity in materials. Things could not be taken for granted: drawing boards, drafting instruments, special pens, even paper. Around the construction sites, many vehicles and machines dated from decades earlier. In the early 1950s, for example, two out of three concrete mixers had been manufactured in prewar Italy. With the exception of five units imported from the Soviet Union in 1949, all rock crushers were also of Italian make. A significant number of these machines lay unused because they were broken or had missing parts. In 1952, more than one in three available heavyweight vehicles were either Italian or American (Fiat, Chevrolet, Ford), but only a third were operational. By the second half the decade, as Salisbury saw in person, shipments of Soviet ZIS and Ural ZIS trucks, GAZ and GAZ Molotovs, and Czechoslovak Praga, Škoda and Tatra vehicles had begun changing the landscape of construction sites.[26] Even then, available vehicles were not enough to match the ambitious planning targets.

Above all, chaotic construction was a reflection of the improvisation pervading planning institutions and the torturous path of decision making. The urban planning section within the ministry would draft a city plan and forward it to the city government, which was supposed to elicit popular feedback on the proposal. Then the plan traveled to a state commission and finally to the Council of Ministers, which had the final say on it. Unsurprisingly, delays were common. Not all levels of government were on the same page about future planning provisions. With each step, officials introduced changes—add buildings here, remove them there—and these in turn necessitated another round of consultations. The management of housing stock, moreover, also went through different hands. There were special housing sectors at city, district (*rreth*), and region (*qark*) levels, and there was also a public works directorate (*drejtoria komunale*). The Construction Ministry oversaw the plan, but local housing agencies were responsible for verifying the results.[27]

Plagued by administrative clutter, the construction industry relied on a seasonal and low- skilled labor force. Like more skilled engineers, these workers also traveled across the country, from project to project. An ill-advised decision to merge the administration of construction with heavy industries and mining in 1953 further reduced the number of workers attached to nonindustrial projects. Workers rushed to seek employment in large industrial projects, which paid better wages, or were eager to carry out manual labor for the "privates" (those individuals permitted to build their own houses). This reorganization converted the entire Construction Ministry, formerly with a staff of one hundred, into essentially a department (a staff of twelve) within the Ministry of Construction and Mines. The move was disastrous, and the decision was reversed the following year. But it reflected the regime's fundamental assumption that construction was just another branch of the industrial plan.

With a labor force dependent on unskilled peasants, the government pushed men and women to join construction brigades. In 1954, about a third (3,000) of all available construction workers consisted of "volunteer youths," while a substantial number (1,330) were prison laborers. This shows the degree to which convicts constituted an important source of labor. The rest consisted of seasonal and predominantly unskilled workers. In many construction sites, the labor force present at any time stood under 80 percent of the minimal numbers required to complete the task. In some, it was below 50 percent. To appease higher-ups, managers sometimes fudged the numbers. For example, they might calculate the total number of workers in the fall after quickly assembling all the men they could find in the local area. As long as that number corresponded to the planned workforce, they had achieved the plan (a situation analogous to that in enterprises preferring large-scale construction projects, which allowed them to report plan fulfillment in terms of currency investments rather than material output).[28]

In reality, however, large swaths of the men wound up leaving the construction site after a month or two. Government investigations found that some so-called workers had been forced to sign up at the construction site simply to make up numbers; these included elderly individuals, young boys, and invalids who were obviously unfit for employment. Others joined to obtain ration cards, including kulaks and alleged antiparty elements. At the construction site of Soviet-style apartment blocks along the Lana canal in Tirana, for example, investigators found that one in four workers was unfit for work.[29] The Ministry of Interior kept a watchful eye, finding irregularities with the use of building materials and naming the culprits.[30] The mobilization of political prisoners and other convicts persisted for decades.[31] "On top of the scaffolding you could see prisoners working," recalled one eyewitness, "Soviet architecture executed for the first time by Albanian architects and built by prisoners' hands."[32] Since inmates slept in very basic barracks and their provisions were minimal, labor costs could be kept low.

The average wage for an ordinary construction worker, by mid-decade, was hardly sufficient to procure all the essentials for a family. Living conditions in the construction camps were ghastly. Workers lived in smoke-filled tin shacks that let in cold winds during wintertime. Few of them had managed to relocate their families with them and thus did not see their wives or children for long stretches of time. Some workers were lucky enough to obtain a pair of boots, but these would often fall apart in a matter of months. It also mattered *where* one worked. Large-scale industrial building projects closer to the bigger cities tended to offer better living arrangements (and at least some guarantee of compliance with central regulations about worker benefits) than remote sites.[33] Workers also resented the fact that they often had to forgo vacations or religious holidays so as to fulfill planning targets. Unsurprisingly, they have not left many written records of their daily struggles. But we can get indirect glimpses into their lives. In 1954, one official admitted that among workers, "one does not see anymore the enthusiasm that one saw in the period between 1951 and 1952."[34]

In the background to all of this was a sharp demand for housing. In the early 1950s, the government instituted a passport program (*pashaportizim*). Like the equivalent Soviet measure of the 1930s, *pashaportizim* was meant to limit the number of peasants moving into a city like Tirana. Still, no matter how much authorities tried to crack down, they found "suspicious elements" had settled in the capital, often taking up menial jobs merely with the aim of obtaining a passport. Whenever civil and military personnel moved to the capital, they brought along their families (in some cases relatives). Some married city inhabitants and thereby became eligible for passports. Faced with these increasingly creative tactics, the government instituted rules in 1957 that further restricted the movement of outsiders. It blamed peasants for moving to urban areas "without doing any productive labor there" and for creating a housing crunch.[35]

Despite the stricter controls, Tirana's population kept on increasing. In 1955, the city's population stood at 108,183 inhabitants. By 1960, it had grown to 136,328.[36] By 1961, almost one in five available hotel beds in the capital was permanently occupied by 74 families who lived there permanently. These included families with small children, soldiers, but also unmarried administrators, barbers, mechanics, nurses, and professors. Many were party members. One family had been living in a hotel since 1950. In these cramped hotel rooms, men and women cooked in communal arrangements, ate, slept, congregated, argued, and guarded their personal belongings.[37] This battle for living space, therefore, touched individuals at all levels, from the heart of the party apparatus to the fringes of the shop floor. In the immediate postwar years, authorities had confiscated large private houses, putting to use every nook and cranny, and they had also drawn up lists of stores, basements, schools, depots, warehouses, and annexes that could be taken over. But the battle persisted for years, as ministries, local city officials, public works agencies, and trade unions competed to house their personnel.[38]

Having an urban plan, or even the labor force, still did not solve the problem of allocation. At first, the government sought to copy the Soviet method of distributing construction funds to a series of agencies that would then execute their own projects. But, as some officials argued, what worked in the Soviet Union, where the construction industry was massive and the size of available funds large, would not necessarily work in Albania, where smaller budgets compelled enterprises to build smaller units, which were, on the whole, less economical.[39] Smaller apartments, however, made sense for enterprises eager to fulfill plans and report total numbers of apartments finished (regardless of whether large families could fit in them).[40] By 1961, the Ministry of Interior occupied some 118 rooms in more than nine different buildings around the capital, many of them originally intended as family apartments.[41] This state of affairs further complicated the adoption of a master urban plan for the capital. With each wave of construction, it became necessary to count and register not only new structures but also the original and alternative functions of older ones.

Unable to meet demand, the government allowed certain individuals, especially peasants, to build their own housing units—a practice that peaked in the late 1950s. Those hoping to obtain an apartment in a new building might volunteer at the construction site and bring along family members too.[42] By 1961, the number of units built in this fashion, independently, was more than six times higher than the number of housing units built by the state (34,010 and 5,266, respectively). This combination of state-led planning with independent local construction also produced widely different results in terms of quality. "Housing is very difficult to obtain," confirmed an old-time ethnic German construction specialist repatriated to Austria in 1958, "but very inexpensive, and unemployment is unheard of."[43] In the Soviet Union, the socialist motto in construction in the second half of the 1950s was to build "faster, cheaper, and better." One construction summary, however, admitted that Albanian enterprises built "cheaper and faster, but *worse*."[44] To address the problem, officials looked to experts in the bloc.

Dimo Angelov, a Bulgarian urban planning expert, came to Albania and discovered that urban planning did not yet exist—either as theory or in practice.[45] He traveled around the country and inspected construction sites. Mirroring a familiar party narrative, Angelov blamed the state of affairs on the legacy of "foreign occupations." He was also careful to point out that scattered ruins he had seen in Krujë, Pogradec, and Durrës attested to an ancient local architectural culture. Angelov admitted that the Italians had shaped some of the cities, but Fascist architectural legacy was of no use to socialist planning. He volunteered to draft plans for two cities and recommended translating Bulgarian urban planning guidelines. Still, he was not overly optimistic. Chaotic construction, he warned, might persist for a long time. He listed all the errors he had seen: houses built at random; blueprints literally falling apart (he suggested storing them in suitcases); missing supplies such as draft paper. Bulgaria, he wrote, had been similarly chaotic until 1949. But now the country boasted 1,500 planned villages and 100 planned cities. Albania could do the same.[46]

Borrowing from the Bloc

In December 1954, Nikita Khrushchev delivered a speech that has acquired, in retrospect, the semblance of a break. Addressing Soviet planners, architects, and construction workers, he took issue with Stalin-era architecture, which he deemed extravagant and wasteful. Young architects, he complained, seemed bent on imitating the old masters, "in a hurry to build monuments to themselves." No wonder that civic buildings resembled churches. Soviet architects obsessed over city silhouettes at a time when ordinary people were desperate for housing. But they could no longer afford to privilege aesthetics over the economy of construction. They could no longer hide, Khrushchev declared, "behind phrases" while "spending the people's funds extravagantly."[47] The construction industry had to adopt rational methods, like mass prefabrication of components and standard prototypes that could be reproduced easily across vast territories.

The speech shook those architects who had taken great pride in the monumental buildings dotting the Soviet capital. In light of the secret speech of 1956, this earlier intervention seems like a rehearsal for reform: the opening shot of de-Stalinization. Rather than signifying a break, however, the speech actually revisited debates that had been going on for decades in the Soviet Union: What was socialist architecture? How was it different from architecture under capitalism? What made a city socialist? Could the urban problems of a great socialist state be solved in isolation from the nonsocialist world? Similarly, discussions about the wonders of industrial methods predated Khrushchev's tirade. He made no break with socialist realism, and neither did he call for a return to the fantastically experimental constructivism of the early Soviet period. Instead, he advocated combating the latter by "sensible means."

Apart from making a case for Khrushchev's technocratic skills, in the context of an ongoing succession struggle in the Kremlin, the speech showed, if anything, a great deal of continuity. Khrushchev delivered it in thoroughly Stalinist form, heaping blame on guilty architects, whom he identified by name, and dismissing the unassailable aesthetics of the Stalin era in the name of the unassailable logic of cost-effectiveness.[48] He hailed the powers of reinforced concrete and the practicality of prototype housing designs. He called for public meetings with architects and specialists "so that they may talk 'heart to heart' and find a common language." What if this push provoked resistance? Those who disagreed, he warned, "should be corrected." In his memoirs, Khrushchev took pride in this vast campaign for cheap housing, insisting that Beria, the powerful security chief, had opposed reinforced concrete. This was not a minor technical disagreement, in other words, but a political victory. Khrushchev wrote that he had overcome all the obstacles—from his colleagues' suspicions to technical hurdles posed by weight and humidity. "I breathed a great sigh of relief," he boasted. "The technological process that I had dreamed of had come true, allowing us to build on an unlimited scale."[49]

The call to architects was linked to the domestic urgency of housing millions of Soviet inhabitants but also a wider push to compete with the capitalist West. This self-induced competition with capitalism led Soviet planners to seek new technologies, prompting US officials in turn to present the material culture of capitalism (private homes, consumer goods, modern art) as signs of a more advanced civilization.[50] That competition, too, had been playing out well before the famous "kitchen debate" at the American National Exhibition in Moscow in 1959, which saw Khrushchev and Nixon debating the merits of their respective political systems while standing in front of dishwashers and washing machines.[51]

Whereas the Soviets were fascinated and frustrated with the Americans and their shiny household goods, Harrison Salisbury was struck by how few questions about the United States he received in Albania. During his trips through the bloc countries, it had seemed as though every intellectual longed to go to Paris or New York. In Albania, he was baffled that there was no "rain of questions about New York, Hollywood, or even the state of the Negro." Instead, young men and women were starry-eyed about Moscow. "It was only with great effort," he wrote, "that a few conceded there might be something of value in the West." One young student of architecture, "hopeful of going to Moscow, said he had heard New York also had some interesting buildings."[52] Salisbury projected his own image of an adversary onto the country ("extremely primitive," he described it to the CIA chief), inexplicably taken by surprise by the fact that someone still living under a ruthlessly repressive Stalinist regime might not have felt comfortable enough to profess curiosity about the United States.

Existing accounts of the Cold War as a battle over consumption—preoccupied as they often are with big countries, big companies, and big money—perpetuate this idea of a defining East-West divide. But the East-West comparison was not the only one available in the 1950s. Socialist leaders had reason to obsess over living standards under capitalism, but there was another, more immediate, comparative field than the one between Moscow and Paris or Washington. Khrushchev had explicitly pointed to it in his 1954 speech to Soviet city builders. "Why, for example, do we not learn from the Czechs, who make remarkable reinforced-concrete ties and save lumber in so doing," he chided his inferiors. "Take a trip there and have a look. They are our friends." The speech quickly appeared in the professional journals of the bloc. From Berlin to Bucharest, architects held meetings to discuss it, and party higher-ups, such as East Germany's Walter Ulbricht, pushed their underlings to adopt cost-saving technologies. If it makes sense to think of this as some kind of mechanical imposition, it is important to note that it was multidirectional. It also came with the awareness that the Czechs, as Khrushchev himself admitted, were *ahead* of the Soviets.

Ironically, Khrushchev's top-down assault on Stalin-era "gigantomania" encouraged, over the years, more gigantic concrete blocks across a vast territory.[53] The preoccupation with aesthetics did not disappear, but planning bureaus in the bloc also became preoccupied with a search for integrated building systems. Gone were the tall, extravagant people's palaces of the early 1950s, with their elaborate façades and stucco moldings. The imperatives of standardization became urgent. The Soviets were not the first to experiment with prefabrication. Around Central Europe, architects had long fantasized about standard housing types.[54] After the Second World War, mass housing spread not just to the Eastern bloc but also to the outskirts of Paris and Seoul. But the Soviets *were* the first in the world to experiment with mass housing and prefabrication at such scale (with the crucial full backing of a party-state). "While making use of a product that had, initially, been designed in the West," writes the architectural historian Adrian Forty, "the Soviet Union developed production of its notoriously inflexible system on a scale that exceeded even the imagination of anyone in the West, producing identical buildings, from Vladivostok to the Elbe, under the control of one organization, which at its height employed thirteen million people."[55]

In Prague or Budapest, the turn away from Stalin-era palace architecture might have seemed like a return to the modern forms of the prewar years. But Albania had had no such modernism to recover.[56] There were a few traces, almost all of them Italian, which architects nevertheless could not openly embrace. So the architectural reversal did not immediately take the form of resistance to Moscow or a revolt against socialist realism—the analytical frame that an American visitor in 1957 (or twenty-first-century scholars) might be tempted to adopt. On the contrary, Albanian planners and architects relied on other socialist countries for literature, codes, specifications, and building systems. Officials attended the Moscow conference and published the proceedings.[57] (The embassy in Berlin also forwarded Ulbricht's related speech to Tirana.) "Reinforced concrete has a great future," declared a resolution from the Ministry of Construction, ordering architects to come up quickly with building prototypes and standard components.[58] Officials called for competitions on devising models for each element of a housing block. The Tirana-based construction enterprise December 21st (honoring Stalin's birthday) designated a prefabrication sector.

Some experiments had already taken place years earlier. Enterprises had proposed a few simple prototypes (*projekte tip*) for a limited range of structures (kindergartens, animal sheds, bridges).[59] In 1952 the construction chief had vouched for the value of building prototypes. "Everywhere in the Soviet Union," he had stated then, "one can see cranes hovering over construction sites but very few workers."[60] That was in sharp contrast to the labor-intensive methods one could see across construction sites. No matter how many Soviet methods workers applied or how much they perfected their skills, construction would still be centered on physical labor and hence on the physical limits of bodies. A different approach was therefore necessary. What the Soviets called *tipizatsiia* (*tipëzim*), however, required a level of coordination that was difficult to attain quickly. It meant standardizing windows, doors, staircases, and bathrooms. At first, Soviet and Eastern bloc state enterprises devised large building blocks, but standardization could be taken to the extreme—factories churning out slabs of concrete that could be simply stacked on top of one other using massive cranes.

Albanian officials took small steps. Within the State Planning Commission, the National Bureau of Standards took on the task of establishing norms for a range of articles slated for mass production (bricks, concrete blocks, decorative tiles, but also consumer articles, pieces of furniture, and home appliances).[61]

In October 1955, the minister of construction, Josif Pashko, traveled to Prague and observed that prefabrication was the talk of the town. Hungary did not trail far behind either. In comparison, Albanian building methods looked embarrassingly old-fashioned. Some things about construction in Czechoslovakia and Hungary made no sense to the visitor (the effort to minimize lumber in construction so as to preserve forests, for example, seemed peculiar), but Pashko nevertheless called for emulating Czechoslovak examples.[62] Two years later, Albanian specialist teams visited Bulgaria, East Germany, Czechoslovakia, and Romania, where they surveyed the construction industry and prefabrication techniques.[63]

At the first construction conference in December 1955, delegates still heard about "the correct application of Soviet methods," but the turn to industrial mass production was apparent.[64] So were the stakes for those caught on the wrong side of the debate. Precisely because the regime looked at architecture as a branch of construction (and construction as secondary to industrial plans), errors could be costly. In preparation for the conference, officials prepared lists of errors and culprits.[65] The security police blamed construction officials for plan failures, shortages, and waste. Buildings looked good on the outside, the security police charged, but they were dark, crowded, and uncomfortable inside.[66] Someone like Strazimiri, who only a few years earlier had been the face of socialist architecture, now came in for criticism, as did the housing designs for workers at the Stalin textile mills in Yzberish. Tirana's buildings featured too many floors and too many ornaments. The chief of the design enterprise declared that the "outward flourishes" of Strazimiri's apartment blocks stood "in sharp contrast to the bleak interiors" of the workers' apartments.[67] Almost in the blink of an eye, Strazimiri's designs went from being models of a Soviet style to examples of formalism.[68] In 1956 he was booted out of the design institute.

There was irony to this charge: in earlier years, the battle against formalism in architecture had swept through the Polish, Hungarian, and Czech circles. But charges of formalism were dangerous precisely because the offense could be so loosely applied to design choices. It was not necessary, then, to have had a modernist architectural tradition in the 1920s and 1930s or a history of functionalism or developed theories of architecture to participate in the debate over what was proper socialist architecture and urban planning. Just as it could borrow machines and ready-made plans, Albania could also borrow (from Moscow and the Eastern bloc) a vocabulary—terms that meant something different in Prague and Warsaw but nonetheless became operative in Tirana too. It fact, since anyone could fall prey to charges of formalism, Albanian architects were in an even more precarious situation. In the absence of well-developed professional debates or professional associations, it was harder to defend oneself against charges raining from above.

Here, once more, was a demonstration of the contradictions of socialist exchange: yesterday's architectural borrowings from the Soviet Union quickly turned into a form of professional liability. In some countries, the backlash against Stalin-era architecture made careers and helped nurture myths of national expression. But did the essential orientation of construction within the central plan change? One Albanian architect later insisted that it did not. In a country with 70 percent of its people locked up in villages, the state continued to prioritize the construction of industries.[69] Albanian officials kept translating Soviet speeches, and they kept sending delegations abroad to study mass construction. They kept receiving building blueprints and catalogs of industrial consumer products from East Germany, as well as reports on the administration of hotels in the Soviet Union, on parks and recreation in Czechoslovakia, on the design of electrical plants in Poland, on housing stock administration in Bulgaria, and on municipal services in Hungary.[70] For years, bilateral agreements had prevailed. In the second half of the decade, however, Soviet and Eastern bloc officials discussed the idea of a common agency to oversee such exchanges.

Going to Berlin

East Germany emerged as the center of transnational coordination in matters of construction. To be sure, Soviet officials were directly involved in overseeing the collaboration.[71] But the East Germans also enthusiastically took on the role of guides, pointing to their considerable planning achievements. Between 1953 and 1957, the rate of personnel devoted solely to *Typung* in East Germany grew threefold.[72] By 1958, East German designers had reportedly developed more than one hundred modular housing units, as well as prototypes for kindergartens, schools, shops, and an array of interior elements. They also created similar prototypes for rural settings (cattle sheds, stalls, barns, and power stations). In urban planning, planners embraced the *sozialistische Wohnkomplex* concept, built around the idea of a residential unit of several thousand inhabitants with access to standard social, commercial, and leisure services.

Socialist representatives convened in Berlin, between the twenty-first and twenty-seventh of May 1957. They came from Albania, Bulgaria, China, Czechoslovakia, East Germany, North Korea, Poland, Romania, Hungary, and the Soviet Union.[73] One of the principal hosts was a man by the name of Gerhard Kosel (shown with his guests in figure 23), who admitted that coordination in construction and urban planning posed some obstacles. It would not do, for example, to mechanically transfer blueprints from Berlin to Pyongyang. But Kosel also argued that socialist countries had a unique opportunity to draft common

FIGURE 23. Going to Berlin: delegates from socialist countries visit the prefabrication complex in Hoyerswerda, 29 May 1957. BArch, Bild 183-47090-0002 / Erich Schutt.

standards. More advanced countries could serve as models for the less developed.[74] The meeting's program reflected this outlook. Visitors toured Stalinstadt, the first socialist city in East Germany, where reactions varied from awe (the North Korean representative reportedly hailed the city as "an example for us"; the Czech seemed envious of the abundant resources) to criticism of the lack of balconies (by the Soviet representative) and the size of the blocks (by the Pole).[75]

The hosts explicitly framed socialist cooperation as a weapon against the capitalist West. They compared their designs, on display at the Deutsche Sporthalle, with examples in West Germany, including at the Interbau housing project in West Berlin's Hansaviertel. Interbau had brought together some of the biggest-name architects of the world (Walter Gropius, Le Corbusier, Alvar Aalto, Hans Scharoun), experimenting with housing solutions addressing problems of cost and scale. The East German press panned the experiment.[76] Kurt Liebknecht, the chief of the Soviet-styled Bauakademie, wrote in a similar vein, "The city of tomorrow," he declared, "cannot be built in the society of yesterday."[77] Gerhard Kosel added that the Interbau stood for "fashion-architecture." It was the duty of East German architects and civil engineers to "convince" their West German counterparts of the "right path of socialist countries." There were familiar echoes in the talk about the supremacy of socialist interactions. Only in those countries where "the power of the capitalist monopoly had been broken," the host argued, was genuine exchange possible. Western architectural and urban planning experiments were plagued by fierce "competition and company trade secrets."[78]

Gerhard Kosel's biography reflected better than most the unexpected turns of socialism. Born in 1909, he had studied under the Weimar-era visionary Bruno Taut at Berlin's Technische Hochschule. He had joined the Communist Party in 1931. The following year, when Taut had decided to move to the Soviet Union, Kosel had followed suit. Stripped of his German citizenship, he later found himself in Siberia. He designed an opera house for Ulan Bator, the Mongolian capital. In his memoirs, he later presented his choice to play along with Stalin-era classicism as a kind of compromise. He agreed to employ the classical elements and the flourishes but with the growing realization that rational industrial methods would be the way of the future.[79] He returned to East Germany in October 1954, rose through the ranks, and eventually became president of the Bauakademie—where he continued to champion industrial methods—as well as deputy minister of construction.[80]

The irony is that for someone so interested in production, Kosel's activities were mostly those of a bureaucrat.[81] Architectural histories tend to privilege authors and their designs more than collective enterprises or bureaucratic structures like the Comecon committees or the design agencies and the endless, dull conferences that were common under central planning. Accordingly, Kosel makes few appearances in architectural histories of the German Democratic Republic. But his personal papers reveal a man who combined the tedious bureaucratic work with the kinds of opportunities for socialization that stood at the core of socialist exchange: vacations in Albania and on the Black Sea; cure resorts for party types; cocktail receptions; study trips to Sofia, Shanghai, and India; camel rides in Mongolia; and speeches in Zanzibar, where East German planners developed prototype housing projects. His diary entries comfortably switch between German and Russian. Beyond the formalities and the speeches, internationalism in architecture also meant opportunities for access, travel, and an expanded horizon.

The discussions in Berlin centered on a vexing question that does not seem surprising in retrospect: Was it possible to devise common planning principles and building standards that were applicable to wildly different economies, climates, and cultures? The North Korean delegate, for example, explained that Eastern bloc countries, and especially East German architects and engineers, had provided significant aid and expertise to his country. But he also pointed out that the foreigners had introduced different technologies and building practices, which had produced confusion and disagreements with locals about the right approach to urban planning.[82] The Albanian representative admitted to the *Neues Deutschland* paper that each country had its own building traditions.[83] If anything, the Albanian displays in Berlin showed how vast the technological gap was between socialist countries. Albania was still building socialism the old-fashioned way (bricks and mortar). Only a few industrial elements were standard.[84]

How could one create a unified building system from Germany to China? For a start, national technical systems were different: Germany had once developed a set of unified technical standards, but the East Germans developed their own system, different from the Soviet one.[85] Then there were the multitudes of machines. To take one example, concrete mixers, which were crucial for the task of creating components, were hardly standard from one country to the next.[86] Finally, translation was an additional hurdle. The vaster the expanse of socialist states, the bigger the challenge. The Chinese delegate in Berlin pointed out that his country had adopted some building prototypes (copied from the Soviets) since 1953. But it had quickly become apparent that they required modification. Still, the East German hosts insisted that it was possible to create a unified system of standards (floors, roofs, staircases, walls, sanitary units). China could be part of that too.[87]

The Berlin meeting left some of these questions, and others, unresolved. Participants called for more bureaucracy: more conferences, more publications, and more exhibitions. In other words, more paperwork.[88] One reason for this was the fact that many of the attendees were bureaucrats: ministry officials, chiefs of enterprises and institutes, or planning functionaries. Many were party members too. Tasks associated with "socialist cooperation" were often supplementary to other duties. Coordination at the transnational level was thus secondary to national programs, and this problem would continue to plague socialist integration for decades. Nevertheless, attendees agreed to create a special standing commission on construction within the Comecon. Tasked with overseeing multilateral exchanges in technology and urban planning, the commission had its first meeting in September 1958.[89] Kosel again took the lead. The program included a visit to Hoyerswerda, where delegates could witness the production of concrete panels (*Plattenbauweise*).[90] To woo the visitors, the East German hosts had prepared showcase apartments complete with furnishings.[91] The commission established sections covering specific areas: construction materials (based in Moscow), prototype designs (Warsaw), the construction industry (Prague), urban planning (Budapest), and building economy (Bucharest).[92]

Meeting after meeting, it became clear that technical coordination depended on a *shared register*, which was something more than a shared language. The East Germans spoke of *eine einheitliche Maßordnung*, which required unified norms across national planning agencies. Cooperation, moreover, depended on unified modes of *presentation* of technical data.[93] The idea was for Germans,

Czechoslovaks, Hungarian, Poles, Romanians, Bulgarians, and Albanians to agree on a nomenclature of building types, a proper classification of design processes, and a shared terminology. If socialism necessitated this kind of shared register—a mode of communication between engineers, architects, and planners—the bloc kept on producing a confounding mix of acronyms and specifications. Integration was supposed to be far-reaching, so many other Comecon-related agencies sprang up, specializing in machine building, ceramics, plastics, chemical works, glass, and transportation. They scheduled regular meetings on the basis of preapproved topics (one example: "On the optimal size of cities and the limits of urban growth in large cities").[94]

Members prepared reports, submitted study materials, and obtained "tasks" from the central administration.[95] In 1959, for example, a meeting on building prototypes convened in Leningrad. The East German delegation proposed an exhibition that would show, among other things, how a Soviet standard design had been "appropriated" by a German town.[96] Other meetings hailed the powers of plastics for quickly and massively satisfying the popular appetite for industrial and consumer goods.[97] When one examines these piles of yellowed paper, the daunting technical reports, and the formulaic letters shuffling back and forth between Moscow, Berlin, Warsaw, Prague, Budapest, Sofia, Bucharest, and Tirana, it is hard to look beyond the endless hurdles and the stuffy socialist formalities. They are transcripts of wishful thinking. But officials kept trying anyway, across national borders, and the underlying aspirations still seem remarkable.[98]

Albanian Soil, Italian Traces, Socialist Slabs

Khrushchev had championed it with vigor in his 1954 speech, and in a matter of years, prefabrication became the urgent task for planners throughout the bloc. Leading the revolution, the Soviets, the Czechoslovaks, and the East Germans exchanged technical details and kept an eye on one another's factories.[99] The expansion of concrete in the Eastern bloc encouraged comparisons: Was the Polish model more cost-effective than the East German?[100] By 1960, some 17 percent of all construction in Czechoslovakia involved prefabrication. Two years later that figure rose to 29 percent.[101] The Soviet Union presented itself as being at the forefront of designing cheap mass industrial housing, and the United Nations dispatched architects from Latin America, Asia, Africa, and the Middle East to study the country's approach.[102]

Eastern bloc countries developed "national types," often named after the places where the building models came to life. Picking up on prewar prefabrication experiments, for example, the Czechs designed their own prototypes

("G-building"). The East Germans created sections of three- to five-story units (Lübbenau, Berlin, Hoyerswerda). In Hungary, housing blocks rose in Dunaújváros and Pécs, even as architects continued to debate the social implications of family homes, which were a large share of the country's stock. Polish planners devised the WUF-60 (Warsaw Universal Form), a system of arranging concrete slabs. The Romanians built experimental five-story prefab units. When East German colleagues paid a visit in 1959, the Romanian counterparts explained that cutting costs had become the single most important task across the country's construction industry.[103]

There was nothing inherently ideological about prefabrication, and socialist planners readily looked to the capitalist West for examples. At earlier points, Eastern Europeans "turning to the West" might have been a problem for Soviet officials. Back in 1955, a Soviet Ministry of Foreign Affairs memorandum noted that a Hungarian member of the Academy of Sciences had complained that Hungarian experts had such a hard time dealing with the Soviet journal *Stal'* (*Steel*) that they had been forced to examine American professional journals instead. Scientific and technical institutes in Bucharest and Budapest, similarly, complained that they did not receive enough technical literature from their Soviet counterparts. The East Germans, moreover, apparently found it easier to get the necessary technical Soviet literature from West Germany or Denmark than from the International Book service in Moscow.[104]

By the late 1950s and early 1960s, however, keeping an eye on private companies in the capitalist world was common. In fact, some Eastern bloc countries paired with West European counterparts for the purpose of adopting technical expertise.[105] The process was complicated, since European countries employed a variety of prefabrication systems. This meant that it was necessary to survey the industries, calculate the costs, and assess the flexibility of each system. How many hours did it take a Western factory or a private company to build a housing unit? Was the French Camus system more effective than the Larsen-Nielsen? In addressing the problem, Hungarian and East German planners drew, among others, from French sources and examples like the Laing Industries in Britain.[106]

The precise details of this story varied from country to country. For the Albanian industry of the 1950s, prototypes, mass production, and reinforced concrete were aspirations rather than reality. Some architects attended congresses. Catalogs made their way to planning bureaus. Delegations toured factories in Czechoslovakia, Bulgaria, and Romania. They took notes and wrote memos: How do state authorities in Czechoslovakia feed the workers? Who secures the construction material in Sofia and Plovdiv? What does a prefab factory actually look like?[107] The orientation toward factory-made housing was also reflected in academic work. For example, officials approached Czechoslovakia for pedagogical and technical guidance.[108] Soviet Academy of Sciences members, moreover, reviewed drafts of the university's curriculum, underscoring serial housing construction, prefabrication, and the expansion of reinforced concrete (singling out appropriate models for Albania).[109]

Here too, Albanian officials appeared self-assured but also deeply aware of lagging behind. "The whole country has turned into a construction site," proclaimed a draft resolution for the national construction conference.[110] Socialist construction had assumed its own heroic figures since the 1940s: men who had collapsed or died in the midst of backbreaking tasks, famed norm-busters, and pioneers of *racionalizim*.[111] And in this ongoing battle, party functionaries declared, industrial methods and new materials were the way of the future.[112] A few years earlier, laborers had been expected to heroically master Soviet bricklaying techniques, turning their bodies into machine-like instruments. Now they had to master the processes of a new heroic material: concrete.[113]

Within a few years, *projekte tip* became so ubiquitous that administrators and architects grew concerned about uniformity. In order to maximize savings, government officials recommended reducing types, so that in addition to *tipëzim*, designers were bombarded with calls for *thjeshtëzim* (simplification). The result was an increasing wave of complaints about the monotony of socialist panoramas. As one 1958 report put it, Albanian towns were starting to look alike: "the same façades (with the same standard windows)."[114] In 1960, the Central Committee criticized planners for employing *projekte tip* "without regard to any architectural or planning criteria," thus contributing to "monotony and uniformity" across urban landscapes.[115] One party chief warned engineers not to forget "that they can learn a great deal from their more able Soviet, German, and Czech colleagues" but that they should not reproduce those blueprints mechanically.[116] There it was once more—the recurrent theme of building socialism, endlessly recapitulated in different contexts: copying was expected, but mechanical copying was problematic. A system devised *explicitly* for the purpose of easy replication—from city to city, country to country—was supposed to be adapted to a local context.

The more routine the complaints about uniformity became, the more uniformity seemed to spread.[117] Whatever they might be able to copy from the bloc, Albanian planners could not replicate Soviet, Czech, or East German material advantages. Up until the middle of the decade, each building enterprise had been responsible for securing its own building material. Enterprises focused on satisfying short-term planning targets, and as a consequence, there was little industry-level coordination. Top-down directives called for simplifying designs, but the incentive among enterprises was to work "on their own account" in order to obtain the necessary materials to achieve immediate planning targets. If an enterprise waited until the very last moment to get its construction plan approved, it could bypass the regular technical supervision and get approval from the deputy minister directly. That way, the enterprise could use whatever building material it deemed necessary to get the job done, meeting only the minimum standards.[118]

Cutting costs meant cheaper materials. And what was cheaper than soil? For years, enterprises had made use of *qerpiç* (mud bricks), and East Germans came to Albania to experiment with low-rise mud-brick dwellings. The savings were obvious (transportation costs and coal), and local workers could qualify by taking a special course lasting less than two weeks.[119] Stones might have been another option, but they required vehicles, which were in short supply. *Qerpiç*, on the other hand, offered a number of advantages. Craftsmen could make bricks using the right kind of soil and laying the pieces out to dry on a nearby field that they had cleared beforehand. Then they would use clay to hold the units together. The whole process demanded only basic tools: mattocks, shovels, hoes, carts, and small pieces of wood used to flatten the bricks. There were downsides too. The appropriate construction period was limited to the warmest months. Moisture was a major problem, and surfaces came out uneven. The available soil around the site, finally, determined the consistency of the material.

Authorities employed master craftsmen who had used mud bricks for many years and who informally passed on their knowledge to apprentices. This shows the continuity of local knowledge under central planning; the material of socialism was a kind of amalgam. Take the example of *populit*, a Fascist-era material. It was a high-resistance composite made of wood shavings bound with cement, which could be pressed to obtain relatively lightweight slabs providing durability and insulation.[120] *Populit* seems to have arrived in Albania from the Italians before the Second World War, though the details are obscure. Some accounts mention the involvement of an Italian engineer by the name of Dario Pater, known to Mussolini's wife, and a fixture at Villa Torlonia, Il Duce's residence.[121] The Fascist regime reveled in material innovations that showed Italian ingenuity and self-reliance, so *populit* fit into an obsession with giving autarky material form (*materiali autarchici*).

Over the years, the material underwent a transformation from an Italian autarkic invention to a solution for socialist problems. Like *qerpiç*, it was relatively cheap.[122] It was better suited than soil to industrial methods. The fact that *populit* may have been associated with Italian planning does not seem to have bothered socialist authorities. In fact, a team of industry experts visited Italy in 1958 precisely for the purpose of gathering technical intelligence on prefabrication methods using the composite material. Hoping to get a tour of a factory near Venice, the visitors posed as businessmen interested in buying the "Eraclit" panels (wood elements treated with magnesium). The Italian owner, however, agreed to only a five-minute visit and refused to provide detailed technical specifications. The technology was patented, he told the guests. They could not simply walk in and obtain the technical formulas. If they wanted to buy the machines, the price was 250 million lire.[123]

As with earlier fits of Stakhanovism, the battle over new materials and construction methods became synonymous with the battle for socialism. Virtually everyone learned to speak the language of "mechanization" and "industrial methods," but there are also indications that managers often reverted to old-fashioned, manual-intensive techniques, in addition to continuing to use mud bricks and other primitive materials.[124] In response, the government made the use of certain construction materials obligatory in 1960. For example, it decided that foundations had to be made of stone and that floors were made of reinforced concrete. It also called for expanding the use of lime.[125] Up until then, "finished" apartment buildings still looked "unfinished" because enterprises, under the planning crunch, left them with exposed walls. The government ordered that the walls facing streets should be plastered.[126] Then, when enterprises plastered façades, the prime minister lashed out at officials for choosing bright yellow. Apparently, the "conditions of our country" dictated the need not only for frugality but also for socialist modesty. Appropriate colors for Albanian cities, a memo clarified, were grays, whites, and light hues.[127]

When the government finally registered all the country's dwellings in 1959, it determined that two-thirds dated from before the Second World War. One-fourth of the populace lived in structures deemed "poor." Forty-four percent lived in buildings deemed "somewhat adequate." Six percent were in housing deemed "uninhabitable." Living space was also crowded space; statistics show that the average city housing unit in the late 1950s contained 1.4 families. In some cities, the average was as high as 1.7 and 1.8. At the national level, each individual reportedly had 4.7 square meters of living space (excluding kitchens), but the number was lower (3.5) in industrial areas. Almost one in five industrial workers had less than 2 square meters of living space. Workers in general were more cramped than farmers and administrators. The typical family in an industrial town or an agricultural center was composed of 5.2 members and included, on average, more than two couples living together in fewer than two rooms. It was common, in other words, for a single room to be divided between three or four people.[128]

Older neighborhoods were cast in adobe and limestone, but some of the newer buildings were made of concrete blocks. This difference in materials was made more evident by changes in height. By the end of the 1950s, almost 90 percent of all of the country's dwellings had no more than two floors. Very few buildings had more than four floors. Soon thereafter, the government called for building standard five-story apartment blocks, but it was not easy to get enterprises to comply.[129] Reliance on an unskilled workforce and volunteers contributed to the continued construction of low dwellings.[130] Albanian authorities never replicated the dizzying heights of prefab housing estates that came to dominate the edges of Moscow, Berlin, and Prague. But precisely because the typical Albanian structure was so low, a five-story addition made a visual difference. More important, the experience of inhabiting an apartment was new. The ethos of "rationalizing" life, after all, extended beyond the construction site and into the interior of a home. In 1959, industry experts designed the model of a standard kitchen composed of a stove, a sink, and cupboards for groceries and utensils.[131]

Early experiments produced awkward results. Prototype housing blocks featured unsealed windows, haphazard plastering, and floors finished in a composite made of scraps, chips, and wood shavings (mixed with mortar instead of concrete).[132] One standard apartment layout (*tip 59/2*) came with such a tiny hallway that the door to the apartment blocked access to the kitchen.[133] A number of bathrooms got no direct light. Some kitchens were barely big enough to hold a sink unit. Exposed water pipes occasionally meandered through apartment rooms. Women reported difficulties in cleaning the rough, shoddily finished floors. They complained of having no place to store foodstuffs or clean carpets. Consequently, they did laundry in the bathroom if there was room to do it there. Carpet cleaning had to be done outside. To address some of these concerns, the Union of Women issued several recommendations to the Ministry of Construction in 1961 calling for the adoption of kitchen designs from East Germany, which they deemed "comfortable and most appropriate."[134] The kitchen, initially a nook, grew over several proposals into an *aneks* (a semiseparate kitchenette).

The move into a new apartment was something special for those lucky enough to get off the waiting list. A 1958 survey asked 220 such families to evaluate their new homes (58 responded). Most of the apartment buildings were centrally located in Tirana, but the survey also included respondents who lived in the blocks around the Stalin textile complex outside the city. Almost all families (except for two) had their own apartment. Some complained about small bedrooms, but the report's author dismissed the demands as "exaggerated." The author acknowledged, nevertheless, that the hallways were tiny. Warm water was in high demand, as were windows and balcony doors that did not let rain into the apartment. One inhabitant had the audacity to ask that the neighborhood get a pharmacy, emergency room, and cinema. Trash chutes were missing, so inhabitants reportedly collected their trash by the front entrance to the apartment, treating their neighbors to foul odors. The apartments, admitted the memo, did not yet provide all the necessary comforts. They made it complicated "for housewives to do household chores."[135]

Reports on newly erected housing from 1960 abound with references to crooked balconies, uneven floors, and lousy furnishings.[136] Some enterprises reportedly used concrete of a lesser quality than the plan called for. Under the pressure of deadlines, managers declared housing units finished and signed off on them, even if they featured untreated walls, exposed floors, missing sanitary fittings, and deficient masonry. Some prototypes featured lower ceilings and narrower staircases (as well as thinner walls on the upper floors).[137] As budgets took a cut, so did ceiling heights—from over three meters to slightly above two and half. When contemplating reductions, Albanian officials drew from Soviet publications such as *Arkhitektura SSSR*. In one instance, they consulted Soviet journals to gather information about ceiling heights *in the West*.[138] Some proposed getting rid of hallways altogether. After all, one architect explained, moving from one room directly into the next, without passing through a hallway, "is considered normal in the Soviet Union because it saves floor space."[139] There was no detail too small for the party leadership to ponder. The Secretariat took up the merits of building materials, locations, and ceiling heights. The party chief extended advice on where to put the shops and on the appropriate number of floors for an apartment building (four).[140]

Tirana to Beijing to Havana

Out of this mixture of top-down planning in the absence of urban plans; desire for mass production and constant improvisation with soil, composites, and other rudimentary materials; borrowed blueprints and scarcity; calls for reducing *monotoninë* and also for combating *teprimet* (excesses) emerged the Albanian socialist city. It was the kind of landscape that confounded Salisbury in 1957: cities teeming with rural elements and expanding industrial settlements staffed with overworked peasants. One Western visitor described the country as a "dreary little island of Stalinism" in a letter to Harrison Salisbury. "Wherever I went," he wrote, "I was vividly reminded of my years in North Africa, and astonished every time I remembered I was in Europe."[141] The country was somewhere and nowhere—suspended between Western arrogance, socialist expectations of plenty, and plain misery. The mud was predominant. The past was still alive. "We should destroy old buildings," insisted the chief in charge of construction at a meeting of the party Secretariat. "Agreed," Hoxha responded, "we should destroy the old buildings," recommending not compensation to current residents but new apartments in socialist buildings.[142]

When Nikita Khrushchev visited the country in 1959, he witnessed local construction and found it primitive. Introducing reinforced concrete and mechanized systems, he lectured his hosts, would cut costs by half. They could build a five-story apartment building made of concrete blocks in one month. Bricks and mortar were a thing of the past; low-rise dwellings were not economical. The Albanians could look around the Eastern bloc for models. The Politburo promptly took up the issue, and within a year, there was talk of obtaining an Eastern bloc–designed prefabrication factory.[143] The Berlin-based Comecon commission on construction promised technical assistance.[144] Each member state would focus on specific areas within the construction industry: East Germany, for example, would renovate Albania's brickworks and introduce industrial construction technology.[145]

The year 1960, however, also saw the beginning of a messy break between the Albanian and Soviet parties—the subject of the following chapter—and the effects rippled in relations with the rest of the bloc. By the following year, the Soviet advisers were gone, as were the East Germans and the Czechs, replaced with Chinese technical teams. Here too there were echoes of the disagreements with East German engineers in Kurbnesh. Albanian representatives accused their Comecon counterparts of failing to live up to their aid program, refusing to attend the commission's meeting in November 1961.[146] Just as socialist states sought more integration, Tirana cut itself off. Still, political detachment did not preclude continued material borrowings and shared planning practices. Socialist states did not need to have good political relations to execute similar planning objectives.

With the Soviets gone, the party declared that reinforced concrete and rational methods would help solve the housing crisis by 1975. In a memo on the subject, the party chief underlined the magic word: "prefabrication."[147] In the early 1950s, Soviet methods had stood for the future, building awareness of the need to catch up with the rest of the socialist world. By the decade's close, government and party higher-ups pointed to the powers of concrete and the virtues of mass construction—at first visiting the Eastern bloc and then going around it. Construction specialists also began to look elsewhere for technology: for example, the capitalist West. Specialists visited Italy to observe the construction industry, and trainees also traveled to France to study prefabrication.[148] Officials also pondered sending trainees to Denmark and Sweden for the same purpose.[149] Needless to say, the country's isolation from the Eastern bloc made it harder to keep up with what was happening in Berlin and Prague. Architects and planners had limited access to foreign design journals. This contributed, over time, to a sense of isolation and reliance on outdated technical solutions.

There were a few indirect routes. Government officials, for example, pressed the Chinese for equipment and funds and asked for blueprints of modular housing, interior furnishings designs, and descriptions of assembly processes, as well as standard designs for toilets, sinks, and showers. Albanian housing designs, in turn, turned up in exhibitions in China—illustrations of the advancements made in the outer frontiers of the socialist (and developing) world.[150] In the early 1950s, Albania had shipped asphalt to North Korea. A decade later, with vanishing Soviet credits, Albanian functionaries sought assistance from Pyongyang. Architects visited the North Korean capital to observe housing construction, hydraulic projects, and the application of urban planning principles. The visitors were impressed with the rapid rate of construction in the People's Republic (made possible in part by Eastern bloc technical assistance).[151] Published reports, moreover, extolled the discipline of North Korean steelworkers, whose crusade for development resonated with the tasks back at home.[152]

The other site of socialist possibilities was Cuba. In 1963 the party apparatus encouraged the embassy there to expand local cultural contacts.[153] When a team of Albanian architects traveled to Cuba to attend a congress of the International Union of Architects that same year, they were moved by the architectural culture of Havana. They took note of the fact that the Cubans had made considerable advances in industrial technology and that they were applying reinforced concrete in mass housing. Particularly enthralling were Havana's vivid colors. "As a southern country, endowed with strong sunlight and rich horticulture," the two visiting architects wrote, "we should also apply light colors to our constructions."[154]

The Cubans, in fact, received a prefabricated panel factory from the Soviet Union: a gift after hurricane Flora in September 1963. Yugoslavia, Afghanistan, and Chile similarly got Soviet prefabrication technology.[155] Officials in Tirana wanted a factory of their own, but they could no longer get one from the Soviet Union. At one point, they considered purchasing one in Romania. They settled for a Chinese-made panel factory instead, asking to send seventeen specialists for training abroad.[156] All artisanal methods in construction, the Politburo ordered, had to be replaced by prefabrication.[157] Under continued pressure, specialists went back to Bulgaria and Romania to study large panel technology. In other words, socialist exchange also happened despite what East German, Soviet, and the other representatives had decided in Berlin in 1957. Albania took much longer to develop large-scale prefabrication but then applied it widely—in housing, in hydraulic works, roads, bridges, and agriculture.[158]

The politically divided socialist world was thus unified in the unmistakable expansion—across continents—of the concrete slab. There was a distinct chronology to this story, shaped by geopolitics but also defying the usual diplomatic breaking points, because it points to the overlooked stubbornness of material culture. Concrete expanded through the interplay of domestic factors (housing crisis), national ones (centralization, professional infighting), Eastern bloc exchange (Comecon), and more broadly international competition (capitalism

FIGURE 24. Socialist types: residential complex composed of prototype housing units in Tirana, June 1966. ATSH.

and socialism). There was copying and there was also unplanned isomorphism. Socialism produced unexpected entanglements. In Albania, it was precisely the tension between an orthodox ideological program supervised by a party-state and shifting alliances that created a recognizable material culture. The built environment came to embody the possibilities of mass construction, as well as its shortcomings and shoddiness. Once adopted, a prefabrication system created a set of new problems to be solved.

From the Albanian periphery to Hungarian towns or to Santiago de Cuba, prefabrication gave rise to questions of adaptability. What panel systems offered in terms of cost and speed, they sacrificed in aesthetics. It became necessary, therefore, to deal with outward appearance. "Domesticating" concrete entailed designing flourishes for the naked concrete panels or other national motifs (along with the architectural debates that such choices provoked). The state-driven approach to construction as a social problem raised similar conceptual problems across national borders and ideological divides—about the social role of the architect, the function of consumption under central planning, and individual spatial needs in a collectivist society.[159]

Some authors have been at pains to show that grayness was not endemic to socialist apartment life. Yet officials, planners, and architects themselves obsessed over monotony and uniformity. It is not so much that socialism was only about grayness but that the battle against grayness became a thoroughly socialist preoccupation across national borders. Rather than as aesthetics, we might think of socialist construction in terms of time: the time it took to get an apartment but also the desperate push to cut down the time it took to build housing; the time it took to fix any small problem along the chain of production, which would be compounded by the massive scale of central planning; the time spent dealing with the fact that each modification required other moves across the industry; the time spent coordinating across state agencies and, increasingly, national borders.

The economic factor in construction was not the only factor, but central planning made it a priority. "The architects did not welcome the arrival of reinforced concrete," Khrushchev admitted in his memoirs, adding, "Every standardized production process limits individuality. May the architects forgive me." He admitted, too, that the architects were not the only ones who had been suspicious. "Later a lot of jokes sprang up about people coming home slightly 'under the weather' and not being able to find which neighborhood or which building was theirs," he recalled. "Well, after all, someone who is not sober can lose his way between three pine trees." What mattered was the fact that the state had built quick cheap housing on an unprecedented scale. "No other country built as much housing as we did," Khrushchev boasted. "I was proud of it and am proud of it today."[160] Derision, monotony, irritation, pride, and a sense of home: these were hardly mutually exclusive in the life of a socialist city dweller.

THE GREAT LEAP

Nikita Khrushchev: We think that you are doing quite well and that
maybe if you were to give us a loan, we would take it. (Laughter)
Mehmet Shehu: We have a lot of rocks, sea, and air.
Nikita Khrushchev: We have more of those things than you do. Do you
have dollars?

Tirana (1959)

We said to Nikita Khrushchev, "You are economically powerful, but we
are also powerful because of Marxism-Leninism."

Enver Hoxha in conversation with Li Xiannian (1961)

Some people say that we are isolated. Maybe they are right. It is also
possible that they are wrong.

Mao Zedong (1963)

The regime was desperate for a big square. Like other parties in the bloc, the Party
of Labor of Albania was keen on holding parades: endless rows of workers wav-
ing small red flags every May, soldiers marching in lockstep to project strength,
gigantic portraits of the classics of Marxism-Leninism floating above the crowds.
But such parades required proper boulevards. Crowds needed large open spaces.
Moscow, for example, had the glorious space around the Lenin Mausoleum. The
Bulgarian capital had another dead body to serve as a backdrop (Dimitrov's mausoleum). Warsaw had its Parade Square, stretching out in front of the Palace of
Culture and Science, the gargantuan Soviet gift towering over the capital and permanently infringing on Polish pride. In Budapest, the leadership set up a tribune
at the base of Stalin's massive statue—before angry crowds tore it down in 1956.
The Albanian party had no such tribune. It had no big socialist square to fill with
the chanting masses. What it did have was a crammed Ottoman bazaar—smack
in the middle of the socialist capital of the People's Republic. Next to the bazaar
stood a splendidly crafted mosque (Et'hem Bey's).

When Hoxha asked Khrushchev for a Soviet-designed Palace of Culture in
1958, the Soviet leader did not appear enthusiastic.[1] Moscow had provided many
concessions already, only to have the Albanian party come back, lists in hand,

asking for more rubles. Add to that the fact that the Albanian side kept asking the Kremlin to put pressure on the Eastern Europeans to purchase the country's inferior goods. As usual, Soviet higher-ups insisted on investments in agriculture. The Albanian establishment, however, kept obsessing over industries—and a Palace of Culture. Tirana did not yet look like a socialist city. There were the petty traders of the bazaar and the Fascist-era buildings. The city center was a constant memory of the past; local administrators spoke of it as "a wound." They resented the squalor of the bazaar, which they equated with darkness and the despotism of an Ottoman past. Like an illness, the Ottoman vestiges in Tirana had to be eradicated. A Soviet Palace of Culture would not only transform the center, they argued, but also "make eternal the friendship of a new kind between our people and the people of the Soviet Union."[2] The blow to the architectural past would also be a symbolic blow to the institution of the market.

The two sides signed an agreement for the Palace of Culture in July 1959.[3] Later that year, the razing began. The small shops of the bazaar were gone and then a few of the surrounding low-rise dwellings. The following March, authorities approved the blueprints. Soviet-Albanian dealings, however, were uneasy. As the Soviet journal *Arkhitektura SSSR* acknowledged, the Moscow-based design team went through several drafts, though it did not explain that this was due to constant pushing, from the Albanian side, for a bigger building. Officials in Tirana envisioned something monumental, and they were adamant about a tribune at the palace's base. It was not the Soviets who pushed for something grand and imposing—it was the Albanian side. Design in the center of the socialist world, in other words, had to reflect priorities in the periphery.[4] This explains the building's awkward façade; to appease their partners, Soviet designers recessed the front of the building and opted for large colonnades, likely to facilitate the functioning of the platform as a tribune. The idea was to make Skanderbeg Square, after expansion, the central focus of socialist parades and mass gatherings.

Just as the Palace of Culture got its foundation in the summer of 1960, however, political relations between Tirana and Moscow began to show cracks. By the following spring, Soviet advisers sent to oversee the construction of the building had left the country permanently.[5] A large, empty site stood in the middle of the capital, looking more like a gaping ruin than the birth of a landmark (figure 25). With the Soviets gone, local managers were forced to finish the edifice on their own. Having made the palace a symbol of friendship, party and government authorities now turned it into a symbol of resolve *against* Moscow. They quickly urged city residents to volunteer at the construction site. They organized local women in special work brigades and took photographs of their labor (figure 26) to show that solidarity could overcome "great-power chauvinism." And they

FIGURE 25. Ottoman-Italian-Soviet: construction of the Soviet-designed Palace of Culture on the site of the former *pazar* (market), Tirana, early 1960s. In the background, the city's clock tower and mosque, which survived the demolitions, and the Italian-designed government buildings and the National Bank. ATSH.

FIGURE 26. The ruins of friendship: women join in the construction work for the Palace of Culture after the departure of Soviet specialists, 1962. ATSH.

removed specialists from other important industrial projects, assigning them to work on the palace.[6]

Ironically, the authorities' indulgence in a massive project made the task of completion more difficult. Budgets now had to be stretched.[7] Trade officials approached the Chinese and the East Germans for building materials, furniture, and fixtures. Originally planned to be finished in 1962, construction of the edifice continued into 1966. The result was an elevated rectangular structure with a prominent white colonnade spanning the entire length of the façade and dwarfing the nearby mosque and the clock tower.[8] At the inauguration, officials fired off passionate speeches declaring the palace a monumental achievement. It was, they emphasized, a feat of *Albanian* construction and engineering, a triumph over revisionism.[9] To make the point, authorities also organized a tour for the foreign diplomats. (The Czechoslovak representative, who also looked after Soviet interests, did not participate.)[10]

In light of the story so far, this bitter end of the Albanian-Soviet bond appears puzzling. For one thing, there was the economic uncertainty. Vanishing Soviet credits and technical assistance put planning targets into question. It would become necessary to find new sources of aid, possibly turning to capitalist countries for imports. Above all, it became necessary to explain this Soviet "betrayal" to the population. After intense campaigns in the name of emulating the Soviet Union, how could a small country go against Moscow? As a local manifestation of the bigger Sino-Soviet confrontation, Albania's turn shows how socialist relations, which produced considerable uniformity on a large scale, also highlighted and exacerbated differences. But while the Sino-Soviet split had far-reaching consequences for international socialism, it is also possible to see continuities across the 1960–61 point. Practices and knowledge gathered from the Soviet Union and the Eastern bloc in the 1950s persisted after the schism. The capitalist-socialist divide remained crucial in the Cold War, but some of the fiercest battles took place *within* the socialist sphere. Recognized similarities bred vicious conflict.

The fact that ideology mattered in all of this can be appreciated precisely by looking at how a small country on one side of the globe could extract capital from a rising power, like China, on the other. It was more than machines and imports, however. The Albanian party, having grown painfully conscious of big-power politics, exploited the contradiction between Soviet ideological speech and Soviet behavior in the international system. Resistance (to de-Stalinization) and regional insecurity (Yugoslavia, isolation, capitalism across the border) help explain behavior that might otherwise seem, looking back, recklessly aggressive and yet also cast in a desperate defensive key. The Albanian alliance with China was, from the beginning, a marriage of misplaced expectations. But China was also a massive window into the Third World—and the same mechanisms that the Soviets and East Europeans had developed in the 1950s could now be used to establish contacts with countries such as North Korea, Cuba, or former colonies in Africa and Asia.

The Sino-Soviet split was not only a matter of global competition between two socialist powers.[11] It was also, as Tony Judt has put it, "a genuine conflict for the soul of 'world revolution.'"[12] For Khrushchev's leftist critics, the Soviets had failed to live up to the task of leading the socialist world, with the consequence of alienating true believers. Khrushchev and his allies in Eastern Europe had thus betrayed their roots. But the Chinese were also prone to ideological errors, Enver Hoxha warned in the 1960s. Stalinism thus persisted in Albania thanks to Chinese credits and shipments, coercion, waves of purges and executions, and a widespread campaign to place insecure Albania at the heart of an alternative socialist world made up of militant revolutionaries. To dismiss this orthodoxy as a national peculiarity offers no explanation for why Stalinism could prove so persistent. In the 1950s the country had been a kind of laboratory for Soviet modernity. A decade later, it unexpectedly turned into a microcosm of Cold War antagonisms and a big battle over the proper ownership of Marxism-Leninism.

A Garden of Rocks

In the early 1950s, Albanian visitors to the Soviet Union had drawn parallels between their country and the Soviet republics in the Caucasus and Central Asia. After Stalin's death, Khrushchev and his collaborators spoke of Albania as an example of successful Soviet-financed modernization for *other* underdeveloped countries. A September 1956 memo forwarded to Mikhail Suslov, for example, argued that aid to Albania was significant given the country's Muslim majority, its historical ties to the Middle East, and the possibility of propping it up as an example of development for formerly colonized peoples.[13] Soviet officials recommended that Albania, as "the only predominantly Muslim country of the European people's democracies," expand religious and cultural contacts to the Middle East and eastern and northern Africa.[14]

The following year, Khrushchev again boasted that the country would become an example for the Arab world (whereas East Germany would be the counter example to Western Europe). "The Americans are now helping out Yugoslavia with the intention of exploiting it to divide the socialist camp," he told a delegation in 1957. "We help out Albania with the intention of raising the material well-being and cultural level of the Albanian people." From there, the Soviet leader added, "we will launch our ideological offensive against the enemy's ideology" and into Africa and Asia.[15] In his memoirs, the Soviet party chief insisted that his country had been a benevolent force, trying to help the Albanians "restructure the Albanian economy, bringing it to a modern level, thus making Albania, as it were, a precious gem that would attract the rest of the Muslim world toward Communism, especially in the Middle East and Africa."[16]

For a while, Albania's party boss played along. "The imperialists need to recognize," he told Eastern bloc diplomats in Tirana in 1957, "that a small backward country like Albania can turn into a blooming garden in a short amount of time, when the powerful Socialist Camp comes to its aid."[17] Arab visitors could see for themselves how "selfless" Soviet development assistance was helping Albania's majority Muslim population overcome backwardness.[18] But the boastful talk betrayed contrasting ideas about the country's place in the world. Moscow may have begun fretting about the fate of decolonized countries, but party higher-ups in Tirana hardly thought of themselves as Muslims building socialism. Rather, they thought of themselves as European Communists and partners on an equal footing with other Communist-led states—albeit presiding over a less developed economy. Soviet leaders, moreover, projected their own ideas and anxieties about Muslims and the Third World onto the Albanians, whose history of multiple coexisting religions and secular calls in the name of the nation, which preceded and in fact has outlived Communist rule, was far more complicated than the Soviet ready-made formulas.[19]

As important as misperceptions were, they did not make the Soviet-Albanian rupture inevitable. More pertinently, Soviet rhetoric was underlined by economic implications. The Albanian party-state was preoccupied with developing an industrial basis for a self-sufficient socialist economy. But Moscow complained that Tirana pursued the wrong priorities. There was a reason for the "garden" metaphor: Albania was to become an agricultural supplier to the camp. The Adriatic location made it attractive for establishing touristic and cure resorts for the exhausted workers of the Eastern bloc. On one level, this orientation had troubling resonances in an insecure country that had endured Rome's expansionist plans in the 1930s. Albanian officials understood the problem of feeding the populace, the necessity of eradicating marshlands, improving irrigation, and gaining arable land. But the regime never thought of the country as essentially a source of plants, fruits, and vegetables, as well as a handful of other raw minerals, for Moscow, Prague, and Berlin.[20] In 1949, Stalin had quipped, "We will help you, but will your people ever get to work?"[21] Less than a decade later, Mikoyan and his comrades still kept "joking" that the Albanians would always keep coming back to Moscow, cup in hand.[22]

Recall, moreover, the dilemma posed to the Albanian leadership by Khrushchev's gamble in 1956. Back then, the Soviet party boss had embarked on a course of rapprochement with Yugoslavia, throwing the Albanian leadership into utter panic. For them, an opening to Yugoslavia was not only a matter of policy—it was an existential problem. First of all, a new course would raise fundamental questions about Albanian-Yugoslav relations going back to the party's founding in 1941. Belgrade insisted on the retraction of the charges that the Party of Labor had levied back then. Additionally, Hoxha had sustained a myth around his heroic stance vis-à-vis Belgrade—with Stalin's backing. Tirana's separation from Belgrade had been bloody: one minister (Spiru) had committed suicide; Xoxe, the security chief, had been placed in front of a firing squad. Who was to take responsibility for their dead bodies?[23]

Add to this the fact that Khrushchev had shocked Stalinists throughout the bloc by attacking Stalin and thus ushering in a chorus of protests in the name of reforming socialism. What might have made sense for the Soviet leader was utterly unacceptable for Hoxha and Shehu, who had presided over the purges of their former comrades in arms. The problem in 1956, therefore, was one of survival but also of a fundamental irony: Stalinism had been important for both Hoxha's and Tito's continued rule. The difference was that Khrushchev acted as if Stalinism was a problem of the past. But for the Albanian leadership it was very much a problem of the present. Khrushchev's crusade against Stalin, to put it another way, had both personal implications (for the party clique) and troubling implications for the entire history of Albania's party and its crimes. Some lower-ranking party members began to gripe, but Hoxha stood firm: no rehabilitation for the slain former security boss Xoxe.

Compounding the frustration, Khrushchev did not even bother to consult with the Politburo in Tirana when dealing with the Budapest uprising in November 1956. The Soviet leader, however, consulted with Tito, in the Brioni Islands, when he decided to replace the troublesome Hungarian leader Imre Nagy with the more pliable János Kádár. Hoxha was furious. How could the leader of the socialist world belittle the leader of another Communist party in this fashion? (Recall how Churchill had "forgotten" Albania in conversations with Stalin in October 1944.) Were Communist relations not supposed to differ from typical great-power politics? The offense taken in Tirana may seem naive to a reader keen on seeing a Communist party's rhetoric as a kind of mask for the usual behavior of big and small powers in the international system. But the ideology made such contradictions hard to swallow.

Albania might be left alone, Hoxha told his Politburo colleagues, but it would not give up its principles. The Hungarian mess, as the party leader saw it, had developed under Moscow's nose. The Hungarian chief Mátyás Rákosi had rehabilitated the slain interior minister László Rajk, and the situation had snowballed into a counterrevolution. There would be no such concessions in Albania. And sure enough, in November 1956, Albanian authorities charged three former party officials, including a woman, for conspiring with "a foreign power" (understood to be Yugoslavia) and had them shot. The "Stalinist-style" executions worried even the Stalinist Gheorghe Gheorghiu-Dej in Romania.[24] Still, there was no obvious alternative to Moscow for the time being, and so Albanian party leaders kept their reservations private.

All this helps explain the background to an uncomfortable reality unfolding in socialist relations in the late 1950s: Hoxha stuck to a hard line within his party and kept lambasting Belgrade at every turn. By the spring of 1957, however, Khrushchev had had enough. To him, Hoxha's obsession with Tito seemed pathological. In vain, the Albanian leader tried to make an argument for why his Yugoslav counterpart could not be trusted. The Albanians were "warm-blooded" southerners, Khrushchev fumed, and they approached the issue "nervously."[25] Hoxha presented his case, the Soviet boss added, as if stable relations between Tirana and Belgrade were impossible. Moreover, Khrushchev took issue with the decision to execute a woman in late 1956. Times had changed, he explained, and it no longer made sense to condemn people to death for political offenses. Toasts about friendship continued at dinner, but the Soviet leader went even further—inviting the Yugoslav ambassador in Moscow to toast with the Albanian delegation. "We all toasted and shook hands," Hoxha later reported. "Truth be told, the atmosphere at dinner was warm but we felt hurt inside."[26] Losing sleep that night, the delegation had agreed to change tactics vis-à-vis Belgrade.

The obsession with Yugoslavia, however, did not die down. (Instead of flying over Yugoslavia, the Albanian delegation traveled to the Soviet Union by ship; the ship reportedly came back loaded with Soviet advisers.) When reporting on the Moscow talks to the ambassadors of other socialist countries, Hoxha insisted that there were no disagreements with Moscow at all. Khrushchev, he told them, planned on transforming Albania into a socialist "garden in bloom."[27] He acknowledged that his party might have made mistakes, but he played down the contradictions.[28] In short, the Albanian party boss tried to play an uneasy balancing act, promising restraint in Moscow and reverting to a hard line at home. "If Khrushchev had not taken this stand," he told his Politburo colleagues, "we would have done as before, said that we agreed with them but in practice we would have acted differently." The heated exchanges in Moscow had left him with the impression that "the Soviet comrades do not appear to know the issues related to the development of our country very well." For example, the delegation had sworn to Molotov about the profound love for the Soviet Union among the people of Albania only to have Molotov raise his eyebrows: How could a non-Slavic people love the Soviets so much?

The Party of Labor leaders did not need to see Soviet tanks rolling into Budapest to understand the existential threat posed by calls for reforming socialism.

This was an unreconstructed Stalinist party—the Soviet ambassador was the first to admit that the "Leninist principle of collective leadership" had not been restored in Albania in 1956.[29] At a party plenum two years later, Hoxha declared Albania the "living proof of the fair Marxist-Leninist character of relations between socialist countries and the Soviet Union" and in the same breath continued to lambast Belgrade's "revisionism."[30] (It helped that Soviet-Yugoslav relations cooled that year.) Khrushchev may have been furious in private, but he had no trouble using Hoxha's outbursts whenever convenient in dealings with the Yugoslav leadership. Beijing, which at one point had also tried to expand contacts with Yugoslavia, joined the attacks against Belgrade after the Seventh Yugoslav Party Congress in 1958.

The Albanian party boss must have felt vindicated. In December of that year, he told the Politburo that the Soviets must "have no objections to our political standing, because if they had any, they would not have failed to tell us."[31] De-Stalinization had been shown to amount to self-destruction. Having purged "hostile elements" on trumped-up charges of conspiring with Belgrade, Hoxha was able to frame reformism as an effort to liquidate the party. The Soviet Union had decided to release political prisoners, but in Tirana the Politburo pondered asking the Soviets for *more* security police training. Party tactics on specific issues may be subject to changes, Politburo members agreed in the spring of 1959, but the main party line would go unchanged: fierce war against enemies— foreign and domestic.[32]

The Ruins of Friendship

For several years Albania's party had pleaded with Khrushchev for an official visit. He finally made it to Tirana in May 1959, laying the first stone for the Soviet-designed Palace of Culture. Before the trip, however, the Soviet chief sent word that Yugoslavia would be off limits in speeches ("for obvious reasons") and asked for reassurances from Tirana that the government would not bring it up.[33] Unsurprisingly, the Politburo did not take the request well. In a tense meeting, Hoxha explained that the Soviet leader might cancel the visit if they refused to comply. The hosts therefore decided to keep Yugoslavia off the table. "Our party line is correct," Hoxha reassured his colleagues. "There is no doubt about this."[34] Then he promptly brought up Yugoslavia in conversation with Khrushchev, much to the Soviet guest's irritation.[35]

As propaganda, the visit served the Party of Labor well: here was the leader of the socialist world lending support to a small and isolated country. During conversations, however, a different picture unfolded. When the hosts broached the subject of a new round of Soviet technical assistance, Khrushchev demurred. To estimates presented by local planning bureaucrats, he responded by recommending that they redo the calculations.[36] "Do you think 300 million [rubles] is small change?" he retorted to the prime minister during a brief conversation. The guest was irritated by the fact that the visit had quickly turned into pleas for rubles. "You fed us lunch and then promptly demand all these things from us," he mocked the hosts. "If we had known about this, we would have brought lunch with us."[37] Yet again, Hoxha presented all of this to the Politburo as the Soviets *joking*. The visit, he ensured them, had secured Albania's future.[38]

Khrushchev urged the hosts to invest in agriculture. Instead of oil extraction, which would be costly and adventurous, given the quality of the country's reserves, he suggested cultivating grapes, oranges, lemons, peanuts, tea, and olives. During tours around the country (figure 27), he visited the major Soviet-funded projects of the decade, including the Stalin textile complex, the Marx hydropower plant, the Lenin cement factory in Vlorë, and a number of cooperative farms.[39] But he shrugged whenever the hosts spoke of complex industries. Albania was endowed with "minerals, good soil and climate, as well as the sea," he pressed. Fruits and vegetables—not oil—were the country's "gold."[40] It was imperative for Albania to grow self-sufficient, but Khrushchev's idea of self-sufficiency was

FIGURE 27. Nikita Khrushchev discusses land reclamation plans for Tërbuf, Albania, May 1959. ATSH.

different from his hosts'. As usual, the Albanian aid requests kept coming. Unable to pay back earlier loans, authorities requested an additional 500 million rubles from the Soviet Union and other Eastern bloc countries in early 1960.[41]

Against this backdrop of economic dependency, Hoxha and Shehu received news of Sino-Soviet disagreements in February 1960. Anastas Mikoyan summoned Hoxha to a private meeting during a visit to Moscow. The Soviets made it clear that the meeting was to be kept at the highest party level, but Hoxha insisted on bringing Shehu along. (It was not the first time that the party chief correctly sensed that something important was going on.) The two did not immediately report to the Politburo on what Mikoyan had told them. In that meeting, Hoxha only hinted at some discrepancies with the Chinese but underscored the primacy of the Soviet Union and the correct standing of his own party. "Our position on Yugoslavia is correct," he added, admitting that the Soviets "do not use the same language as we do" but that the leaders in Moscow were largely in agreement anyway.[42]

Then, in early June, Moscow informed Tirana that a meeting of Communist parties would be held later that month in Bucharest, on the occasion of the Romanian party congress. The meeting's purpose was to discuss the international situation.[43] (The Albanians initially assumed it might have to do with the recent U-2 incident, in which an American spy plane had been shot down over Soviet territory.) At the same time, Hoxha was in contact with Beijing, where an Albanian parliamentary delegation was on a high-level visit. The delegation included Politburo member Liri Belishova, who informed Hoxha that the Chinese party officials had spoken to her at length about their divergences with the Soviets. The Chinese, moreover, wished to know what Tirana thought of the April 1960 articles (the so-called Lenin Polemics) they had put out, in which they took issue with Moscow's thesis of "peaceful coexistence" in international affairs.[44] Caught unprepared, Belishova asked for instructions from Tirana.[45]

The Politburo convened on June 6. Hoxha warned that the situation was complicated and serious. They agreed to send a delegation to Bucharest, but what should they say to the Chinese? Some Politburo members pressed: Should they not voice their unanimous support for the Soviet Union, as they had always done? Hoxha was cautious. He kept insisting on the importance of the Soviet Union. But he also pointed out that Moscow and Tirana did not exactly agree on everything. "The point here is for us to judge this issue on principle," he went on, "meaning that we should avoid making any mistakes, avoid any wavering vis-à-vis Marxism-Leninism, avoid leaning a bit to the left."[46] The ultimate goal would be for Communist parties "to close ranks around the USSR," so the Albanian Politburo would emphasize unity in the camp. Nevertheless, the party chief also made the point that Beijing seemed to hold Albania in esteem. This was no small matter. Hoxha instructed the delegation visiting Beijing to praise the Chinese articles on Leninism.[47]

The following weeks of June were a dangerous time to be caught between Beijing and Moscow. The Politburo got word that the meeting of Communist parties would be postponed after all. Still, the party delegations might exchange some views in Bucharest. Hoxha suspected that Sino-Soviet disagreements might come up in Bucharest anyway, which explains his cunning approach—to keep a distance. Instead of traveling himself, he decided to send Hysni Kapo, the party's third-ranking man. Belishova, meanwhile, was far away from what was happening in Europe. She stood out—in Tirana and elsewhere in the social-ist world. For a start, she was a woman in a sea of men in gray suits. She had studied Marxism-Leninism in Moscow in the early 1950s. She was young—in her thirties—and she was energetic. She told me that she had become enrap-tured with the idea of Communism as a young girl after reading Gorky. She had become a fervent believer.[48] Back in Beijing, Belishova did what seemed reason-able to her: she informed the Soviet embassy about what the Chinese hosts had told her. Moscow took this as a sign of support for the Soviet line. It would spell Belishova's undoing.

Days before the Bucharest meeting, Alexei Kosygin, the Soviet deputy pre-mier, caught up with Mehmet Shehu (in Moscow for health reasons) and let it be understood that the Soviets would not back down with the Chinese.[49] On June 21, the Soviet officials distributed a long document condemning the Chi-nese party to those present in Bucharest. Kapo immediately informed the Polit-buro in Tirana. He had been instructed not to take sides, but it was Hoxha who benefited from the distance from what was taking place in Bucharest. To the frustration of the Soviets, Kapo kept repeating the same line over and over: his party had not authorized him to take a position. The Albanians stalled, in other words, insisting on procedures.

The party urgently convened another Politburo meeting on June 22. Hoxha warned his colleagues that the issue was serious and also urged party unity. It was necessary not to err, he explained, and he praised the "unbreakable" friendship with the Soviet Union but also worried lest the Chinese get the wrong impres-sion.[50] There was more than a hint here of the kinds of calculations and fears that had driven behavior at the height of the Stalin-Tito split in 1948. Two days later, when the Soviet attack against the Chinese in Bucharest culminated, Hoxha pre-dicted that the Bucharest meeting's communiqué would have "terrible repercus-sions across the world, just like the speech on Stalin's cult."[51] He instructed Kapo not to sign anything that criticized the Chinese. By June 25, the party adopted a position of generally supporting the Soviet proposal for a common statement from the Communist parties but criticizing the *tactics* employed at the meeting.

The frustration with Soviet tactics was genuine. The Soviet representatives supplied Kapo with their lengthy criticisms of the Chinese only the night before the actual meeting where the documents would be discussed. Khrushchev, moreover, insisted that the Albanian party take a stand, sending Yuri Andropov to convince Kapo to fall in line, without success. All of this created a sense of helplessness in the face of Soviet strong-arm tactics. Khrushchev's arrogance, moreover, struck a chord in light of his 1959 visit and years of disagreement. By itself, the Bucharest meeting does not explain why Albania ended up on China's side. But the combination of disgruntlement over Soviet tactics going back to 1955, long-standing disagreements over Yugoslavia, and especially the broader ideological and practical implications of reforming socialism provides a better sense of the overlapping dilemmas in Tirana.

As Khrushchev prepared his attack against the Chinese, Belishova found herself in Moscow, showered with praise for having taken a courageous stand in Beijing. Soviet officials told her that Hoxha had to make a decision: Was it better to have an ally comprising two hundred million (referring to the Soviet Union) or six hundred million (China)?[52] They insisted that Moscow deserved a friendship "without zigzags." Events in Europe had precipitated too quickly for Belishova. After her return to Albania, her "error" gradually took on the proportions of a deviation from the party line. There was bitter irony in the fact that she found herself accused of doing what Albanian party officials had done for a long time. After all, it had long been common practice to consult with Soviet representatives. Indeed, the habit of seeking out advice on every trivial matter had frequently irritated Soviet officials. For Belishova, however, the praise in Moscow quickly turned into a torrent of abuse back home.

The country had been on the brink before. The schism with Yugoslavia had fed into Hoxha's anxieties about foreign developments he could not control. Receiving news of how the party men in Moscow were lauding Belishova probably also struck a chord of resentment. Hoxha knew that Belishova's passing of information to Moscow hardly provided them with anything they did not already know. Still, he used the opportunity to punish the youthful and energetic Politburo member. In vain, Belishova submitted to hours of reflection and self-criticism. For some Central Committee types, the opportunity to tear down a young woman at the height of her powers might have been irresistible. Having been thoroughly tactical in handling Bucharest, Hoxha later insisted that he had been principled all along (a déjà vu of 1948 all over again).

In July, the party chief brought the complications with Moscow to the plenum. There, too, he framed the disagreements as a matter of principle. Hysni Kapo gave a resume of the Bucharest meeting, which now acquired a kind of chauvinistic character. Hoxha then got up and delivered a detailed account of political relations between the two countries, tracing "Soviet mistakes" back to 1955. He lingered on the heated exchange in Moscow in April 1957. That meeting, he admitted, had left the Albanian delegation feeling "as if the Kremlin had fallen on our heads." The entirely unexpected turn of events in June 1960 now assumed the form of a historical arc. Hoxha skillfully cast the rebellion against the Soviets as a sign of maturity: "We, comrades, are Marxists," he told the attendees, then adding,

> We used to be young but we are older now, and I am not talking about us as individuals but the party as a whole. We are no longer a one- or two-year-old party but a party that will soon count twenty years. We have not spent all this time lying on a bed of roses but in a bloody war against Fascism, the National Front, the English, the Americans, the Trotskyites, the Yugoslavs, the Greek monarcho-Fascists and all kinds of other enemies. We have thus learned Marxism from books, from war, from life.[53]

When Albania approached the Soviet Union for grain that summer, Moscow did not comply. This was the beginning of Soviet pressure tactics, which would backfire. On 1 August 1960, Mehmet Shehu met with the Chinese chargé d'affaires in Tirana. Beijing agreed to grant Albania a total of fifty thousand tons of grain. The diplomat explained that China's party "admired the heroic stand that comrade Hysni Kapo adopted at the Bucharest meeting."[54] The Central Committee of the Chinese Communist Party, he added, has supported and would support Albania's position in the battle over Marxism-Leninism. For his part, Shehu reconfirmed Albania's support. "A friend in need," he told the diplomat, "is a friend indeed." Mao had his own saying: "One good friend," he reportedly told an Albanian delegation later, "is just enough."[55]

A party plenum in September purged Belishova and Koço Tashko, the Harvard-educated activist who had been involved in Hoxha's introduction to the party.[56] Both stood accused of passing information about internal party matters to the Soviets—again, something that Hoxha himself had done repeatedly. At the time, these purges gave the impression of intraparty factional conflict.[57] Given the secrecy of the state and the absence of reliable sources, the myth of factional struggle lives on in scholarship. It also has not helped that Hoxha's so-called memoirs—fanciful collages of half-truths—have informed Western scholarship for decades. Existing accounts describe "pro-Khrushchevite" and "pro-Stalinist" groups.[58] But there was no intraparty struggle. It was all manufactured after the fact. Belishova was a genuine enthusiast of the Soviet Union, but she was not a faction. Tashko was also a lifelong partisan of the Soviet Union. He had long been sidelined, however. With their fluent Russian and extensive personal history of Soviet contacts, both individuals were effective scapegoats. What is astonishing, in retrospect, is precisely the opposite of what existing accounts claim: the absence of actual challenges to Hoxha's rule. This is what needs to be explained.

The purges sent a clear message to the lower ranks. In dealing with Moscow over the following weeks, Hoxha took on a warlike tone. When the Soviets suggested a meeting to avoid "turning the spark into a fire," the Albanian side refused to discuss Sino-Soviet relations in Moscow in the absence of Chinese officials. Instead, the party leader went looking for instances of "provocation" and found them in the behavior of the Soviet ambassador, who now seemed suspicious. When Shehu traveled to the United Nations in New York in September 1960, Hoxha signed the missives he sent to him with his wartime pseudonym (Shpati). He reported developments back at home as news "from the home front."[59] As things got heated at the United Nations, Hoxha gleefully enjoyed the show from a distance. "Let them be unmasked once and for all," he wrote to his prime minister, calling the critics of Albania and China "trash."[60] Shehu's missives from New York piled on the insults toward the "gravediggers of revolution."[61]

To read this secret back-and-forth communication is to appreciate how self-consciously militant these two former guerrilla fighters were, how thoroughly seeped in an ideological outlook of world affairs. And sure enough, at the meeting of eighty-one Communist parties in Moscow in November, the militancy turned into spectacle. Loud and boisterous himself, Khrushchev became exasperated with the Albanian delegation.[62] The more pressure the Soviet party boss exerted, the tougher the Albanian stance became. Ahead of the meetings, Hoxha's delegation had consulted with the Chinese. But the Albanian team even outdid the Chinese in opposition against the Soviet party. In a sense, the Stalinist project in Albania had worked *too well*—to the point that the man who had taken on Stalin's legacy now found himself unable to keep a Stalinist under control.

The Communist world had once fractured in 1948, inaugurating witch hunts and show trials. Then Soviet tanks had crushed the Hungarian uprising. Albania's challenge was serious, but Albania was no Yugoslavia, Poland, or Hungary. It mattered, moreover, that Khrushchev was no Stalin and that Beijing had made it clear that it stood on Tirana's side. Still, Soviet retaliation was quick, culminating in the withdrawal of Soviet specialists in the spring of 1961. The fate of technical transfer agreements with the rest of the Eastern bloc also became uncertain. China stepped in to provide some relief. Confronted with the disastrous famine produced by the Great Leap Forward in the late 1950s, officials in Beijing nevertheless agreed to import grain and ship it to the Balkans.[63] Moscow had always urged caution and "stages of development," but Mao championed the formula of "'more, faster, better, and cheaper' socialism."[64] Incidentally, this also was in line with the thinking of the Albanian party leadership. During a December 1960 meeting, Deng Xiaoping assured his Albanian guests that China would assist the small country with "every difficulty."[65] Officials in Tirana also asked for thousands of tons of rice, oils, and sugar and a million and a half US dollars. The following year, the countries signed technical transfer agreements.

A dispute over the joint Albanian-Soviet submarine base, off of the southern coastal city of Vlorë, was the culmination of the Soviet-Albanian row. Party officials announced that they had identified a supposed coup attempt under the leadership of a Soviet-trained navy admiral, who was reportedly working for the imperialist American, Yugoslav, and Greek powers.[66] The implication was clear: outside threats to Albania were real. Unimpressed with the ploy, Moscow first used the Warsaw Pact as a lever to discipline Tirana, and then, faced with aggressive Albanian resolve, decided to pull the submarines. An attempt by Ho Chi Minh to mediate between Moscow and Tirana in the summer of 1961 bore no fruit. The Soviets recalled their ambassador, and Khrushchev attacked the Albanian party at length at the Twenty-Second Soviet Party Congress in October. It was in response to those attacks that Hoxha famously declared, on November 7, that regardless of what might happen, "we say to Nikita Khrushchev that the Albanian people and the Party of Labor will survive on grass—if necessary—rather than sell themselves for thirty silverlings, because they prefer to die standing and honorably rather than live with shame and on their knees."[67]

The tone was aggressive, but the Albanian leadership appears to have panicked that year—fearing threats not from the imperialists but from the Soviet Union. "We did not have weapons in 1961," Mehmet Shehu told a Chinese delegation years later, adding, "We couldn't care less about bread, but we were desperate for weapons because the revisionists could attack us."[68] This perceived insecurity also explains the Albanian officials' insistence on military assistance (artillery, missiles) and a security treaty with Beijing in 1963.[69] But in reality the government could not ignore the bread problem either. The schism with Moscow coincided with years of drought. The winter of 1962–63 caused extensive flooding. Before the rift, socialist countries had planned on supplying around 600 million rubles in loans and credits. (Moscow would have provided half.)[70] It was possible to keep trading with other Eastern bloc countries, but the terms changed. One East German diplomat warned that the country's third Five Year Plan (1961–65) was in danger of becoming "a scrap of paper."[71]

In some respects, the Chinese replaced the Soviets, but Albanian political behavior was different from that in earlier years. Though party officials courted Beijing for aid, they abandoned the submissive position they had assumed in dealings with Moscow. In part, this was a reflexive response to the fact that Albania effectively became a target for political statements against China. This turned the small party into a proxy, though its leaders thought of themselves as partners. During a visit in June 1962, the Chinese hosts admitted as much, telling the guests that the Soviets "indirectly castigate us by castigating you, so by defending you, we also defend ourselves."[72] The Tirana ruling circle embraced this sudden international relevance, just as it had vigorously embraced Stalinism in the 1940s. There were, moreover, signals that Pyongyang was on board too. An October 1960 dispatch from the embassy there pointed out that "even after the Bucharest meeting we can see that relations between our countries have not been perturbed one bit."[73] In the spring of 1961, Kim Il-Sung reassured Albanian representatives of his full support. "Both of us are defending socialism," he told a diplomat, "you on the western frontier of the socialist camp, and we on the eastern one."[74]

Internal discussions about Soviet policies had been deferential in the 1950s, whereas in the early 1960s the Albanian Politburo did not shy away from taking issue with the Chinese leadership. For example, the party objected to Chinese pleas to attend a meeting of Communist parties in 1962.[75] In internal documents, Albanian higher-ups argued that Beijing's wavering position toward Moscow was in line with repeated Chinese missteps in foreign policy. Chinese criticism of Stalin, similarly, was cause for concern in Tirana. Not only did Hoxha and his party comrades reject de-Stalinization, but they also argued that the Soviets had managed to *dupe the Chinese* into believing some of the allegations against Stalin. In light of this, Hoxha reasoned that Albania needed to employ different tactics from China. "We ought to fight so that China will be with us," he told the Politburo in the summer of 1962.[76]

Saving the Revolution

How could the "eternal friendship" with the Soviet Union, well rehearsed and enforced, be so readily dismissed? Part of the answer is that it could not. Breaking the Soviet bond involved more than purging Belishova and Tashko, reshuffling a handful of cadres, or adjusting the propaganda machine. Soviet influence had been too far-reaching to be quickly corrected through administrative measures. For a small battalion of apparatchiks, bureaucrats, midranking functionaries, and all the way down to managers, factory workers, and other individuals, the schism raised serious questions about the future. In this protracted adjustment, the party engaged on several fronts, by reframing Albania's position in the socialist world and by rearranging the mechanisms of socialist exchange to mirror new geopolitical realities. In striving to save the legacy of socialism from Khrushchev, Hoxha and his associates were of course saving their unreformed selves. But the party line was sustained by broader social anxieties and hopes.

At first, the party head was at pains to distinguish between the Communist Party of the Soviet Union and the Soviet Union itself. At the party congress, he invoked the "great and unbreakable friendship" with the Soviet Union, "which there is no force or intrigue in the world that can weaken."[77] Cadres had to understand, thus, that the Albanian leadership was not breaking with the Soviet Union per se. On the contrary: it was Khrushchev who was responsible for betraying Lenin's revolution and for defiling Stalin. If anything, the Albanians were upholding the *true* Soviet legacy. In this spirit, a November Central Committee letter urged party members to distinguish "between Khrushchev the renegade and those who follow him on the one hand, and the Soviet people and the Communist Party of the Soviet Union on the other." Communists were not to confuse "the hostile position and battle waged by Khrushchev against our party with the friendship, love and respect that we harbor for the Soviet people and the party of the great Lenin."[78]

To preempt confusion, the Tirana party organization called meetings to instruct members on Albanian-Soviet relations. In June, some two hundred circulated with the purpose of talking to local youths. During these meetings, participants asked what precise mistakes Khrushchev had committed, why the Soviet specialists had left the country, and why they had abandoned construction work for the Palace of Culture. Toward the end of the year, party organizations around the country conducted more meetings.[79] The ideological aspect of such instruction was also tied to practical concerns. In addition to surveying international relations, propagandists urged workers to cut down production costs and save more raw materials—a necessity in light of the prospect of vanishing Soviet aid. Accordingly, government branch offices arranged special commissions tasked with overseeing "saving" campaigns.[80] Party organizers also set up "voluntary" work brigades to help at construction sites, clear the streets, plant trees, and paint façades. Newspapers prodded enterprises to make up for imports by manufacturing products themselves. Popular mobilization took on the characteristics of a psychological battle.

For months, the regime acted as if the country's place in the socialist world had not changed. With the Soviets gone, authorities celebrated a Soviet Friendship Month in 1961. One East German witness noted that the party leaders probably would have preferred not to celebrate the Soviet Union at all. But, he reasoned, such a thing might have been too confusing for the inhabitants.[81] Earlier that year, at May Day celebrations, the crowds kept calling Hoxha's name. The East German diplomats counted all the portraits on display: Marx, Engels, Lenin, Stalin, Yuri Gagarin (displayed twice), one of Patrice Lumumba, but none of the other leaders of the bloc.[82] With Khrushchev condemned, factory managers kept talking about "Soviet experience." There were still celebrations of the October

Revolution. There were still seminars on the anniversary of the Red Army. And there were still rallies and concerts on Lenin's birthday.

In the summer of 1962, Hoxha again declared that "no force in the world could destroy this friendship" with the Soviet people.[83] At the same time Albanian propagandists blasted the Kremlin's great-power chauvinism. It might seem like a paradox, but it made ideological sense: Khrushchev did pose a fundamental challenge to Stalinists everywhere, having offered no viable alternative. Reformism, moreover, did threaten the stability of the socialist world, sending angry crowds to the streets in Central Europe and concluding with Beijing's refusal to fall in line. Cold War scholars have scrutinized the elite-driven causes of the Sino-Soviet split, but it was the outcomes of the split that shed light on the consequences for people's lives. The socialist global project was broken. But that fact did not kill hope. In fact, socialist conflict created even more illusions. The Sino-Soviet split laid bare the vicious infighting in the socialist world, but it was precisely those animosities that endowed minor regimes—like Albania's—with a voice.

There was no shortage of committed Stalinist patriots in the Albanian Central Committee who responded emotionally to Khrushchev's bullish ways. But nonparty members could also see in the split an opportunity for a possible opening to the West. Perhaps, they speculated, the West might accept Hoxha, now that he was free from the Soviets (as it had accepted Tito), gradually pushing the regime to soften. For some, China appeared too distant to become a permanent solution. Those who had come to discover the Soviet Union bemoaned the loss, in private, not because they were necessarily fond of Nikita but because they saw the possibility of Soviet-style de-Stalinization vanish. Others still, especially the children of the establishment, did not care too much about what China had to offer. They cared for Italian TV. They listened to Western music. They were engrossed with their privileged life.[84] In short, the Sino-Albanian convergence, which to some foreigners appeared "grotesque," needs to be understood in the context of such contradictory expectations.[85]

It is also important to keep in mind that the party apparatus pushed hard against the idea of isolation. It professed ideological purity and vowed self-reliance, but the Eastern bloc did not vanish. The socialist world, which the Albanian regime had celebrated, could not be erased by decree. So the party agitprop apparatus devised a parallel effort to convince lower ranks that inhabitants in the Eastern bloc felt equally betrayed by Khrushchev and that they actually sympathized with Tirana and Beijing. Thus, Albanian students in Bulgaria reported conversations in which locals spoke highly of Albania's stand vis-à-vis Moscow.[86] Diplomatic missives from a number of socialist countries confirmed local support for the "principled position" of the Albanian comrades. On several occasions, Chinese officials echoed the idea that Tirana (and, by implication, Beijing) enjoyed widespread support among inhabitants in the people's democracies.[87] Radio propaganda would now target individuals in the people's democracies who harbored, as Hoxha put it, "feelings of friendship and love for our people." These individuals supported Albania out of principle, he asserted, but they nevertheless "could easily accept a donation or two."[88]

No matter how improbable these claims may seem, the ideological terms employed by Chinese diplomats, foreign Marxist-Leninists, and reports from abroad converged to create the illusion of some external support. There were, after all, plenty of Stalinists who despised Khrushchev, just as there were non-Stalinists who might have despised living under the Albanian dictatorship but who were captivated by the fact that a small state had stood up to the domineering men in the Kremlin. Jokes about Khrushchev used to be forbidden before, but now they could be seen as evidence of popular frustration with Soviet power in Eastern Europe. The break with Moscow, in other words, created a mirror effect: Albania could continue to reflect socialist achievements in the people's democracies, purporting to speak for the people there, even as it denounced those establishments as revisionist. Geographically and ideologically cut off from the bloc, the country remained nevertheless crucially tied to it, even if only as a counterexample to the "betrayed socialism" of East Germany, Poland, and the others.

The party propaganda sector was consumed with the fact that, as one memo put it, Yugoslavia and Western countries "spread lies and constantly speak against us," whereas Soviet, East European, and West European Communist newspapers and media would not even mention Albania, opting to "keep silent and isolating us."[89] Accordingly, central party officials advised diplomats to expand their activity and not—as they had instinctively done in fear of committing political errors—isolate themselves.[90] The other vehicle for breaking Albania's isolation was something that the Soviets had themselves helped promote in Albania: radio. In the early 1960s, Radio Tirana operated programs in English, French, Italian, Greek, Serbian, and Arabic.[91] The party Secretariat decided to create three separate radio sectors targeting Europe and the United States, neighboring countries, and Albanian immigrants abroad. Radio was now supposed to also target Moscow and the Eastern bloc through special programs in Russian and East European languages.[92] To achieve these goals, technicians traveled to China for training.

In May 1959, Tirana had hosted celebrations for the Comecon's tenth anniversary. Bloc delegates had vowed to increase technical aid to the poorest member of the bloc. Three years later, the picture had changed dramatically. Tirana was now a site of Cold War division. The scene at a Ghanaian reception in the capital in 1962, described in East German documents, is like something out of a novel. Officials congregated in four groups: one composed of the Albanians and the Chinese; one composed of the socialist countries of Europe (including

Yugoslavia); a third with the capitalist representatives; and, finally, a fourth group of the "neutrals."[93] Gone were the days when Eastern bloc specialists tried to coordinate Albania's ascension into an integrated international economy. Now Eastern bloc diplomats coordinated with one another (with the East Germans acting as mediators) to make sense of Albanian-Chinese contacts. There was still a division of socialist labor, then, even as the socialist world turned into a world of hostilities.[94]

Geopolitics Is Personal

For many years, propagandists had encouraged personal contacts across national borders. Such contacts were now sources of suspicion. This is why, in September 1961, East German industrial enterprises received instructions on how to handle fraternal requests from Albania.[95] In light of political relations, exchanged letters now became potentially compromising evidence. Take the example of an Albanian man by the name of Jaho, who wrote to Richard in East Germany. The two had become friends during a training program. In his letter, Jaho wrote at some length about the old days. He mentioned a recent bout with the flu. Then he turned to Khrushchev. "I don't want to conduct propaganda with you," he promised, then launching into an analysis of Soviet-Albanian relations. He assured Richard that Moscow had abandoned his homeland at a time of severe need.[96] Jaho's letter ended up at the East German party's Central Committee. It is not clear who prepared a four-page draft response to Jaho there, but it included this line: "Have you forgotten the heroic deeds of the Soviet people during the anti-Fascist battle and the peaceful reconstruction, deeds that served you and me, and all of us?"[97]

A few months later, Siegfried, a student at the Weimar School of Architecture also received a letter from an Albanian friend, Vasillaq. Like Jaho, Vasillaq was at pains to explain that his country was not at fault in the Soviet-Albanian dispute. Khrushchev, he charged, had dealt a blow to the anti-imperialist struggle among formerly colonized people, to the German unification problem, and to the class struggle in the West. "Do you even know why we cannot come to study in Germany anymore?" Vasillaq wrote. "Maybe what you are being told is that this is the fault of the Albanian leaders, that they do not want to send students to East Germany. This is not true." He insisted that Berlin was responsible for cutting off socialist exchange. "One thing is clear, dear Siegfried," Vasillaq's letter announced, "time will tell who chose the right path."[98]

It is impossible to say what motivated these letters. They are contained in a party archive—framed by an institution that made sense of them as political

artifacts. Siegfried seems to have asked Vasillaq to explain the political situation in Albania in previous correspondence, and once Vasillaq obliged, he then
seems to have turned the letter in to the authorities. The tone of the Albanian
letter, on the other hand ("our party is led by the teachings of Marxist-Leninism,"
"under the leadership of our party, our people have made giant steps forward in
the construction of socialism"), seems ready-made, as if the sentences had been
culled from a party speech. It is not far-fetched to suppose that Albanian specialists received encouragement to propagandize in this fashion. After all, Albanian
embassies routinely spread antirevisionist leaflets and speeches around the Eastern bloc. This was communication of a specific kind—grounded in the all-too-
familiar rhetorical rituals of socialism but all the more poignant because of the
sense of a shared past bond.

Geopolitics had become a personal matter. Nowhere was this drama more
pronounced than in the fate of mixed Albanian-Soviet marriages. In the early
1950s, party and security officials had been hesitant to allow marriages between
Albanian citizens and foreigners. Earlier laws had stipulated that petitioners had
to obtain official approval prior to such marriages. In reality, some individuals
seem to have overlooked the procedures all together. The Politburo took up the
issue in 1959, on account of a letter sent to Hoxha by a young Soviet woman,
pleading to be allowed to marry an Albanian officer. The party boss appeared
conciliatory, as he was often keen to do, recognizing that they could not "forbid
people from being in love." But too many mixed marriages could turn into a
problem. The Politburo maintained that marriage requests from "students and
trainees who have been licentious with women" (*bredhur me shumë vajza*) would
be rejected, as would requests to marry women of questionable morals. Hoxha
drew on moral considerations, cautioning against "whoring and immorality."
Immorality, a memo explained, "not only destroys the family and the partner's
life, but also creates political dangers."

The Politburo decided to establish a set of criteria for petitioners, including
political loyalty, on the basis of which requests could be considered. It also placed
particular restrictions on marrying East German, Polish, and Hungarian citizens, since, it claimed, "reactionary elements" had attempted to seduce Albanian
cadres by securing them local women in these countries. But this association of
foreign women with "political danger" was not merely a reflection of the dispro-
portionate number of Albanian men (as opposed to women) who chose foreign
partners. Intentionally, the central party apparatus sought to embed its policy
into an "Albanian mentality" that allegedly rejected the choice of foreign women
as spouses. "Let our comrades keep in mind," the Politburo decision continued,
"that marriages with foreign citizens [the Albanian text uses the female noun]
are generally frowned upon by our people, because they are deemed to imply

disregard for Albanian girls." Albanian mentality, it concluded, may not always be "fair," but it could not be transformed overnight either.[99]

Choices of romance and marriage but also sexual behavior were framed within considerations of ideological, social, and geopolitical threats. For those Soviet consorts who had moved to Albania with their partners, the 1960s were marked by isolation and surveillance. As diplomatic relations were suspended in late 1961, these individuals were faced with the choice of returning to their homeland or renouncing their citizenship and becoming Albanian citizens.[100] Some of the Soviet spouses left the country, but the security police kept a watchful eye on letters and phone conversations, fretting that Soviet women would use the children they took with them as leverage to possibly corrupt the Albanian husbands left behind. If a husband sought to keep the relationship going by writing to his wife abroad, the security police warned of the potential of espionage.[101] Those foreign women who stayed in Albania were similarly subject to surveillance and intimidation. "It was as if the women of the Warsaw Pact," one author later wrote, "were far more dangerous than its artillery."[102]

As Soviet women faced pressure to renounce their ties, the Soviet friendship journal continued publication until 1966. It featured articles on Soviet science, kolkhozes, and factories, and the construction of prefab apartment blocks in places like Krasnodar or the wonders of mass-produced housing in Moscow's Cheremushki district.[103] In November 1962, the anniversary of the Bolshevik Revolution got more coverage than the anniversary of Albanian independence. (Two key differences were the appearance of Chinese musicians and farmers on the cover and the expansion of coverage of North Korea, Cuba, Vietnam, and decolonized African countries.) Mechanisms and practices that had once served Soviet and Eastern bloc propaganda could now be effectively used *against* Soviet and Eastern bloc interests. Techniques once hailed by Soviet advisers could be employed in the interest of improving productivity, thus countering the Soviet "blockade." Some of the continuities, like the journal's content, reflected party tactics. But some of the continuities across 1961 were informal; the isomorphism across socialist states did not have to be planned. Tirana's youths, for example, continued to congregate in a city corner they baptized Broadway (*Broduej*) in the 1960s, just as stylish Soviet youths (*stiliagi*) had done years earlier with Gorky Street in Moscow and Nevsky Prospekt in Leningrad.[104]

The tools, practices, and technological systems that the Soviets had championed, after all, were flexible enough to be borrowed, selectively employed, modified, and retooled to reflect shifting elite interests and geopolitical circumstances. Precisely because it had been thoroughly Sovietized in the 1950s, Albania's Stalinist challenge to Khrushchev seemed all the more surreal. This was not merely the case of a small peripheral state standing up to the powerful imperial center (that dynamic was interesting in its own right, especially at a time of decolonization). The Soviets' own civilizational mission ended up turning against them—from an outpost in the Balkans—emboldening Albanians to object to the negation of a shared legacy (Stalinism). Khrushchev fumed in his memoirs about Hoxha's irrational ways ("That damn Enver Hoxha is simply a gangster"), but Hoxha was a familiar type.[105] Albania's radical positioning was also thoroughly logical within a world system that the Soviets had themselves helped shape. Tirana continued to publish Marx and Engels but also added Mao to the mix.[106]

When coupled with pervasive and continued coercion, this gradual realignment begins to explain why there was no greater pushback against the split with Moscow among midlevel apparatchiks and state employees. The party leadership had already enacted purges in the mid-1950s, and the memory of the executions from 1956 was still fresh. By the early 1960s, party ranks had closed in the name of vigilance against enemies and the ongoing battle against "revisionism." In fact, looking at the party hierarchy in 1960, it becomes clear that Hoxha's orthodoxy at the top was enabled and sustained by a robust system of appointments based on proven political loyalty. At the top of Tirana's party organizations, for example, were 196 secretaries, of whom some 75 percent had joined the party in the crucial years 1941–48, when political loyalty to Hoxha had become paramount. Even though the ranks of educated Communists had expanded in the 1950s, only a third of these party chiefs in 1961 had higher education. This suggests that personal connections and loyalty, rather than credentials, kept them in their positions.[107] The party, moreover, functioned like a networked information society, carefully screening rumors and crafting a narrative that seemed plausible even to the most committed antiparty types.[108]

As for coercion, realignment away from Moscow came with intensive campaigns to identify and punish antiparty elements. The security police had long placed individuals under surveillance, including former party members, diplomats from bourgeois countries, relatives of executed individuals, and others suspected of antistate activities. Once relations with Moscow deteriorated, army officers, writers, Russians, and those known to have Soviet connections became subjects of interest. In the summer of 1961, in fact, party higher-ups appeared eager to remove all suspects and perceived enemies from the capital. "Cleaning," as Hoxha put it during a Secretariat meeting, "is to be carried out at all times."[109] This became particularly important in light of the Sino-Soviet split. The result was that by 1965, the security police counted some 15,700 operatives (including informers), almost 1 in 5 of whom was a party member. One in four of the people placed under surveillance by that point were suspected of the infamous charge of "agitation and propaganda." This represented a considerable increase from 1962–63.[110]

Soviet-trained cadres posed a problem for a regime trying to distance itself from Moscow. Unlike construction plans, journals, and radio programs, they could not easily be reprogrammed. As a result, students enrolled in Soviet and Eastern bloc universities came under scrutiny. During the Soviet-Albanian confrontation, security operatives reported on their conversations and political attitudes, and party organs meted out punishments accordingly.[111] Hysni Kapo and Ramiz Alia, a former youth activist who became Politburo member in 1961, told Mao in 1962 that Moscow had tried to turn Albanian students against their country by "using girls and promises, or by threatening them with their security agents."[112] The government needed Eastern bloc technical assistance but was wary of keeping students there. This was especially true for students in the humanities and in cultural studies, whom apparatchiks deemed especially at risk of succumbing to revisionist propaganda. Initially officials found it necessary to keep some students in the bloc, but Poland and East Germany were now undesirable. Candidates to be sent to any of the other countries now had to be screened even more closely than before for ideological purity. China, moreover, would become a primary destination, as would North Korea to a much lesser extent.[113]

The party's response to the loss of the Soviet Union thus combined internationalist rhetoric with pushback against the idea of isolation, promotion of China, private caution about Beijing's foreign policy, and stricter controls on foreign borrowings. In the case of marriages and personal contacts, the party appealed to "an Albanian mentality," thus asserting itself as mediator between threatened tradition and big, ruthless powers in the international system. Hoxha was particularly adept at this, shedding his petit bourgeois ways in an instant, charming a peasant with localisms, remembering war veterans by name (and kin). Standing up to Khrushchev became associated, in his long fiery speeches, with Albanian pride in the face of long-standing injustice by the big powers. Years earlier, party propagandists had gone back in history to unearth the deep roots of a friendship with the Soviet Union. They had crafted a genealogy of Bolshevism's appeal in Albania. Now those same people crafted a story of Albanian subjugation and resistance. An immediate sense of righteous solitude—Albania as the one true socialist state left in Europe—added a sense of drama to the rhetoric. As one part of the socialist world declined in the horizon, another perspective opened up farther east.

701 Million

Party and government authorities spoke of the disappearance of Soviet and Eastern bloc experts as a form of betrayal. The Comecon, they charged, had reneged on signed agreements. Much effort went into documenting the financial losses associated with this withdrawal. For their part, East German bureaucrats culled quotes and figures from past Albanian publications, speeches, and planning estimates. Hoxha himself had admitted, they pointed out, that 90 percent of all industrial machines and installations in the country stemmed from the Soviet Union.[114] The effusive past pronouncements about selfless socialist aid now contradicted the Albanian officials' insistence on unfairness and betrayal. In the spring of 1962, the government sought to revive contacts with Eastern bloc partners to "force them," as one memo put it, "to make a statement whether they want to continue cooperating with us or not." After all, Eastern bloc governments had arrangements with Western Europe; denying technical agreements to Albania, the reasoning went, would "shame" the East Europeans.[115]

This abrupt change in relations, however, did not entail a practical end to the diffusion of socialist knowledge and techniques. In fact, after the suspension of technical aid from other socialist countries, administrators seem to have become even more interested in Eastern bloc expertise. Partly in response to this new reality, ministry functionaries pushed employees to scrutinize archived technical materials and blueprints sent by their Eastern bloc partners prior to 1961.[116] These included descriptions of technical processes, construction methods, and industrial formulas that bureaucrats had set aside, formally reviewed, or even forgotten about. Some proposals, which might never have been implemented had official relations persisted, now saw the light of day.[117] Another factor contributing to this sudden surge of interest in Eastern bloc innovations was the state-led campaign to cut down production costs.[118] Agencies signed fresh agreements with China, North Korea, and Vietnam (Romania was added later).

This was no match for Soviet expertise, which seems to have produced uncertainty. Recalled one eyewitness, "In my conversations with them, professors of Tirana University tried to play down the consequences of the Soviet scientific boycott, proudly pointing to the capability of the University's own teaching staff." Nevertheless, this commentator added, "their eyes betrayed their anxiety."[119] Across the country, this visitor saw the same pattern: East Europeans moving out and Chinese specialists trickling in. The latter came to take up jobs in factories and plants, design hydraulic projects, and work on tunnels and dams.[120] This signaled the other major development in the postwar period: China's rise in the socialist world. From a recipient of Soviet technology, China began the difficult transition into a new role as a source of technical aid for another developing country. As Beijing became more and more interested in Afro-Asian collaboration, it also kept the Albanian side abreast of the ongoing struggle with Moscow in asserting leadership in Africa and Asia.[121]

Beyond grain shipments, China pledged cement and brick factories, a tractor spare parts plant, a hydroelectric power station, consumer manufacturing plants, a superphosphate plant, a copper refinery and textile plants, a metallurgic complex, and more. In the spring of 1963, some 284 Chinese specialists were due to arrive in Albania to help with the construction of nineteen industrial projects. Another 104 Albanians were scheduled to move to China to learn how to operate the new factories.[122] Some stores in the capital still carried East German radios, but Chinese-made pens, textiles, and other goods were quickly becoming commonplace.[123] Chinese professors of English came to teach at the state university in Tirana. Through special arrangements, Beijing also supplied plants, seeds, and other raw materials for experiments.[124] At one point, Albanian officials sought to adopt Chinese popular medicine, including acupuncture, though the technique appears to have had little success among locals.[125] By mid-decade, 80 percent of Chinese development assistance reportedly went to four countries: Vietnam, Korea, Outer Mongolia, and Albania.[126]

Talk of fraternal China was effusive, but Albanian economic requests were a burden for Beijing. "We try to do our job in assisting your economy," Chinese premier Zhou Enlai told Albanian interlocutors in 1962, "but you must rely first and foremost on your own strength."[127] Using party channels, the Albanian side pleaded for chemical fertilizers, machines, industrial goods, and even technology that the Chinese lacked.[128] In response, Zhou urged them to achieve economic self-reliance. A few years earlier, Albanian party functionaries had urged Moscow to force Eastern bloc governments to buy unmarketable Albanian goods. Now it was Beijing's turn to complain about having to purchase them. "Nobody in China likes your tobacco," Zhou told his Albanian counterparts in 1965. "We have only imported it because you have insisted."[129] He pointed to the fact that the living standard was *lower* in China than in Albania. During a visit to the country, he warned the hosts that industrial requests had become onerous. Here was a notable socialist development: Beijing provided more aid to a European country than to North Korea (only Vietnam received more by 1965).[130]

China's distance meant that the country could hardly exert the kind of far reaching cultural influence (or pressure) that Moscow could—even if Beijing had wished to do so.[131] But it also complicated transportation to the Adriatic, which was a costly logistical ordeal. Other obstacles that had accompanied technical transfer from the Eastern bloc in the 1950s also resurfaced in dealings with the far-flung Asian partners. Some specialists worked on the basis of special technoscientific arrangements; others were attached to industrial projects. Here too there were Sino-Albanian disagreements on procedures.[132] Vehicles, dwellings, furnishings, and consumer goods were scarce. Agencies fought for every single resource. At times, Chinese specialists came by the hundreds, but there were no

FIGURE 28.   Two revolutions: a delegation of the China-Albania Friendship Society visits a tractor factory, 28 September 1967. ATSH.

vehicles to even take them to work. (Some metallurgy workers went on foot.)[133] Previously, specialists' apartments had had two beds per room. Administrators considered stacking three. Others kept sleeping in hotels.[134] Only in the early 1970s did the government decide to build a special hotel to house them.

The Soviet-driven discovery of a socialist world had expanded the number of Russian speakers in Albania, but speakers of Chinese were hard to come by. Chinese specialists, in turn, were unable to translate from or into Albanian. Materials therefore had to go through double translation—Albanian to Russian and then Russian to Chinese or vice versa.[135] When requesting contracts and technical materials from China, Albanian officials asked to receive them in Russian.[136] As difficult as it was to overcome the language barrier with the Chinese, it was even harder with the North Koreans. When a team of specialists came to Albania to experiment with rice and hops crops, it became clear that there was only one person in the whole country who spoke Korean. The language barrier was not the only obstacle to be overcome. According to one report, local inhabitants were suspicious about the potential of these crops, quipping that "the peasants of Shkodër and Kavajë are neither Chinese and nor Korean."[137]

In the 1950s, learning the language of Lenin had been a political imperative. Blasting Lenin's heirs in the Kremlin now also required more language learning. When it came to translating Hoxha's speeches, the party was willing to spend good resources. But much of the propaganda effort was amateurish. By the early 1960s, almost 80 percent of state-employed translators were around sixty years old. "The majority of them don't have a healthy political standing," added a memo, admitting that some of the translators had in fact been prisoners.[138] (Prison labor produced some of the outstanding Albanian translations of world literature.) A handful of Albanian trainees studied English in China, Vietnamese in Vietnam, Spanish in Cuba, and Arabic in Iraq and, for a short time, in the United Arab Republic. But Russian persisted as the lingua franca of international socialism well after the split. Mao's teachings, for example, were obtained through their Russian translations.[139] Albanian students traveled to China to learn Russian in addition to English.

"If someone asks how large our population is," Albanian authorities were fond of saying in the 1960s, "we say that it is 701 million." The outward signs of the great friendship with China were conspicuous. There were Chinese film festivals, radio broadcasts dedicated to Chinese music, and festivals featuring Chinese writers. Journalists and authors traveled on state-backed pilgrimages to revolutionary China. Still, compared with the Soviet-Albanian relationship, which had been a mass effort involving hundreds of language courses and thousands of specialists, propaganda for the Chinese was circumspect, kept under tight party control, and made more difficult by geography and a steep language barrier.[140] In fact, Sino-Albanian contacts accentuated differences and reinforced distinctions. Established in 1959, the Sino-Albanian Friendship Society never became a mass organization as the Soviet one had been.

This was not incidental. In 1962, as we have seen, the Politburo had voiced suspicion over Chinese foreign policy tactics. Propaganda for the Soviet Union had backfired, so the party was careful with the promotion of China. The Central Committee kept receiving requests to name—in proper Stalinist form—cooperative farms after Mao Zedong. And, indeed, authorities did name one such farm after him, in Lushnje, though the statue of Mao they erected there did not look like Mao at all and had to be taken down.[141] The Twenty-Second Soviet Party Congress, Mao told an Albanian delegation in 1963, had made the Party of Labor of Albania famous around the world. Sino-Albanian discussions, like those with the Koreans, hailed the legacy of anti-Fascism (drawing a parallel between Japan and Fascist Italy and Nazi Germany).[142] The conversations recounted at tedious length the respective party genealogies—the Trotskyites, the sinister plotters, the ever-expanding lists of traitors. Still, none of this socialist international bonding was a guarantee for agreeing on big questions. Mao kept highlighting the dangers of imperialism, but the Albanian higher-ups were obsessed with revisionism.

After Khrushchev's ouster in 1964, Beijing signaled to Tirana that the change presented an opportunity for a thaw in relations with Moscow. Hoxha compared this position with Khrushchev's rapprochement with Tito a decade earlier. Provincial party chiefs received instructions stating that relations with Moscow were inconceivable as long as the Kremlin continued on a revisionist path. They also learned that the Chinese had a different position on this issue.[143] Beijing's "wavering," the Albanian party boss fumed, was a sign of "anti-Marxism." He also called for a complete rehabilitation of Stalin. As he put it, "Stalin is Marxism-Leninism," whereas disarmament had proven "a big bluff."[144] The realization that the Chinese had also been talking to Romanian party leaders "behind our back" caused further irritation. The party boss warned that "in the future relations between us will become aggravated, our disagreements will increase." Nevertheless, he suggested that differences of opinion be kept away from the public. "We will tell them that we are friends," he explained, "but that you can't buy us."[145]

Propaganda for China, and especially for Mao, had to be kept under control. Exaltation of the Soviet Union, Hoxha warned, had been excessive, and the aggrandizement of Mao was similarly misguided. Apparatchiks placed too much emphasis on "the great assistance from China," which made it seem like Albania could not survive without a powerful patron. "What about now, when we are confronted with difficult situations, what will we do?" he asked the Politburo. "Will we perhaps die?" The answer was no: "We might have to tighten our belts, but we will not die." If the choice would be between factories and principles, the party would pick principles. If Beijing, like Moscow, cut credits and deliveries, they would not hold back. "Our generation," Hoxha affirmed, "has fought against the Italians, the Germans, the Greeks, the Yugoslavs, the Americans, the Khrushchevites, and now against Mao. Our whole lives we have waged war against our enemies."[146]

As Sino-Soviet relations tumbled, however, Sino-Albanian relations picked up again. In 1965, after a visit from Zhou and promises of substantial aid, the Albanian party leadership gushed about China's "internationalist" aid. Requests to Beijing (for loans, machines, factories, armaments) kept flowing. Internally, the party chief insisted that Chinese assistance was "not the decisive factor" for the country's planning goals—far more important, rather, was "the power of our people and our party."[147] The following year he assured the Chinese ambassador Xu Jianguo that the two parties had no disagreements.[148] "Our friendship is untouchable, unbreakable, eternal," Mehmet Shehu declared in China shortly after that.[149]

Broken World, New World

Political breaks, so important to diplomatic history, can be misleading. Ruptures in state, party, or diplomatic relations help frame a story of disagreement. They magnify the nuances. But there was continuity across the Sino-Soviet split, just as Stalinist methods outlived Stalin. The idealism that underlay transnational socialist efforts in the 1950s, whether born out of fear, duty, patriotism, or a sense of sacrifice, could survive under the tyrannical rule of a decisive party that ostensibly spoke in the name of a world without the Soviets at the helm. It is possible to question the idealism, to deride the professions of intense solidarity and the overblown language of unreconstructed Stalinists, but that does not explain what sustained them. The loss of Moscow raised troubling economic questions, but it also incidentally opened up room for a small group of Communists to assume an aggressive voice outside their national borders.

In the early 1960s, China saw its revolutionary past as a blueprint for formerly decolonized countries in Africa and Asia. But China could also serve as a window into the Third World for a European country. Party authorities now pondered expanding relations with Afro-Asian countries—something that Khrushchev had personally emphasized years earlier.[150] When Belgrade hosted the meeting of the Non-Aligned Movement in 1961, officials in Tirana took Tito's involvement to mean that Washington was trying to keep the movement divided. There was a sense of competition not just between Moscow and Beijing, in other words, but also between smaller European states ruled by leaders with outsize egos. Regardless of what Beijing might do, the party leadership emphasized working with "the peoples in the Congo, Vietnam, Laos, in Latin America and everywhere else to fight, because that is how American imperialism is weakened."[151] Accordingly, political teams circulated around provincial party organizations to explain revisionism, Soviet ideological errors, the Romanian and Cuban resistance to Moscow, and the broader international situation, in addition to answering questions about the Congo, Vietnam, and Cyprus.[152]

The country's internationalist aspirations, which had been articulated through Soviet support and Eastern bloc circulations, were reformulated—through Chinese resources but independent of Beijing's tactics—to mirror revolutionary efforts in the Third World. The East German representative in Tirana complained that Hoxha's regime was still Stalinist and that it enjoyed no popular support (recall that US intelligence had also insisted on this point, a decade earlier).[153] But the regime combined coercion, forced mobilization, with a sense of revolutionary purpose. Moreover, the party used tactical openings to the rest of the world to encourage the idea of a broader struggle. In retrospect this seems like an act of desperation. Could Iraq, Brazil, Vietnam, Cuba, and Algeria make up for the loss of the Soviet Union, Czechoslovakia, or East Germany?[154] Still, authorities could also effectively employ tactical openings with France and Italy—particularly in terms of technology agreements and cultural programs. (In 1964, the missions in Rome and Paris were upgraded to embassies.)

In the 1950s the Stalin textile works outside Tirana had been a showcase of Soviet modernity. Now the factories stood for *Albanian* resolve against revisionism. Instead of corresponding with textile workers in some Soviet republic,

Albanian teams now corresponded with the Chollima brigade of the Sinuiju Woolen Textile Mill in North Korea.[155] The October 1963 bulletin of the Albanian Working Youth Union carried a picture of Cuban, Chinese, and Albanian young people ("symbol of the unity of youth in the struggle for peace and friendship against imperialism").[156] The union organized days of solidarity with the youth of Angola, Venezuela, and Puerto Rico, while the party played host to a procession of delegations from the formerly colonized world: the Union of Mothers, Widows, and Orphans of the Algerian Martyrs; Indonesian Communists and their family members; and Marxist-Leninist groups from Latin America and the Middle East. Within two years of the opening of a Cuban embassy, authorities organized a week of Cuban culture in Tirana, featuring a piano concert, an exhibition on Cuban architecture, films, and a book fair.[157] Officials looked into more openings to Ghana too, but Accra's representative noted that his country was far more developed than Albania, whose cigarettes, he scoffed, consisted of "raw tobacco wrapped up in pieces of paper." Albanians, he pointed out, "rather have much to learn in our country."[158]

Intent on projecting strength, Albania's party devised a special hard currency solidarity fund to assist Marxist-Leninist groups around the world. Initially it consisted of 700,000 US dollars. China issued half a million, and the rest came from internal funds.[159] Here was the ruling party of a country that still struggled to feed its inhabitants, projecting itself as a source of revolutionary activism in the Third World *and* in Western Europe. In 1964, the party Secretariat disbursed money to marginalized Polish Marxist-Leninists; the Belgian Communist Party; the Communist Party of Brazil; the Communist Party of Peru; the Italian Marxist-Leninist paper *Nuova Unità*; and groups in Spain, Portugal, the Netherlands, and Columbia.[160] Activists in Australia and Ceylon were hired as foreign correspondents for the party daily. Small sums also went to a coterie of Marxist-Leninist characters in Paris and London (the short-lived Committee to Defeat Revisionism, for Communist Unity), as well as in Vienna. The United States–based Hammer and Steel received modest contributions as well. Beyond the funds, Albanian officials established direct links with Iranian Marxist-Leninists (the Revolutionary Organization of the Tudeh Party held its first congress in Tirana in 1965). Indonesian students enrolled in Tirana's university, and a few Indonesian Communist officials were treated to paid vacations.[161]

Within a few years, however, the revolutionary moment in the Third World had been dealt serious blows. The Indonesian Communist Party stood accused of a coup in 1965 and collapsed under army-led brutal mass reprisals. In Algeria, Ben Bella's regime was overthrown that same year. In February 1966, so was Ghana's Kwame Nkrumah. At the same time, Fidel Castro loudly denounced Beijing for using development aid as a form of political blackmail. Neither did Chinese prospects in North Vietnam fare a lot better. Albanian openness to the Third World, moreover, was not openness to all; foreigners were carefully scrutinized for ideological trustworthiness and proper Marxist-Leninist credentials. Because the party framed resistance to the Soviet Union as a national form of assertion, it increasingly encouraged antiforeign anxieties. Thus one security report from 1965 complained that foreigners "negatively influence our people with the way they dress, the way they behave, and their activities."[162]

To avoid cultural contamination from the capitalist world, higher-ups began to scrutinize more closely requests for foreign trips, screening individuals for proper political standing. Attending international symposia and scientific conferences—unless they took place in China, North Korea, Cuba, or a limited number of other friendly countries—became difficult, often requiring special permission from the central party apparatus. Back in 1962, one Albanian exiled scholar had perceptively noted that Soviet cultural influence was bound to outlive the Soviet-Albanian split "if unchallenged." He had asked, "How could the powerful influence of Soviet culture on Albania be opposed?" One possibility was "to stress Albanian native culture," which meant "more studies of Albania's past, folk creations, and material culture, and for more literature that would deal with the Albanian people, and not with the workers alone."[163]

Such an assertion of national character required creating a mental and material map of a native "revolutionary patriotic tradition," just as Soviet friendship had required a different kind of mapping in the 1950s. It was precisely this earlier Soviet-era experience that made this later reorientation possible. At that time, agitators had worked hard to connect Albania's civilizational path to the Soviet Union's. But now there was a twenty-year history of struggles they could draw from, including years of contacts with a sixth of the globe, and themes of betrayal, conspiracy, and heroism. As the party rewrote its history, it also celebrated a distinct material culture. The Tirana house where the Communist Party had been founded in 1941, for example, came under state protection, as did Hoxha's childhood home in Gjirokastër. Churches and mosques, on the other hand, increasingly fell into disrepair. Local city committees often denied requests for repairs and maintenance. A Central Committee letter from March 1964 warned about neighborhood requests for money to build new places of worship, advising local party authorities to deny them.[164]

Because Albania also witnessed a revolutionary campaign in 1967, it seemed, on the outside, as if this was a copy of the Chinese version—the Great Proletarian Cultural Revolution launched by Mao in 1966 to purge and purify the party through an all-out attack against bureaucrats. In his widely used memoirs, the Albanian party boss perpetuated the myth that Beijing had tried to force Maoism on his country. In fact, the Albanian upheaval in 1967 was not some sudden mass hysteria; it had been years in the making. Well before the party establishment even knew about Mao's gamble, it had launched a crusade to "eradicate the remnants of the past" (*zhukje e mbeturinave të së kaluarës, mbeturina* being the same word used for "rubbish"). These included bourgeois beliefs and attitudes, as well as "religious prejudices," which were supposed to be combated by way of "atheist-scientific propaganda." For years, the party apparatus had lambasted "bureaucratic practices," the "mentality" of administrators, and their "style and method of work."[165] The goal of "revolutionary dynamism" was to be met by sending administrators to production work, by reacquainting them with the discipline of manual labor. Anti-intellectualism did not have to be imported from China; it was already there.

If anything, Mao's Cultural Revolution initially baffled the Albanian leadership. Why would a powerful party in a powerful country unleash this kind of madness? Hoxha panicked that Mao might lose his grip on the party and that Albania might lose China. Only when the chairman sent his assurances during the fifth Albanian party congress (1–8 November 1966) was there some relief in Tirana.[166] Mao sent a glowing greeting to the congress, via Kang Sheng, calling Albania a beacon of Marxism-Leninism. Chinese officials also admitted *that they had made mistakes* and that they needed to conduct self-criticism in front of their Albanian counterparts. At times, the paranoia of Mao's Cultural Revolution seemed baffling even to the paranoid Stalinists in Tirana. But did a party with a twenty-five-year history of uninterrupted internal purges and executions really need much prodding to give in to stories of devious traitors and Khrushchevite "roaders"? With its willful isolation, Beijing alienated many countries in Asia, but it carefully cultivated the Albanian partnership. The more Mao and his followers ritualized self-criticism and underscored Soviet danger, the more sympathy they evoked in Tirana.[167] The year 1967—a year of destruction—was also the peak of the Sino-Albanian alliance.

Destruction: A Crossroads with China

Mao's self-destructive gamble incidentally created an opening for the Albanian party to speak, to be heard, and to receive wild praise in the register of militant Marxism-Leninism. Chinese officials themselves championed Enver Hoxha as an example of ideological purity. The Albanian and Chinese domestic realities were worlds apart in 1967, but the two militant parties—masters of conspiratorial thinking and ruthless in its execution—found their rhetoric aligned.[168] The path to socialism had been endless war, Mao and Mehmet Shehu agreed during a meeting in 1966, and it was through constant internal struggle against enemies that socialism could be kept alive.[169] Caught at the epicenter of the Sino-Soviet conflict in the early 1960s and then as Beijing's sole foreign partner during the mayhem of Mao's revolution, Albania came to reflect the achievements (by way of its continued Stalinist policies) and also the costs (relative development vis-à-vis other Eastern bloc economies) of socialist exchange. Continued Chinese industrial and military assistance made possible ambitious planning goals, with an emphasis on heavy industries, rigid party controls, class struggle, and a strong leader cult. Beijing helped Tirana keep Stalinism alive.

Even as the two parties spoke the same militant language, however, the two revolutions took distinct paths. The Albanian *revolucionarizim* was always framed in the context of an *international* struggle, but the Chinese example was also a warning of how things could go wrong. The party leadership was careful not to copy Chinese methods wholesale. It retained full control of events on the ground but tactically framed much of the upheaval as initiated from

FIGURE 29. Sino-Albanian signals: a Chinese delegation inspects Albanian-made television sets. Chinese technical assistance helped Albanian authorities develop regular broadcasts, n.d. ATSH.

below.[170] Local youths in the city of Durrës were said to have started a campaign against backward practices. But there is no doubt that the Albanian movement was guided from the highest levels. Hoxha delivered a mobilizing speech in early February 1967.[171] The party apparatus, moreover, sent clear guidelines on how the campaign was supposed to unfold.[172] Small youth detachments attacked churches, stripping them of religious icons and placing *dazibao*-style large posters (*fletë-rrufe*, literally, lightning sheets) on the walls.[173] The posters were meant to attack negative practices and name the offenders, and the party also closely supervised their dissemination.[174]

These examples also point us to the other important local characteristic of the Albanian revolutionary movement: the ruthless war against religion and especially against the Catholic Church, long considered an anti-Communist stronghold in the country's north. Muslim and Orthodox figures, the party leader argued, were ignorant and thus of no political importance. Many of the Catholic figures, however, were intellectually more advanced. He warned that they might continue to "advance Catholicism as a philosophy."[175] After years of neglect, some churches and mosques were falling apart. "Do not repair a single one," was the directive from the party command.[176] Authorities counted some 1,536 active churches, mosques, monasteries, and Bektashi *teqe*, with an eye toward repurposing them into depots, worker clubs, and reading rooms.[177] Religious holidays had to be replaced with secular celebrations of labor (days devoted to miners, oil workers, or other socialist heroes). The ritual washing of the bodies of the dead, party memos pronounced, was a backward tradition. Everything was up for reconsideration: Which way would the dead be buried? What ornaments were appropriate for graves?[178]

An analysis of this upheaval would surely have to deal with the cultural dimensions of the war against backwardness. But it would be deficient if it failed to acknowledge that the revolutionary movement was also an economic campaign, in light of the struggles of central planning in the 1960s, to squeeze the populace further: confiscate valuables, diminish personal plots of land, lower wages, extract unpaid labor and time through frenzied volunteering drives. The attack on religion was a claim on knowledge, additionally, and an answer to the question of who had the right to produce it under socialism. As authorities took possession of churches, mosques, and deeds, they also confiscated manuscripts and old wedding and death records, which had been held locally until that point.[179] Finally, this cultural offensive laid bare the bleak living conditions of the country's peasantry—families carving out a pitiful livelihood under a regime obsessed with industry.

There was, to be sure, backlash against all of this. Secret surveillance reports mention peasants' complaints about the destruction of their local churches and mosques.[180] The older generation in particular seems to have resented the attack.

In a southern province near Saranda, a small group of women apparently beat up a local chief and the party secretary when these two tried to take down the religious icons in their church.[181] But consider, also, that many other women, especially in the poorer areas of the country, experienced the frenzy of the late 1960s—the full-blown offensive against social conservatism—as personally liberating and an opportunity for physical mobility. A group of thirty-eight women from Mirditë wrote to the party boss in 1969 to tell him that they had traveled all the way to Vlorë, in the south, for a three-month stay. Many of them had never traveled outside Mirditë in their lives. "The Party," they wrote, "brought Mirditë women outside the narrow world of the family, outside the walls of the house."[182] They vowed to continue the fight against backwardness, to improve hygiene, to combat fanaticism back at home, and to organize women in active work.

Albania's revolutionary campaign was designed not to attack the party but to present the party as a mediator between generations. That is why when reports of local backlash and incidents reached the capital, the Central Committee intervened to school "zealous" provincial officials, whom it criticized for not properly preparing their local communities ahead of the revolutionary measures. Hoxha in particular excelled at coming across as the voice of reason in a time of turmoil, as evidenced by the letters and complaints he received and his handling of them.[183] The party apparatus, to put it another way, acted like a social valve: people's problems, their needs, their anger, and their resentment circulated across villages and mountain ranges all the way to the party headquarters in Tirana, along the Boulevard of the Martyrs of the Nation, and then, once addressed or redirected, back again to the periphery.

Such differences with the Chinese Cultural Revolution help us make sense of how Maoism served as a conduit of confusion rather than as a mechanism of understanding. Precisely because the Albanian party never intended to give up control, it found some of the Chinese revolutionary practices bewildering. Diplomatic memos tried to get Albanian travelers prepared for the mass rituals they would encounter in China (group readings of Mao's quotations, public confrontations, grueling displays of self-criticism).[184] Albanian delegates to China were also taken to local revolutionary committees, where they were asked to criticize the Chinese guests to their faces—something they found difficult to do. When an Albanian art exhibition toured China (a long journey on a Soviet train, via Bucharest), one Red Guard complained that the show did not feature enough portraits of comrade Enver and Chairman Mao. Caught off guard, the Albanian artists rushed to craft on the spot small models and drawings of militant Red Guards, thus injecting the show with some of the missing revolutionary spirit.[185]

Some Chinese individuals wrote to Hoxha directly, like the Shanghai Red Guards who sent him badges and banners, photos of Mao, and red flags. They

FIGURE 30.   A Chinese musical ensemble entertains Albanian railroad construction volunteers, Guri i Kuq, Pogradec, October 1975. ATSH.

called Albania, as the chairman had done in 1966, a beacon of socialism in Europe.[186] Chinese students and peasants described in their letters their family background, their lives, their work, and what the revolution meant to them. None of them placed the ruler of the tiny Party of Labor of Albania on the same level with the chairman (one of the letters called Mao "the greatest teacher of the people of the world"). But some of the letter writers also called Hoxha "a great leader." Many years later, in his old age, the Albanian party boss claimed to have resented how the Chinese were making a god out of Mao. Perhaps he was indeed bothered by it. But this hardly stopped him from building his own cult at home. At the height of this revolutionary moment in the late 1960s, *mësimet e shokut Enver* (the lessons of comrade Enver) also became commonplace. It is no coincidence that these years marked the beginning of a decades-long party-led effort to document and globally disseminate Hoxha's contributions to Marxism-Leninism.[187]

In the context of shortages and herculean efforts on the part of workers to comply with production goals, the language of warfare increasingly permeated workplaces, classrooms, and homes. The country was under a blockade; ordinary men and women had "to take up arms." The appeal to Albanian nationalism is clear here, but let's also recall the warlike thinking that had permeated internal party discussions since the 1940s, the militant anti-imperialist rhetoric around the Third World, and the fact that upheaval could be productive for a country—like Albania—stuck between enemy camps. When Shehu met with Yao Wenyuan, a member of the Cultural Revolution Group, both of them agreed that the greatest danger to socialism was internal. "It is clear to us today," the Albanian prime minister explained, "that internal enemies are far more dangerous than external ones."[188] It is too easy to Orientalize the militancy of this Sino-Albanian moment, to dwell on the bizarreness of such an unequal alliance, as if that militancy were not a hallmark of many other revolutionaries in a Cold War world.

Marxism-Leninism had a way of turning insecurity into an advantage, defeat into a symptom of a better world to come. The Albanian party leaders decided that they did, after all, have something to offer to the oppressed people of the world: their history of decades of struggle. Hence the Albanian Politburo developed a number of theses about what the building of socialism in Albania could teach militants around the world. These were some of the lessons. Capitalism was not a necessary condition for the creation of a Communist party. It was not necessary to wait for revolution to develop organically. Youth (instead of workers) could take the lead in overturning the social order. The party could lead even in conditions of economic backwardness. A liberation war also had to be, at the same time, a class war. War could start with the towns and then move to the villages. It was crucial for the party to take leadership of the popular front. A country could go from feudalism or semifeudalism to Communism without an intermediate capitalist stage.[189]

Seen from the longer perspective of two decades, it is not so much the nationalism of this Communist Party that comes across as its defining feature but how much the party was shaped by its difficult struggle to inhabit an international system. Unexpectedly, a country struggling for survival in one corner of Europe had become a Soviet partner under Stalin in the 1940s. Exchange had enabled it to engage with this imperfect socialist world, struggling to make sense of its strange connectivity and myriad contradictions. If the Soviet Union had been a path to modernity and a formula for catching up, Marxism-Leninism had also become a form of currency, allowing Albanians to express themselves, to make demands, and to disagree, much to the frustration of Soviet and, eventually, Chinese party officials. Soviet blunders, in turn, like Chinese ambitions, enabled a small state to go against the more powerful. Elsewhere in the Eastern bloc, going against Moscow ended in bloodshed and trauma. The party clique in Tirana came out with a fighting voice in a fragmented socialist world. But the people it ruled also paid the terrible price of continuing to live as if in a state of war.

1991

In early August 1991, a well-worn commercial ship loaded with Cuban sugar reached the Albanian port of Durrës. A large crowd gathered outside the port. It pushed past the gates, eventually taking hold of the vessel, which bore the name of another seaside city (*Vlora*). Rumors spread fast that the port in Durrës was open. More and more people headed there. "Within ten minutes," one participant later recalled, "there were ten thousand of us."[1]

These people were trying to get out of Albania. It is not clear how many of them made it on board that ship on that day; estimates range from ten thousand to twenty thousand individuals. Once they took over, they ordered the captain to set sail for Italy. (He later recalled that some had specifically asked for Germany because in their mental geography, the West was simply something across the Adriatic.) But there were engine problems. After some back-and-forth, the ship started to move. Thousands of people filled every nook and cranny on deck. It was so hot that most of the men stood shirtless. Film sequences show wary faces marked with excitement. When the newcomers reached Italy, however, hope gave way to despair. Caught unprepared, local authorities in Bari did not know what to do. They eventually locked the foreigners inside a soccer stadium, waiting to process them. They pleaded with them to go back to their country. These Albanians had gone looking for the West, finding instead a Western country that seemed shocked they existed at all. Hunger, thirst, desperation, and anger quickly set in.

Chaos had gripped Europe's last Communist dictatorship before *Vlora* set sail for Italy. Thousands had tried to flee the country earlier that year. The previous summer, large groups had stormed Western embassies in the capital. They refused to get out, embarrassing the party-state and the feared security police, who proved ineffective. At the helm of the party was Ramiz Alia, the successor to Hoxha, who had died in 1985 after a forty-year rule. Born in Shkodër in 1925, Alia had joined the Communist youth and then the newly formed party in 1943. He held a number of military positions during the war and became youth secretary at the age of twenty-four. Alia quickly rose through the ranks, joining the Central Committee, serving as minister of education and culture, and becoming a Politburo member during the Soviet-Albanian crisis. Through the years, he managed to survive the party purges. But Alia was no Hoxha. After the embassy debacle in the summer of 1990, he did not order a crackdown. Neither did he manage to quell the agitated mood in the capital.

A year after the fall of the Berlin Wall, the Party of Labor was still in charge in this corner of the Balkans. Images of Romanian dictator Nicolae Ceaușescu's bullet-ridden body had made the rounds across the world. But the Communist regime pressed on. It was as if the party was convinced (or wanted to convince itself) that events in the bloc had no bearing on it. Officials blamed the embassy incidents on hooligans, rotten individuals, and "international reactionaries" who were said to have instigated them.[2] Later that winter, however, students in Tirana's frigid and overcrowded dormitories—lacking heat and power—took to the streets to protest their living conditions. The crowds grew bigger and bolder. More residents joined them. The youth's economic woes quickly assumed political meaning—after all, in a socialist state, the economic plight of young people, who represented the state's supposed promising future, was a political problem.

The unreformed party did not lack committed types willing to use violence to put down these protests. After all, the regime had not hesitated before to execute people for attempting to cross over into Greece or Yugoslavia. It routinely threw individuals into prison for a lot less. This time, however, Alia invited representatives from the protesters to meet with him. Then, shockingly, he declared that other parties could be established. (There was some back-and-forth over the meaning of the word "pluralism" because most individuals involved were not clear on how a multiparty system was supposed to function.) Alia did not seek to destroy the party's hold on the country, but he also wanted to appear conciliatory. This decision ushered in the liquidation of the party-state. The following months were chaotic. The Party of Labor, still enjoying the full backing of the state and the police, won the elections in the spring of 1991, setting off further protests and skirmishes. Seeing no hope, thousands tried to flee to Greece across the southern borders. Others turned to the ports, hoping to make it across the sea—to "the West." After years of self-enforced isolation in the name of building a socialist fortress on the Adriatic, the whole country seemed on the run.

This intense desperation during the final hours of Communist rule was a far cry from the hopes of the postwar years. The break with the Soviet Union in the early 1960s had been economically destabilizing, especially given how reliant the state had become on Soviet subsidies. Yet the break also convinced the party leadership that it had to pursue self-reliance, which it interpreted as a continuation of the industrialization drive.[3] The lesson was that the country might be left alone—a lesson that the North Korean leader Kim Il-Sung, for example, had already taken to heart.[4] This also helps explain the massive amounts of technical aid that the Albanian side asked from Beijing throughout the years—anything from textile factories and hydroelectric plants to copper and iron smelting plants, oil refineries, truckloads of ammunition, and fighter airplanes. As much as the Chinese grumbled, they kept furnishing credits and supplies, financing the party's industrial dreams.

This is because ideology mattered. And the Albanian ideologues understood that it mattered, and so they panicked when Beijing decided to abandon the isolation of the Cultural Revolution in the late 1960s—a reordering of China's world in which tiny Albania would lose its privileged position. All the talk of brotherhood and being "bound by blood" notwithstanding, the alliance with China ended up reinforcing a sense of geographic isolation.[5] Chinese overtures to the Soviet Union and Yugoslavia and especially the decision to host US president Richard Nixon infuriated the Albanian party leadership. "Ever since we openly opposed modern revisionism," Hoxha told his colleagues in early August 1971, "we were best friends, the closest and most loyal friends of the Chinese. This is a fact. But now, we must realize that this is no longer true." A power-hungry China might leave Albania behind. "The time will come when we will be in conflict with the Chinese," he explained, urging vigilance, sacrifice, and careful control over party members.[6]

The roots of the so-called self-reliance in the 1970s can be found in these earlier years. The notion of encirclement went back all the way to the Stalin-Tito schism of 1948. But with each dramatic shift in the geopolitics of the socialist world, the stakes of encirclement took on ever more dramatic meaning. The party boss had long denounced the Soviet "blockade," which, he asserted, required the construction of socialism "through our own forces" (*duke u mbështetur në forcat tona*). In practice, this meant squeezing as much as possible from China, round-the-clock volunteering drives that were anything but voluntary, grueling saving campaigns, intense coercion, and uninterrupted mobilization. Albania *was* encircled—Yugoslavia, eventually entering an economic crisis, was still far better off, to say nothing about Italy, whose radio and television channels many Albanians followed religiously. Ironically, it was Chinese technology that helped boost Albanian television reception in the 1970s, blanketing the country with the signal of the state channel but also creating room for smuggled "capitalist" signals and a tedious battle, ultimately lost by the state, to jam Western stations.[7]

As diplomatic history, the Sino-Soviet conflict serves to highlight divergences. There have been analyses of the split as an elite affair, focusing on Communist parties, their internal squabbles, and the interplay between domestic power struggles and foreign policy moves. The Sino-Soviet split also complicated the future of socialism in the Third World. In the 1960s, Maoism gained admirers internationally, including among radical Western activists and militant revolutionaries from Latin America to Asia. (It has been easier to miss how Maoism confounded Mao's closest ally in the Balkans.) The failure to maintain unity within the socialist world in the 1960s was followed by more socialist failures in the decolonized world: Iraq, Angola, Mozambique, Somalia, South Yemen, Afghanistan. And yet, framing the Sino-Soviet competition in these terms—a grand contest between two powers—also misses important continuities and unexpected entanglements along the periphery.[8] Geopolitics eventually caught up with the socialist world-making project, but socialism was always bigger than the calculations in Moscow and Beijing.

Consider how the split made room for Stalinist continuity and how it deepened the possibilities for continued repression. It enabled an insecure regime in the Balkans to keep speaking in the name of a Soviet civilization that the post-Stalin leadership in Moscow often found embarrassing. And that regime pressed on through coordinated attacks against key social and economic sectors: After the assault on religion, the party uncovered all kinds of fantastic-sounding plots and conspiracies among officials in cultural affairs, in the army, and in planning. The 1976 constitution declared Marxist-Leninism the country's official ideology and prohibited credits from or concession to foreign companies or "capitalist, bourgeois and revisionist states."[9] In cultural affairs, the regime combined brief periods of relaxation with waves of censorship and repression. As China began to engage with the broader world in the 1970s, the Albanian party-state retreated further into isolation. It channeled considerable resources into the construction of military fortifications (tunnels, bunkers, underground depots) that were supposed to help in the event of a military attack.[10] This evolving siege mentality appears bizarrely paranoid. And it was. But was paranoia not at the core of the Cold War conflict?

A global perspective on the Sino-Soviet struggle should not obscure just how rooted it was, as an extended event, in the history of socialist internationalism, how it could take on local meaning that neither the Soviets and nor the Chinese could control. The split made it possible to imagine a socialist world without the Soviets at the helm. To put it another way, it encouraged a kind of intellectual labor in reinterpreting the socialist past and the imperfect present. For their part, the Chinese treated their Albanian interlocutors as ideological brothers but then recoiled when the white, European brothers returned the favor by taking Mao to task for his dumbfounding foreign policy zigzags. It is beside the point to ask whether ideology mattered more than security, because the Albanian regime did not see them as distinct. The country continued to be part of the socialist world, undeniably bound by a shared past. And yet it also willingly chose not to be a part of it. It was an unapologetically Stalinist regime at a time when Stalinism was somehow considered to be the past—including among many Western left-ists who were willing to ignore the Albanian dictatorship or dismiss it as some nationalist oddity, a bizarre eastern joke.

The split within socialism also ushered in a period of heightened nationalist claims, which in retrospect have served to further detach this history of Stalinism after Stalin from the main current of the postwar period. In 1968, the year of the Soviet crushing of the Prague Spring, state officials moved Stalin's monument from Tirana's center and replaced it with an equestrian statue of the Ottoman-era national hero Skënderbej (Skanderbeg). This was followed by campaigns to project back into Albania's history a sense of national cohesion, to show how Albanians had fought heroically against formidable adversaries—Ottoman, Italian, German, Yugoslav, and Soviet. Such an approach presented Albanian nationalism as a linear story, flattening a tangled imperial past. It cast it as something preexisting and concrete, obscuring how nationalism has been enabled and activated by international engagement. After all, Stalin's monument did not disappear in 1968. City authorities merely moved him—from Tirana's central square to the Boulevard of the Martyrs of the Nation, a short walk away. Stalin stood there until 1991.

Viewing the international history of Cold War antagonism exclusively through the lens of high-level deliberations also misses the upheaval it unleashed in individual lives. For many of the protagonists of this book, the break with the Soviet Union had far-reaching intellectual, creative, and professional consequences. Ismail Kadare, the young student at the Gorky Institute, eventually became his country's most celebrated writer. Over the years, he conceived a sprawling literary universe, dramatizing Albania's unlikely Cold War alliances and walking a thin line between parodies of the Soviet Union (or, later, Mao's China) and what could be interpreted as allegories of socialism as an interconnected world of squalor. During the Great Proletarian Cultural Revolution, he found himself in Shanghai, sent to "exchange ideas" with fellow Chinese writers.[11] Gani Strazimiri, the once-celebrated architect of the 1950s, continued to labor in relative obscurity following the rejection of the monumentality of the Stalin era. He left a mark on the profession, however, by establishing the country's first program of historical preservation. It took many years for a state obsessed with industry to appreciate historical preservation. Nevertheless, this development later dove-tailed with the regime's increasingly nationalist invocations. (Ottoman-era archi-tecture, for example, once cleansed of its Ottoman context, could be hailed as a distinct Albanian legacy.)

The two younger architects mentioned in earlier chapters came of age profes-sionally in the 1960s and 1970s. Petraq Kolevica, the student who grew to appre-ciate Russian literature, designed buildings and issued an acclaimed translation of Mikhail Lermontov's "Demon." Maks Velo, an extraordinary talented architect and artist, fared a lot worse. Where many others touted the values of socialist realism, Velo was captivated by modern architecture. He also found inspiration in vernacular forms but stripped them of the socialist character that authorities demanded. In other words, he never properly fit the mold of the socialist artist. In 1979, he was put on trial for agitation and propaganda against the state. Dur-ing the proceedings, a number of other artists testified against their colleague. Authorities scrutinized his paintings and architectural projects for "foreign influ-ences," which now assumed the characteristic of a crime. They had many of his works burned. Velo was sentenced to ten years and spent a long stretch at the notorious Spaç labor camp.

Keen on disciplining the intellectuals, the party devoured its most commit-ted servants. As in the Soviet Union, the terror routinely turned against former executioners and loyal believers. Hoxha thrived on instigating internal rivalries and conflicts, which is how the erstwhile champions of Stalinism eventually found themselves accused of imaginary devious crimes. Liri Belishova, scape-goated during the Sino-Soviet split, spent the next thirty years in internment. Her husband, the former agriculture minister, was also expelled from the party, interned, and eventually imprisoned. Koço Tashko, the longtime champion of the homeland of Lenin, spent his aging years in internment camps and then, at the age of seventy, was thrown into the Burrel prison. According to the account of an official who himself fell victim to the 1970s purges, Tashko kept hoping for a Soviet "liberation" of Albania. In prison, he religiously celebrated Soviet holidays.[12]

Mehmet Shehu, the Spanish Civil War veteran, onetime security police chief, and prime minister since 1954, had done everything expected of him—and more. He was unflinchingly loyal to his boss for close to forty dramatic years. To many, it seemed like a foregone conclusion that he would be the successor. In 1981, however, Shehu was found lying dead on his bed. The official cause was given as suicide. All of a sudden, Hoxha announced that his longtime comrade-in-arms had been a sworn enemy all along. He now stood accused of having been recruited by *both* the Americans and the Soviets. To have served as interior min-ister between 1946 and 1983, in fact, proved to be one of the most secure paths to death. The two other interior ministers (Kadri Hazbiu and Feçor Shehu) were also executed in 1983. Each wave of repression came with even more fantastical fabricated charges and witch hunts for alleged coconspirators. Punishment was not confined to the chosen individual; it was a plague that fell on the victim's immediate family too.[13]

The terror, the paranoia, and the purges were not of the past. In Albania, they were the never-ending present. In the 1950s, socialism had been about the creation of international identities in addition to instilling a sense of national pride. Socialism had come with Soviet blueprints and a ready-made language for interpreting the world, brand-new factories and urban plans, sounds, texts, and new references, including forbidden ones. When we look back, with the knowledge of Albania's later years, this early internationalism may seem doomed, the capitalist-driven globalization of the late twentieth century inevitable. And yet Albania's recent history also serves as a reminder that exchange does not necessarily lead to more openness, that there was nothing inevitable about the path from Stalinism to "socialism with a human face" to the collapse of Communist regimes in 1989. From a laboratory of Soviet modernity in the 1950s, the country turned into an exaggerated reflection of Soviet socialism's own legacy—the strange but familiar outcome of a kind of socialist connectivity across national borders that the Soviets launched, the Chinese momentously joined, but that no big country, no matter how powerful, seemed able to control.

Materially, socialism connected far-flung places, even as the political project of international unity failed. In the early 1960s, Albanian party higher-ups had panicked that a Soviet military attack might be imminent. To prepare for the fight, they pleaded with the Chinese for weapons and ammunition. Beijing was willing to help, but the problem was how to get the supplies across such a long distance. With Chinese funds, authorities purchased a commercial ship. They named it *Vlora*. They sent *Vlora* around the globe, to China, loaded it with ammunition and brought it back to fight a war that never came.[14] Thirty years later, *Vlora* made its way to the Italian coast, carrying thousands of desperate, exhausted, dazed, but hopeful Albanian men and women looking for the West. The West seemed so close—just a few hours on a ship. But the journey across the Adriatic seemed endless. Beginning in 2015, images of *Vlora* bearing those thousands of Albanians fleeing from a brutal past resurfaced on Facebook and Twitter. History plays cruel tricks, and so commentators online panicked at the sight of the photograph, thinking that it showed Syrians fleeing the catastrophic civil war in the Middle East and threatening to invade Europe's shores.

Note on Sources

How does one write the history of a largely illiterate society? During the first half of the twentieth century, most Albanians could not read or write. In researching this book, I had to rely on what archival sources told me. But what about those who lived through these heady years of socialism but left no trace behind? What about those who saw a Soviet film for the first time—perhaps the first film they had ever seen—or witnessed a show trial, or completed a grueling shift at the Stalin textile mills, or attended a party organization-led study session afterward, but never wrote a word about any of it?

This is a particularly serious problem for a history of a dictatorship that claimed *to speak for everyone*. It is necessary to look beyond the state (even as this book insists on the relevance of the state and the need to understand how the state constituted itself in large part by coming up with a vocabulary that illiterate men and women could learn). To do so, I have used fiction, films, memoirs, and newspapers, including limited editions of provincial titles (like *Përpara*), which came out irregularly, whenever there was printing paper available. I also spoke with some of the individuals whose names appear in the text. Each of them experienced socialism in some fashion but at different times and with different consequences. I explicitly went looking for perspectives that contradicted my hunches—placing party documents next to personal letters, surveillance reports, and a few Italian-language 1960s witness accounts of Albanian exiles, procured by Radio Free Europe. Finally, I looked at thousands of photographs at the dedicated archives of the socialist-era news agency. The images were sometimes the first clues—only later was I able to piece together a story through archival records.

When writing about the construction of the Stalin textile mills in the outskirts of Tirana, I knew that I might be able to tell the bureaucratic story of construction: this many hours of labor, that many tons of steel. What was lacking was the lived experience of the place. This was crucial for an argument about how a distant Soviet reality became locally meaningful in one corner of Europe. For those men and women working at that site, a new Soviet factory was about more than textiles. It was about catching up—as individuals, as a nation. For women, this episode was of great importance because a factory job signaled a social shift as well. To go beyond the numbers, I used full runs of the journals *Shqipëri-B.R.S.S.* and *Miqësija*, held in the reserve collections of the National Library in Tirana.

This book, however, could not have been written without access to the archives of the Central Committee of the Party of Labor: high-level meetings and preparatory memos of the Politburo and the Secretariat, as well as the correspondence of various Central Committee departments covering personnel, propaganda, education, foreign affairs, and the economy. The party thought of itself as the driver of Albania's modernity. Party officials increasingly inserted themselves into the social, cultural, and intellectual life of Albanians. Still, the party was young, inexperienced, and uneducated. This inexperience allowed me to peer into the archive and see firsthand the messy process of administering lives. Documents from the 1940s are often written by hand. They are confusing: people from various parts of the country used nonstandard Albanian (language standardization came later). They made mistakes in reporting. They referred to the same institutions by many names. Only gradually, in the 1950s, did the party develop mechanisms for systematic record keeping. As frustrating as it was to make sense of this world, it also taught me to see the archive as a process.

As a native speaker of Albanian, I occupied a specific place inside the archives. I was intimately familiar with the bureaucratic procedures and the anxiety over "state secrets" that still lingers in a country where the memory of terror is still raw. And yet I was also an outsider to the institution and its unspoken rules. Some of the archivists were hospitable but anxious that I might use my findings to shame powerful Albanian public figures. In post-Communist Albania, archival records can quickly transform into weapons against adversaries. Daily newspapers and news websites carry separate sections (titled "dossier") where they print archival documents ripped out of context, shaming this or that political figure or indulging the public's curiosity about the private lives of the former Communist elite. The history of the postwar period remains fraught, and periodic scuffles erupt in public about the legacy of wartime collaboration, anti-Fascism, and the crimes of the Communist dictatorship. One result has been that many Albanian historians have decided to steer clear of the most contentious themes.

There are also administrative hurdles in place. Some party collections still remain off-limits to researchers. The finding guides are kept away from the public. The laws governing access to archival materials are contradictory. Generally, documents are available no earlier than twenty-five years after their date of production. This rule also governs materials produced under the Communist regime. Routinely, documents that should have been declassified in accordance with this provision have not been. An additional law restricts access to state secrets (in my experience, no distinction was made between secrets under the Communist regime and those after 1991). One outcome is that the same file may be accessible under one rule but classified according to the other. Moreover, archivists tend to apply privacy restrictions to socialist-era files, regardless of how long ago they have been produced. It is the kind of chaotic situation that discourages serious engagement with the dictatorship's past. Often it is not possible to determine the precise status of a given document. On privacy grounds, I have refrained from revealing names when there was any doubt.

The archives of the security police (Sigurimi) remain inaccessible, despite routine government commitments to make them available. I was able to work in them for brief periods of time and found the material in disorganized piles on floors and desks. Nevertheless, it is also possible to get at some of the security police material from the party angle, since security chiefs regularly reported to the Politburo. Some general reports were forwarded to other Central Committee departments. As important as these records are, this book makes the case for the importance of *state* records, including the vast amount of government correspondence (construction, mining, education, culture) and the many administrative bodies that covered technical and scientific affairs. It is impossible to understand the way the socialist state operated without taking stock of this material. For a country like Albania, there was no other choice: I lacked even basic details on the economy, since the minuscule secondary literature is built on guesswork. Finally, I had unlimited access to the separate archives of the Ministry of Foreign Affairs, where declassification was taking place on the table next to me, as I was researching the files.

Albanian archives contain documents written in Italian, German, Serbo-Croatian, Russian, and Chinese. But I also wanted to look at the country from the outside. Transnational history works when it is possible to capture contacts and conflicts from multiple perspectives. This was particularly important in the case of countries driven apart by ideological squabbles during the Cold War. Albania's regime not only broke with Yugoslavia and the Soviet Union but also crafted distinct narratives about why it did so.

Therefore, I researched Soviet-Albanian contacts from the Soviet angle in Moscow. Italian and British archives were crucial for the wartime years. British officers stationed in Albania provided fine-grained reports on dynamics between the Communist-led partisans and the other forces, in addition to good details that cannot be found in official Albanian records. Many myths emerged in later socialist-era historiography about the National Liberation War. Ironically, declassified CIA memos sometimes contain richer details than Albanian records, too, especially for the early years, along with exaggerations and interpretative leaps. The state, party, and diplomatic archives in Berlin were important for conveying the multifaceted transnational exchanges in the Eastern bloc. I tried to trace the same incident, reference, or event in multiple national archives. Some German diplomatic cables from Tirana offered detailed descriptions of day-to-day affairs in the capital. The unexpected insights of capable foreign diplomats allowed me to read Albanian records against the grain.

The fact that some of the more compelling sources on Albania's modern history are to be found in Rome, London, Berlin, and Moscow may seem like a tragedy to the nationalist-minded. But it seemed to me like a good opportunity to write a kind of European history that takes the national frame seriously without being bound by it.

Notes

INTRODUCTION

1. I use "Eastern Europe" as a geopolitical term, not a geographic one. Akira Iriye sees internationalism as "an idea, a movement, or an institution that seeks to reformulate the nature of relations among nations through cross-national cooperation and interchange." See his *Cultural Internationalism and World Order* (Baltimore: Johns Hopkins University Press, 1997), 3. Socialist internationalism sought to reformulate those relations on the basis of a distinct ideology. To emphasize that fact, I refer to both Communism and socialism, as did the subjects of this study, preferring the former when referring to beliefs and party structures.

2. Whereas a first wave of books on the Eastern bloc privileged captivity, a handful of later accounts emphasized diversity and division. Hugh Seton-Watson, *The East European Revolution* (New York: Praeger, 1951); Zbigniew Brzezinski, *The Soviet Bloc: Unity and Conflict* (Cambridge, MA: Harvard University Press, 1967); François Fejtő, *A History of the People's Democracies: Eastern Europe since Stalin* (New York: Praeger, 1971). After the initial opening of Russian archives in the 1990s, Russian scholars also revisited the debate along familiar lines: T. V. Volokitina, G. P. Murashko, and A. F. Noskova, *Narodnaia Demokratiia: Mif ili real'nost'? Obshchestvenno-politicheskie protsessy v Vostochnoi Evrope, 1944–1948 gg.* (Moscow: Nauka, 1993); T.V. Volokitina, G. P. Murashko, A. F. Noskova, and T. A. Pokivailova, *Moskva i Vostochnaia Evropa: Stanovlenie politicheskikh rezhimov sovetskogo tipa, 1949–1953* (Moscow: ROSSPEN, 2002). The preoccupation with Stalin's objectives endures: Stefan Creuzberger and Manfred Görtemaker, eds., *Gleichschaltung unter Stalin? Die Entwicklung der Parteien im östlichen Europa, 1944–1949* (Paderborn: Ferdinand Schöningh, 2002).

3. Exceptions include two important chapters by Mark Kramer: "Stalin, the Split with Yugoslavia, and Soviet-East European Efforts to Reassert Control, 1948–1953," in *Stalin and Europe: Imitation and Domination, 1928–1953*, ed. Timothy Snyder and Ray Brandon (New York: Oxford University Press, 2014), and "Stalin, Soviet Policy, and the Consolidation of a Communist Bloc in Eastern Europe, 1944–1953," in *Stalinism Revisited: The Establishment of Communist Regimes in East-Central Europe,* ed. Vladimir Tismaneanu (Budapest: Central European University Press, 2009). See also Melvyn P. Leffler and David S. Painter, eds., *Origins of the Cold War: An International History*, 2nd ed. (New York: Routledge, 2005); Norman Naimark and Leonid Gibianskii, eds., *The Establishment of Communist Regimes in Eastern Europe, 1944–1949* (Boulder, CO: Westview, 1997).

4. The other explanation is the fact that the Albanian-Yugoslav split complicated the problem of the significant Albanian population living in Kosovë/Kosovo, a cause that Hoxha could self-servingly mobilize after 1948.

5. A characteristic move has been to mistake insecurity for xenophobia. A. A. Fursenko and Timothy J. Naftali, *Khrushchev's Cold War: The Inside Story of an American Adversary* (New York: Norton, 2006), 345. A useful book on post-Communist Albania nevertheless manages to get the earlier history wrong in the first sentence: "For four decades after World War II, tiny Albania was hermetically sealed." Fred C. Abrahams, *Modern Albania: From Dictatorship to Democracy in Europe* (New York: NYU Press, 2015), xi. Whereas Polish, Hungarian, and Czechoslovak intellectuals later relegated Stalinism to a kind of

non-European form of barbarism, Albanian commentators often seem embarrassed by the longevity of Stalinism in the country's past. But Stalinism is a European legacy too.

6. I owe my approach in starting from the "anomalous," as a strategy toward understanding the greater whole that constitutes it, to the works of Carlo Ginzburg. As an example, see his "Witches and Shamans," in *Threads and Traces: True False Fictive* (Berkeley: University of California Press, 2012), 215–27.

7. The parallel with Romania's "anti-Soviet Stalinist" regime is striking. The political scientist Vladimir Tismaneanu has argued that Nicolae Ceaușescu's regime and much of the country's intelligentsia were bound by a "contract" celebrating autonomy vis-à-vis Moscow. See his *Stalinism for All Seasons: A Political History of Romanian Communism* (Berkeley: University of California Press, 2003), 24.

8. Much scholarship exists on how some Communist regimes became nationalized, but it is worth acknowledging that antireformism also became nationalized. The Albanian regime, for example, treated calls for reform after 1956 as signs of hatred for the party, as potential evidence of Yugoslav conspiracies, or, increasingly, as symptoms of a mental disorder.

9. Maria Todorova, "The Trap of Backwardness: Modernity, Temporality and the Study of Eastern European Nationalism," *Slavic Review* 64, no. 1 (Spring 2005): 140–64. For all the emphasis on Balkan nationalism, which sometimes takes the form of an explanation for everything, one rare American visitor to the country in the 1950s saw not even "the faintest hint of any separate national pathway towards socialism." Harrison Salisbury, "Chance for West Seen in Albania: A New Approach, It Is Felt, May Reorient Country's All-Soviet Outlook," *New York Times*, 13 September 1957, 8.

10. One compelling study captures socialism as a multifaceted ideological, political, social, cultural, and economic project, but it also continues the tendency to make "Central Europe" emblematic of "Eastern Europe." Anne Applebaum, *Iron Curtain: The Crushing of Eastern Europe, 1944–1956* (New York: Doubleday, 2012).

11. Decades ago, Leszek Kołakowski remarked that Stalinism "was an international and not merely a Soviet phenomenon" and that its variations could not be properly understood "only from the point of view of Russian internal policy and sectional strife." See his *Main Currents of Marxism: Its Origin, Growth, and Dissolution*, vol. 3 (Oxford: Clarendon Press, 1978), 5. Nevertheless, a great deal of Soviet history pursued an internal framework of analysis, shaped by Russian historical legacies or the revival of "traditional" systems and patterns of authority. One landmark volume acknowledged that Stalinism was transferred "wholesale" to Eastern Europe but its contributions were confined to the Soviet Union. Sheila Fitzpatrick, ed., *Stalinism: New Directions* (London: Routledge, 2000), 2. A wider chronological and spatial frame is offered in David L. Hoffman and Yanni Kotsonis, eds., *Russian Modernity: Politics, Knowledge and Practices, 1800–1950* (New York: Macmillan, 2000), and Balázs Apor, Péter Apor, and E.A. Rees, eds. *The Sovietization of Eastern Europe* (Washington, DC: New Academia Publishing, 2008). Michael David-Fox has made a useful argument for entanglement. See his "Multiple Modernities vs. Neo-Traditionalism: On Recent Debates in Russian and Soviet History," *Jahrbücher für Geschichte Osteuropas* 54, no. 4 (2006): 535–55.

12. Stephen Kotkin, "Modern Times: The Soviet Union and the Interwar Conjuncture," *Kritika* 2, no. 1 (2001): 160. Kotkin's work is pervaded by the view of modernity not as "some inherent sociological process, a move out of tradition, but of a vicious geopolitical competition." See his *Stalin*, vol. 1 (New York: Penguin, 2014), 4–5.

13. Stephen Kotkin, "Mongol Commonwealth? Exchange and Governance across the Post- Mongol Space." *Kritika* 8, no. 3 (Summer 2007): 525.

14. What does it mean to adopt ideas? "Acceptance is possible only on the condition of adaptation," wrote Zygmunt Bauman in a pioneering volume, "and adaptation means transformation. The required adaptation may on some occasions leave to the initial

pattern the role of a first push only." See his "East European and Soviet Social Science: A Case Study in Stimulus Diffusion," in *The Influence of East Europe and the Soviet West on the USSR*, ed. Roman Szporluk (New York: Praeger, 1976), 92.

15. In addition to external threats—real, imagined, manufactured—the regime also faced domestic resistance. An important legacy of the long Ottoman period was the continued existence of separate social spheres, especially in remote areas and the highlands. They proved resistant to central authority in the early years, and the Communist Party waged a determined and ruthless battle to integrate them within the new socialist order.

16. In one of the most perceptive analyses of the Albanian regime, François Fejtő wrote that it was based on two crucial elements: "fanatical hostility against Yugoslavia and, domestically, Stalinism to the bitter end." François Fejtő, "La deviazione albanese," *Comunità*, no. 107 (1963): 25.

17. Arne Westad emphasizes pessimism, rather than a sense of euphoria, as contributing to Stalin's handling of postwar Eastern Europe in addition to the Third World. See his *The Global Cold War: Third World Interventions and the Making of Our Times* (Cambridge: Cambridge University Press, 2005), 57–66.

18. Drawing from the history of the French estates, the French demographer Alfred Sauvy wrote about three worlds: "Trois mondes, une planète," *L'Observateur*, 14 August 1952. China's position within this framework became a matter of disagreement. Mao later devised his own development-based model of three worlds, collapsing both the United States and the Soviet Union into a single category of First World imperial powers. See Chen Jian, "China, the Third World, and the Cold War," in *The Cold War in the Third World*, ed. Robert J. McMahon (New York: Oxford University Press, 2013), 85–100.

19. At the founding of the Communist Information Bureau (Cominform) in September 1947 in Poland, the Soviet ideology chief Andrei Zhdanov spoke about two "camps." Many see the speech as some kind of turning point, but a Russian scholar has argued that plans for a similar organization predated that event. Leonid Gibianskii, "Forsirovanie sovetskoi blokovoi politiki," in *Kholodnaia voina, 1945–1963 gg.: Istoricheskaia retrospektiva: Sbornik statei*, ed. N. I. Egorova and A. O. Chubar'ian (Moscow: OLMA-PRESS, 2003), 137–86.

20. "Deklaratsiia Pravitel'stva Soiuza SSP ob osnovakh razvitiia i dal'-neishego ukrepleniia druzhby i sotrudnichestva mezhdu Sovetskim Soiuzom i drugimi sotsialisticheskimi gosudarstvami," *Pravda*, 31 October 1956, 1. One author found "commonwealth" misleading because it merges "the normative with the descriptive." Of course, this was precisely the problem that Communist authorities also faced. Zvi Y. Gitelman, "The Diffusion of Political Innovation: From East Europe to the Soviet Union," in Szporluk, *The Influence of East Europe and the Soviet West*, 16. At the time of Gitelman's analysis (1976), the socialist sphere was still "very much in the process of self-definition." This process of self-definition persisted until the system collapsed.

21. Mark Mazower, *Governing the World: The History of an Idea* (New York: Penguin, 2012), 247.

22. David C. Engerman, "The Second World's Third World," *Kritika* 12, no. 1 (Winter 2011): 183–211; Frederick Cooper, "Writing the History of Development," *Journal of Modern European History* 8, no. 1 (January 2010): 5–23. Studies of development are often cast in terms of center-periphery dynamics, including the more recent studies of Soviet-Third World interactions, but this should not obscure the persistence of peripheral contacts circumventing the center.

23. In his memoirs, Nikita Khrushchev characteristically boasted that the creation of a "socialist commonwealth" had been "something new in the world." Nikita Khrushchev, *Memoirs of Nikita Khrushchev*, vol. 3, *Statesman (1953–1964)*, ed. Sergei Khrushchev, trans. George Shriver (University Park: Pennsylvania State University Press, 2007), 390.

24. On the need to take seriously illiberal internationalism, see Jessica Reinisch, "Agents of Internationalism"; David Brydan, "Axis Internationalism: Spanish Health Experts and the Nazi 'New Europe,' 1939–1945"; and Ana Antic, Johanna Conterio, and Dora Vargha, "Beyond Liberal Internationalism," all in *Contemporary European History* 25, no. 2 (2016): 195–205, 291–311, 359–71.

25. Austin Jersild, "The Soviet State as Imperial Scavenger: 'Catch Up and Surpass' in the Transnational Socialist Bloc, 1950–1960," *American Historical Review* 116, no. 1 (February 2011): 112.

26. Dipesh Chakrabarty, "The Muddle of Modernity," *American Historical Review* 116, no. 3 (June 2011): 674. Via Baudelaire, Michel Foucault defined modernity as "a mode of relationship that has to be established with oneself." See "What Is Enlightenment?," in *The Foucault Reader*, ed. Paul Rabinow (New York: Pantheon, 1984), 41.

27. James Scott paints a sweeping picture of the ills of "high modernism," which, he writes, "could be found across the political spectrum from left to right but particularly among those who wanted to use state power to bring about huge, utopian changes in people's work habits." His analysis of Soviet schemes, however, relies heavily on Bolshevik texts rather than the specifics of the institutions put in place. James C. Scott, *Seeing Like a State: How Certain Schemes to Improve the Human Condition Have Failed* (New Haven: Yale University Press, 1998), 5.

28. "It is counterintuitive to suggest that the best way to understand a global process is by narrowing the focus," David Engerman and Corinna Unger offer, but "local studies offer an excellent avenue to the study of global studies of modernization without losing sight of regional, national, and international circumstances." David C. Engerman and Corinna R. Unger, "Towards a Global History of Modernization," *Diplomatic History* 33, no. 3 (June 2009): 377.

29. György Péteri, "Nylon Curtain—Transnational and Transsystemic Tendencies in the Cultural Life of State-Socialist Russia and East-Central Europe," *Slavonica* 10, no. 2 (November 2004): 113–23; Michael David-Fox, "The Iron Curtain as Semipermeable Membrane: Origins and Demise of the Stalinist Superiority Complex," in *Cold War Crossings: International Travel and Exchange across the Soviet Bloc, 1940s–1960s*, ed. Patryk Babiracki and Kenyon Zimmer (College Station: Texas A&M University Press, 2014), 14–39. The importance of Khrushchev-era internationalism also emerges in some of the contributions in Anne Gorsuch and Diane Koenker, eds., *The Socialist Sixties: Crossing Borders in the Second World* (Bloomington: Indiana University Press, 2013).

30. Some scholars of globalization have stressed differentiation rather than some kind of inevitable uniformity in the process. The chronology associated with globalization is also a matter of debate. Some date it to the late twentieth century. Others go back to the convergence of the Atlantic economies in the nineteenth century. Jürgen Osterhammel and Niels P. Petersson, *Globalization: A Short History* (Princeton: Princeton University Press, 2005); A. G. Hopkins, ed., *Globalization in World History* (New York: Norton, 2002); Kevin H. O'Rourke and Jeffrey G. Williamson, *Globalization and History: The Evolution of a Nineteenth-Century Atlantic Economy* (Cambridge, MA: MIT Press, 1999); Eric Hobsbawm, "Guessing about Global Change," *International Labor and Working-Class History* 47 (Spring 1995): 39–44.

31. "Rech' tovarishcha N. S. Khrushcheva na deviatoi obshchegermanskoi rabochei konferentsii v gorode Leiptsige 7 marta 1959 goda," *Pravda*, 27 March 1959, 2.

32. In a different context, Sebastian Conrad has noted that nationalization and globalization were not "two stages of a consecutive process of development, but rather were dependent on each other." Sebastian Conrad, *Globalisation and Nation in Imperial Germany* (New York: Cambridge University, 2010), 2–3.

33. Arjun Appadurai, *Modernity at Large: Cultural Dimensions of Globalization* (Minneapolis: University of Minnesota Press, 1996), 4.

34. Patricia Clavin has observed that despite a certain tendency to view transnational flows and circulations as emancipatory, they need not be "consistently progressive and co-operative in character." See her "Defining Transnationalism," *Contemporary European History* 14, no. 4 (November 2005): 424.

35. In North Korea's engagement with the world, Charles Armstrong also sees "a vivid reminder that the homogenizing forces of globalization, and the reach of American power, have their limits." Charles K. Armstrong, *Tyranny of the Weak: North Korea and the World, 1950–1992* (Ithaca: Cornell University Press, 2013), 9.

36. While the book is largely chronological, certain themes and individuals show up repeatedly, from chapter to chapter. The idea has been to avoid the presentation of a linear story of planning and exchange in favor of showing multiple forces interacting, clashing, and constituting one another. This also explains the focus of the chapters, which do not attempt to offer a comprehensive history of the country in the postwar period.

37. One of the best studies on the linguistic and symbolic strategies of a Communist dictatorship is Ardian Vehbiu's *Shqipja totalitare: Tipare të ligjërimit publik në Shqipërinë e viteve 1945–1990* (Tirana: Çabej, 2007).

38. Václav Havel, *Redevelopment, or, Slum Clearance* (London: Faber and Faber, 1990); György Konrád, *The City Builder* (New York: Harcourt Brace Jovanovich, 1977).

39. Ismail Kadare, *The Palace of Dreams* (New York: William Morrow, 1993).

1. TEN YEARS OF WAR

1. Lev Pavlovich Sukacev typescript, "Soldier under Three Flags: The Personal Memoirs of Lev Pavlovich Sukacev," Hoover Institution Archives, box 1, p. 144.

2. Robert Austin, *Founding a Balkan State: Albania's Experiment with Democracy, 1920–1925* (Toronto: University of Toronto Press, 2012).

3. Other early prominent leftist figures included Ali Kelmendi, Lazar Fundo, Sejfulla Malëshova, Tajar Zavalani, and Skënder Luarasi, among others. An early overview was provided by Ernest Koliqi, "Il comunismo in Albania (1935)," Archivio Storico Diplomatico del Ministero degli Affari Esteri (ASMAE), Direzione Generale Affari Politici 1943–1945 (DGAP), Albania, busta (b.) 55, fascicolo (f.) 11 ("Partiti politici"). See also Kristo Frashëri, *Historia e lëvizjes së majtë në Shqipëri dhe e themelimit të PKSh-së, 1878–1941: Vështrim historik me një shtojcë dokumentare* (Tirana: A.SH.SH., 2006), esp. 31–88.

4. See, for example, Office of the Prime Minister, Central Police Directorate-General (Tirana) to Chief of Police (Rome), 15 February 1940, Archivio Centrale dello Stato (ACS), Ministero dell'Interno (MI), Direzione Generale Pubblica Sicurezza (DGPS), Divisione Affari Generali e Riservati (DAGR), cat. K-1 B, b. 56/A. By 1941, Italian authorities recognized an increase in Communist activity in Albanian towns. Luogotenenza Generale, "Propaganda comunista," 14 July 1941, ACS, MI, DGPS, DAGR, cat. K-1 B, b. 63. For earlier reports of Bolshevik propaganda in Albania, see "Appunto per la Direzione Generale degli Affari Politici—Ufficio Albania" (Riservato), 21 August 1935, ASMAE, DGAP, b. 55, f. 11 ("Partiti Politici").

5. Mugoša and Popović were followed by Velimir Stojnić, Nijaz Dizdarević and Savo Zlatić. Svetozar Vukmanović-Tempo also became involved in Albanian party affairs for a period of time. See his *Revolucija koja teče: Memoari* (Zagreb: Globus, 1982), 2:455ff.

6. Vladimir Dedijer, *Jugoslovensko-albanski odnosi (1939–1948)* (Belgrade: Borba, 1949), 15–16; 17th CIC Detachment Trust, "A Survey of Albania" (Secret), 15 September 1950, in CIA Records Search Tool (CREST), National Archives and Records Administration (NARA), College Park, MD, CIA-RDP83-00415R006100200002-9.

7. Ironically, the more Albanian propagandists later denied their early Yugoslav sympathies, the more they contributed to the idea that they had been under Yugoslav control (with the implication, popular among émigrés, that Communism was therefore "foreign").

8. Many authors, for example, have repeated the myth that Hoxha wrote for the French Communist paper *L'Humanité*. Arshi Pipa disputed the intellectual myths created later around the party boss, speculating that Hoxha might not have read Marx at all. See his *Albanian Stalinism: Ideo-Political Aspects* (New York: Columbia University Press, 1990), 131. Of course, whether Hoxha had read Marx or not (and when) offers no explanation about how he was able to navigate the thorny power struggles of the postwar period.

9. Petro Marko, *Intervistë me vetveten (Retë dhe gurët)* (Tirana: OMSCA, 2000), 439–41. The leading Albanian historian of the left has written that Hoxha started calling himself "a communist" only in 1939 and that a number of old-time leftist intellectuals who had abandoned Bolshevism were purposefully kept out of the founding meeting. Frashëri, *Historia e lëvizjes së majtë në Shqipëri*, 225. Years later, while serving a prison sentence, Tashko is said to have admitted that he had supported Hoxha's membership in the Korçë Communist group because they needed a Muslim; the group was otherwise dominated by Orthodox Christians. "After all," he is said to have explained, "did Lenin not also bring along [Roman] Malinovsky, who was later found to be a spy for the tsarist secret police?" Todi Lubonja, *Nën peshën e dhunës* (Tirana: Mësonjëtorja, 1998), 70.

10. For this argument, see Nicholas C. Pano, "Albania," in *The Columbia History of Eastern Europe in the Twentieth Century*, ed. Joseph Held (New York: Columbia University Press, 1992), 30.

11. British Military Mission in Albania, Periodical Political Report (Secret), 22 June 1945, The National Archives of the United Kingdom (TNA), Records of Special Operations Executive (HS) 5/54.

12. Central Intelligence Group (CIG), "Albanian Political Situation" (Confidential), August 1947, CIA-RDP82-00457R000800310005-8.

13. CIG, "Albania" (Secret), 15 August 1947, in Declassified Documents Reference System (DDRS), Gale Group, document no. CK3100439949.

14. Besnik Pula, "State, Law and Revolution: Agrarian Power and the Nation-State in Albania" (PhD diss., University of Michigan, 2011), 348.

15. On British support, see the correspondence contained in "Finance and Relief. Including Russian Finance in Albania," 1944–45, TNA, HS 5/102.

16. Rudolf Vogel, "Brot für ganz Albanien," *Donauzeitung*, 25 January 1944; "Die Feindfront in Verlegenheit [. . .]," *Donauzeitung*, 16 December 1943, both newspaper clippings in Friedrich Katz Collection, Hoover Institution Archives, box 24. See also Hubert Neuwirth, *Widerstand und Kollaboration in Albanien 1939–1944* (Wiesbaden: Harrassowitz, 2008), 136–50. The German perspective on occupation is given in Hermann Neubacher's *Sonderauftrag Südost 1940–1945: Bericht eines fliegenden Diplomaten* (Göttingen: Musterschmidt-Verlag, 1956), 105–21. The author was the Nazi envoy to southeastern Europe.

17. "SOE activities in Albania," n.d., TNA, HS 7/69, 8. One author has observed that the partisans did only limited damage to the Nazi troops. Bernd J. Fischer, "Enver Hoxha and the Stalinist Dictatorship in Albania," in *Balkan Strongmen: Dictators and Authoritarian Rulers of Southeast Europe*, ed. Bernd Fischer (West Lafayette, IN: Purdue University Press, 2007), 248. A sense of a partisan triumph, however, could be heightened by German cruelty. One British report noted that the more German morale declined, the more ruthless Nazi officers became, directing their violence against civilians. "German Methods during Battle of Tirana" (Secret), 30 November 1944 [forwarded 17 December 1944], TNA, HS 5/17.

18. "Albania—Political," n.d., TNA, HS 5/4 ("Assessment of situation inside Albania. March 1941–December 1944").

19. "SOE activities in Albania," n.d., TNA, HS 7/69; Foreign Office to Washington (for Cairo and Algiers), 15 July 1944, TNA, Foreign Office (FO) 371/43561 R 1471/1471/90, 34.

20. One British participant later recalled that his compatriots assigned to the various camps were compelled "to live Albanian—to eat, drink, sleep, breathe and think Albanian." And thus: "Those with the Partisans became very pro-Partisan and those with the nationalists or Zogists tended to become very attached to the chieftains with whom they personally were in contact, and very anti-Partisan." Reginald Hibbert, *Albania's National Liberation Struggle: The Bitter Victory* (London: Pinter Publishers, 1991), 241.

21. Albanian Country Section of Force 399, "Allied Military Mission, Albania 1942–1945," n.d. [1945], TNA, HS 7/70, 31.

22. In the spring of 1946, the Tirana Communist Party committee counted 867 members, 60 percent of whom were between the ages of eighteen and twenty-five. Roughly a third of all members had attended high school. More than 4 out of 10, however, had attended only primary school. See Tirana party committee to Central Committee, 20 April 1946, Arkivi Qendror Shtetëror (AQSH), fondi (f.) 14/AP, struktura (str.), Seksioni Organo-Instruktiv, viti (v.) 1946, dosja (dos.) 13, fleta (fl.) 9.

23. "Extract from Report by Major The Hon. A.V. Hare, M. C., Household Cav. who was in Albania from November 1943 to November 1944" (Top Secret), n.d., TNA, FO 371/48078 R 460/46/90. The author observed that when Communists understood that "the danger of political influence we are developing in Albania outweighs the value of the supplies we are sending, it is considered that occasion will be found to bundle all our representatives out of the country, without a day's delay." Another British assessment noted that without Yugoslavia, "it is unlikely that a country with as small a population as Albania, under a regime such as the [Front], will be able to exist independently in the Balkans in the circumstances of to-day." See "Allied Military Mission, Albania 1942–1945," n.d. [1945], TNA, HS 7/70, 39.

24. Jacobs to Secretary of State, 26 May 1945, *Records of the Department of State Relating to the Internal Affairs of Albania, 1945–1949*, microfilm, record group 59, decimal file 875, roll 1 (Wilmington, DE: Scholarly Resources, 1987). Relations worsened throughout the spring and summer of 1946, and Washington withdrew the mission in November 1946.

25. British Military Mission in Albania, Periodical Political Report (Secret), 12 October 1945, TNA, HS 5/55. Consider the Soviet "staging" of elections in eastern Poland after the invasion of 1939. "It was a practical lesson in intimidation and collaboration," Jan Gross has argued, "superb conditioning for both the subjects of the new order and its enforcers." Jan T. Gross, *Revolution from Abroad: The Soviet Conquest of Western Ukraine and Western Belorussia* (Princeton: Princeton University Press, 1988), 113.

26. The party apparatus, which started campaigning ahead of time, sent teams of agitators to towns and villages to stir up enthusiasm. It also worked with individuals known to exert influence in local communities in the interest of drawing additional support. And it encouraged local officials to mobilize journalists and photographers ahead of time and to pay special attention to veterans, their families, and women. Correspondence between central and local party offices contained in AQSH, f. 14/AP, str., v. 1945, dos. 147, esp. fl. 1–79. Since most of the population was illiterate, voting involved dropping a rubber ball into a box. According to official results, over 90 percent of the votes went to the Democratic Front.

27. Fischer, "Enver Hoxha" 251; Peter R. Prifti, "Albania's Expanding Horizons," *Problems of Communism* (January–February 1972): 30–39 (esp. 33).

28. Besnik Pula, "Becoming Citizens of Empire: Albanian Nationalism and Fascist Empire, 1939–1943," *Theory and Society* 37 (2008): 567–96. It should not be surprising, then, that Communist officials invoked other foreign powers in the name of nationalism.

A confirmation of the new regime's suspicion of the West is provided in I. R. H Black, "New Year Reception in Tirana" (Secret), 4 January 1945, TNA, FO 371/48078 R 1781/46/90.

29. Back in October 1944, Anthony Eden had informed Winston Churchill that a partisan takeover was the likely scenario in Albania. The exiled king Zog would not regain his throne. "Another King gone down the drain!" Churchill wrote on October 11, at the time of the so-called percentages agreement with Stalin over spheres of influence. "We did not mention Albania the other night," he added, "but personally I think we should insist upon a fifty-fifty arrangement with the Soviets." Churchill to Eden, 11 October 1944, TNA, Prime Minister's Office (PREM) 3/41, 9.

30. Executive committee of the Liberation Council of Tirana, 27 March 1945, AQSH, f. 489, v. 1945, dos. 131, fl. 5. For other examples from Kukës, in the country's northeast, see fl. 91–95. An Italian official's confirmation of the popular expectation that an Allied landing might happen: "Stralcio relazione Col. Corti Antonio," n.d., ASMAE, Aff. Pol. (Albania), b. 1, fasc. 2 ("Italia ed Albania").

31. See, for example, Instituti i Studimeve Marksiste-Leniniste pranë KQ të PPSH, *Historia e Partisë së Punës të Shqipërisë* (Tirana: 8 Nëntori, 1981), 181–238. On the relationship between state building and historical writing: Michael Schmidt-Neke, "Zwischen Kaltem Krieg und Teleologie: Das kommunistische Albanien als Objekt der Zeitgeschichtsforschung," in *Albanische Geschichte: Stand und Perspektiven der Forschung*, ed. Oliver Jens Schmitt and Eva Anne Frantz (Munich: R. Oldenbourg Verlag, 2009), 131–47.

32. Jan Gross, "Social Consequences of War: Preliminaries for the Study of the Imposition of Communist Regimes in East Central Europe," *East European Politics and Societies* 3, no. 2 (Spring 1989): 198–214.

33. Bernd J. Fischer, *Albania at War, 1939–1945* (West Lafayette, IN: Purdue University Press, 1999), 3.

34. François Fejtő, "La deviazione albanese," 19.

35. Stoyan Pribichevich, "Albania: Key to the Adriatic," *Current History* 50, no. 1 (March 1939): 40.

36. Sukacev typescript, "Soldier under Three Flags," pp. 129–30.

37. Investments focused on ports, roads, bridges, public buildings, and land reclamation projects (two-thirds of all construction projects were reportedly carried out by Italian companies). Società per lo sviluppo economico dell'Albania, *Un decennio di vita della "S.V.E.A." Relazione presentata all'assemblea generale degli azionisti del 15 maggio 1936-XIV* (Rome: La libreria dello stato, 1936), 21ff; Italian Ministry of Foreign Affairs, DGAP, "Memoria sull' opera svolta dall' Italia in Albania dal 1925 al 1943," n.d., ASMAE, Aff. Pol. (Albania), b. 2.

38. One author has written that Ciano came to view the country as his "personal fief." Davide Rodogno, *Fascism's European Empire: Italian Occupation during the Second World War* (Cambridge: Cambridge University Press, 2006), 30.

39. Sestilio Montanelli served as a technical adviser to the government on education reform prior to 1939. Jacomoni to Rome, 30 May 1938, ASMAE, Aff. Pol. (Albania), b. 90 (1938–39), fasc. 14 (Scuole, Educazione Fisica). His son, Indro, a prominent journalist in postwar Italy, also visited the country and published a detailed account of Albania's bid for modernization. Indro Montanelli, *Albania una e mille* (Torino: G.B. Paravia, 1939).

40. Starace to Ciano (Riservata), 29 September 1939, ACS, Partito Nazionale Fascista (PNF), Direttorio Nazionale (DN), b. 1736F, fasc. 12 ("Federazioni di Tirana"). Under the directorship of Giovanni Giro, the Albanian Fascist Party issued a newspaper (*Fashizmi*). ACS, PNF, DN, b. 1735 ("Quotidiano Fashizmi"). The party had a totalizing vision for its role in Albania, despite its limited capacities, considering, for example, using sports as a mechanism to attract ordinary Albanians. Albanian Fascist Party (Partija Fashiste Shqiptare), "Relazione sul bilancio di previsione dei proventi e delle spese del direttorio centrale

del Partito Fascista Albanese," 18 September 1939, ACS, PNF, DN, b. 1736F, fasc. 10 ("Fasci Albania"). Albanian women, similarly organized in *fasci*, also paid visits to Italy. "Rassegna Politica," *Rivista d'Albania*, fasc. 2 (July 1940): 213–19.

41. Mark Mazower, *Hitler's Empire: How the Nazis Ruled Europe* (New York: Penguin, 2008), 343.

42. Rodogno, *Fascism's European Empire*, 47–54. Rodogno's important analysis is nevertheless limited to the view from the imperial center.

43. Mostra della Rivoluzione Fascista, ACS, PNF, MRF, b. 93, "Sala della Spagna e Albania."

44. Vittorio Santoianni, "Il Razionalismo nelle colonie italiane 1928–1943. La 'nuova architettura' delle Terre d'Oltremare" (PhD diss., Università degli Studi di Napoli Federico II, 2008), 86–89.

45. Giuliano Gresleri, "Albania: Una dimensione sospesa tra opere pubbliche e rifondazione delle città," in *Architettura italiana d'oltremare: Atlante iconografico*, ed. Gresleri, Pier Giorgio Massaretti, and Stefano Zagnoni (Bologna: Bononia University Press, 2008), 434.

46. Giorgio Ciucci, *Gli architetti e il fascismo: Architettura e città, 1922–1944* (Torino: Einaudi, 1989), 81.

47. Maria Adriana Giusti, *Albania: Architettura e città, 1925–1943* (Florence: Maschietto, 2006); Mia Fuller, *Moderns Abroad: Architecture, Cities and Italian Imperialism* (London: Routledge, 2007), 129–32; Giuseppe Miano, "Florestano di Fausto from Rhodes to Libya," *Environmental Design: Journal of the Islamic Environmental Design Research Centre* 8, no. 9–10 (1990): 56–71. After his Albanian excursion, di Fausto ended up in Libya, where he designed government buildings, churches, and hotels.

48. David Rifkind, "Gondar: Architecture and Urbanism for Italy's Fascist Empire," *Journal of the Society of Architectural Historians* 70, no. 4 (2011): 492–511.

49. Marie Lou Busi, "Vita e opera di Gherardo Bosio," in *Gherardo Bosio: Architetto fiorentino, 1903–1941*, ed. Carlo Cresti (Florence: A. Pontecorboli, 1996), 49–52.

50. Regulatory plan for the city of Tirana and related documentation, Arkivi Qendror Teknik i Ndërtimit (AQTN).

51. See Carlo Cresti, "Gherardo Bosio: Una breve intensa apparizione nell' architettura degli anni Trenta," in Cresti, *Gherardo Bosio*, 9–20.

52. Bosio quoted in Lucia Billeri, "Bosio e i piani urbanistici per le città dell'Albania," in Cresti, *Gherardo Bosio*, 77.

53. The Italian architect Mario Cereghini took an interest in Albanian vernacular buildings, photographing towns and villages during a volunteering stint with the Italian mountain troops on the way to Greece in early 1941. See "Corriere architettonico," *Architettura: Rivista del Sindacato Nazionale Fascista Architetti* 20 (July 1941): 296–97.

54. Alessandro Roselli identifies several reasons for Italy's reluctance to promote industrialization in Albania: the direction laid out by the League of Nations for the country, which largely focused on agriculture and roads; the desire to limit social upheaval; the objective of keeping Albania in the role of a supplier of raw materials; and, not least important, Rome's immediate military objectives in the Balkans. See his *Italy and Albania: Financial Relations in the Fascist Period* (London: I.B. Tauris, 2006), 151. Yet another iteration of the failure argument can be found in Giovanni Villari, "A Failed Experiment: The Exportation of Fascism to Albania," *Modern Italy* 12, no. 2 (June 2007): 157–71.

55. "Ligjë Nr. 158 d. 14–11–1945 mbi aprovimin e Planit Rregullues të Qytetit Tiranës," 14 November 1945, AQSH, f. 489, v. 1945, dos. 101, fl. 1.

56. "Gjenda urbanistike në qytetet t'ona," n.d., AQSH, f. 499, v. 1960, dos. 430, fl. 1.

57. Ministry of Public Works, "Qarkore," 22 May 1946, AQSH, f. 499, v. 1946, dos. 355, fl. 1. The British, however, cited different figures, which the representative in Tirana found suspect. The "stone cottage of the average Albanian mountaineer," he wrote, was hardly

worth 2,800 pounds sterling, as the Tirana government would have it. British Military Mission in Albania, Periodical Political Report (Secret), 10 November 1945, TNA, HS 5/55.

58. For examples, see the correspondence from the Ministry of Public Works contained in AQSH, f. 499, v. 1945, dos. 243, fl. 2–4, and AQSH, f. 499, v. 1948, dos. 11, fl. 1 verso.

59. The winter of 1946–47 saw an intensifying battle against so-called speculators (*matrapazë*) and saboteurs, as provincial authorities reportedly targeted gold collectors, petty traders of foreign coins, and state employees charged with pilfering anything from food to bars of soap. With store shelves lying empty, police officials targeted small shop-keepers and their homes, reportedly unearthing hidden stocks of shoes, clothes, and other goods. *Përpara*, 25 January 1947, 2.

60. Ministry of Economy to Ministry of Public Works, 11 May 1946, AQSH, f. 499, v.1946, dos. 154, fl. 1.

61. For example, see a complaint (13 May 1946), related correspondence with the Ministry of Public Works (30 May 1946), and the intervention of the Ministry of Justice (6 July 1946), contained in AQSH, f. 499, v. 1946, dos. 62, fl. 3, 5–6, 9.

62. One such action took place in Durrës: memo from the local executive committee, 3 January 1947, AQSH, f. 490, v. 1947, dos. 226, fl. 31.

63. For this argument, in the context of the pre-1945 economy, see Michael Kaser, "Economic System," in *Albanien*, ed. Klaus-Detlev Grothusen (Göttingen: Vandenhoeck & Ruprecht, 1993), 291. On continued Italian attention to the Fascist-era economic enter-prises in Albania: "Appunto," 23 July 1944, ASMAE, Archivio di Gabinetto, Gabinetto del Ministro (GM), Rapporti Politici (1944–47), pacco no. 47, fasc. 11 (Ris.).

64. General Committee of Albanian Cooperatives (Artisans) to Office of the Prime Minister, 7 February 1949, AQSH, f. 490, v. 1949, dos. 362, fl. 1–3.

65. Ministry of Industry to Office of the Prime Minister, "Mbi maqinerinë private që nuk shfrytëzohet," 20 December 1950, AQSH, f. 490, v. 1950, dos. 1303, fl. 5–8.

66. Berat National Liberation Council to Office of the Prime Minister, 30 June 1945, AQSH, f. 490, v. 1945, dos. 373, fl. 85. Rumors and complaints among inhabitants about house confiscations by the army were also confirmed by monthly reports from the local National Liberation Council in Gjirokastër, in AQSH, f. 489, v. 1945, dos. 131, fl. 38–41. Needless to say, not everyone sent letters of complaint. Not all letters may have been kept. Issues related to property remain—to this day—largely unsolved, a source of deep resent-ment, crime, and widespread corruption in the country.

67. Berat executive committee to Office of the Prime Minister, 3 December 1948, AQSH, f. 490, v. 1948, dos. 753, fl. 82.

68. There was another possibility: those who aided neither the partisans nor their opponents. These became known as *indiferent*, a less damning category than "enemy" but damaging nonetheless. For example, see Pukë executive committee to Office of the Prime Minister, 4 September 1948, AQSH, f. 490, v. 1948, dos. 753, fl. 77.

69. An April 1948 report from the prosecutor general noted that the owners had not been convicted of anything. Still, local officials in Fier took over homes and furniture, arguing that these people "are our enemies and they have amassed all of this [property] by drinking our blood." AQSH, f. 490, v. 1948, dos. 694, fl. 39.

70. Office of the Prosecutor General, 29 October 1947, AQSH, f. 490, v. 1947, dos. 106, fl. 55–57.

71. The note is contained in AQSH, f. 490, v. 1949, dos. 671, fl. 15.

72. Catalog of complaint letters sent to the Office of the Prime Minister between 1947 and 1949, AQSH, f. 490, v. 1949, dos. 671, fl. 1–43.

73. Council of Ministers correspondence with city and district party committees with attached lists of names, AQSH, f. 490, v. 1948, dos. 743, fl. 1–19.

74. "Mbledhje e d. 31/I/48," 31 January 1948, AQSH, f. 14/AP, Organet Udhëheqëse (OU), v. 1948, dos. 57, fl. 5. In February, speaking to an urban planning commission, Hoxha warned that workers, officers, and other functionaries were suffering because of a shortage of housing, which made it necessary to "purge Tirana from parasitic elements that do not have any connections to the city." See "Mbledhje 19/II/1948 mbi komisjonin për urbanizimin e Tiranës dhe të qyteteve të tjera të Shqipërisë," 19 February 1948, AQSH, f. 490, v. 1948, dos. 729, fl. 2.

75. One Italian representative visiting the interior minister noted that a large section of the building was still unfinished. Italian Mission (Tirana) to Rome, "Visita a Koçi Xoxe," 29 August 1945, ASMAE, Aff. Pol. (Albania), b. 4.

76. Italian Mission (Tirana) to Rome, "Visita a Enver Hoxha," 26 August 1945, ASMAE, Aff. Pol. (Albania), b. 4.

77. A list of these houses, filed under "private state-owned buildings," is contained in AQSH, f. 495, v. 1947, dos. 74, fl. 1–16.

78. Committee of Arts and Culture to Office of the Prime Minister, "Kërkim mbi dorëzimin e librave të libraris Stavro Skëndi dhe të Dr. Harisiadhit Bibliotekës Shtetnore," 24 February 1947; Office of the Prime Minister to Ministry of Finance, 21 July 1947, both in AQSH, f. 490, v. 1947, dos. 365, fl. 1, 6. Skendi left Albania shortly after the war, settled in the United States and joined the faculty at Columbia University. See his "Albania within the Slav Orbit: Advent to Power of the Communist Party," *Political Science Quarterly* 63, no. 2 (1948): 257–74.

79. "Raport justifikues mbi mbrojtjen e monumenteve," forwarded 18 June 1947, AQSH, f. 490, v. 1947, dos. 366, fl. 18.

80. Office of the Prime Minister to all administrative offices, 13 February 1947, and response from the Committee of Arts and Culture, 14 February 1947, AQSH, f. 513, v. 1947, dos. 43, fl. 1–2.

81. Ministry of Public Works to Ministry of Foreign Affairs, 9 January 1946, AQSII, f. 499, v. 1946, dos. 251, fl. 10.

82. Ardian Vehbiu, *Kulla e Sahatit* (Tirana: K&B, 2003), 26–29.

83. "Memoria sull' opera svolta dall'Italia in Albania dal 1925 al 1943," n.d., ASMAE, Aff. Pol. (Albania), b. 2.

84. Ministry of Public Works to Maliq construction site (Korçë), "Dërgohen projekte të Ingj. Omodeo," dated by hand 31 May 1947, AQSH, f. 499, v. 1947, dos. 257, fl. 23. See also "Aksioni i Maliqit—Aksion kombëtar dhe më i madhi në vendin tonë," *Bashkimi*, 19 September 1946, 2.

85. Ministry of Public Works to Ministry of Industry, dated by hand 11 February 1947; Technical Archive, "Raport," 2 June 1947, both in AQSH, f. 499, v. 1947, dos. 257, fl. 1, 9. On the Italian road construction studies: "Proces verbal dorëzimi," 22 May 1947, AQSH, f. 499, v. 1947, dos. 350, fl. 3–4 verso.

86. "Proçes-verbal," 30 June 1947 [revised], AQSH, f. 499, v. 1947, dos. 861, fl. 7–11.

87. Italian technical designs for the water supply, for example, could not be located. Ministry of Public Works to State Building Enterprise (Noçka), "Kërkohen informata mbi studimin e projektit të ujit pijshëm Selitë e Madhe Tiranë," dated by hand 18 March 1947, AQSH, f. 499, v. 1947, dos. 257, fl. 4.

88. Harry Fultz, the American director of the technical school in Tirana, estimated that between eighteen thousand and twenty thousand Italian military and service personnel remained at the end of 1944, as well as eight thousand civilians. The treatment of the Italians, he noted, "has been remarkable in its restraint and humanity," especially considering Italian "excesses" in 1941–43. Harry T. Fultz, "Italian Interests in Albania," 17 May 1945, *Records of the Department of State Relating to the Internal Affairs of Albania, 1945–1949*, record group 59, decimal file 875, roll 1. Albanian estimates put the number of Italians in

1944 at twenty-seven thousand, including around seven thousand civilians. "Mbi riatd-hesimin e italianëve," n.d., Arkivi i Ministrisë së Punëve të Jashtme (AMPJ), v. 1948, dos. 146, fl. 131.

89. Command of Italian Troops in Albania (Piccini) to Bari, 13 December 1944, TNA, War Office (WO) 204/9563. Some Italian soldiers surrendered to the Germans, but others joined the partisans in a special battalion named after Antonio Gramsci, and the rest were forced to go from village to village in search of food and shelter. In a letter dated only a few days later, addressed to Italian political parties, the soldiers described themselves as "torn apart, hungry and overwhelmingly sick." See "Copia," 19 December 1944, ASMAE, Aff. Pol. (Albania), b. 6. The Circolo Garibaldi, an organization set up to assist the Italians, also increasingly saw infighting between Italian officials and Albanian representatives of "the new democracy" who took up seats in the council. "Circolo Italiano Giuseppe Garibaldi, Statuto" (Berat), 7 November 1944, ASMAE, Aff. Pol. (Albania), b. 6; Magnoni to Turcato, 5 August 1946, ASMAE, Aff. Pol. (Albania), b. 1, fasc. 2 ("Italia ed Albania").

90. Italian Ministry of Foreign Affairs, DGAP, "Italiani in Albania (November 1946)," n.d., ASMAE, Aff. Pol. (Albania), b. 1, fasc. 2 ("Italia ed Albania").

91. National Anti-Fascist Council, 3 November 1945, AQSH, f. 489, v. 1945, dos. 154, fl. 8.

92. Ministry of Public Works to State Prosecutor, dated by hand 4 September 1945, AQSH, f. 499, v. 1945, dos. 453, fl. 3. The response specified that there was no law allowing for the release of a prisoner in such circumstances.

93. Black, "New Year Reception in Tirana."

94. "Verbale riassuntivo delle conversazioni che hanno avuto luogo a Tirana nei giorni 10, 11, 12 e 14 marzo 1945 fra S.E. il capo del governo Enver Hoxha e S.E. il sottosegretario di Stato alla Guerra Mario Palermo," n.d., ASMAE, Aff. Pol. (Albania), b. 2.

95. "Appunti consegnati al Console Generale Gen. Turcato prima della partenza," "Specialisti," dated by hand July 1945, ASMAE, Aff. Pol. (Albania), b. 4. Lists of Italian specialists contained in AQSH, f. 499, v. 1947, dos. 212, fl. 18–19.

96. Italian Mission (Tirana) to Rome, "Visita a Enver Hoxha," 26 August 1945, ASMAE, Aff. Pol. (Albania), b. 4; Italian Mission (Tirana) to Rome, "Specialisti e contratti di lavoro," 1 September 1945, ASMAE, Aff. Pol. (Albania), b. 1.

97. Many of those who were allowed to leave the country reported having their pos-sessions confiscated. The repatriated Italians, including Olivetti's former representative in Tirana, described a "reign of terror" in Albania and attested to widespread popular discon-tent against the regime. Italian Mission (Bari) to Rome, "Informazioni," 25 February 1946, ASMAE, Aff. Pol. (Albania), b. 4. On the implications of these "national refugees" for postwar Italy, see Pamela Ballinger, "Borders of the Nation, Borders of Citizenship: Italian Repatriation and the Redefinition of National Identity after World War II," *Comparative Studies in Society and History* 49, no. 3 (2007): 713–41.

98. "Sasija e italianëve që kemi," 16 March 1948, AQSH, f. 499, v. 1948, dos. 116, fl. 88. One Foreign Ministry memo put the total number of Italians working without contracts at 258, out of a total of 624 Italians in the country that year. "Mbi riatdhesimin e italia-nëve," n.d., Arkivi i Ministrisë së Punëve të Jashtme (AMPJ), v. 1948, dos. 146, fl. 131.

99. State Roads Enterprise to Ministry of Public Works, "Mbi dërgimin e relacionit Italjanve mbi lidhjen e kontratave," 5 June 1948, along with the signed memo, "Relacion," AQSH, f. 499, v. 1948, dos. 120, fl. 178–79.

100. Ministry of Public Works to Ministry of Foreign Affairs, 31 May 1948, AMPJ, v. 1948, dos.146, fl. 77.

101. Office of the Prime Minister circular, 24 August 1946, AQSH, f. 499, v. 1946, dos. 498, fl. 8.

102. In 1947, the personnel section of the State Building Enterprise informed the security police that an Italian employee was giving Italian language private lessons. The clientele reportedly included other Italians but also a member of the Soviet mission in Tirana. The official deemed it "not natural that an Italian, who is politically suspect no less, conduct himself as a teacher of our Youth." State Building Enterprise to State Security section, dated by hand 18 May 1947, AQSH, f. 499, v. 1947, dos. 390, fl. 1.

103. "Karakteristikat 6 mujore të nëpunësit (teknik i botores)" [C. Z.], 12 July 1947, AQSH, f. 499, v. 1947, dos. 156, fl. 14. Those who had worked for Italian companies were often suspected of hiding gold or other valuables. See, for example, "Appunto," 2 August 1946, ASMAE, Aff. Pol. (Albania), b. 1, fasc. 2 ("Italia ed Albania").

104. On the wartime experiences of Italian soldiers, see a memo by an eyewitness, "Stralcio relazione Col. Corti Antonio," n.d., ASMAE, Aff. Pol. (Albania), b. 1, fasc. 2 ("Italia ed Albania").

105. Ministry of Public Works to Central Directorate of the State Building Enterprise, 26 November 1946, AQSH, f. 499, v. 1946, d. 498, fl. 18. A handwritten note from Spiro Koleka, the future planning chief, instructed, "Italians are to be employed in technical matters and all care should be taken that Albanian managers benefit as much as possible from their technical expertise" (fl. 21).

106. For examples of denunciation reports against Italian and Albanian construction specialists, see letters dated 11–12 November 1946, AQSH, f. 491, v. 1946, dos. 8, fl. 59–62.

107. Italian Ministry of Foreign Affairs to Turcato, 17 January 1946, ASMAE, Aff. Pol. (Albania), b. 4.

108. The Italian Ministry of Foreign Affairs, for example, prepared lengthy memos outlining all the contributions made to Albania over decades. For an example of an article arguing along similar lines, see "Italia e Albania," *Messaggero di Roma*, 16 May 1946.

109. On the Italian understanding of the Soviet position on meddling in the internal affairs of countries within its sphere: Italian embassy in Moscow (Quaroni) to Rome, 28 January 1945 [the memo has been misdated]; Rome (Zoppi) to London, Washington, Paris, and Bari (Turcato), 8 February 1946, ASMAE, Aff. Pol. (Albania), b. 4.

110. Italian Mission (Tirana) to Rome (Castellani), 27 September 1945, ASMAE, Aff. Pol. (Albania), b. 4.

111. Eugenio Reale, the Italian Communist Party member, met with the Albanian ambassador in Paris in June 1948 to discuss the issue.

112. Letter signed "Arkitekt Moz," to Ministry of Foreign Affairs, Ministry of Public Works, State Design Enterprise, and the party's Central Committee, 25 November 1948, AQSH, f. 499, v. 1948, dos. 116, fl. 73; personnel file with short biography, "Pasqyrë," n.d., AQSH, f. 499, v. 1948, dos. 117, fl. 168.

113. Letter signed by a group of Italian specialists to Office of the Prime Minister, Central Committee et al., 3 December 1948, AQSH, f. 499, v. 1948, dos. 116, fl. 76.

114. An April 1948 meeting on devising unified building standards for new housing, for example, included Albanian construction officials, Yugoslav engineers, a Russian technician who had worked in Albania since the 1920s, an Italian specialist, and a Czech carpenter who had been working in Albania since 1926. "Proçes-verbal," 1 April 1948, AQSH, f. 499, v. 1948, dos. 315, fl. 1. Lists and biographies of Italian, Yugoslav, and other foreign construction specialists: "Pasqyrë," AQSH, f. 499, v. 1948, dos. 117, fl. 145–53.

115. "Mbi çështjen e teknikëve Italjanë," 20 June 1949, in AQSH, f. 14/AP, OU, v. 1949, dos. 71, fl. 16–17. Two years later, at a time when the administration was focused on expelling "party enemies" from its ranks, construction officials pleaded with the Interior Ministry to release an Italian specialist—imprisoned for "political faults, as a Fascist"—whom they urgently needed. This man had apparently already been released from prison once,

at the urging of construction officials in the Vlorë district, and had been sent to prison again. Ministry of Construction to Ministry of Interior (Prisons Branch), dated by hand 22 January 1951, AQSH, f. 499, v. 1951, dos. 125, fl. 50.

116. Enver Hoxha, *The Titoites: Historical Notes* (Tirana: 8 Nëntori, 1982), 129–222.

117. CIG, "Albanian Political Situation."

118. "Dje u nënështkrua Traktati i miqësisë dhe i ndihmës reciproke ndërmjet Shqipërisë dhe Jugosllavisë," *Bashkimi*, 10 July 1946, 1.

119. Volunteers formed study brigades, where they read political works and conducted agitation in the makeshift barracks put together at the construction site. One of the youths laying tracks in the Albanian countryside (out of "solidarity," as he would later put it) was Ion Iliescu, the first post-Communist president of Romania. "Problemet e Ballkanit përballohen me vullnet e dëshirë të mirë nga të gjitha vendet ballkanike," 28 September 1990, Plaza Hotel, New York, AQSH, f. 489, v. 1990, dos. 315, fl. 37–39.

120. Lists of Yugoslav specialists expected in Albania, 24 May 1945, contained in AQSH, f. 494, v. 1945, dos. 643, fl. 1. As an example, Marjan Mušič, a Slovenian architect, was supposed to conduct ethnographic surveys of traditional Albanian towns in need of preservation (it is unclear if Mušič ever made it to Albania). Ministry of Public Works to Gjirokastër executive committee, 21 May 1947, AQSH, f. 499, v. 1947, dos. 883, fl. 1.

121. Albanian-Yugoslav Company for the construction and exploitation of the Durrës—Elbasan railway (Bogner), "Izvestaj o radu Uprave za gradjenje za mesec juli 1947 g.," 9 July 1947, AQSH, f. 499, v. 1947, dos. 91, fl. 4.

122. Hoxha's speech at the CPA plenum, 18 December 1946, printed in Ndreçi Plasari and Luan Malltezi, *Marrëdhëniet shqiptaro-jugosllave 1945–1948, Dokumente* (Tirana: Drejtoria e Përgjithshme e Arkivave, 1996), 69–70.

123. I have surveyed published radio programs in local newspapers. For example, see *Përpara*, 24 April 1946, 4; and 1 May 1946, 4.

124. Kukës party regional committee to Central Committee, 2 August 1946, AQSH, f. 14/AP, Probleme Ekonomike (PE), v. 1946, dos. 170, fl. 1.

125. By comparison, Hoxha fumed at the Americans for voting to place the border issue on the agenda of the Peace Conference, which, he claimed, was evidence that Washington backed Greek claims. Henderson (acting representative in Albania) to Secretary of State (Secret), 16 October 1946, in United States Department of State, *Foreign Relations of the United States 1946*, vol. 6 (Washington, DC: United States Government Printing Office, 1969), 28–31.

126. "Radiogram" (very urgent), 30 April 1946, AQSH, f. 14/AP, str., v. 1946, dos. 131/1, fl. 1. The previous summer, British representatives in Tirana had observed that the Greek statements over northern Epirus had "the tendency of uniting the country" behind the Communist-led Front. British Military Mission in Albania, Periodical Political Report (Secret), 13 July 1945, TNA, HS 5/54.

127. Central Committee (Organization-Instruction Section) to regional party committees [1946], AQSH, f. 14/AP, str., v. 1946, dos. 131/3, fl. 5. According to surveillance records, rumors about a possible war with Greece persisted for years. "Parulla të hedhura nga elementi kundërshtar prej datës 10 deri 20–1–1948," n.d., AQSH, f. 14/AP, str., v. 1948, dos. 118, fl. 6–8.

128. "Parrullat me rastin e përvjetorit të konventës ekonomike me R.F.P. të Jugosllavis," n.d., AQSH, f. 14/AP, PE, v. 1946, dos. 170, fl. 19.

129. Letter (Xoxe), dated by hand 15 December 1946, AQSH, F. 14/AP, PE, v. 1946, dos. 170, fl. 2–3; "Letër gjithë qarqeve," forwarded 23 December 1946, AQSH, f. 14/AP, PE, v. 1946, dos. 170, fl. 8. Still, some individuals seem to have made the obvious comparison with prewar economic arrangements with Italy. See Shkodër party committee to Central

Committee, "Në lidhje me konventën," 2 February 1947, AQSH, f. 14/AP, PE, v. 1946, dos. 170, fl. 24/2.

130. "Format që duhet ndjekun për agjitasionin dhe propagandën," n.d., AQSH, f. 14/AP, str., v. 1947, dos. 300.

131. Shkodër party committee to Central Committee, "Në lidhje me konventën," 2 February 1947, AQSH, f. 14/AP, PE, v. 1946, dos. 170, fl. 24/1.

132. Report of the Albanian-Yugoslav Control Commission on Joint Companies, 13 April 1948, AQSH, f. 490, v. 1947, dos. 47/2, fl. 35.

133. "7.VI.1947" [Politburo meeting protocol], 7 June 1947, AQSH, f. 14/AP, OU, v. 1947, dos. 18, fl. 17–18. Such were the bitter ironies of postwar Communist relations that Zlatić, who worked to unite Albania with Yugoslavia, first alienated the Albanian leadership and then fell victim in the Yugoslav anti-Cominform purges after the Stalin-Tito split. He was interned at the Goli Otok camp. Ivo Banac, *With Stalin against Tito: Cominformist Splits in Yugoslav Communism* (Ithaca: Cornell University Press, 1988), 185n136.

134. See, for example, "Izvestaj o radu Uprave za gradjenje za mesec juli 1947 g.," 9 July 1947, AQSH, f. 499, v. 1947, dos. 91, fl. 4.

135. Some Italian technicians demanded that they receive the same kind of food allowance that Yugoslavs received. "Relacion," forwarded 5 June 1948, AQSH, f. 499, v. 1948, dos. 120, fl. 179.

136. See, for example, biographical files on Yugoslav construction specialists, dated by hand 9 September 1947, AQSH, f. 490, v. 1947, dos. 47/2, fl. 4.

137. Berat Executive Committee (Personnel Office) to Ministry of Public Works, 9 September 1947; "Karakteristikat e teknikut Ivan Boraç," 21 January 1948, AQSH, f. 499, v. 1947, dos. 212, fl. 137, 258.

138. "Relacion mbi hekur-udhën në lidhje me mosmarëveshjet të shokëve tanë dhe jugosllavë," n.d., AQSH, f. 14/AP, PE, v. 1947, dos. 331, fl. 30–42.

139. State Building Enterprise to Ministry of Public Works, "Mbi personelin tek. jugosllav (Rez.)," 13 November 1947, AQSH, f. 499, v. 1947, dos. 212, fl. 4 verso. As Yugoslav-Albanian relations deteriorated, reports of Yugoslav misbehavior took on— retrospectively—specific political meaning. All kinds of other "faults" and suspicious behavior came into focus. In particular, "leniency" against the supposed technical shortcomings of Yugoslav specialists could suddenly assume the quality of political misjudgment. One memo claimed that the mining company had employed hostile elements, accusing the Yugoslav deputy director of being unwilling to fire them. Dated 19 July 1948, the document is contained in AQSH, f. 490, v. 1947, dos. 47/2, fl. 89.

140. Making the joint Albanian-Yugoslav companies independent from ministries, as Albanian Politburo members pondered in early 1948, in reality meant creating more opportunities for administrative competition and conflict. Who would oversee whom? "Mbledhje e d. 31/I/48," 31 January 1948, AQSH, f. 14/AP, OU, v. 1948, dos. 57, fl. 1–2.

141. The preparatory materials and the Soviet recommendations are contained in AQSH, f. 14/AP, Marrëdhënie me Partinë Komuniste (bolshevike) të Bashkimit Sovjetik (M-PK(b)BS), v. 1947, dos. 1; "Iz zapisi besedy s. E. Khodzhei ob otnosheniiakh Albanii c CCCR i sosednimi balkanskimi gosudarstvami" (Secret), 15 July 1947, in *Vostochnaia Evropa v dokumentakh rossiiskikh arkhivov 1944–1953* gg., ed. T.V. Volokitina et al. (Moscow: Sibirskii khronograf, 1997), 1:677–81; "27.VII.1947" [Politburo meeting protocol], 27 July 1947, and points from conversations with Soviet leaders between 14 and 26 July 1947, AQSH, f. 14/AP, OU, v. 1947, dos. 23, fl. 5–7; "Shënime të E. Hoxhës nga bisedimet me Stalinin në Moskë," 16 July 1947, in Plasari and Malltezi, *Marrëdhëniet shqiptaro-jugosllave 1945–1948*, 117; D. S. Chuvakhin, "S diplomaticheskoi missiei v Albanii, 1946–1952 gg." *Novaia i noveishaia istoriia*, no. 1 (1995): 114–31.

142. "Fjala e Komandantit drejtuar popullit shqiptar," *Bashkimi*, 27 July 1947, 1. The newspaper prominently displayed a photograph of Hoxha standing next to Stalin and Vyacheslav Molotov in Moscow.

143. For the crucial communications from the summer of 1947, see particularly Plasari and Malltezi, *Marrëdhëniet shqiptaro-jugosllave 1945–1948*, 105–16, 120–46.

144. Ana Lalaj, "Shqipëria dhe Informbyroja," *Studime historike*, no. 3–4 (2009): 107–11. The ongoing work of Daniel Perez at Stanford University has significantly helped my understanding of the treacherous Albanian-Yugoslav relations in 1947–48.

145. One author has outlined the range of Albanian choices in 1948 as "'Yugoslavization' with Soviet-type ruling methods or 'Sovietization' on the basis of a much more distant political and ideological center in Moscow." Peter Danylow, "Sieg und Niederlage der Internationale: Die Sowjetisierung der Kommunistischen Partei in Albanien," in *Gleichschaltung unter Stalin? Die Entwicklung der Parteien im östlichen Europa 1944–1949*, ed. Stefan Creuzberger and Manfred Görtemaker (Paderborn: Ferdinand Schöningh, 2002), 263.

146. An Albanian version can be found in Hoxha's *The Titoites*, esp. 24–41. A Yugoslav version can be found in Dedijer, *Jugoslovensko-albanski odnosi*.

147. Excerpts from the 8 January 1948 Politburo meeting were published in Malltezi and Plasari, *Marrëdhëniet shqiptaro-jugosllave 1945–1948*, 176–99.

148. "Proçes-verbal i mbledhjes së Këshillit të Ministrave mbajtur më 30 qershor 1948 mbi informimin për rezolucionin e Byrosë Informative mbi çështjet e marrëdhënieve tona me Jugosllavinë," 30 June 1948, AQSH, f. 490, v. 1948, dos. 49, fl. 4.

149. See "Komunikatë mbi mbledhjen e Byrosë Informative të Partive Komuniste dhe Punëtore," *Bashkimi*, 30 June 1948, 1. Albania did not take part in the founding meeting of the Cominform in 1947. At the time, Belgrade was understood to "represent" Tirana. The Albanian party was not invited to the June 1948 meeting either.

150. In his pioneering study of the aftershock of the Soviet-Yugoslav split, Ivo Banac argued that the schism "was related most directly to Stalin's fear that Yugoslavia was beginning to see itself as a regional Communist center, with all the possibilities for mischief in relations with the West that such a role implied." Banac, *With Stalin against Tito*, 29. See also Leonid Gibianskii, "Ideia balkanskogo ob"edieniia i plany ee osushchestvleniia v 40-e gody XX veka," *Voprosy istorii*, no. 11 (November 2001): 38–56; Jeronim Perović, "The Tito-Stalin Split: A Reassessment in Light of New Evidence," *Journal of Cold War Studies* 9, no. 2 (Spring 2007): 32–63; Aleksandar Životić, *Jugoslavija, Albanija i velike sile: (1945–1961)* (Belgrade: Arhipelag, Institut za noviju istoriju Srbije, 2011), esp. 295–356. Precisely the fact that Yugoslavia had been so loyal to Moscow, Mark Kramer has written, made Stalin all the more intent to seek "Belgrade's abject capitulation as an example to the other east European countries." See his "Stalin, the Split with Yugoslavia, and Soviet-East European Efforts to Reassert Control, 1948–1953," in Snyder and Brandon, *Stalin and Europe*, 297.

151. See, for example, Ministry of Public Works to Office of the Prime Minister [July 1948], AQSH, f. 499, v. 1948, dos. 11, fl. 1.

152. "Marrëdhënie me teknikët," n.d., AQSH, f. 490, v. 1947, dos. 47/2, fl. 83. It is unclear why these records are filed under the year 1947, since some of them refer to events in 1948.

153. See, for example, "Relacion rreth marrëdhënieve të shoqërive shqip-jugosllave që janë krijuar në vendin t'onë qysh në muajin shkurt 1947 e deri më sot," 19 July 1948, AQSH, f. 490, v. 1947, dos. 47/2, fl. 85–95.

154. "The more explanatory meetings took place," one Albanian historian has written, "the clearer it became that Yugoslav heritage was extensive." Lalaj, "Shqipëria dhe Informbyroja," 131.

155. "Gjithë dikastereve" [draft list of forbidden literature], AQSH, f. 490, v.1948, dos. 591, fl. 3–4; Central Committee to all party committees [signed Nexhmije Hoxha], with

list attached [March 1949], AQSH, f. 14/AP, str., v. 1949, dos. 550, fl. 9–10; Central Committee Secretariat, "Vendim Nr. 166/1," 22 March 1950, "Lista e librave që duhen tërhequr nga çdo qarkullim" [1951], AQSH, f. 490, v. 1951, dos. 1683, fl. 3, 6.

156. One group of engineering students had been enrolled in Zagreb before the crisis and then ended up enrolled in civil engineering in Wrocław, Poland. The Poles, they complained, did not recognize some of the Yugoslav exams they had taken, so they were forced to start their studies from the first year. "Ministris s'Arsimit" [handwritten letter], 1 October 1949, AQSH, f. 499, v. 1949, dos. 63, fl. 74–75.

157. "From Belgrade to Foreign Office" (Confidential), 10 August 1948; British Embassy (Belgrade) to London (Confidential), 15 August 1948, both in TNA, FO 371/72114 R 666/6106/90.

158. "Situation in Albania" (Confidential), 18 October 1948, CIA-RDP82-00457R001900840007-6, CREST.

159. "Economic and Political Situation in Albania," 8 November 1948, CIA-RDP82-00457R002000390004-7, CREST.

160. "Public Opinion and Anti-Communist Resistance in Albania" (Confidential), January 1949, CIA-RDP82-00457R002700460003-3, CREST. The reported figure was upgraded several months later to 90 percent "of the Albanian people," who were said to oppose the regime. "Miscellaneous Information on Albania" (Secret), 31 May 1949, CIA-RDP82-0045R002800380007-7, CREST.

161. Hibbert, *Albania's National Liberation Struggle*, 235. See also Vojtech Mastny, *The Cold War and Soviet Insecurity: The Stalin Years* (New York: Oxford University Press, 1996), 81ff.

162. A proper study of the Albanian security police is yet to be undertaken. Given the state of the archives, however, it may not materialize for a while. Little also exists on the precursor to Sigurimi. See Kastriot Dervishi, *Shërbimi sekret shqiptar, 1922–1944: Historia nga fillimi deri në mbarim të Luftës së Dytë Botërore* (Tirana: "55," 2007). The author was in charge of the Interior Ministry archives.

163. In the 1960s, according to Dervishi, the People's Assembly declared that the security police had been established in 1943, when Hoxha had delivered a speech at a party conference in Labinot. This choice of a founding date served to highlight the leader's personal contribution while diminishing the legacy of Koçi Xoxe and the Yugoslav advisers. Kastriot Dervishi, *Sigurimi i Shtetit: 1944–1991. Historia e policisë politike të regjimit komunist* (Tirana: "55," 2012), 11–12.

164. The security police, however, also included a small contingent of officers who had been active before 1944 and some who had been members of the Fascist Party. By the end of 1952, over 60 percent of Sigurimi officers and deputy officers had a fifth-grade education, or lower. One in twelve was, as the interior minister put it in a Politburo meeting, an "autodidact." See "Mbi gjendjen e brendshme të Republikës Popullore të Shqipërisë" (Top Secret), 20 January 1953, AQSH, f. 14/AP, OU, v. 1953, dos. 8, fl. 30.

165. "Mbledhje e Byros Politike të P.P.SH. më datë 22/IV/1949" (Top Secret), 22 April 1949, AQSH, f. 14/AP, OU, v. 1949, dos. 28, fl. 1; "Organization and Functions of the Ministry of State Security" (Confidential), June 1948, CIA-RDP78-02546R000100130001-3, CREST.

166. "Shënime mbi takimin që u bë në KQ të PPSH midis delegacionit të PPSH dhe delegacionit parlamentar kinez të kryesuar nga shoku Pen Çen më 16/1/1957," 16 January 1957, AQSH, f. 14/AP, Marrëdhënie me Partinë Komuniste të Kinës (M-PKK), v. 1957, dos. 1, fl. 18.

167. An official Sigurimi study on so-called antiparty groups (undated but likely from after 1972) illustrates the crucial legacy of 1948. Arkivi i Ministrisë së Punëve të Brendshme (AMPB), bound undated book, n.d. [likely after 1972], pp. 72ff.

168. "Kërkime shpjegimesh nga P.K.(B)," 27 September 1948, AQSH, f. 14/AP, M-PK(b) BS, v. 1949, dos. 5, fl. 5–6.

169. "Zapis' besedy I. V. Stalina s E. Hodzhei ob albano-iugoslavskikh otnosheniakh, vneshnei i vnutrennei politike Albanii" (Secret), 23 March 1949, in Volokitina et al., *Vostochnaia Evropa*, 2:44–57; "Pritja e Delegacionit Shqiptar të kryesuar nga Gjen. Kol. Enver Hoxha nga Gjeneralisimi Stalin në Kremlin në 23.III.49 ora 22:05" [handwritten notes], AQSH, f. 14/AP, M-PK(b)BS, v. 1949, dos. 18, fl. 1–7; "Mbledhja e Byrosë Politike më 12/IV/1949" (Top Secret), 12 April 1949, AQSH, f. 14/AP, OU, v. 1949, dos. 23, fl. 1–2.

170. "Biseda e parë me shokun Suslov më 18.2.1949," AQSH, f. 14/AP, M-PK(b)BS, v. 1949, dos. 6, fl. 1; "Raport i delegacionit që shkojti në Moskë më 9 shkurt 1949 për të marrë eksperiencë nga Partija Bollshevike," n.d., f. 14/AP, M-PK(b)BS, v. 1949, dos. 7, fl. 1–7.

171. "Dega e agit-propit," n.d., AQSH, f. 14/AP, M-PK(b)BS, v. 1949, dos. 9, fl. 1–40. The reorganized Central Committee, on the basis of Soviet advice from 1949, would consist of departments of propaganda, administrative issues, personnel, agriculture, industries, and trade and finance. "Komiteti Qendror i P.P.SH.," 13 July 1950, AQSH, f. 14/AP, M-PK(b)BS, v. 1950, dos. 5, fl. 1.

172. "Komitetit Central të V.K.P.(B.), Moskë," with notes on Suslov's responses, 8 September 1950, AQSH, f. 14/AP, M-PK(b)BS, v. 1950, dos. 5, fl. 3–11.

173. "Zapis' besedy I.V. Stalina s E. Hodzhei ob albano-iugoslavskikh otnosheniakh, vneshnei i vnutrennei politike Albanii" (Secret), 23 March 1949, in Volokitina et al., *Vostochnaia Evropa*, 2:54–55. On the resulting decisions from the Soviet government to assist the Albanian side, see also excerpts published in *Sovetskii faktor v Vostochnoi Evrope, 1944–1953: Dokumenty*, ed. T. V. Volokitina et al. (Moscow: ROSSPEN, 2002), 2:77–78n3.

174. "Zapis' besedy I.V. Stalina s E. Hodzhei ob nekotorykh vneshnepoliticheskikh i vnutrennikh problemakh Albanii" (Top Secret), 2 April 1951, in Volokitina et al., *Vostochnaia Evropa*, 2:507. See also the related Soviet decisions, 514–15, 525.

175. "Vendim Nr. 418 mbi dërgimin e 65 kuadrove të Ministris së Punëve të Brendshme në B.R.S.S.," 13 October 1953, AQSH, f. 14/AP, OU, v. 1953, dos. 34, fl. 52. United States intelligence reports noted the presence of Russian security police instructors in Albania. "Assignment of Foreign Officers to the Albanian Army," and "School for Secret Agents in Tirana" (Secret), 12 January 1953, CIA-RDP82-00457R015900100003-6.

176. Dervishi, *Sigurimi i Shtetit*, 47. The number of collaborators also increased. For example, the year 1953 saw the highest number (16,850) of them (at p. 187).

177. Ministry of Public Works to Office of the Prime Minister and State Planning Commission, 1 October 1948, AQSH, f. 499, v. 1948, dos. 11, fl. 17; "Marrëveshtje" [agreement between Ministry of Public Works and Gaidarov], 5 May 1947, AQSH, f. 499, v. 1948, dos. 480, fl. 1–2. Gaidarov, the Soviet construction adviser, attained higher status and privileges during the summer of 1948.

178. "Shoku Komandant" [handwritten letter to Hoxha], 1 August 1948; Tirana (Kapo) to Albanian Embassy (Moscow), 3 September 1948, both in AQSH, f. 14/AP, PE, v. 1948, dos. 309.

179. See British Embassy (Belgrade) to London (Confidential), 24 September 1948, TNA, FO 371/72114 R 11201/6106/90.

180. "Miscellaneous Information on Albania" (Confidential), 28 April 1952, CREST, CIA-RDP82-00457R011600300001-3.

181. Amik Kasoruho, *Një ankth gjysmëshekullor* (Tirana: Çabej, 1996), 69.

182. The anti-Nazi offensive also produced an assertive Soviet subject. "The redemption of past sins through wartime exploits," writes Amir Weiner, "particularly the stain of wrong social origin, was ordained by the regime itself." See his *Making Sense of War: The Second World War and the Fate of the Bolshevik Revolution* (Princeton: Princeton University Press, 2001), 367.

183. "Ministrisë P. Botore" [memo from Yugoslav personnel in Maliq, Sindic and Ivan], 19 July 1946, AQSH, f. 499, v. 1946, dos. 147, fl. 3.

184. "Raportim" [signed declaration from an assistant mechanic in Maliq], 12 November 1946, AQSH, f. 499, v. 1946, dos. 503, fl. 2.

185. Zog was diagnosed with cancer in Egypt. Bernd Fischer, *King Zog and the Struggle for Stability in Albania* (Boulder, CO: East European Monographs, 1984), 302.

186. Arshi Pipa, *Libri i burgut* (Rome: Apice, 1959), 71.

2. THE DISCOVERY OF A WORLD

1. Vladislav Zubok, *Zhivago's Children: The Last Russian Intelligentsia* (Cambridge, MA: Harvard University Press, 2009), 29.

2. A comparative approach has served to highlight in particular the differences in Soviet engagement with the largest Eastern bloc countries. See Jan C. Behrends, *Die Erfundene Freundschaft: Propaganda für die Sowjetunion in Polen und in der DDR* (Cologne: Böhlau, 2006), and John Connelly, *Captive University: The Sovietization of East German, Czech and Polish Higher Education, 1945–1956* (Chapel Hill: University of North Carolina Press, 2000).

3. Norman Naimark, *The Russians in Germany: A History of the Soviet Zone of Occupation, 1945–1949* (Cambridge, MA: Belknap Press of Harvard University Press, 1995), 467.

4. On the failure of the Soviet cultural program in Poland, see Patryk Babiracki, *Soviet Soft Power: Culture and the Making of Stalin's New Empire, 1943–1957* (Chapel Hill: University of North Carolina Press, 2015). On the failures of Sino-Soviet friendship, see Austin Jersild, *The Sino-Soviet Alliance: An International History* (Chapel Hill: University of North Carolina Press, 2014), esp. 177–207.

5. Tuk Jakova, a high-ranking party official, had a similar reaction during his 1948 visit. "Si e pash Moskën," *Shqipëri B.R.S.S.*, no. 13–14, 1948, 11–12.

6. Koço Tashko, "Nga Parizi në Moskë me Halim Xhelon," *Miqësija*, no. 2, February 1959, 26–27.

7. "Eksperienca Sovjetike në Kooperativën e Yzberishit," *Shqipëri B.R.S.S.*, no. 2, February 1950, n.p.

8. "Me delegacionin fetar në Bashkimin Sovjetik," *Bashkimi*, 21 October 1950, 3.

9. Il'ia Ehrenburg, *European Crossroad: A Soviet Journalist in the Balkans* (New York: Knopf, 1947), 117. An excerpt was translated from the Russian and published in Albanian as "Shqipëria," *Shqipëri B.R.S.S.*, no.1, August 1947, 35–37. The Italian ambassador in Moscow, Quaroni, took offense to Ehrenburg's critical stance toward the Italian legacy in Albania. "Not even a word," he wrote to Rome, "on the building of the National Bank of Albania, which is an architectural gem, or the new hotel or the building of the new maternity ward." Italian Embassy in Moscow (Quaroni) to Rome, "L'Albania vista da Ilya Ehremberg," 5 December 1945, ASMAE, Rappresentanza italiana in Russia, b. 297, A1 ("Rapporti Politici").

10. "Njëzet ditë me delegacionin sovjetik," *Shqipëri B.R.S.S.*, no. 12, 1948, 25.

11. Ehrenburg, *European Crossroad*, 123–24.

12. Hasan, a peasant who visited the Soviet Union in 1949, was reportedly impressed that Soviet peasants drank alcohol and ceremoniously toasted "just as we do." In Dagestan, he reported, "They drink from bull horns." Soviet people also seemed to worship physical labor. ("Women prefer those men who work the most.") The peasant delegation had the chance to speak with Lysenko, the famous Soviet agrobiologist ("modest, like everyone else"). In fact, Soviet agronomists seemed strikingly simple in demeanor, Hasan declared, "unlike ours." See "Si e pa Bashkimin Sovjetik fshatari Hasan Mbolani nga rreth i Beratit," *Shqipëri B.R.S.S.*, no. 22, October 1949, 19.

13. Musaraj came to appreciate the Soviet Union as an incredibly vast mass of people, cultures, and languages. But he also insisted that the anti-Fascist struggle was a fierce bond that transcended localisms. After all, Musaraj was a veteran of the National Liberation War; war constituted a central theme in his writings. Throughout the trip, the author reportedly met Russians, Ukrainians, and Georgians who had heard of Albania's quest for freedom. During the long train ride to Georgia, for example, the visitors were asked to sing traditional Albanian songs, and the cabin's passengers apparently toasted to "the freedom and happiness of the Albanian people." Following the example of the Soviet Union, Musaraj concluded, "means getting to know the labor methods of Soviet people, their attachment to labor, their civility, their patriotic spirit, their socialist humanism and proletarian internationalism." Shevqet Musaraj, *Njëzet ditë në Bashkimin Sovjetik* (Tirana: Naim Frashëri, 1950), 9, 68, 73, 110–16. The excerpt on the train ride to Georgia was reprinted in the Albanian-Soviet friendship journal: "I gjerë është vendi i sovjetëve," *Shqipëri B.R.S.S.*, no. 7, July 1950, 9.

14. "Propozime nga delegacioni i dërguar në Bashkimin Sovjetik," n.d., AQSH, f. 14/AP, M-PK(b)BS, v. 1950, dos. 10, fl. 1. Yet another delegation visited kolkhozes and oil fields near the Caspian Sea, in Azerbaijan. "Nga vizita e delegacionit të Shoqërisë së Miqësisë nëpër Bashkimin Sovjetik," *Miqësija*, no. 10, October 1957, n.p.

15. "Informatsiia o rabote s delegatsiei obshchestva druzhby Albanii s SSSR" (Secret), n.d., Rossiiskii Gosudarstvennyi Arkhiv Noveishei Istorii (RGANI), fond (f.) 5, opis' (op.) 28, delo (d.) 14, listy (ll.) 165–67.

16. "Mbledhja e Byrosë Politike më 12/IV/1949" (Top Secret), 12 April 1949, AQSH, f. 14/AP, OU, v. 1949, dos. 23, fl. 2.

17. "We should take all necessary measures," a Politburo decision stated, "to popularize our people, our Republic, our Party, and our country in the Soviet Union first and foremost." The reason? "The Soviet Union is the shield and guarantee of our national independence." Moreover, the Soviets needed to get to know Albania, "because by getting to know us better, they will be able to help us better." Important targets were also Bulgaria (because it bordered Greece) and, of course, Yugoslavia. See "Vendim no. 3 mbi popullarizimin e vendit t'onë jashtë," 2 February 1949, AQSH, f. 14/AP, OU, v. 1949, dos.8, fl. 16.

18. Some 339,574 formerly illiterate persons had reportedly learned how to read and write by the end of 1955. However, officials admitted that these numbers were probably inflated. "Informacion mbi realizimin e planit I-rë pesëvjeçar të luftës kundër analfabetizmit," 31 December 1955, AQSH, f. 490, v. 1956, dos. 992, fl. 6. A decade and a half later, some 113,000 individuals aged ten to forty-nine were still illiterate, the vast majority of them peasant women. "Relacion informues mbi gjendjen dhe masat për zhdukjen e mbeturinave të analfabetizmit," 30 June 1971, AQSH, f. 490, v. 1971, dos. 107, fl. 1.

19. "Informatsionnaia zapiska K. D. Levychkina V. A. Zorinu o povestke dnia predstoiashchei vstrechi s zamestitelem predsedatelia Soveta Ministrov Albanii S. Kolekoi" (Secret), 13 December 1949, in Volokitina et al., *Sovetskii faktor*, 2:230–31.

20. "Mbledhja e Byrosë të K.C. të Partisë më 4/V/1948" [Politburo meeting protocol], 4 May 1948, AQSH, f. 14/AP, OU, v. 1948, dos. 83, fl. 21.

21. "Relacion mbi gjendjen e studentave jashtë shtetit dhe mbi masat që duhen marrë për përmirësimin e punës me ta," n.d., AQSH, f.14/AP, OU, v. 1958, dos. 34, fl. 5. The 1958 plan called for sending another 175 students abroad.

22. The very effort to accurately define social class had echoes of the Soviet past. As decided by the central party apparatus, these were the available categories of social origin: worker, poor peasant, middle peasant, wealthy peasant, estate owner (*çifligar*), craftsman with apprentices, individual craftsman, ordinary clerical worker, midlevel clerical worker, high-level clerical worker, petty trader, middle trader, and large trader. However, such

categories initially meant little to people, including party officials, who kept mischaracterizing people's supposed correct class standing. But it became imperative to engage with such categories—and youths looking for a scholarship abroad hardly needed a reminder of this fact. "Mbi funksionimin e organizatave bazë të partisë të studentëve tonë jashtë shtetit për vitin shkollor 1955–1956," dated by hand August 1956, AQSH, f. 14/AP, str. Drejtoria Administrative (DA) (Administrative Department), v. 1956, dos. 192, fl. 21. Such supposed failures in class-based social categorizing could later be used as justification for the existence of party reformists: "Ob izuchenii i obsuzhdenii materialov i reshenii XX s"ezda KPSS v Albanskoi Partii Truda" Secret, 14 June 1956, RGANI, f. 5, op. 28, d. 391, ll. 81–82.

23. The relevant State Planning Commission memo, dated 5 April 1955 (Top Secret), is contained in AQSH, f. 495, v. 1955, dos. 85, fl. 4–6. The Central Committee, however, also had separate mechanisms to send students to Moscow to receive training in Marxism-Leninism and international relations. Ultimately, that year the government decided to send 170 students abroad, including 59 in the Soviet Union, 27 in Czechoslovakia, and smaller contingents in Bulgaria, Romania, Poland, Hungary, and East Germany.

24. "Arqitekti i ri," *Miqësija,* December 1953, n.p.

25. "Karakteristikë e shokut Gani Strazimiri," 24 March 1963, AQSH, f. 511, v. 1965, dos. 48, fl. 40. Strazimiri's brother served a prison sentence until 1953.

26. Gani Strazimiri, handwritten letter to Shinasi Dragoti, 22 June 1949, AQSH, f. 499, v. 1949, dos. 201, fl. 1–2.

27. Ministry of Construction to the Ministry of Foreign Affairs, "Dërgohen disa plane për Moskë," 5 September 1949, AQSI I, f. 499, v. 1949, dos. 201, fl. 3–4. Strazimiri, however, appears to have received them in early 1950. Ministry of Foreign Affairs to Ministry of Public Works, "Mbi një material," [multiple dates for 1950], AQSH, f. 499, v. 1949, dos. 201, fl. 6.

28. Various materials refer to a professor Poliakov, who is said to have assisted with Strazimiri's master plan for Tirana. It is not fully clear whether they mean Leonid Poliakov, the prominent author of Moscow's ten year construction plan, who within a few years, like Strazimiri, would fall out of favor with authorities, bent on curbing the "gigantomania" of the Stalin years. Timothy J. Colton, *Moscow: Governing the Socialist Metropolis* (Cambridge, MA: Belknap Press of Harvard University Press, 1995), 371.

29. Ministry of Construction to the Office of the Prime Minister, n.d., AQSH, f. 490, v. 1950, dos. 1687, fl. 3.

30. "Relacjon. Mbi projekt iden e Planit Rregullues të Tiranës," n.d., AQSH, f. 490, v. 1950, dos. 1687, fl. 5 verso.

31. Ibid., fl. 8 verso, 9.

32. "Protokoll Nr. 18 datë 4/7/1952 i mbledhjes së Byrosë Politike të K.Q.," 4 July 1952, AQSH, F. 14/AP, OU, v. 1952, dos. 43, fl. 37–38. Two Soviet architects assessed the draft city urban plan before the next government discussion in 1954. At the meeting, Strazimiri asked for more Soviet assistance with urban planning. Hoxha concluded, "We should also walk on our own feet. We have our own architects now. And we will have more of them in the future." See "Proçes-verbal i mbledhjes së Këshillit të Ministrave mbajtur më 27 shkurt 1954 mbi shqyrtimin e relacionit për skicë-idenë e planit rregullues të qytetit të Tiranës," 27 February 1954, AQSH, f. 490, v. 1954, dos. 712, fl. 1–4 (at fl. 4). When authorities decided to build a museum dedicated to Lenin and Stalin in 1954 (on the occasion of the tenth anniversary of liberation), Albanian party officials similarly asked for Soviet interior designers. "Sekretariu TsK KPSS tov. Suslovu M.A.," dated by hand 11 March 1954, RGANI, f. 5, op. 16, d. 652, ll. 52–53.

33. A prevailing preoccupation with limiting costs is confirmed by the fact that when the government finally approved an urban plan for the capital—again, supervised by

Soviet planners—it warned that "measures be taken to absolutely limit the destruction of existing buildings." See "Vendim Nr. 130, mbi aprovimin e projekt-idesë të planit rregullues të qytetit të Tiranës," 7 April 1958, AQSH, f. 490, v. 1958, dos. 893, fl. 16.

34. "Zapis' besedy c general'nym sekretarem obshchestva kul'turnoi sviazi Albanii i CCCR N. Natanaili o sodeistvii v poluchenii sovetskoi p'esy dlia postanovki v Narodnom teatre, proektirovanii i sozdanii monumenta I. V. Stalinu v Tirane i dr." (Secret), 13 March 1950, in Volokitina et al., *Sovetskii faktor*, 2:283–84 (esp. note 3); "Monumenti i Stalinit," *Shqipëri B.R.S.S.*, no. 10–11, 1951, 16.

35. Examples can be found in *Arkhitektura SSSR* 11 (1954): 15; *Arkhitektura SSSR* 4 (1957): 21.

36. In his memoirs, Khrushchev explained that Albania was originally not even included in the draft plans for the Warsaw Pact. Molotov was reported to have had reservations about including a country so geographically remote from the socialist camp. In the event of an attack, he pointed out, Albania "was situated right next to a powerful opponent, and we could not provide it with any aid." In his own telling, Khrushchev dismissed this kind of thinking. "Molotov," he shot back, "was Stalin's shadow in his understanding of world politics." Khrushchev, *Memoirs*,3:394.

37. "Një libër i çpuar nga plumbi fashist," *Miqësija,* March 1961, 10–11. Note that this article came out when Soviet-Albanian relations were at a low. As we will see, it was also possible to champion the Soviet-Albanian bond *in spite of* Stalin's successors in Moscow.

38. "Dokumenta të reja të miqësisë shqiptaro-sovjetike," *Miqësija,* February 1957, 19. The home was known to have hosted partisans during the war, and officials also found Communist Party propaganda in the case, suggesting that the materials probably dated from the early 1940s. The archaeological dimension of Soviet involvement in Albania was broader than this. Requests also went out to Moscow to bring experts who could help unearth the country's Illyrian roots. Moreover, there was hope that Moscow might help establish anthropology as a discipline in the country. "Kërkesë qeverisë sovjetike për formimin e ekspeditës së përbashkët arkeollogjike shqiptaro-sovjetike," 29 June 1957; "Relacion mbi zbulimet arkeologjike të viteve të fundit në Shqipëri dhe mbi punën për mbrojtjen e monumenteve të kulturës, n.d., both in AQSH, f. 490, v. 1957, dos. 1133, fl. 16–17, 23.

39. "Protokoll Nr. 43 datë 27/7/1950 i mbledhjes së Byrosë Politike të KQ," 27 July 1950, AQSH, f. 14/AP, OU, v. 1950, dos. 49, fl. 45.

40. "Relacion mbi gjendjen e teksteve shkollore," n.d. [discussed in Politburo meeting on 13 October 1953], AQSH, f. 14/AP, OU, v. 1953, dos. 34, fl. 11–14.

41. "Relacion mbi diskutimin e maketit të historisë së Shqipërisë në Institutin e Historisë pranë Akademisë së Shkencave të B.S. në Moskë," n.d., AMPJ, v. 1958, dos. 63, fl. 38.

42. "Marrëdhëniet midis Republikës Popullore të Shqipërisë me Bashkimin e Republikave Socialiste Sovjetike," dated by hand December 1953, AMPJ, v. 1953, dos. 44, fl. 11–12. See also *Mbi miqësinë shqiptaro-sovjetike (përmbledhje dokumentash e materialesh kushtuar 40 vjetorit të Revolucionit të Madh Socialist të Tetorit)* (Tirana: Universiteti Shtetëror i Tiranës; Instituti i Historisë së P.P.SH; Shoqëria e Miqësisë Shqipëri-B.R.S.S., 1957), 72–76.

43. Michael David-Fox, *Showcasing the Great Experiment: Cultural Diplomacy and Western Visitors to the Soviet Union, 1921–1941* (New York: Oxford University Press, 2011), 9.

44. "Spravki o zarubezhnykh obshchestvakh i kulturnoi sviazi s SSSR," Gosudarstvennyi Arkhiv Rossiiskoi Federatsii (GARF), f. 9576, op. 2, d. 69, ll. 65–66. The large numbers reflected the fact that membership was open, as in the case of Romania, to anyone above a certain age.

45. Julian Chang, "The Mechanics of State Propaganda: The People's Republic of China and the Soviet Union in the 1950s," in *New Perspectives on State Socialism in China,* ed. Timothy Cheek and Tony Saich (Armonk, NY: M.E. Sharpe, 1997), 99.

46. For the North Korean example, see Charles K. Armstrong, *The North Korean Revolution, 1945–1950* (Ithaca, NY: Cornell University Press, 2003), 169–73.

47. "General'nomu sovetu obshchestva druzhby "Albaniia-Sovetskii Soiuz," 27 March 1958, GARF, f. 9576, op. 4, d. 1, l. 85; Albanian embassy (Moscow) to Tirana (Top Secret), 25 April 1958, AMPJ, v. 1958, dos. 61, fl. 2. See also Ragna Boden, *Die Grenzen der Weltmacht: Sowjetische Indonesienpolitik von Stalin bis Brežnev* (Stuttgart: Franz Steiner, 2006), 258; David-Fox, *Showcasing the Great Experiment*, 323. The post-1953 dilemmas around Soviet-Czechoslovak relations are captured in Rachel Applebaum, "The Friendship Project: Socialist Internationalism in the Soviet Union and Czechoslovakia in the 1950s and 1960s," *Slavic Review* 74, no. 3 (Fall 2015): 484–507. On the reorientation in Soviet friendship work, also see Eleonory Gilburd, "The Revival of Soviet Internationalism in the Mid to Late 1950s," in *The Thaw: Soviet Society and Culture During the 1950s and 1960s*, ed. Denis Kozlov and Eleonory Gilburd (Toronto: University of Toronto Press, 2013), 362–401.

48. "Informatsia," n.d., GARF, f. 9576, op. 4, d. 45, l. 200.

49. Victoria de Grazia, *Irresistible Empire: America's Advance through 20th-Century Europe* (Cambridge, MA: Belknap Press of Harvard University Press, 2005); Mary Nolan, *The Transatlantic Century: Europe and America, 1890–2010* (New York: Cambridge University Press, 2012).

50. David-Fox, *Showcasing the Great Experiment*, 16.

51. The telegram, dated 14 November 1945, is contained in GARF, f. 5283, op. 17, d. 8, l. 18.

52. Soviet director Il'ia Kopalin's 1948 documentary feature *Novaia Albaniia* (*New Albania*) depicts a building formerly used by King Zog, now hosting the league. Kopalin, *Novaia Albaniia* (Order of the Red Flag Central Studio of Documentary Films and Committee of Arts and Culture of the People's Republic of Albania, 1948).

53. "Rubrika e Shoqërisë për lidhje kulturale midis Shqipërisë dhe B.R.S.S," *Shqipëri B.R.S.S.*, no. 16, February 1949, 28–31.

54. Central Committee to all party committees, 11 February 1949, AQSH, f. 14/AP, str., Drejtoria Agitacionit e Propagandës (DAP) (Agitation and Propaganda Department), v. 1949, dos. 529, fl. 1. Reports from various localities mentioned public rallies, veterans parades, concerts, and speeches on the feats of the Red Army, which some complained had been lengthy and boring.

55. "Projekt-plan për 70 vjetorin e lindjes së shokut STALIN," n.d.; "Vendim no. 54," 15 November 1949, both in AQSH, f. 14/AP, OU, v. 1949, dos. 63.

56. "Veprimtarija e Shoqërisë për lidhje kulturale me Bashkimin Sovjetik," *Shqipëri B.R.S.S.*, no. 1, August 1947, 41.

57. An accusation that circulated after Spiru's suicide was related to the Soviet practice of sending Albanian visitors to the outer republics. According to this rumor, Spiru had been baffled by the suggestion that he visit Azerbaijan as an example of successful socialist modernization. He was reported to have asked, "What, you think we are Asiatic?" See the notes from the party *aktiv* following the resolution of the Eighth Party Plenum, 13 April 1948, published in Plasari and Malltezi, *Marrëdhëniet shqiptaro-jugosllave 1945–1948*, 446.

58. "Mbledhja e Byrosë të K.C. të Partisë," 4 May 1948, AQSH, f. 14/AP, OU, v. 1948, dos. 83, fl. 17–24.

59. Payroll records from 1950 placed society personnel at thirty-five. These included editors, language instructors, translators, and agitators. By comparison, a budding society for cultural relations with Bulgaria had a staff of two. "Tabela e kategorizimit të punonjësve të Lidhjes Kulturale me B.R.S.S.," 1 February 1950, AQSH, f. 490, v. 1950, dos. 66, fl. 2. In addition to *Miqësija* (name revised to *Miqësia* in 1961), the society also published short-lived journals targeting workers (*Punëtori sovjetik*) and peasants (*Kolkozjani sovjetik*).

60. "Jeta e shoqërisë," *Shqipëri B.R.S.S.*, no. 2, February 1950, 22.

61. Albanian Embassy (Moscow) to Tirana, "Rreth dokumentave të Partisë dhe disa çështjeve të tjera," 25 July 1949, AQSH, f. 14/AP, M-PK(b)BS, v. 1949, dos. 21, fl. 1.

62. "Vendim," 24 August 1951, AQSH, f. 14/AP, OU, v. 1951, dos. 89, fl. 20–21; Albanian Embassy (Bucharest) to Nexhmije Hoxha (Top Secret), 18 September 1951, AMPJ, v.1951, dos. 240, fl. 55; "Promemorje," n.d., AMPJ, v. 1952, dos. 83, fl. 53.

63. Russian Embassy (Tirana), "Zamestiteliu ministra inostrannykh del SSSR tov. Zorinu V. A.," 2 September 1954, RGANI, f. 5, op. 28, d. 153, l. 127. The sentence was underlined by hand in the memo.

64. "Relacion rreth ekspozitës luftës N. Çl.," n.d., AMPJ, v. 1949, dos. 22, fl. 7.

65. Albanian Embassy (Moscow) to Tirana (Secret), 15 January 1953, AMPJ, v. 1953, dos. 26, fl. 1–2. The exhibition, which opened in Moscow in November 1952, was due to travel to Leningrad, Yerevan, Sofia, and Berlin.

66. "Pis'mo predsedatelia pravleniia VOKS A.I. Denisova" (Secret), 7 July 1951; and "Pis'mo D. S. Chuvakhina A. Ia. Vyshinskomu o nedostatkakh v rabote obshchestva druzhby Albaniia-SSSR," 7 November 1951, with explanatory notes, in Volokitina et al., *Vostochnaia Evropa*, 2:561, 643–44.

67. Numbers are derived from extensive screening of articles and published statistics in the issues of the society journal from 1947 to 1960. See also *Kongresi I-rë i Shoqërisë për lidhje kulturale midis R.P. të Shqipërisë dhe B.R.S.S.* (Tirana: Shoqëria për lidhje kulturale midis R.P. të Shqipërisë dhe B.R.S.S., 1948); *Mbi miqësinë shqiptaro-sovjetike*, pp. 310–319; "Spravki o zarubezhnykh obshchestvakh i kulturnoi sviazi s SSSR" ("Obshchestvo druzhby Albanii s Sovetskim Soiuzom"), GARF, f. 9576, op. 2, d. 69, l. 61; "Si punon rrethi jonë i Miqësisë," *Miqësija*, January 1953, 28.

68. "Proçes-verbal," 7 May 1948, and related Council of Ministers documentation, contained in AQSH, f. 490, v. 1948, dos. 23, fl. 1–198.

69. "Raport për analizën e punës n'organizatën e grues të rrethit Kukës," dated by hand 28 December 1950, AQSH, f. 14/AP, str., Drejtoria e Organizimit dhe Inspektimit (OI) (Organization and Inspection Department), v. 1950, dos. 170, fl. 40–44.

70. The low level of education within the propaganda sector was recognized by the Soviet representative. "Zamestiteliu ministra inostrannykh del SSSR tov. Zorinu V.A." (Secret), 2 September 1954, RGANI, f. 5, op. 28, d. 153, l. 126.

71. "Nekotorye sovety albanskim druz'iam" (Top Secret), 24 September 1956, RGANI, f. 5, op. 28, d. 391, l. 189. The figure of the share of workers in the party's membership was underlined in the report.

72. Between 1947 and 1948, party membership increased significantly: from 20,215 in 1947 to 29,950 in 1948, not accounting for party candidates (whose number increased by 5,064). This posed a problem after 1948, when party ranks had to be cleansed from supposed antiparty elements. "Bilanc," AQSH, f. 14/AP, str., Sektori Organo-Instruktiv, v. 1947, dos. 4, fl. 18; "Statistika e P.P.SH.," [December 1948], AQSH, f. 14/AP, str., Drejtori e Organizim-Inspektimit, v. 1948, dos. 445, fl. 1.

73. By September 1959, the share of Central Committee personnel with higher education had risen to 49 percent. Still, when provincial party chiefs and instructors were included, only about 31 percent had a high school education or higher. "Informacion," n.d., AQSH, f. 14/AP, OU, v. 1960, dos. 32, fl. 37.

74. "Me ekipin e shoqërisë në malësitë e Veriut," *Shqipëri B.R.S.S.*, no. 5, May 1950, 26. Films received in the late 1940s included documentaries on Lenin, socialist Hungary, Latvian music, the Russian church, kolkhozes in the Urals, and Alma-Ata. The reels for *Chapaev* (1934) and *Nasreddin v Bukhare* (1943) were reportedly worn out to the point of failure from overuse. Over four hundred Soviet films, documentaries, and newsreels

had made it to Albania by 1950. The statistics are contained in AQSH, f. 513, v. 1950, dos. 18, fl. 18–23.

75. The details of the van (model GZA-651) are contained in GARF, f. 5283, op. 17, d. 26, l. 41; "Dhuratë e çmueshme," *Shqipëri B.R.S.S.*, no. 8, August 1951, 21. In the interwar period, Italian Fascist officials also used projection trucks, modeled on Soviet examples. Ruth Ben-Ghiat, *Fascist Modernities* (Berkeley: University of California Press, 2001), 70–71.

76. "Festivali i filmit sovjetik në fshat," *Miqësija,* September 1956, 27.

77. By 1964, the Friendship Society had nineteen mobile projectors, slightly fewer than half of all such machines in the country. "Relacion për projekt-vendimin 'Mbi kalimin për administrim të autokinemave nga Kinostudio 'Shqipëria e Re' Komiteteve Ekzekutive të K.P. të Rretheve,'" dated by hand 22 August 1964, AQSH, f. 490, v. 1964, dos. 378, fl. 5. See also "Spravka ob obshchestve sovetsko-albanskoi druzhby," n.d., GARF, f. 9576, op. 4, d. 106, l. 202.

78. "Shoqëria e Miqësisë Shqipëri-B.R.S.S. pregatitet për muajin e miqësisë Shqiptaro-Sovietike," *Zëri i Popullit,* 27 July 1951, 1.

79. "Predsedateliu Azerbaidzhanskogo obshchestva kul'turnoi sviazi s zagranitsei," n.d., GARF, f. 9576, op. 4, d. 1, l. 118; "Zav. otdelom sotsialisticheskikh stran Evropy soiuza sovetskikh obshchestv druzhby i kul'turnoi sviazi s zagranitsei," 18 October 1958, GARF, f. 9576, op. 4, d. 2, l. 48; "Java e miqësisë shqiptaro-ukrainase," *Miqësija,* August 1959, 16–17. Azerbaijani officials in turn organized a week in honor of Albania. "Spravka ob obshchestve sovetsko-albanskoi druzhby," n.d., GARF, f. 9576, op. 4, d. 106, l. 196.

80. "Plan zur Anleitung für die Arbeit der Grundeinheiten im Monat der Deutsch-Sowjetischen Freundschaft 1951," Gesellschaft für Deutsch-Sowjetische Freundschaft, Kreisverband Jena, Hoover Institution Archives, box 1.

81. Central Committee to all party committees, 31 July 1950, AQSH, f. 14/AP, DAP, v. 1950, dos. 368, fl. 10–11.

82. "Radio në Shqipëri," n.d., AQSH, f. 509, v. 1952, dos. 2, fl. 41.

83. A government decision on Radio-Difuzioni, dated 21 March 1949, is contained in AQSH, f. 490, v. 1949, dos. 610, fl. 11–16.

84. In 1949, for example, the broadcaster reserved forty minutes per week for Bulgarian music, in addition to a daily fifteen-minute program in the Bulgarian language. "Drejtorisë së Radiopërhapjes së Shtetit," 2 June 1949, AMPJ, v. 1949, dos. 132, fl. 29. Radio Tirana similarly transmitted Romanian music and short sessions on science, industrialization, and metallurgy in Romania. Bucharest radio's broadcasts, on the other hand, included sessions of Albanian folk music and special editions devoted to the arts and culture in socialist Albania. Albanian Mission (Bucharest) to Tirana, 18 July 1951, AMPJ, v. 1951, dos. 244, fl. 19–21.

85. For the purposes of comparing radio broadcasts, I have systematically examined published daily programs in the party newspaper *Zëri i Popullit* for July, August, and September in the 1950s.

86. A notice of a meeting between Deputy Premier Kapo and the Shkodër radio chief, 21 October 1950, is contained in AQSH, f. 490, v. 1950, dos. 1228, fl. 16. No matter how far and wide the society blanketed the country's north, the regime continued to view the region as a holdover of antisocialist resistance and, in certain areas, subversive Catholicism.

87. "Foreign Broadcasting Reception Potential in Albania" (Secret), 4 February 1954, CIA-RDP79-01093A000400130001-0. Western daily broadcasts to Albania, however, did not exceed thirty minutes, compared with those in Moscow and Belgrade, which transmitted a full hour. Richardson to Dunning (Strictly Confidential), 14 June 1961, Radio Free Europe/Radio Liberty corporate records, Hoover Institution Archives, box 1665.

88. Petraq Kolevica, *Arkitektura dhe diktatura* (Tirana: Logoreci, 2004), 40–41.

89. Ibid, 41. Years later, when planning a post office building, he would be told that the building needed to be located in the city center. After all, "didn't Moscow have the post office in the city center?" (90).

90. "Ideologicheskoe rukovodstvo Albanskoi Partii Truda" (Secret), 30 June 1954, RGANI, f. 5, op. 28, d. 153, l. 54.

91. "Relacion mbi profesorët dhe ingjinierët e huaj që kanë punuar në sektorin e arësimit," dated by hand 21 February 1953, AQSH, f. 511, v. 1953, dos. 83, fl. 2; "Universiteti—simbol i miqësisë jetëdhënëse shqiptaro-sovjetike," *Miqësija,* October 1957, 24–25.

92. Dmitri Shostakovich, *Testimony: The Memoirs of Dmitri Shostakovich,* ed. Solomon Volkov (New York: Limelight, 2004), 173; Kolevica, *Arkitektura dhe diktatura,* 42.

93. Detailed lists of foreign language speakers, based on 1946 party correspondence, are contained in AQSH, f. 14/AP, str., v. 1946, dos. 111, fl. 1–55. Unsurprisingly, the number of Italian speakers was especially high in Shkodër, the center of Albanian Catholicism.

94. "Zapis' besedy I. V. Stalina s E. Khodzhei o nekotorykh vneshniepoliticheskikh i vnutrennikh problemakh Albanii" (Top Secret), 2 April 1951, in Volokitina et al., *Vostochnaia Evropa,* 2:509.

95. "Mbi metodën rusisht" (Secret), dated by hand 31 March 1951, AMPJ, v. 1951, dos. 42, fl. 2; Nina Potapova, *Gjuha ruse (Metodë)* (Moscow: Shtëpia Botonjëse e Letërsisë në Gjuhë të Huaja, 1951), 3. The two student translators were Llazar Siliqi and Arben Puto. Both had long careers in Albania: the first as a poet, the second as a scholar of diplomacy.

96. "Jeta e shoqërisë," *Shqipëri B.R.S.S.,* no. 4, April 1950, 22.

97. "Të mësojmë gjuhën ruse," *Miqësija,* September 1953, 29.

98. "Raport mbi gjendjen e Shoqërisë së Miqësisë Shqipëri-Bashkimi Sovjetik," n.d. [discussed in Politburo on 4 August 1955], AQSH, f. 14/AP, OU, v. 1955, dos. 27, fl. 52.

99. "Informacion mbi zbatimin e vendimit të Byrosë Politike mbi punën e Shoqërisë së Miqësisë Shqipëri-Bashkimi Sovjetik," n.d., AQSH, f. 14/AP, OU, v. 1956, dos. 62, fl. 6.

100. On society measures: "Zapis' besedy s general'nym sekretarem obshchestva druzhby 'Albaniia-SSSR' Nasho Natanaili," 18 and 25 January 1961, GARF, f. 9576, op. 4, d. 106, l. 72.

101. "Mbledhja e Byrosë të K.C. të Partisë," 4 May 1948, AQSH, f. 14/AP, OU, v. 1948, dos. 83, fl. 22; "Relacion mbi profesorët dhe ingjinierët e huaj që kanë punuar në sektorin e arësimit," 21 February 1953, AQSH, f. 511, v. 1953, dos. 83, fl. 1–3. The last memo also noted the activities of a number of Yugoslav instructors, who, it charged, undermined the work of their Soviet colleagues and did not benefit the schools. ("They have sabotaged them" was handwritten under the text.)

102. "Lista e teknikëve—specialistave të huaj që kanë ardhur në bazë të marrëdhanjeve për bashëpunimin shkencor-teknik," n.d., AQSH, f. 511, v. 1953, dos. 83, fl.73–74.

103. "Vendim No. 237 mbi marrjen e masave për futjen e gjuhës ruse në shkollat 7-vjeçare," 18 August 1953, AQSH, f. 490, v. 1953, dos. 1020, fl. 2.

104. "Raport mbi gjendjen e shoqërisë së Miqësisë Shqipëri-Bashkimi Sovjetik," fl. 56–57.

105. Meliha, a member of the socialist brigade in the tobacco factory in Shkodër, was said to have fifteen Soviet pen pals. One of her letters was published in the Friendship Society's journal. "Letër Zina Bishininoj, Stravropol B.R.S.S.," *Miqësija,* October 1961, 8.

106. "Zamestiteliu ministra inostrannykh del SSSR tov. Zorinu V. A." (Secret), 2 September 1954, RGANI, f. 5, op. 28, d. 153, l. 123.

107. "Vendim Nr. 355 mbi punën e Shoqërisë së Miqësisë 'Shqipëri-Bashkimi Sovjetik' dhe masat për përmirësimin e saj," 4 August 1955, AQSH, f. 14/AP, OU, v. 1955, dos. 27, fl. 77 verso.

108. The Albanian party sent a request to Prague for help with the publication of Stalin's works. "Protokoll i mbledhjes së Byrosë Politike të KQ," 27 July 1950, AQSH, f. 14/AP, OU, v. 1950, dos. 49, fl. 45. The request went out to Prague in August: Tirana (Spahiu) to Prague (KSČ), 18 August 1950, Národní archiv (NA), KSČ-ÚV-100/3, sv. 23, a.j. 82, 34.

109. Tirana (Belishova) to SED Central Committee, 22 September 1956, in Bundesarchiv (BArch), Stiftung Archiv der Parteien und Massenorganisationen der DDR (SAPMO-BArch) DY 30/IV 2/20/94, 76; "Relacion mbi zbatimin e pllanit të botimit të veprave të klasikëve të Marksizëm-Leninizmit për vitin 1955 dhe mbi pllanin për vitin 1956," n.d., AQSH, f. 14/AP, OU, v. 1956, dos. 62.

110. The publication of Lenin's complete works was finalized in 1962. "Relacion. Mbi përkthimin dhe botimin e veprave të K. Marksit dhe F. Engelsit në gjuhën shqipe dhe mbi masat që duhet të merren për këtë punë" [addressed to Enver Hoxha], dated by hand 15 July 1961, f. 14/AP, OU, v. 1961, dos. 55, fl. 136. By 1957, 26 newspaper titles and 350 journals had entered the country, most of them published in the Soviet Union. Translations included ideological texts but also specialized journals (agriculture, science, youth, and construction). "Në vendin tonë vijnë 19861 copë gazeta e revista," Miqësija, May 1957, 14; "Dopolnitel'nyi spisok," n.d., GARF, f. 9576, op. 4, d. 1, l. 34.

111. The protocols presented to the Central Committee secretariat and the discussions from 9 November 1953 are contained in AQSH, f. 14/AP, OU, v. 1953, dos. 73, esp. fl. 25–30, 116.

112. For details, see memos on foreign delegations (from September 1955), contained in AQSH, f. 490, v. 1955, dos. 752, esp. fl. 4–6.

113. Transcript of Politburo meeting, 27 June 1955, AQSH, f. 14/AP, OU, v. 1955, dos. 22, fl. 175.

114. DAP report to Politburo, n.d., AQSH, f. 14/AP, OU, v. 1955, dos. 27, fl. 53–55. One year later, Soviet representatives confirmed that Albanian ideological work lagged behind. "O khode vypodneniia reshenii aprel'skogo 1955 g. Plenuma TsK APT po voprosu ideologicheskoi raboty partii," 28 June 1956 (Secret), RGANI, f. 5, op. 28, d. 391, l. 109.

115. Information to the Central Committee secretariat from the Friendship Society, and the DAP [secretariat meeting of 3 February 1956], AQSH, f. 14/AP, OU, v. 1956, dos. 62.

116. Emboldened by post-Stalin developments in the Soviet Union, Jakova and Spahiu challenged the official party history and something that no one dared discuss publically—Hoxha's cult of personality. A bitter irony, however, was the fact that both men were implicated in the anti-Yugoslav hysteria of the late 1940s. Ana Lalaj, "Detanta e parë dhe Shqipëria," Studime historike 3–4 (2009): 337–43.

117. "Proçes-verbal i mbledhjes së Byrosë Politike të Komitetit Qendror të P.P.SH," 4 August 1955, AQSH, f. 14/AP, OU, v. 1955, dos. 27, esp. fl. 96–97.

118. On the "normalization" years with Yugoslavia: Svetozar Rajak, Yugoslavia and the Soviet Union in the Early Cold War: Reconciliation, Comradeship, Confrontation, 1953–1957 (New York: Routledge, 2011).

119. Elidor Mëhilli, "Defying De-Stalinization: Albania's 1956," Journal of Cold War Studies 13, no. 4 (Fall 2011): 4–56.

120. In the Soviet Union, for example, there were some forty-five party organizations for students and officers in training. "Raport mbi përfundimin e zgjedhjeve në organizatat bazë të partisë me studentat dhe kursantët civila dhe ushtarakë në Bashkimin Sovjetik," 15 January 1956, AQSH, f. 14/AP, str., DA, v. 1956, dos. 177, fl. 45. In one example, officials told an Albanian male student not to date an Eastern German, whom they deemed "immoral." Albanian Mission (Berlin) to Leipzig student organization, 15 September 1956, AQSH, f. 511, v. 1956, dos. 25, fl. 63.

121. "Komunikatë operative no. 79" (Top Secret), 19 October 1953, AMPB, v. 1953, dos. 15, fl. 53.

122. "Buletin informativ i datës 30.VII.1953. Sektori K.P. e K.P. Jashtme" (Top Secret), 30 July 1953, AMPB, v. 1953, dos. 14, fl. 103.

123. Interior Ministry records from 1953–54 contain references to letters detailing hardships, complaining about the price of corn, sugar, cooking oil, and fantasizing about living in a capitalist country. Examples: "Buletin informativ i datës 3.7.1953. Sektori K.P. e K.P. Jashtme" (Top Secret), 3 July 1953, AMPB, v. 1953, dos. 14, fl. 26; "Komunikatë operative no. 114" (Top Secret), 25 November 1953, AMPB, v. 1953, dos. 15, fl. 296; "Komunikatë operative no. 42" (Top Secret), 11 February 1954, AMPB, v. 1954, dos. 16, fl. 189.

124. "TsK KPSS," n.d. [August 1958], RGANI, f. 5, op. 35, d. 83, l. 47.

125. "Informacion mbi disa çfaqje të shtrembëra të disa studentëve tonë në Poloni," 30 May 1957, AQSH, f. 14/AP, str., DA, v.1956, dos. 179, fl. 69–72. The total number of students involved seems small, but consider that in 1958, for every three students enrolled at the state university in Tirana, one was enrolled in a university in another socialist country. This helps explains the party's preoccupation. "Zgjerimi dhe zhvillimi i mëtejshëm i rrjetit të shkollave," n.d., AQSH, f. 511, v. 1958, dos. 5, fl. 1–1 verso.

126. "Relacion mbi gjendjen e studentave jashtë shtetit dhe mbi masat që duhen marrë për përmirësimin e punës me ta," n.d., AQSH, f.14/AP, OU, v. 1958, dos. 34, fl. 5–17 (at fl. 10). Students were reprimanded for dating "suspicious" foreigners, including partners with relatives in the capitalist West. Penalties for the students were written by hand on top of their printed biographical summaries. "Projekt-vendim mbi marje masash për disa studenta që studjojnë jashtë shtetit," n.d., AQSH, f. 14/AP, OU, v. 1958, dos. 34, fl. 18–31. During the 1957–58 academic year, twenty-seven students had their scholarships revoked. "Vendim Nr. 272, mbi gjendjen e studentave jashtë shtetit dhe masat që duhen marrë për përmirësimin e punës me ta," 14 August 1958, AQSH, f. 14/AP, OU, v. 1958, dos. 34, fl. 33–36.

127. "Shënime të mbajtura në mbledhjen e Sekretariatit të Komitetit Qendror" (Secret), 14 August 1958, AQSH, f. 14/AP, OU, v. 1958, dos. 34, fl. 77. The party secretariat asked for more political education.

128. "Bericht über die Betreuung der Genossinnen Hodscha und Shehu während ihres Aufenthaltes in der DDR mit der albanischen Partei- und Regierungsdelegation vom 7.—11.1.59," 13 January 1959, Politisches Archiv des Auswärtigen Amts—Ministerium für Auswärtige Angelegenheiten (PA AA, MfAA), A 9.474, 68–69.

129. US Embassy (Athens) to Department of State, 22 December 1958, in *Records of the Department of State Relating to the Internal Affairs of Albania, 1955–1959*, record group 59, decimal file 767, roll 1 (Wilmington, DE: Scholarly Resources, 2002?).

130. "Ismail Kadaré, The Art of Fiction No. 153," *Paris Review* 147 (Summer 1998): 204.

131. Kadare's poems were published in Russian as *Lirika* (Moscow: Izdatel'stvo inostrannoi literatury, 1961).

132. Ismail Kadare, *Ftesë në studio* (Tirana: Naim Frashëri, 1990), 151.

133. David Bellos, introduction to *Twilight of the Eastern Gods*, by Ismail Kadare, trans. David Bellos from the French of Jusuf Vrioni (New York: Grove Press, 2014), x.

134. Vasilii Tiukhin,"Ismail' Kadare: 'Mne snilas' Moskva,'" *Sankt-Peterburgskie vedomosti*, 21 February 2007, 4.

135. *Le crépuscule des dieux de la steppe* (Paris: Fayard, 1981). See also Éric Faye's preface, originally published in 1997, reprinted in the Albanian edition: Ismail Kadare, *Muzgu i perëndive të stepës* (Tirana: Onufri, 2006), 7–10.

136. On the novel and Kadare's Moscow years, see "La Vérité des souterrains: Ismaïl Kadaré avec Stéphane Courtois," in Shaban Sinani, Ismaïl Kadaré, and Stéphane Courtois, *La dossier Kadaré* (Paris: Odile Jacob, 2006), 141–206.

137. Kadare, *Twilight of the Eastern Gods*, 43.

138. Ibid., 42.

139. Faye, preface, *Muzgu i perëndive të stepës*, 8.

140. Philippe Delaroche, "Ismail Kadaré: 'La littérature et la vie sont des mondes différents, deux mondes en lutte,'" *Lire*, no. 380 (November 2009): 99.

141. Czesław Miłosz, *The Captive Mind* (New York: Vintage, 1990), xii.

142. Author interview with Ismail Kadare, 18 July 2008, Mal i Robit, Albania.

143. Delaroche, "Ismail Kadaré," 98.

144. Kadare, *Ftesë në studio*, 145; Delaroche, "Ismail Kadaré," 99; Peter Morgan, *Ismail Kadare: The Writer and the Dictatorship, 1957–1990* (London: Legenda, 2010), 52. Years later, Helena Kadare also discovered the Soviet literary world of the late 1950s, though indirectly, by reading her husband's Moscow diary. See her *Kohë e pamjaftueshme: Kujtime* (Tirana: Onufri, 2011), esp. 54–58.

145. Delaroche, "Ismail Kadaré," 99. In 1960 Moscow had a population closer to six million.

3. THE METHODS OF SOCIALISM

1. Ladislav Mňačko, "When Liri Grows Up," *New Central European Observer* 4, no. 1 (1951): 287. The author also published a travelogue: *Albanská reportáž* (Bratislava: Pravda, 1950).

2. Handwritten letter [Hoxha in Moscow to Tirana], 6 April 1949, AQSH, f. 14/AP, M-PK(b)BS, v. 1949, dos. 19, fl. 1–5.

3. Typed notes on conversation between Hoxha and Stalin in Sukhumi, n.d. [24 November 1949], AQSH, f. 14/AP, M-PK(b)BS, v. 1949, dos. 20. For the issues Hoxha brought up with Stalin (including Greece and Kosovë/Kosovo): "Tsentral'nomu Komitetu Partii Bol'shevikov," 16 November 1949, in Volokitina et al., *Sovetskii factor*, 2:210–14. The theme of modesty runs through the history of Stalin's cult of personality, as it does with Hoxha's. The more the Albanian party boss seemed to resist his inferiors' efforts to build a cult around him, the greater the cult became. Jan Plamper, *The Stalin Cult: A Study in the Alchemy of Power* (New Haven: Yale University Press, 2012), 119ff.

4. "Moskë, më 2 prill ora 10 1/2, orë e Moskës–Mbrëmje" [meeting with Stalin, Molotov, Beria, Malenkov, and Bulganin], 2 April 1951, AQSH, f. 14/AP, M-PK(b)BS, v. 1951, dos. 15; "Zapis' besedy I.V. Stalina s E. Khodzhei o nekotorykh vneshniepoliticheskikh i vnutrennikh problemakh Albanii" (Top Secret), 2 April 1951, in Volokitina et al., *Vostochnaia Evropa*, 2:508.

5. "Pjekje me Mikojanin Kremlin 3 prill ora 10," 3 April 1951, AQSH, f. 14/AP, M-PK(b)BS, v. 1951, dos. 15.

6. In line with the Soviet requests, Hoxha gave up his government positions as prime minister, minister of defense, and minister of foreign affairs. He stayed, however, at the party helm. "Protokoll no. 17 i mbledhjes së Byrosë Politike të KQ," and "Protokoll no. 18 i mbledhjes së Byrosë Politike të KQ," 20–22 June 1953, printed in Ana Lalaj, "1953—udhëheqësit e rinj sovjetikë paralajmërojnë: ose ndryshime ose katastrofë," *Studime Historike* 1–2 (2010): 227. For the Soviet perspective: Mark Kramer, "The Early Post-Stalin Succession Struggle and Upheavals in East-Central Europe: Internal-External Linkages in Soviet Policy Making (Part 1)," *Journal of Cold War Studies* 1, no. 1 (Winter 1999): 3–55.

7. "Komunikatë no. 41" (Secret), 28 July 1953, AMPB, v. 1953, dos. 14, fl. 84. The clarification about Shehu, the security police chief at the time, is included in the surveillance report.

8. Access to ration cards depended on the category under which one's activity fell: there were ordinary workers, "light" workers, "heavy" workers, and special "heavy" workers, corresponding, in government terms, to the difficulty and intensity of the work involved.

9. On continued Soviet criticism: "Proçes-verbal no. 1 i mbledhjes së Byrosë Politike të K.Q. të P.P.SH.," 4 January 1954, AQSH, f. 14/AP, OU, v. 1954, dos. 4, fl. 1–21.

10. Stephen Kotkin, *Magnetic Mountain: Stalinism as a Civilization* (Berkeley: University of California Press, 1995), 279.

11. Two examples are Jochen Hellbeck, *Revolution on my Mind: Writing a Diary under Stalin* (Cambridge, MA: Harvard University Press, 2009), and Igal Halfin, *Terror in my Soul: Communist Autobiography on Trial* (Cambridge, MA: Harvard University Press, 2003).

12. "Bericht über das IV. Quartal 1952," n.d., PA AA, MfAA, A 4.516, 136.

13. "Si e kanë penguar dhe sa e kanë damtuar trockistat jugosllavë industrinë t'onë," *Bashkimi*, 7 January 1949, 2.

14. "Mbi nevojat urgjente për Fab. Sheqerit Korçë" (Res.), 18 July 1948 [corrected by hand], AMPJ, v. 1948, dos. 23, fl. 21.

15. On the land reclamation projects, see Dean S. Rugg, "Communist Legacies in the Albanian Landscape," *Geographical Review* 84, no. 1 (January 1994): 59–73.

16. "Këneta lulëzon, 1944–1959" *Miqësija*, August 1959, 14.

17. "Kombinati i Tekstilit 'Stalin' vepër e madhe e planit dyvjeçar," *Bashkimi*, 19 July 1950, 3. One motorist also published a poem about the construction of the textile works, describing workers toiling "as one body," like "fast arrows," night and day, to build a structure that would carry the name of "the great genius."

18. "Kombinati 'Stalin' po ndërtohet me sukses," *Bashkimi*, 2 December 1950, 3. Another short chronicle ("Stalin Is Life") pointed out that construction workers came from all over the country. They included a veteran donning a military coat, who now worked as a concrete mixer operator. "The blood of his comrades," the article explained, "was not in vain. Their wish has been fulfilled. Albania is free, just as the martyrs dreamed of it." "Stalini është jeta," *Bashkimi*, 27 October 1950, 2.

19. "Relacion mbi gjendjen dhe jetesën e punonjësve të ndërtimit dhe masat që mejtojmë të marim," dated by hand 8 June 1954, AQSH, f. 499, v. 1954, dos. 4, fl. 2.

20. "O nekotorykh voprosakh kooperirovaniia sel'skogo khoziaistva v evropeiskikh stranakh narodnoi demokratii" (Top Secret) [forwarded to Khrushchev], 19 August 1955, RGANI, f. 5, op. 28, d. 286, l. 34. A 1980s textbook written by two of the country's foremost socialist-era historians admitted that agriculture had initially not been a priority, while "the goals for industry also always surpassed realistic possibilities." Stefanaq Pollo and Arben Puto, *The History of Albania: From Its Origins to the Present Day* (London: Routledge & Kegan Paul, 1981), 267.

21. On labor force shortages and the related economic and political stakes: "Protokoll no. 31 i mbledhjes së Byrosë Politike të KQ të P.P.SH.," 3 October 1952, AQSH, f. 14/AP, OU, v. 1952, dos. 56, fl. 72ff.

22. The Central Committee secretariat meeting protocol, dated 23 February 1953, is contained in AQSH, f. 14/AP, v. 1953, OU, dos. 47, fl. 116.

23. To mark the occasion, Hoxha asked Moscow to send the Lenin Prize–winning director of the Trekhgornaia manufaktura, A. A. Sever'ianova. Alexei Kosygin, minister of light industry at the time, did not like the idea. Sever'ianova's husband had been punished in 1937, and she managed to travel abroad only after the Twentieth Soviet Party Congress. "Pis'mo V.G. Grigor'iana M. A. Suslovu o netselesoobraznosti poezdki v Albaniiu direktora kombinata 'Trekhgornaia manufaktura' A. A. Sever'ianovoi" (Secret), 20 September 1951, in Volokitina et al., *Vostochnaia Evropa*, 2:620–21. A Lenin Prize–winning Stakhanovite from Trekhgornaia manufaktura visited in 1953. "Mysafirë të dashur," *Miqësija*, September 1953, 11.

24. Tirana to Moscow (Top Secret), 14 February 1952, AMPJ, v. 1952, dos. 19/1, fl. 11.

25. "Kombinati i Tekstilit 'Stalin' vepër e madhe e planit dyvjeçar," *Bashkimi*, 19 July 1950, 3.

26. Security police operatives kept a close eye on the pace of production and reported the problems to the security chief. "Komunikatë operative no. 84" (Top Secret), 25 March 1954, AMPB, v. 1954, dos. 16, fl. 390.

27. An inspection report at the Stalin textile complex, dated 26 July 1950, is contained in AQSH, f. 499, v. 1950, dos. 190, fl. 39.

28. For example, see a memorandum dated 6 September 1950, contained in AQSH, f. 499, v. 1950, dos. 291, fl. 1–2.

29. "Vendim mbi mbarimin e Kombinatit Tekstilit Stalin no. 106," 8 February 1951, AQSH, f. 499, v. 1951, dos. 363, fl. 1–2.

30. Foreign Trade Ministry to the Office of the Prime Minister and the Ministry of Foreign Affairs, 12 September 1950, AQSH, f. 490, v. 1950, dos. 1435, fl. 1.

31. Albanian Mission (Moscow) to Tirana (Top Secret), 30 September 1950, AMPJ, v. 1950, dos. 31, fl. 74.

32. Arkadii Perventsev, "The New Albania on the Road to Socialism," *VOKS Bulletin* 2 (1953): 135.

33. *Dimitrovgrad* (Sofia: Nauka i iskustvo, 1959).

34. "Relacion mbi përmirësimin e konditave kulturalo-jetësore të punonjësve të Kombinatit Tekst. 'Stalin,'" forwarded 11 October 1952, and the response: "Vrejtje mbi projekt vendimin për përmirësimin e konditave kulturale dhe strehimit në Komb. Tekst. Stalin," 15 October 1952, both inAQSH, f. 499, v. 1952, dos. 351, fl. 6–7 verso.

35. "Relacion mbi ngritjen e banesave dy katëshe në Kombinatin e Tekstilit 'Stalin,'" 5 June 1953, AQSH, f. 490, v. 1953, dos. 603, fl. 1–2. The problem was taken up in a government meeting, where officials argued over the proper materials for the housing structures. The discussion, dated 9 June 1953, is contained in AQSH, f. 490, v. 1953, dos. 600, fl. 5–7.

36. "Relacjon mbi kontrollin punimeve në banesat A+M+B me tulla dhe 2A me blloqe ne Kombinatin e Tekstilit Stalin" [signed Ark. Skënder Luarasi and Ingj. Myzafer Dragoti], 2 March 1954, AQSH, f. 499, v. 1955, dos. 326, fl. 1. Another report mentioned housing units with no windows. "Relacion mbi realizimin e planit si 8 mujor në ndërtesat e banimit,"n.d., AQSH, f. 499, v. 1955, dos. 333, fl. 17.

37. "Kombinati i Tekstilit 'Stalin' vepër e madhe e planit dyvjeçar," *Bashkimi*, 19 July 1950, 3.

38. "Relacion mbi gjendjen dhe jetesën e punonjësve të ndërtimit dhe masat që mejtojmë të marim," dated by hand 8 June 1954, AQSH, f. 499, v. 1954, dos. 4, fl. 1–5; "Relacjon mbi zbatimin e vendimit të Byros Politike të Komitet Qendror të P.P. Shqipërisë 'mbi gjendjen dhe trajtimin e punonjësve të ndërtimit,'" n.d., AQSH, f. 499, v. 1955, dos. 273, fl. 17–20.

39. "Average Day of Average Tirana Factory Worker: Document, Price, Transportation Information/Obligatory Labor and Political Meetings" (Confidential), 8 February 1954, CREST, CIA-RDP80-00809A000500380217-7.

40. "Informacion. Mbi zbatimin e Vendimit Këshillit Ministrave no. 1096 datë 28/12/950 lidhur me sigurimin e shëndetit të punonjësve," dated by hand 21 July 1958, and "Akt kontroll," dated by hand 27 July 1958, both in AQSH, f. 491, v. 1958, dos. 146, fl. 8–10.

41. The Durrës local construction enterprise, for example, which consisted of 340 workers, owned its own cows and benefited from close ties to the consumer enterprise. Hence it enjoyed better provision of foodstuffs. "Analizë e gjendjes hygjenike shëndetësore të punonjësve të Ndërmarrjes Lokale Ndërtimit qarkut Durrës," n.d., AQSH, f. 499, v. 1955, dos. 273, fl. 39–40.

42. "Relacjon mbi zbatimin e vendimit të Byros Politike," n.d., AQSH, f. 499, v. 1955, dos. 273, fl. 21–23.

43. "Në qytetin e Tekstilit," *Miqësija*, June 1959, 8–9.

44. "Kombinati i Tekstilit Stalin," *Shqipëri B.R.S.S.*, no. 10–11, October-November 1951, 20–21. In Poland, similarly, authorities boasted of breaking social taboos but still pushed

women toward "gendered" work (spinning, weaving, sewing). A more reliable path to social advancement was to surpass norms. Malgorzata Fidelis, *Women, Communism, and Industrialization in Postwar Poland* (New York: Cambridge University Press, 2010), 78–79.

45. Mňačko, "When Liri Grows Up," 287.

46. Lev Pavlovich Sukacev typescript: "Soldier under Three Flags: The Personal Memoirs of Lev Pavlovich Sukacev," Hoover Institution Archives, box 1, 125–26 (emphasis in original).

47. Georgy Gulia, "Soviet Union's Friends Abroad. Albania, September 1952 (Travel Notes)," *VOKS Bulletin* 1 (January–February 1953): 77.

48. For attempts to co-opt the religious committees: "Zapis' besedy s E. Khodzhei o khode partkonferentsii na mestakh o polozhenii pravoslavnoi tserkvi v Albanii, o protsesse nad gruppoi K. Dzodze i dr." (Secret), 20 May 1949, and "Zapis' besedy s E. Khodzhei o vstrechakh s deiateliami pravoslavnoi, musul'manskoi i katolicheskoi tserkvei o vyborakh v sel'skoi mestnosti" (Secret), 8 June 1949, both in Volokitina et al., *Vostochnaia Evropa*, 2:120–23, 141–44.

49. "Monatsbericht für Juli," 1 August 1952, PA AA, MfAA, A 4.516, 172–76.

50. US Embassy (Rome) to Department of State (Confidential), 16 September 1958, in *Records of the Department of State Relating to the Internal Affairs of Albania, 1955–1959*. record group 59, decimal file 767 (Wilmington, DE: Scholarly Resources, 2002?).

51. For an interpretation of the unintended outcomes of this labor push in the Soviet Union, see Lewis H. Siegelbaum, *Stakhanovism and the Politics of Productivity in the USSR, 1935–1941* (New York: Cambridge University Press, 1988). For the Eastern bloc: Applebaum, *Iron Curtain*, 318ff.; Padraic Kenney, *Rebuilding Poland: Workers and Communists, 1945–1950* (Ithaca: Cornell University Press, 1997), 237–86; Naimark, *The Russians in Germany*, 198–204; Georgi Markov, *The Truth That Killed* (New York: Ticknor & Fields, 1984), 7. Rather than interpreting chaos or resentment as supposed state failures, Katherine Lebow powerfully shows how Stalinist rhetoric and mobilization "helped shape new ways of talking, thinking, and acting about work and citizenship." Katherine Lebow, *Unfinished Utopia: Nowa Huta, Stalinism, and Polish Society, 1949–56* (Ithaca: Cornell University Press, 2013), 76.

52. "Vendim no. 601," 11 August 1950, AQSH, f. 490, v. 1950, dos. 660, fl. 1; "Në rrugën e stahanovistëve sovjetikë," *Zëri i Popullit*, 2 July 1952, 1; Agron Frashëri, "One Day in Albania," *New Central European Observer* 4, no. 23 (1951): 365.

53. Office of the Prime Minister, untitled circular to ministries and executive committees (Secret), 31 January 1951, AQSH, f. 499, v. 1951, dos. 147, fl. 1–2.

54. One front-ranking construction brigade at the Stalin textile complex was found to have made up hours of work. The investigative report to the Office of the General Prosecutor, dated 29 April 1950, is contained in AQSH, f. 499, v. 1950, dos. 190, fl. 37.

55. Was *copying* Soviet methods sufficient for prizes? Or should Albanian workers also be expected to come up with their innovations? Such questions came up in discussions of the Presidium of the Council of Ministers in 1953. This emphasis on workplace innovation, in fact, persisted long after Albania broke with the Soviet Union, meaning that it did not depend on the Soviet Union to be sustainable. Protocols of high-level government discussions from 1953 are contained in AQSH, f. 490, v. 1953, dos. 706, esp. fl. 73–74.

56. "Rregullore mbi konditat dhe mënyrën e shpalljes së Stahanovistave," *Zëri i Popullit*, 1 July 1952, 3.

57. "Raport—justifikues," n.d., AQSH, f. 490, v. 1950, dos. 660, fl. 3.

58. Donald A. Filtzer, *Soviet Workers and Late Stalinism: Labour and the Restoration of the Stalinist System after World War II* (Cambridge: Cambridge University Press, 2002), 8.

59. Inaugurated in 1948, the Enver Machine Works stood on the foundation of engineering plants built by Italian FIAT in 1939. (Workers kept calling one department by its Italian name, *ufficio pianificazione.*) After the war, authorities finished the project according to the original Italian specifications but installed equipment received from formerly private plants and, according to some accounts, German machines received by way of Yugoslavia. The first director was a man by the name of Artion Spartak, who had reportedly left Albania in the 1920s, settled in the Soviet Union, and joined the party there. He then supervised the adoption of Soviet work methods in Tirana.

60. "Konferenca nacionale e tornitorëve për prerjen e shpejtë të metalit," *Shqipëri B.R.R.S.,* no. 4, April 1951, 29. Bykov also popped up elsewhere in the Eastern bloc. The East German artist Hermann Bruse, for example, immortalized him in a 1951–52 painting titled *Pavel Bykov—Teacher of German Workers,* which depicted the Soviet master advising German counterparts. "Fokus DDR," 7 June–25 November 2012, Deutsches Historisches Museum, Berlin.

61. "Punojmë për t'u bërë 'uzinë stahanoviste,'" *Miqësija,* February 1952, 9.

62. "The Enver Hoxha Machine Works" (Secret), 8 October 1952, CIA-RDP82-00457 R014200050008-5.

63. The October 1952 US intelligence report cited above, for example, pointed out that a special brigade at the plant had been set up by an Italian, who might be replaced by "an Albanian specialist trained in the U.S.S.R. or Czechoslovakia."

64. "Muhanovi në uzinën 'Enver,'" *Miqësija,* August–September 1952, 12.

65. A. Tkachenko "Golos Druzhby," *Pravda,* 10 October 1953, 3.

66. "Si u bana Stahanoviste," *Miqësija,* August–September 1952, 23.

67. "Në konferencën e luftëtarëve pararojë të pesëvjeçarit," *Miqësija,* July 1953, 8. Two years earlier, the rate of those working *me norma* reportedly stood at 80 percent, but the minister insisted that the rate ought to be 100 percent. It was unclear how to achieve this quickly, since it was not possible to establish norms for work routines employed for the first time. An undated memo on Soviet-style work norms is contained in AQSH, f. 499, v. 1951, dos. 282, fl. 64–65.

68. "Protokoll Nr. 17 i mbledhjes së Byrosë Politike të K.Q. të P.P.SH.," 16 June 1953, AQSH, f. 14/AP, OU, v. 1953, dos. 22, fl. 46.

69. Examples: "Udhëzim. Mbi aplikimin e metodave Sovjetike në Ndërtim," n.d.; "Akt-kontroll," n.d. [May 1953], both in AQSH, f. 499, v. 1953, dos. 92, fl. 4–6, 9–10.

70. An untitled and undated memo is contained in AQSH, f. 490, v. 1955, dos. 1039, fl. 99.

71. The Friendship Society's journal routinely published letters from farmers and workers—complete with their portraits—attesting to the value of Soviet techniques. In an early example, it showcased the cotton-gathering techniques of the Soviet hero Basti Bagirova, author of *How I Planted and Gathered In My Cotton Crop,* and the Albanian women who had emulated her. "Arritëm suksese sepse aplikuam metodën e Bastia Bagirovës," *Miqësija,* January 1952, n.p.

72. Tirana Party Committee memorandum on activities carried out during the Friendship Month with the Soviet Union, dated by hand 25 November 1950, AQSH, f. 14/AP, DAP, v. 1950, dos. 368, fl. 31.

73. "Metoda 'Kafarov' një fitore e madhe e këtij viti për punëtorët tonë të naftës," *Bashkimi,* 19 December 1950, 3.

74. "Bericht über das IV. Quartal 1953," n.d., PA AA, MfAA, A 4.516, 138.

75. Notes from a meeting between Deputy Premier Kapo and Minister of Justice Konomi, dated 6 September 1950, are contained in AQSH, f. 490, v. 1950, dos. 1228, fl. 13; for the additional references to Soviet advice, fl. 19, 55.

76. Notes from a meeting between Deputy Premier Kapo and General Prosecutor Floqi, dated 6 December 1950, are contained in AQSH, f. 490, v. 1950, dos. 1228, fl. 92.

77. "Relacion për fjalët dhe emrat e huaja që të shkruhen ashtu siç lexohen," n.d. [1951]; "Vendim no. 670," 24 August 1951, AQSH, f. 14/AP, OU, v. 1951, dos. 89, fl. 14, 16.

78. A survey of cultural politics between 1945 and 1950 is contained in AQSH, f. 513, v. 1950, dos. 18, fl. 2.

79. See a Council of Ministers meeting protocol, dated 18 May 1950, contained in AQSH, f. 490, v. 1950, dos. 227, fl. 1–22.

80. On the Soviet personnel in Maliq: memorandum dated by hand 8 January 1951; National Building Enterprise to Ministry of Construction, 3 July 1951; National Building Enterprise memorandum, 5 May 1951, all in AQSH, f. 499, v. 1951, dos. 160, fl. 3, 14, 29. The provision of separate facilities for foreign specialists continued in later years. See "Soviets in Albania" (Secret), 27 January 1955, CREST, CIA-RDP80-00810A005600130007-2.

81. "Relacion mbi bisedimet që pata me shokët sovjetikë të Kombinatit Naftës më 25 dhe 26 dhjetor 1952," 2 January 1953, AQSH, f. 14/AP, OU, v. 1952, dos. 66/2, fl. 24–34.

82. Office of the Prime Minister, 7 December 1951, AQSH, f. 499, v. 1951, dos. 160, fl. 35.

83. "Protokoll i mbledhjes së Byrosë Politike të KQ të P.P.SH.," 19 December 1952, AQSH, f. 14/AP, OU, v. 1952, dos. 66, fl. 2–7; "Zapis' besedy poslannika SSSR v Albanii Levychkina K. D. s zamestitelem prem'er-ministra i sekretarem TsK APT Mekhmetom Shekhu, 16 dekabrya 1952 goda," cable no. 897 (Secret), 17 December 1952, cited in Kramer, "The Early Post-Stalin Succession Struggle," 39.

84. "Relacion mbi bisedimet që pata me shokët sovjetikë të Kombinatit Naftës më 25 dhe 26 dhjetor 1952," 2 January 1953, AQSH, f. 14/AP, OU, v. 1952, dos. 66/2, fl. 25. The city's party committee concluded that the local enterprise leadership had ignored the advice of Soviet engineers on several occasions and that it had inappropriately held Soviet specialists accountable for technical problems. "Byrosë Politike të P.P.SH. Relacion si janë zbatuar këshillat e ingjinierëvet sovjetikë nga drejtoria e Kombinatit të Naftës dhe si janë marëdhëniet midis tyre dhe shokut [Z.H.], drejtori i Kombinatit dhe [P.M.] n/drejtor i Kombinatit," 29 December 1952, AQSH, f. 14/AP, OU, v. 1952, dos. 66/2, fl. 64–69.

85. "Zapiska D. S. Chuvakhina o khode vypolneniia dvukhletnego narodnokhoziaistvennogo plana NRA za pervoe polugodie 1949 g." (Secret), 30 September 1949, in Volokitina et al., *Vostochnaia Evropa*, 2:240.

86. In 1950, two doctors had faced accusations of "anti-Soviet behavior" for reportedly showing reluctance to follow the advice of Soviet surgeons. See information reports dated 4 September–9 October 1950, contained in AQSH, f. 490, v. 1950, dos. 1228, fl. 5.

87. "Zapis' besedy vremennogo poverennogo v delakh SSSR v Albanie Kabanova A. F. s pervim sekretarem TsK APT Enverom Khodzha" (Secret), 14 October 1954, RGANI, f. 5, op. 28, d. 153, l. 164.

88. "Protokoll i mbajtur në zyrën e nënkryeministrit, shokut Mehmet Shehut, në datën 20.XII.1952" (Top Secret), 21 December 1952, AQSH, f. 14/AP, OU, v. 1952, dos. 66/2, fl. 1–17, esp. 10, 12.

89. The Soviets had long been preoccupied with Taylorism. The Soviet methods of 1950s Albania are reminiscent of Frederick Winslow Taylor's time and motion studies, aimed at identifying more efficient work routines through controlled body movements. Frederick Winslow Taylor, *The Principles of Scientific Management* (New York: Harper & Brothers, 1911). Frank Bunker Gilbreth, similarly, was originally preoccupied with reducing body movements in bricklaying. See his *Bricklaying System* (New York: M.C. Clark, 1909). His wife, Lillian, focused on bringing the insights of efficiency studies into the household. On the Soviet engagement with Taylorism and scientific management, see

Mark. R. Beissinger, *Scientific Management, Socialist Discipline, and Soviet Power* (Cambridge, MA: Harvard University Press, 1988), esp. chap. 1.

90. A *Trud* article from 1 November 1945 provided a short biography of Kulikov, who was said to have been a builder before the war, also pointing out that "during the days of the blockade he worked on bomb shelters and military construction." Referred to in Joseph Aloysius Alexander, *In the Shadow: Three Years in Moscow* (Melbourne: Herald and Weekly Times, 1949), 274–75. A small book of Kulikov's was also translated into Albanian: *Për ndërtimin e shtëpijave për banim* (Tirana: Botim i Këshillit Qendror të B.P.S., 1949).

91. "23 m³ mur në 8 orë," *Bashkimi*, 19 July 1950, 3.

92. "Në qytetin e ri," *Shqipëri B.R.S.S.*, no. 6, June 1950, 4.

93. "Konferenca Nacionale 'Kulikov,'" *Shqipëri B.R.S.S.*, no. 6, June 1950, 24.

94. Perventsev, "The New Albania," 35.

95. Nikolai Pogodin, "In the Spirit of Peace, Friendship, Happiness," *USSR Information Bulletin* 12, no. 8 (1952): 226.

96. Frashëri, "One Day in Albania," 365.

97. "Eksperienca Stakonoviste" [article by I. S. Kovalev translated into Albanian], with drawings and diagrams, n.d., AQSH, f. 499, v. 1953, dos. 92, fl. 48–53.

98. A number of Soviet construction methods also appeared in Albanian translation: *Eksperienca e novatorëve sovjetikë në punimet e ndërtimit* (Tirana: Ministria e Ndërtimit, 1955).

99. Some undated guidelines on Soviet methods are contained in AQSH, f. 499, v. 1949, dos. 182, fl. 6.

100. An undated Ministry of Public Works memorandum on Soviet methods in construction is contained in AQSH, f. 499, v. 1949, dos. 182, fl. 5. Although the file has been archived under the year 1949, the material actually stems from the second half of 1952.

101. For examples of rewards and mechanisms of compliance, see undated reports on Soviet methods contained in AQSH, f. 499, v. 1950, dos. 291, fl. 17–18.

102. "Sot punoj me tri metoda sovietike njëkohësisht," *Zëri i Popullit*, 18 July 1952, 1.

103. "Eksperienca sovietike burim ftoresh në punë," *Zëri i Popullit*, 8 September 1951, 1.

104. "Nderojnë atdheun," *Miqësija*, April 1953, 26–27. Branches of the Friendship Society continued to hand out material rewards to the reported highest achievers. For examples from the second half of the decade, see "Dega e jonë po zhvillon një aktivitet të gjerë," *Miqësija*, September 1958, 15.

105. "Vendime të mbledhjes për analizën e punës gjat dy-vjeçarit 1949–1950," n.d., AQSH, f. 499, v. 1949, dos. 403, fl. 1. Compare with later guidelines: "Qarkore," 12 November 1950, and "Relacion mbi metodën Levçenko-Muhanov," n.d., both in AQSH, f. 499, v. 1950, dos. 109, fl. 1–1 verso, 3–4; "Puntorve Stahanovistëve, sulmuesa, karpentjerve, muratorve, mekanikëve, shoferave, gjithë specialistëve, teknikëve dhe nënpunsave të ndërtimit," n.d., AQSH, f. 499, v. 1951, dos. 282, fl. 34–8.

106. "Evidenca e Stahanovistave, sulmuesave dhe përdorimi i metodave Sovjetike në tremujorin e I-rë 1953," n.d. [first quarter of 1953], AQSH, f. 499, v. 1953, dos. 92, fl. 40. Compare with the numbers reported in a memo from the Ministry of Construction to the Society of Albanian-Soviet Friendship, 22 May 1953, AQSH, f. 499, v. 1953, dos. 265, fl. 13–13 verso. See also "Relacion mbi gjendjen dhe jetesën e punonjësve të ndërtimit dhe masat që mejtojmë të marim," dated by hand 8 June 1954, AQSH, f. 499, v. 1954, dos. 4, fl. 1–5.

107. According to one survey, in one particular sector specializing in apartment construction, Soviet methods took no more than two hundred hours, compared with the total of over twenty-four thousand working hours. This shows that "success" depended on

what prevailing indicator one chose to put forward: total number of workers employing Soviet methods or total effective hours of Soviet-style labor? This dispatch warned that this chaotic state of affairs ended up discrediting Soviet methods. Ministry of Controls to the Minister of Construction, Deputy Prime Minister, and the Central Committee, [1952], AQSH, f. 490, v. 1952, dos. 1210, fl. 8–8 verso. Finally, some enterprise managers faced accusations of having manipulated the numbers indicating savings from the application of Soviet methods. "Të përmirësojmë rrënjësisht punën me studimin dhe projektimin e objekteve të ndërtimit," forwarded 16 November 1955, AQSH, f. 490, v. 1955, dos. 1039, fl. 69.

108. "Komunistët luftojnë për përhapjen e metodave sovjetike," *Miqësija*, May 1956, 10–11. In addition to the Machine Works, the journal also surveyed the capital's shoe factory, which "used to be known for the poor quality of its products and for high costs." Here too the essential factor was party involvement.

109. Enterprises set up special "friendship brigades" tasked with promoting Soviet methods. For example, one such brigade introduced a special Soviet shovel that reportedly carried four to five times more mortar than a traditional trowel. The sheer weight of the tool at first apparently baffled the workers, but a local Stakhanovite swore by its efficiency. "Si punon rrethi i miqësisë në ndërmarrjen tonë," *Miqësija*, December 1956, 21.

110. "Relacion mbi përfitimet nga eksperienca e Sollovjovit P.E. në Sektorin e Ndër-timit," forwarded 10 June 1954, AQSH, f. 490, v. 1954, dos. 1028, fl. 34; "Konsultë për përhapjen e metodave sovjetike në ndërtim," *Miqësija*, April 1954; "Raport në kolegjium. Analizë mbi përfitimet që kemi pasur nga bashkëpunimi tekniko-shkencor midis vendit t'onë, B. Sovjetik dhe vendeve të Demokracis Popullore," n.d., AQSH, f. 567, v. 1955, dos. 360, fl. 1–2 verso.

111. The undated [May 1954] notes from a meeting of the directorate of the Ministry of Industries and Construction are contained in AQSH, f. 491, v. 1954, dos. 3, fl. 1.

112. Memorandum on the benefits of techno-scientific agreements, n.d., AQSH, f. 490, v. 1954, dos. 1028, fl. 35.

113. A protocol of a 14 May 1954 meeting at the Ministry of Industry and Construc-tion is contained in AQSH, f. 491, v. 1954, dos. 3, fl. 3.

114. The Soviet embassy also urged more press attention to the problem of Soviet methods and mentioned the continuing problem of formalism in spreading them. "O khode vypodneniia reshenii aprel'skogo 1955 g. plenuma TsK APT po voprosu ideo-logicheskoi raboty partii," 28 June 1956 (Secret), RGANI, f. 5, op. 28, d. 391, l. 99.

115. "Muratorit Pando Mihali, Ndërmarrja e Furnizimit, Qyteti 'Stalin'—Shqipëri," *Miqësija*, May 1956, 26.

116. "Mbi metodën e suvatimit me emulacion gëlqereje," 26 April 1957, and "Mbi metodën e suvatimit me emulacion gëlqereje. Urdhër [no number]," 10 July 1957, both in AQSH, f. 499, v. 1957, dos. 918, fl. 1–5.

117. "Protokoll Nr. 18 i mbledhjes së Byrosë Politike të K.Q.," 4 July 1952, AQSH, f. 14/AP, OU, v. 1952, dos. 43, fl. 22.

118. Kotkin, *Magnetic Mountain*, 230.

119. One critical review of the work at a Durrës enterprise, for example, contained both the director's signature, suggesting agreement with the assessment of the investigator sent from Tirana, and a handwritten note in which the director further clarified the posi-tion on Soviet methods. "Akt-kontrolli," n.d. [signed 12 May 1953], AQSH, f. 499, v. 1953, dos. 92, fl. 10–10 verso.

120. "Udhëzim i përbashkët i Këshillit Qendror të B.P.SH dhe Ministrisë Ndërtimit për zbatimin e Metodave Sovjetike," forwarded 26 November 1957, AQSH, f. 499, v. 1957, dos. 293, fl. 2–3; "Golden Hands," *B.R.P.SH. Information Bulletin*, October 1963, 4.

4. SOCIALISM AS EXCHANGE

1. "Zusatz zum Abschlußbericht der TWZ-Gruppe (Nur für die deutsche Seite bestimmt!)," 23 September 1961; GDR Embassy (Tirana), "Aktenvermerk" (Vertraulich!), 24 June 1961, BArch DE1(Staatliche Plankommission)/25483.The Kurbnesh copper factory was part of a February 1957 agreement specifying East German loans worth 35 million rubles for the period 1957–60. See "Gesprächsthemen," dated by hand November 1957, PA AA, MfAA, A 9.474, 152; "Schwerpunktaufgaben für den Arbeitsplan der WPA Tirana im Jahre 1960," 14 March 1960, BArch DE 1/25476, 220.

2. Harry Hamm, *Albania–China's Beachhead in Europe* (New York: Praeger, 1963), 45.

3. Minister of Mines and Geology [Çarçani] to Hoxha and Shehu, n.d. [April 1960], AQSH, f. 537, v. 1960, dos. 219, fl. 1–2.

4. "Informacion mbi vënien në shfrytëzim të fabrikës së pasurimit të bakrit në Kurbnesh" (Secret), forwarded 11 August 1960, AQSH, f. 537, v. 1960, dos. 219, fl. 3–7.

5. The East German State Planning Commission referred to an increasingly confrontational attitude of Albanian managers in the spring of 1961. "Bericht über die Arbeit der Spezialisten der Staatlichen Geologischen Kommission in der VR Albanien," 12 May 1961, BArch DE 1/25483, 728–31.

6. "Lista e specialistave të huaj që punojnë në ndërtimin dhe projektimin e veprave në R.P. Shqipërisë," n.d., AQSH, f. 499, v. 1960, dos. 604, fl. 1.

7. "Shpërndarja dhe sigurimi i kuadrit," n.d., AQSH, f. 499, v. 1960, dos. 430, fl. 6.

8. An exceptionally broad comparison was provided in Zoltan Barany, "Soviet Takeovers: The Role of Advisers in Mongolia in the 1920s and in Eastern Europe after World War II," *East European Quarterly* 28, no. 4 (1995): 409–33.

9. In 1953, the Albanian ambassador in Moscow boasted that socialist technical exchange was "a new form of cooperation among our countries"—one that did not and could not exist under capitalism. Albanian Embassy (Moscow) to Tirana (Shtylla), 31 October 1953 (Top Secret), AMPJ, v. 1953, dos. 51, fl. 81.

10. In comparison with other areas of socialist life, the Comecon has not received much attention in post-1989 scholarship. One study, which pushes hard against the idea of Soviet autarky, nevertheless pays little attention to the organization. Calculations within Soviet trade circles notwithstanding, the Eastern bloc did not suddenly disappear as a geopolitical imperative. Oscar Sanchez-Sibony, *Red Globalization: The Political Economy of the Soviet Cold War from Stalin to Khrushchev* (Cambridge: Cambridge University Press, 2014). The classics on the Comecon are from decades ago: Michael Kaser, *Comecon: Integration Problems of the Planned Economies*, 2nd ed. (London: Oxford University Press, 1967); Henry W. Schaefer, *Comecon and the Politics of Integration* (New York: Praeger, 1972); and Randall Stone, *Satellites and Commissars: Strategy and Conflict in the Politics of Soviet-Bloc Trade* (Princeton: Princeton University Press, 1996). Newer work appears in a special issue of *European Review of History: Revue européenne d'histoire* 21, no. 2 (2014): 157–348.

11. Kramer, "Stalin, the Split with Yugoslavia," 297.

12. The Comecon literature painstakingly catalogs anything and everything that went wrong with socialist economic integration. Compare it with the literature on West European integration and the lasting myths around figures such as Jean Monnet and Robert Schuman. Alan Milward argued that Western Europe "had much to thank the Soviet Union for, especially its threatening, unremitting hostility," thus contributing to the process of economic integration. See his *The Reconstruction of Western Europe 1945–51* (London: Routledge, 1984), 385. On socialist integration as, at turns, showmanship, economic interdependence, Soviet domination, and regional forms of integration: Charles

Gati, *The Bloc That Failed: Soviet-East European Relations in Transition* (Bloomington: Indiana University Press, 1990), 118ff; Iván Berend, *An Economic History of Twentieth Century Europe: Economic Regimes from Laissez- Faire to Globalization* (Cambridge: Cambridge University Press, 2006), 169.

13. "Iz zapisi besedy s predsedatelem Soveta Ministrov Albanii E. Khodzhei o tseliakh i zadachakh sozdaniia SEV, nedovol'stve albanskoi storony politikoi v oblasti vneshnei torgovli v ramkakh SEV i dr." (Secret), 10 March 1949, in Volokitina et al., *Vostochnaia Evropa*, 2:31–34. The following year, Molotov had to explain to Hoxha that the Comecon was not meant to assess and approve the economic plans of member states. See "Zapis' besedy tovarishcha Molotova V.M. s t.t. Enver Khodzha i Tuk Iakova" (Top Secret), 5 August 1950, in Volokitina et al., *Sovetskii factor*, 2:371–72.

14. For an assessment of the validity of the argument that Comecon's 1949–53 activity was almost wholly inconsequential, see Włodzimierz Brus, "1950 to 1953: The Peak of Stalinism," in *The Economic History of Eastern Europe 1919–1975*, ed. M. C. Kaser (Oxford: Clarendon Press, 1986), 3:4, esp. note 1.

15. Włodzimierz Brus, "1957 to 1965: In Search of Balanced Development," in Kaser, *The Economic History of Eastern Europe*, 3:73. Michael Kaser noted that the post–World War II East-West divide marked a divergence from a prewar arrangement of wealthy centers dealing with poorer peripheries. Kaser, *Comecon*, 10. In this view, the Stalin-era Soviet Union took an "imperial" approach to the East European economies but with the distinction that parts of the periphery (East Germany, Czechoslovakia) were more developed.

16. "Protokoll i mbledhjes së Byrosë Politike të Komitetit Qendror të P.P.SH.," 28 May 1958, AQSH, f. 14/AP, OU, v. 1958, dos. 13, fl. 39.

17. On the endurance of bilateralism in Soviet–Eastern bloc trade: Gati, *The Bloc That Failed*, 124–35. In 1960, the Soviet Academy of Sciences established the Institute of Economics of the World Socialist System, tasked with research on socialist economies and an international division of labor.

18. Kaser, *Comecon*, 5. A valuable recent study reinforces the point about "structural obstacles built into the very nature of the Soviet system" by bringing into focus the Comecon-based International Investment Bank. David R. Stone, "CMEA's International Investment Bank and the Crisis of Developed Socialism," *Journal of Cold War Studies* 10, no. 3 (Summer 2008): 49.

19. Brus, "1957 to 1965," 116.

20. On the "pricing conundrum" in socialist foreign trade, see Jozef Wilczynski, *The Economics of Socialism after World War II* (1970; repr., New Brunswick, NJ: AldineTransaction, 2008), 200–201.

21. P. J. D Wiles, *Communist International Economics* (New York: Praeger, 1969), 311.

22. "Technisch-wissenschaftliche Zusammenarbeit, das ist Freundschaft," dated by hand November 1950, BArch DE 1/10676, 1–4. The State Planning Commission pitched an article titled "A Higher Form of Collaboration" to *Die Wirtschaft*. See "Artikel 'Eine höhere Form der Zusammenarbeit,'" 27 November 1950, BArch DE 1/10676, 5–11.

23. An overview of socialist technoscientific exchange written by a Comecon official, originally printed in *Planovoe khoziaistvo* (Moscow), is T. Azarov, "Problems in Coordinating the Scientific and Technical Research of Comecon Countries," *Eastern European Economics* 2, no. 4 (Summer 1964): 11–16.

24. For examples from East Germany, see "Die Entwicklung der technisch-wissenschaftlichen Zusammenarbeit im Jahre 1956 (Entwurf)," n.d. [1956], BArch DE 1/12875, 1–7; "Cooperation between ZAFT and TWZ" (Secret), 21 April 1955, CREST, CIA-RDP80–00810A006400550002–2.

25. Council for Mutual Economic Assistance, *A Survey of 20 Years of the Council for Mutual Economic Assistance* (Moscow: CMEA Secretariat, 1969), 64.

26. One source, for example, reported that the Soviet Union sent 31,778 technical documents between 1948 and 1961 to Eastern bloc countries as well as Mongolia, North Korea, North Vietnam, and China. In return, it received 8,877. It named China as the biggest recipient of Soviet technical documents in this period and Czechoslovakia as the largest contributor. A.N. Bykov, *Nauchno-tekhnicheskie sviazi stran sotsializma* (Moscow: Mysl', 1970), 68–69.

27. Jersild, "The Soviet State as Imperial Scavenger."

28. "Relacion mbi rezultatet e aritura në sektorin e B.T. Shkencor dhe masat e mara kohët e fundit për përmirësimin e mëtejshëm të punës," n.d., AQSH, f. 490, v. 1957, dos. 1168, fl. 259.

29. The Albanian planning chief Spiro Koleka admitted as much. "Mbi zhvillimin e punimeve të mbledhjes së përfaqësuesave të partive komuniste dhe puntore të vendeve socialiste" (Top Secret), 27 May 1958, AQSH, f. 14/AP, OU, v. 1958, dos. 13.

30. "Die Stellung der Volksrepublik Albanien im sozialistischen Weltwirtschaftssystem," n.d., BArch DE 1/21355. In 1956, Albania had trade agreements with only twelve countries, including Mongolia, and the only nonsocialist trade partners (not counting Yugoslavia) were Syria and Italy. "Shtetet me të cilët kemi marëveshje ekonomike," n.d., AMPJ, v. 1956, dos. 26/1, fl. 1.

31. For a Soviet assessment of economic planning: "O polozhenii s ispol'zovaniem kreditov, predostavliaemykh Albanii Sovetskim Soiuzom i stranami narodnov demokratii" (Secret), 24 September 1956, in RGANI, f. 5, op. 28, d. 391, esp. ll. 204–5.

32. Technoscientific cooperation agreements were first signed in 1947, though informal arrangements had been reached before then. For example, Albania requested Czechoslovak specialists as early as 1945. Back then, when asking (via Belgrade) for such personnel—for agriculture, water management, fishing, and mining but also for an information expert—the Albanian side spoke of "a moral assistance to our Democratic Government." The correspondence between the Ministry of Economy and the Council of Ministers, dated 26 November 1945, is contained in AQSH, f. 490, v. 1945, dos. 124, fl. 1.

33. Relacion mbi marrëveshjet e përfunduara për pesëvjeçarin 1951–1955," n.d., AQSH, f. 14/AP, OU, v. 1951, dos. 28, fl. 48–49.

34. "Jahresbericht der WPA Tirana über die ökonomische und technisch-wissenschaftliche Zusammenarbeit mit der VRA im Jahre 1959," n.d., and "Berichtsteil 'Wirtschaftliche Beziehungen 1958,'" 4 November 1958, BArch DE 1/25476.

35. One Albanian estimate put the figure for loans delivered between 1949 and 1955 at around 910 million rubles. "Sh. Enver Hoxha" (Top Secret), n.d., AQSH, f. 14/AP, v. 1955, dos. 22, fl. 91. Mehmet Shehu, in turn, mentioned a total of one billion rubles. (The interest rate for the amount of Chinese credit, which was relatively small, was four times lower than what Moscow and other Eastern bloc states provided.) "Shënime nga takimi që u bë në KQ të PPSH midis delegacionit të PPSH dhe delegacionit parlamentar kinez të kryesuar nga shoku Pen Çen," 16 January 1957, AQSH, f. 14/AP, Marrëdhëniet me Partinë Komuniste të Kinës [Relations with the CCP] (M-PKK), v. 1957, dos. 1, fl. 33. Soviet sources provide roughly comparable numbers. One specifies a total of 947 million rubles by 1956. "Nekotorye sovety Albanskim druz'iam" (Top Secret), 24 September 1956, RGANI, f. 5, op. 28, d. 391, l. 184. Another puts the 1949–55 figure at 810 million (plus a special Soviet payment of 165 million). This was the breakdown of assistance provided: Soviet Union (375 million rubles), Czechoslovakia (109.5), Romania (65.2), Hungary (65), GDR (61.5), Poland (60), Bulgaria (50), China (50). "O polozhenii s ispol'zovaniem kreditov, predostavliaemykh Albanii Sovetskim Soiuzom i stranami narodnov demokratii" (Secret), 24 September 1956, in RGANI, f. 5, op. 28, d. 391, l. 211. Later figures are harder to align. For CIA estimates of the 1945–1964 period (USD 550 million) see "Communist Mutual Economic Assistance" (Secret), October 1964, in CREST, CIA- RDP79S01046A001000020001–8.

One economic historian also tried to estimate total Soviet and East European aid in the 1950s (he came up with a figure of USD 400 million). Kaser, "Economic System," 302n47.

36. East German Embassy (Tirana) to Berlin, 8 May 1957, BArch DC 1 (Zentrale Kommission für Staatliche Kontrolle)/4230.

37. "Bericht über das IV. Quartal 1953," n.d., PA AA, MfAA, A 4.516, 136.

38. The Ministries of Agriculture, Construction, and Mining got parallel sectors devoted to technical cooperation in 1955, which were nevertheless poorly staffed. Within the Ministry of Construction, for example, four different people took on the job between 1954 and 1956. "Vendim Nr. 187 mbi organizimin e degës së bashkëpunimit tekniko-shkencor," 31 May 1955, AQSH, f. 490, v. 1955, dos. 327, fl. 6; "Relacion mbi bashkëpunimin tekniko-shkencor," n.d., AQSH, f. 499, v. 1955, dos. 394, fl. 1. The deputy prime minister appeared clueless about the process and the costs involved with technoscientific cooperation. "Informacjon" [handwritten remarks signed K. Th. and dated 3 January 1956], AQSH, f. 490, v. 1955, dos. 1163, fl. 233.

39. "Vendim Nr. 237 mbi disa masa për forcimin organizativ të sektorit për bashkëpunimin tekniko-shkencor," 22 June 1956, AQSH, f. 490, v. 1956, dos. 1062, fl. 17–19.

40. "Disa vrejtje të përgjithshme të konstatuara në sektorin e bashkëpunimit tekniko-shkencor," 21 June 1956, AMPJ, v. 1956, dos. 26/1, fl. 64–66. Another example: "Akt-kontrolli," 21 August 1956, AQSH, f. 491, v. 1956, dos. 2, fl. 55–56 verso. At this point, artisanal cooperatives had received six hundred patents. They reported having translated seventy-six of them, but only four (on lighters, hinges, and door locks) had been adopted. "Raport mbi punën e B.T. Shkencorë (Për shokun Koço Theodhosi)," 1 March 1956, AQSH, f. 490, v. 1956, dos. 1060, fl. 8.

41. "Scandalous!" the unnamed recipient of a State Control Commission report on lost documentation wrote on the margins. "Mbi dokumentat e huaja tekniko-shkencore që kanë humbur" (Secret), 10 September 1956, AQSH, f. 490, v. 1956, dos. 1080, fl. 160. The following year, the prime minister suggested getting the Ministry of Interior involved in finding the missing documents. "Proçes-verbal i mbledhjes së Këshillit të Ministrave mbajtur më 6 shkurt 1957," 6 February 1957, AQSH, f. 490, v. 1957, dos. 1168, fl. 23.

42. "Mbi dërgimin e specialistit Bullgar të xhamit në Bullgari," 4 April 1955, AQSH, f. 490, v. 1955, dos. 1164, fl. 30.

43. "Relacion mbi ruajtjen e përdorimin e materialeve tekniko shkencor nga ana e dikastereve," n.d., AQSH, f. 491, v. 1956, dos. 2, fl. 54.

44. Hungarian Embassy (Tirana) to Ministry of Trade and Communications, "Envoi des spécialistes hongrois," 24 April 1954; "Ministrisë së Arsimit të Republikës Popullore të Shqipërisë," 28 June 1954; "Mbi dërgimin e specialistëve hungarezë ardhur për derdhien në bronz të monumentit të Skënderbeut," 6 October 1954, all in AQSH, f. 490, v. 1954, dos. 1039, fl. 20, 26–27, 34. Then, during talks in November 1954, the Hungarian side complained about the waste of Hungarian expertise: Albanian Embassy (Budapest) to Tirana (Secret), dated by hand 3 December 1954, AMPJ, v. 1955, dos. 129, fl. 1–2.

45. "Informacion mbi gjendjen e B.T.SH. (i shkurtër) dhe masa për përmirsimin e sajë," 14 February 1955, AQSH, f. 490, v. 1955, dos. 1163, fl. 110 verso.

46. Albanian Embassy (Budapest), "Kryeministrisë, Degës për Bashkëpunim Tekniko-Shkencor," n.d., AMPJ, v. 1955, dos. 129, fl. 9. It is worth pointing out that much of the criticism directed at technoscientific cooperation targeted a lack of awareness of the *terms* of exchange without questioning any of the assumptions behind it.

47. An example, related to a conference on chemistry in the GDR: Institute of Sciences to Ministry of Foreign Affairs, 6 April 1955, AMPJ, v. 1955, dos. 111, fl. 25.

48. A good part of the technical documentation was supposed to be free of charge. "Finanzierung der technisch-wissenschaftlichen Zusammenarbeit zwischen der Deutschen Demokratischen Republik und der Volksrepublik Albanien," dated by hand

1956; "Zusammenstellung," n.d.; "Begründung," 23 January 1956, all in BArch DE 1/1963. However, there was such chaos in technoscientific affairs that one critical report that year raised the possibility that some enterprises might have paid hard currency for the documentation. "Vërejtje të përgjithshme mbi punën e bashkëpunimit tekniko-shkencor" n.d., AMPJ, v. 1956, dos. 26/1, fl. 10.

49. "Raport mbi përdorimin e materialeve të bashkëpunimit tekniko-shkencor dhe përhapjen e eksperiencës së përparuar në prodhim," 11 August 1958, AQSH, f. 490, v. 1958, dos. 998, fl. 3.

50. "Vendim no. 214 mbi përdorimin e materialeve të bashkëpunimit tekniko-shkencor dhe përhapjen e eksperiencës së përparuar në prodhim," 4 July 1958; "Byroja Politike," 4 July 1958 (Top Secret), AQSH, f. 14/AP, OU, v. 1958, dos. 16, fl. 135–39, 197.

51. "Proces-verbal i mbledhjes së Këshillit të Ministrave mbajtur më 30 gusht 1958 mbi shqyrtimin e raportit për problemin e ndihmës së marrë në rrugën e bashkëpunimit tekniko- shkencor dhe mbi përhapjen e eksperiencës së përparuar në prodhim," 30 August 1958, AQSH, f. 490, v. 1958, dos. 998, fl. 37.

52. "Relacion mbi gjendjen dhe funksionimin e bashkëpunimit tekniko-shkencor," 25 May 1956, AQSH, 490, v. 1956, dos. 39, fl. 1–8; "Raport mbi punën në sektorin e B.T.SH.," n.d., AQSH, f. 490, v. 1956, dos. 1060, fl. 40.

53. Eastern bloc partners also struggled to figure out what Albania could offer them. East German officials, for example, pointed out that they largely subsidized technical aid to the small Balkan country. The reasons provided included the fact that other socialist countries did so and the admission that Albania was the poorest socialist partner and that the sums involved were not large. "Begründung zum Beschluss der Staatlichen Plankommission vom 6.7.1956 über eine Finanzierung der technischen und technisch-wissenschaftlichen Hilfe seitens der Deutschen Demokratischen Republik an die Volksrepublik Albanien," n.d., BArch DE 1/25482; "Die Stellung der Volksrepublik Albanien im sozialistischen Weltwirtschaftssystem," n.d., BArch DE 1/21355. East German planning officials also took issue with the one-sided nature of technical cooperation, and the implication that their advanced country had little to gain from countries like Albania, Bulgaria, and China. "Die zweiseitige wirtschaftliche und technisch-wissenschaftliche Zusammenarbeit," n.d., BArch DE 1/25483.

54. "Përshkrim i shkurtër mbi marrëdhënjet e B.T. Shkencore të R.P. Shqipërisë me vendet e demokracisë popullore" (Confidential), dated by hand 16 January 1957, AQSH, f. 490, v. 1956, dos. 1080, fl. 224–25.

55. "Bericht über die in Tirana mit dem Aussenministerium der Albanischen Volksrepublik geführten Besprechungen," 17 March 1950, SAPMO-BArch NY4090 (Nachlass Otto Grotewohl)/475, 17–20.

56. "Protokoll über Besuch einer Delegation der Albanischen Volksrepublik beim Genossen Ministerpräsidenten Otto Grotewohl im Amtszimmer des Ministerpräsidenten," 11 November 1954, SAPMO-BArch NY4090/475, 34. Socialist solidarity had its limits. At one point, Albanian representatives had pressed their Romanian counterparts about oil shipping costs. They explained that they had no hard currency to cover them. After all, they did not trade with capitalist countries. Seemingly irritated, the Romanian deputy minister of trade said that he was actually aware that Albania traded with Italy, causing his guests to take offense. A memo from the Albanian Mission in Bucharest, dated 28 February 1950, is contained in AQSH, f. 490, v. 1950, dos. 1374, fl. 5–6.

57. "Zapis' besedy vremennogo poverennogo v delakh SSSR v Albanie Kabanova A.F. c pervom sekretarem TsK APT Enverom Khodzha, 2 October 1954" (Secret), 6 October 1954, RGANI, f. 5, op. 28, d. 153, ll. 185–93; "Zapis' besedy vremennogo poverennogo v delakh SSSR v Albanie Kabanova A.F. c pervom sekretarem TsK APT Enverom Khodzha" (Secret), 14 October 1954, RGANI, f. 5, op. 28, d. 153, l. 163–66; "Protokoll i mbledhjes së Byrosë Politike të KQ të PPSH," 18 December 1958, AQSH, f. 14/AP, OU, v. 1958, dos. 24.

58. An example from Polish-Albanian contacts: Albanian Mission (Warsaw) to Tirana, 14 April 1950, AMPJ, v. 1950, dos. 88, fl. 6 verso. In 1951, Polish official Hilary Minc pointed out that it was easier "to provide credits than technicians." See "Relacion mbi marrëveshjet e përfunduara për pesëvjeçarin 1951–1955," n.d., AQSH, f. 14/AP, OU, v. 1951, dos. 28, fl. 48.

59. Later in the decade, one group of Polish civil engineers and planners volunteered to plan the capital city's transportation system. "Varshava, 5.12.1959" [letter typed in Russian], AQSH, f. 490, v. 1959, dos. 1199, fl. 53.

60. Ministry of Education to Office of Prime Minister (Secret), 27 September 1951, AQSH, f. 490, v. 1951, dos. 1629, fl. 1; "Mbi caktimin e rrogave të specialistëve dhe teknikëve sovjetikë t'ardhur për ndihmë teknike," 5 July 1952, AQSH, f. 490, v. 1952, dos. 464, fl. 1. In the 1950s, fifty lekë were officially equivalent to one US dollar.

61. "Zapis' besedy s E. Khodzhei o netselesoobraznosti peresmotra zarabotnoi platy sovetskikh spetsialistov v Albanii, uchastii sovetskikh predstavitelei v mesiachinke albano-sovetskoi druzhby, priniatii na uchebu v vuzy SSSR albanskikh studentov i dr." (Secret), 9 August 1952, in Volokitina et al., *Sovetskii faktor*, 2:678–80.

62. Meeting protocols of the Presidium of the Council of Ministers are contained in AQSH, f. 490, v. 1953, dos. 706, fl. 43 verso.

63. "Kryetarit të Këshillit të Ministrave, shokut Mehmet Shehu" (Top Secret), 2 June 1955, AMPJ, v. 1955, dos. 79, fl. 53.

64. Office of the Prime Minister, "Gjithë dikastereve, gjithë enteve," 8 January 1949, AQSH, f. 490, v. 1949, dos. 616, fl. 3.

65. Office of the Prime Minister, Section on Organizational Structures and Categorizations, dated by hand 25 August 1951, AQSH, f. 499, v. 1951, dos. 160, fl. 2.

66. State Roads Enterprise to Ministry of Construction, 10 September 1951, AQSH, f. 499, v. 1951, dos. 160, fl. 46.

67. Immediately after the Stalin-Tito split, some seventy-three Russians moved to Albania from Yugoslavia. As Hoxha explained in a letter to Moscow, these were Russians who "had left the Soviet Union, according to their paperwork, after the victory of the Great October Revolution," eventually settling in Yugoslavia. Then they had been expelled from that country. The Albanian party boss also deemed them politically suspect, claiming that they "threaten the reverence that our people have for the Soviet Union." He urged Stalin to have them repatriated. "Tovarishu Stalinu," 6 March 1951, AQSH, f. 14/AP, M-PK(b) BS, v. 1951, dos. 4, fl. 1. One small group of Russians was attached to the design enterprise, where they had started work between December 1949 and January 1950. "Lista e sovjetikëve që kanë patur nënshtetësi Jugosllave dhe janë kthyer në Shqipri," dated by hand 4 March 1950, AQSH, f. 499, v. 1950, dos. 104, fl. 6.

68. "Mbi gjendjen e brendëshme të Republikës Popullore të Shqipërisë. (Raport i Ministrit të P. të Mbrendëshme për Byronë Politike)" (Top Secret), 20 January 1953, AQSH, f. 14/AP, OU, v. 1953, dos. 8, fl. 14–15. Note, however, that the figure included 18,622 *Chams* (Muslim Albanians expelled from Greece).

69. "Protokoll no. 3 i mbledhjes së Byrosë Politike të KQ të PPSH," 26 January 1953, AQSH, f. 14/AP, OU, v. 1953, dos. 8, fl. 107.

70. Czechoslovak Embassy (Tirana) to Dragoti, 9 January 1956; "Relacion mbi propozimin e ambasadës Çeke (Degës së Tregëtisë) në lidhje me rregullimin e shpërblimit të specialistëve çekë mbas heqies së pjesëshme të triskave në vendin tonë," 31 January 1956; "Sh. zv. Kryeministër i I-rë, Hysni Kapo," 11 February 1956, all in AQSH, f. 490, v. 1956, dos. 1079, fl. 1–2, 4–5, 11.

71. Czechoslovak Embassy (Tirana) to Ministry of Foreign Affairs, 19 July 1956, AMPJ, v. 1956, dos. 74, fl. 7. Later that year, Hungarian government officials also asked the freshly arrived Albanian ambassador in Budapest for higher salaries for their specialists.

Apparently, the Hungarians made this request after asking the Czechs and the Romanians about the kinds of agreements they had with Tirana. Albanian Embassy (Budapest) to Tirana, "Relacion. Mbi takimet me trupin dipllomatik dhe personalitetet e vendit gjat muajit shtator 1956," 10 September 1956, AMPJ, v. 1956, dos. 14/6, fl. 18–21.

72. "Informatsiia o nauchno-tekhnicheskom sotrudnichestve v 1955 godu" (Secret), n.d., AQSH, f. 490, v. 1955, dos. 1163, fl. 151–69. References to how the Czechoslovaks organized technoscientific cooperation could be deployed as illustrations of how far behind Albania was in the Eastern bloc. "Raport mbi punën e B.T.Shkencorë (Për shokun Koço Theodhosi)," 1 March 1956, AQSH, f. 490, v. 1956, dos. 1060, fl. 18.

73. Shen Zhihua, *Sulian zhuanjia zai zhongguo, 1948–1960* (Beijing: Zhongguo guoji guangbo chubanshe, 2003); Jersild, *The Sino-Soviet Alliance*, 33–38; Zhihua Shen and Yafeng Xia, *Mao and the Sino-Soviet Partnership, 1945–1959* (Lanham, MD: Lexington Books, 2015), 28.

74. "Relacion mbi çështjen e këshilltarëve dhe specialistëve të vendeve miq që ndodhen në vendin t'onë (me përjashtim të ushtarakëve)," 24 December 1956, AQSH, f. 490, v. 1956, dos. 1079, fl. 62. Payroll records from two years later show that the construction branch ministry employed sixteen foreigners who were paid significantly more than Albanian employees, except the minister, the deputy ministers, and several chiefs of national construction enterprises. "Lista e pagesës së rrogave të personelit" [August–September 1958], AQSH, f. 499, v. 1958, dos. 956/2, fl. 2, 160.

75. "Aktennotiz. Betr.: Reklamation über 3 in der 'Mechanischen Werkstatt Enver Hodscha' in Tirana aufgestellten Werkzeugmaschinen," 16 February 1956, BArch DG 3 (Ministerium für Maschinenbau)/5553, 8.

76. "Mbi rangun e mjekut Sovjetik Shokut Tullupov Nikollaj Ivanoviç," dated by hand 18 June 1952, AQSH, f. 490, v. 1952, dos. 464, fl. 6.

77. Sixty-five families of high-ranking party officials and Soviet advisers enjoyed access to a separate food store. The discussion of guidelines at the Central Committee Secretariat and the ensuing decision dated 23 November 1953 are contained in AQSH, f.14/AP, OU, v.1953, dos. 75, fl. 25–31.

78. Soviet specialists living in the hotel included professors, deputy directors at various institutes, and advisers attached to ministries and other state agencies. "Mbi lëvizjet e teknikëve dhe specialistave të huaj në Dajti, me rastin e festës 29 nëntor," 29 December 1952, AQSH, f. 14/AP, OU, v. 1952, dos. 66/2, fl. 71–72.

79. "Bericht für die Zeit vom 15.5.–31.5.1952," 2 June 1952, PA AA, MfAA, A 4.516, 224.

80. "Informacion," 6 April 1956, AQSH, f. 499, v. 1956, dos. 190, fl. 6.

81. "Pasqyra e normativës për mobilimin dhe pajisjen e banesave të spec. e teknikëve të huaj ndarë në kategori," n.d., AQSH, f. 499, v. 1956, dos. 194, fl. 1–3.

82. "Buletin i datës 17/VII/1953" [date corrected by hand to 17 July 1953], AMPB, v. 1953, dos. 14, fl. 50.

83. "Raport mbi punën e B.T. Shkencorë (Për shokun Koço Theodhosi)," 1 March 1956, AQSH, f. 490, v. 1956, dos. 1060, fl. 37.

84. "Zusatz zum Abschlußbericht der TWZ-Gruppe (Nur für die deutsche Seite bestimmt!)," 23 September 1961, BArch DE 1/25483.

85. "Mbi fotografitë që bëhen nga disa turistë Polakë" (Top Secret), 22 September 1955, AQSH, f. 490, v. 1955, dos. 743, fl. 1.

86. "Relacion përfundimtar i ekspertit çekosllovak sh. Antonin Stupka në kohën prej 24/Janar/1957 deri 30/Qershor/1959," 18 June 1959, AQSH, f. 490, v. 1959, dos. 1188, fl. 6.

87. Examples of technical intervention: "Plan i vënies në zbatim i materialeve të marruna në kuadrin e B.T.Shkencore nga B.R.S.S. dhe vëndet e demokracisë popullore," forwarded 20 January 1956, AQSH, f. 490, v. 1955, dos. 1166, fl. 46.

88. Information to the deputy prime minister, n.d., AQSH, f. 490, v. 1956, dos. 1061, fl. 76.

89. "Informacion," 18 June 1956, AQSH, f. 490, v. 1956, dos. 1061, fl. 70–73.

90. "Histori me zhurmues," interview with Mark Alia, TV Klan (Albania), 3 December 2011.

91. "Proçes-verbal i mbledhjes së Këshillit të Ministrave mbajtur më 6 shkurt 1957," 6 February 1957, AQSH, f. 490, v. 1957, dos. 1168, fl. 23.

92. Ibid., fl. 30.

93. "Informacion Zv. Kryeministrit shokut Koço Theodhosi," 6 August 1959, AQSH, f. 490, v. 1959, dos. 1195, fl. 1.

94. "Studienbericht zur Vorbereitung eines TWZ—Beschlusses DDR—VRA zur Förderung der Holzspielwaren—Produktion in der Volksrepublik Albanien," 22 October 1958, BArch DE 1/26906.

95. Tensions were not limited to Albania. East German planning officials mentioned instances of disagreement with the Romanian side on technical aid terms. See Comisia mixtă de colaborare tehnico-ştiinţifică Romino-Germana, 12 June 1958, BArch DE 1/25478; "Weiterführung der zweiseitigen Zusammenarbeit mit der Volksrepublik Bulgarien," 19 October 1960, BArch DE 1/25484.

96. Office of the Prime Minister to Deputy Minister of Construction, 26 November 1958, AQSH, f. 499, v. 1958, dos. 867, fl. 116; "Vermerk für Genossen Strei," 22 October 1959, BArch DE 1/25483. An East German-sponsored effort to cultivate small potatoes in Albania between 1957 and 1959 produced discouraging results.

97. A November 1960 letter from the deputy prime minister warned that Albanian enterprises wasted too much money on living expenses for foreign specialists. "Mbi disa çështje të trajtimit të specialistëve të huaj," 5 November 1960, AQSH, f. 499, v. 1960, dos. 916, fl. 3–4.

98. The leader of one East German team working in nickel mining returned on vacation to East Germany in March 1961 and reported that the situation in Albania was so tough that he would rather not go back. The Albanian side was told that comrade Mertke, the team leader, was ill and could not return. "Ergänzung zum Vermerk über die TWZ-Situation mit der VR Albanien," BArch DE 1/25484.

99. Hamm, *Albania*, 47–48.

100. The East German Politburo revised credit and technical aid terms. Foreign Ministry and planning officials also reasoned that exchange terms with Albania would have to follow the same rules as with any other country. "Protokoll Nr. 26/61 der Sitzung des Politbüro des Zentralkomitees am Dienstag, dem 13. Juni 1961 im Sitzungssaal des Politbüros," 13 June 1961, SAPMO-BArch DY 30/J IV 2/2/768; East German Embassy (Tirana) to Berlin, "Thesen," 14 August 1961, BArch DE 1/25484; "Abschrift/Hi." (Top Secret), 26 October 1961, BArch DE 1/12307, 2–3.

5. MUD AND CONCRETE

1. Harrison Salisbury, "Albania Is Emerging from Isolation: 'Stalinist' Satellite is Changing Under Soviet Prodding," New York Times, 9 September 1957, 6.

2. Harrison Salisbury, "Albania Industry Still Far Behind: A Thin Edge of the Twentieth Century Cuts into Backward Albania," New York Times, 11 September 1957, 12.

3. Harrison Salisbury, "Chance for West Seen in Albania: A New Approach, It Is Felt, May Reorient Country's All- Soviet Outlook," New York Times, 13 September 1957, 8.

4. Harrison Salisbury Papers, Columbia University, Rare Book and Manuscript Library, box 320, folder 1.

5. US Embassy (Belgrade) to State Department (Confidential), 17 October 1957, in Records of the U.S. Department of State Relating to the Internal Affairs of Albania, 1955–1959, microfilm, record group 59, decimal file 767, roll 1 (Wilmington, DE: Scholarly Resources, 2002?).

6. Harrison Salisbury, "Diversity in East Europe Replaces Stalinist Rigidity: Student Protest of Censorship in Poland and Rock 'n' Roll Fad in Bulgaria Illustrate Change in Atmosphere," *New York Times*, 21 October 1957, 1.

7. "Stenographic Notes of Conversation between DCI and Harrison Salisbury with Mr. Amory and Col. Grogan on 23 October 1957" (Secret), CREST, CIA-RDP80 R01731R000900010010-5.

8. US Embassy (Rome) to Department of State (Confidential), 16 September 1958, in *Records of the Department of State Relating to the Internal Affairs of Albania, 1955–1959*, microfilm, record group 59, decimal file 767, roll 1.

9. "Ndërtimet t'ona gjat gjashtë vjetë të pushtetit popullor," n.d., AQSH, f. 499, v. 1951, dos. 56, fl. 2.

10. In 1955, planning authorities had on file two Italian studies and one postwar draft for Durrës, several Italian studies and a 1953 draft plan for Tirana, an Italian plan and partial 1953 studies for Elbasan, and Italian draft plans or studies for Berat, Vlorë, Shkodër, Sarandë, Burrel, Milot, Lushnje, and Kavajë. "Gjendja urbanistike në qytetet t'ona," n.d., AQSH, f. 499, v. 1955, dos. 470, fl. 59. Many of the big cities got their urban plans only in the 1960s: Durrës, Elbasan, and Pogradec (1957); Tirana (1958); Sarandë and Lezhë (1960); Korçë, Lushnje, Përmet, Kavajë, Peshkopi (1962); Fier and Berat (1962). "Gjendja si dhe masat për zgjidhjen e problemeve që ngrihen në informacionin e Lidhjes së Shkrimtarëve dhe Artistëve të Shqipërisë mbi takimin kombëtar të arkitektëve," n.d., AQSH, f. 490, v. 1971, dos. 303, fl. 31.

11. "Mbledhje e dt. 11/II/48," [Politburo protocol dated 11 February 1948], AQSH, f. 14/AP, OU, v. 1948, dos. 61, fl. 26.

12. Mbledhje 19/II/1948 mbi komisjonin për urbanizimin e Tiranës dhe të qyteteve të tjera të Shqipërisë," 19 February 1948, AQSH, f. 490, v. 1948, dos. 729, fl. 2.

13. Between 1947 and 1957, the capital got 1,615 new residential structures, more than twice as many as the next biggest recipient (Vlorë). "Analiza mbi regjistrimin e ndërtesave të banimit," 22 September 1959, AQSH, f. 499, v. 1959, dos. 345, fl. 8.

14. "Mbi disa çështje urgjente të urbanistikës," forwarded 7 August 1956, AQSH, f. 499, v. 1956, dos. 421, fl. 15.

15. "Protokoll mbi disa çështje urgjente të urbanistikës," forwarded 30 August 1956, AQSH, f. 499, v. 1956, dos. 421, fl. 22.

16. "Parashtresë mbi projekt-idenë e planit rregullues të Tiranës," n.d., AQSH, f. 490, v. 1958, dos. 893, fl. 52–57.

17. "Relacion Sekretariatit mbi të metat në projektimin dhe zbatimin e ndërtesave të banimit (Relacion për B.P. të P.P.SH.)," n.d., AQSH, 499, v. 1955, dos. 333, fl. 22.

18. "Parashtresë mbi kriteret që janë ndjekur në hartimin e projekt-ideve të planeve regulluese të qyteteve," forwarded 13 October 1958, AQSH, f. 490, v. 1958, dos. 893, fl. 35–36.

19. Kimberly Elman Zarecor, *Manufacturing a Socialist Modernity: Housing in Czechoslovakia, 1945–60* (Pittsburgh: University of Pittsburgh Press, 2011), 69–112; Anders Åman, *Architecture and Ideology in Eastern Europe during the Stalin Era: An Aspect of Cold War History* (Cambridge, MA: MIT Press, 1992), 23.

20. "Vendim Nr. 20 mbi Komisionin dhe zyrat e Arkitekturës dhe Urbanistikës," 10 January 1955, AQSH, f. 567, v. 1955, dos. 219, fl. 1; "Protokoll mbi mbledhjen e Komisionit të Arkitekturës dhe Urbanistikës datë 31 dhjetor 1955," 31 December 1955, and "Mbi disa çështje urgjente të urbanistikës," forwarded 7 August 1956, AQSH, f. 499, v. 1956, dos. 421, fl. 7, 17.

21. "Raport mbi planet rregulluese të qyteteve, qendrave industriale dhe bujqësore dhe masat që duhen marë për gjëndjen e krijuar," 3 December 1956, AQSH, f. 499, v. 1956, dos. 461, fl. 35.

22. The plan called for expanding the numbers to eight architects, four planners, two economists, and fifteen geometers by 1960. "Skema e Komitetit të Arteve dhe Urbanistikës pranë Këshillit Ministrave R.P.SH," n.d., AQSH, f. 499, v. 1960, dos. 430, fl. 2.

23. Maks Velo, *Paralel me arkitekturën* (Tirana: njeriu, 1998), 29.

24. Kolevica, *Arkitektura dhe diktatura*, 38.

25. The minister blamed construction errors on the inexperience of recent graduates, lack of discipline, and the stubbornness of the technical personnel. "Raport mbi të metat në ndërtim dhe masat që duhen marrë," 10 November 1954, AQSH, f. 567, v. 1954, dos. 215, fl. 65.

26. "Promemorje. Mbi nevojën e mekanizimit të punimeve në ndërtimet," 29 January 1953, AQSH, f. 499, v. 1953, dos. 257, fl. 1–3.

27. When a housing unit was finished, it would be handed to the local governing committee, which was then responsible for issuing apartments to the various housing sectors of enterprises. "Administrimi i banesave shtetërore," n.d., AQSH, f. 502, v. 1954, dos. 82, fl. 9–10.

28. Figures in this section are derived from "Raport mbi të metat në ndërtim dhe masat që duhen marrë," 10 November 1954, AQSH, f. 567, v. 1954, dos. 215, fl. 51–52.

29. Ibid., fl. 52.

30. "Komunikatë operative no. 114" (Top Secret), 25 November 1953, AMPB, v. 1953, dos. 15, fl. 295.

31. In 1958, the Ministry of Interior suggested mobilizing soldiers and prisoners in plants producing bricks and standard construction elements, hoping to build quick and cheap housing units for its officers. "Mbi ndërtimin e një punishteje për prodhim populiti" (Secret), 10 March 1958, and "Relacion mbi pregatitjen e materialit ndërtimit" (Secret), 28 March 1958, both in AQSH, f. 490, v. 1958, dos. 896, fl. 4–8.

32. Velo, *Paralel me arkitekturën*, 32–33.

33. "Mbi gjendjen e ndërtimeve," n.d., AQSH, f. 499, v. 1959, dos. 70, fl. 32.

34. "Raport mbi të metat në ndërtim dhe masat që duhen marrë," 10 November 1954, AQSH, f. 567, v. 1954, dos. 215, fl. 57.

35. "Udhëzim Nr. 25 mbi kufizimin e ardhjes së personave në qytetet kryesore," 4 December 1957, AQSH, f. 490, v. 1957, dos. 735, fl. 1–2. The prosecutor general reported that more than 1,200 families from the villages of Përmet had settled in Tirana. Another 223 families, mostly peasants from other districts, had settled in villages around the capital. "Mbi pashaportizimet e paligjëshme në periferin e Tiranës" (Secret), 27 June 1959, AQSH, f. 490, v. 1959, dos. 1168, fl. 1–6.

36. "Raport mbi gjendjen e popullsisë të qytetit Tiranës dhe shtimin e saj gjatë viteve 1955–1960 dhe vitit 1961," n.d., AQSH, f. 490, v. 1961, dos. 1107, fl. 1.

37. "Relacion mbi zënejen [*sic*] e hoteleve në qytetet e Tiranës për banim të përherëshëm," 5 August 1961, AQSH, f. 490, v. 1961, dos. 290, fl. 1.

38. "Mbi shpërnguljen e disa zyrave në Tiranë nga ndërtesat e banimit në dyqane ose binca" (Secret), 1 April 1957, and "Mbi zgjerimin e sipërfaqes së banueshme nëpërmjet ngushtimit dhe sistemimit të zyrave në Qytetin e Tiranës," 25 October 1957, AQSH, f. 490, v. 1957, dos. 1048, fl. 1–2, 15–20.

39. "Mbi ndryshimin e procedurës së shpërndarjes së banesave në qytetin e Tiranës" (Secret), 15 June 1956, AQSH, f. 499, v. 1956, dos. 348, fl. 2.

40. Mauricio Bego, *Skeda arkitekture: 1965–2004: Në kronikën e një jete të dallgëzuar* (Tirana: DEA, 2009), 58.

41. Ministry of Interior to deputy prime minister and minister of construction, 20 June 1961, AQSH, f. 490, v. 1961, dos. 895, fl. 9.

42. "Relacion mbi organizimin e ndërtimit të apartamenteve të banimit nga vetë punonjësit," 22 October 1957, AQSH, f. 490, v. 1957, dos. 588, fl. 1–2.

43. US Consulate General (Munich) to Department of State (Confidential), 3 December 1958, *Records of the U.S. Department of State Relating to the Internal Affairs of Albania, 1955–1959*, microfilm, record group 59, decimal file 767, roll 1.

44. "Relacion Sekretariatit mbi të metat në projektimin dhe zbatimin e ndërtesave të banimit. (Relacion për B.P. të P.P.SH.)," n.d., AQSH, 499, v. 1955, dos. 333, fl. 22 (emphasis in original).

45. Bulgaria also supplied four brickworks between 1958 and 1959, but the Albanian side was unhappy with the results and the related construction costs. "Mbi disa çështje për tu shikuar me palën Bullgare," 13 October 1959, AQSH, f. 490, v. 1959, dos. 723, fl. 35–36 verso.

46. "Raport," 20 June 1956, AQSH, f. 499, v. 1956, dos. 421, fl. 23–26; "Me Republikën Popullore Bullgare," n.d., AQSH, f. 490, v. 1956, dos. 1080, fl. 124. The report does not mention Angelov by name, but the context makes it obvious.

47. "O shirokom vnedrenii industrial'nykh metodov, uluchshenii kachestva i snizhenii stoimosti stroitel'stva," *Pravda*, 28 December 1954, 2–3.

48. Earlier in the proceedings, when the president of the Academy of Architecture had delivered his report on Soviet architecture, Khrushchev had interrupted him and demanded to know the figures for construction costs per square meter. R.W. Davies, "The Builders' Conference," *Soviet Studies* 6, no. 4 (1955): 443–57.

49. Nikita Khrushchev, *Memoirs of Nikita Khrushchev*, vol. 2, *Reformer (1945–1964)*, ed. Sergei Khrushchev (University Park: Pennsylvania State University Press, 2006), 275.

50. de Grazia, *Irresistible Empire*, esp. 453ff; Susan E. Reid, "The Khrushchev Kitchen: Domesticating the Scientific-Technological Revolution," *Journal of Contemporary History* 40, no. 2 (2005): 289–316.

51. Greg Castillo, *Cold War on the Home Front: The Soft Power of Midcentury Design* (Minneapolis: University of Minnesota Press, 2010). On how Soviet inhabitants experienced the Thaw through the advent of mass housing: Steven E. Harris, *Communism on Tomorrow Street: Mass Housing and Everyday Life after Stalin* (Washington: Woodrow Wilson Center Press, 2013).

52. Salisbury, "Chance for West Seen in Albania," 8.

53. On Soviet gigantomania as a product of "the fascination and commitment to a technology of display" but also of the state's "exaggerated interest in mass production owing both to egalitarian ideological precepts and resource scarcities": Paul R. Josephson, "'Projects of the Century' in Soviet History: Large-Scale Technologies from Lenin to Gorbachev," *Technology and Culture* 36, no. 3 (July 1995): 519–59.

54. Elidor Mëhilli, "The Socialist Design: Urban Dilemmas in Postwar Europe and the Soviet Union," *Kritika: Explorations in Russian and Eurasian History* 13, no. 3 (Summer 2012): 635–65. "When we occupied part of Germany," the Soviet party boss wrote, "that's where we learned the technological process for producing reinforced-concrete panels for the floors between the stories of buildings." Khrushchev, *Memoirs*, 2:273.

55. Adrian Forty, *Concrete and Culture: A Material History* (London: Reaktion, 2012), 158.

56. On the need to consider architectural modernism also through the prism of geopolitics: Vladimir Kulić, "The Scope of Socialist Modernism: Architecture and State Representation in Postwar Yugoslavia," in *Sanctioning Modernism: Architecture and the Making of Postwar Identities*, ed. Vladimir Kulić, Timothy Parker, and Monica Penick (Austin: University of Texas Press, 2014), 37–62.

57. *Thirje e pjesëmarësve të konferencës së ndërtonjësve, arkitektave, punonjësve të industrisë së materialeve të ndërtimit, të prodhimit të maqinerisë së ndërtimit dhe rrugëve, t'organizatave të projektimit dhe kërkimeve shkencore të B. Sovjetik, organizuar nga Komiteti Central i Partis Komuniste të B. Sovjetik dhe Këshillit të Ministrave të B.R.S.S.*

për të gjithë punonjësit e industrisë së ndërtimeve (Tirana: Ministria e Ndërtimit dhe Komunikacioneve, 1955).

58. "Rezolucion," n.d. [forwarding letter drafted 24 January 1955], AQSH, f. 567, v. 1955, dos. 275, fl. 2–5.

59. For examples: "Projekt Vendim mbi projektet e vitit 1952," with attached list of prototypes, n.d., AQSH, f. 499, v. 1951, dos. 499, fl. 1–9.

60. "Raport mbi pregatitjen për prodhimin e materialeve të parafabrikuara në ndërtimet," n.d., AQSH, f. 499, v. 1952, dos. 178, fl. 1.

61. "Standardizimi i artikujve për vitin 1956," with attached lists, 5 November 1955, AQSH, f.499, v. 1955, dos. 441, fl. 4–6; "Vendim no. 546 mbi planin e artikujve që do të standardizohen gjatë vitit 1959," with attached tables, 20 December 1958, AQSH, f. 499, v. 1958, dos. 33, fl. 1–6.

62. "Informacion mbi zhvillimin e konferencës të ndërtimit në Çekosllovaki," 9 November 1955 [also dated by hand 10 November], AQSH, f. 499, v. 1955, dos. 87, fl. 5; Tirana to Albanian Embassy (Prague) (Top Secret), 20 October 1955, AMPJ, v. 1955, dos. 94, fl. 35.

63. "Informacion," n.d., AQSH, f. 499, v. 1957, dos. 115, fl. 1–14; State Planning Commission to Ministry of Construction, 5 December 1957, AQSH, f. 499, v. 1957, dos. 135, fl. 1.

64. "Tezat," 25 August 1955, AQSH, f. 499, v. 1955, dos. 269, fl. 4–8.

65. "Mbi të metat në organet dhe organizatat e ndërtimit dhe masat që duhen mare për likuidimin e këtyre të metave," n.d., AQSH, f. 490, v. 1955, dos. 1039, fl. 5–10.

66. "Mbi punën e bërë në sektorin e ndërtimit" (Secret), forwarded 5 [month unclear] 1955, AQSH, f. 490, v. 1955, dos. 1039, fl. 26.

67. "Të përmirësojmë rrënjësisht punën me studimin dhe projektimin e objekteve të ndërtimit," 8 November 1955, AQSH, f. 490, v. 1955, dos. 1039, fl. 34 verso.

68. "Ndërtimet në qytetin e Tiranës gjatë pesë-vjeçarit të parë dhe në pesë-vjeçarin e dytë," dated by hand 16 May 1956, AQSH, f. 499, v. 1956, dos. 461, fl. 48–49.

69. Bego, *Skeda arkitekture*, 8.

70. "Drejtoria Komunale," n.d., AQSH, f. 502, v. 1954, dos. 82, fl. 13. The correspondence on exchanged materials is contained in AQSH, f. 499, v. 1957, dos. 730.

71. "Besprechung im Ministerium für Aufbau, HA Technik, Abt. Forschung und TWZ," 11 August 1956, BArch DH 2 (Bauakademie der DDR)/21881; "Begründung," and Institut für Typung beim Ministerium für Aufbau, "Internationale Tagung über Typenprojektierung," 25 January 1957, BArch DH 1 (Ministerium für Bauwesen)/44994; "Aktennotiz," 23 July 1958, SAPMO-BArch DY 30/IV 2/6/06/17, 19–22.

72. "Stand und Perspektive der Entwicklung des Bauwesens in der DDR," n.d. [1958], BArch DH 1/8087. On East German interest in Soviet prototypes: "Zur verbesserung der Planung von Wohnungstypen," n.d., BArch DH 2/21882.

73. "Tagungsbericht (1957)," BArch N 2504 (Nachlass Gerhard Kosel)/193. The results of the meeting were reportedly also conveyed to Mongolia, Vietnam, and Yugoslavia. The latter had been invited to the Berlin meeting but did not participate.

74. "Zur internationalen Tagung über Typenprojektierung," BArch DH 1/44994. In 1955, Kosel had led a group to the Soviet Union to study the uses of reinforced concrete and prefabrication. "Bericht über die Durchführung der Delegationsreise in die Sowjet-Union in der Zeit vom 7–30.12.1955," BArch N 2504/231.

75. "Stalinstadt ist ein Vorbild für uns," *Märkische Union*, 5 June 1957.

76. "While in Berlin they are putting up an international exhibition for a handful of star architects catering to a small circle of clients," noted one article. "We are discussing the best details from the best projects, which bring forward useful solutions based on harmony and functionality." See "Internationaler Typenaustausch,"*Die Wirtschaft*, 30 May 1957.

77. "Internationale Ausstellung: Typenprojekte,"*Berliner Zeitung*, 23 May 1957. See also the meeting's protocol, "Stenografisches Protokoll," 27 May 1957, BArch DH 1/44994.

78. Kosel cited in a *Neues Deutschland* article clipping, BArch DH 1/44993; "Beschluß über die Zusammenarbeit der sozialistichen Länder in der Typenprojektierung," 27 May 1957, BArch DH 1/45334.

79. Gerhard Kosel, *Unternehmen Wissenschaft: Die Wiederentdeckung einer Idee: Erinnerungen* (Berlin: Henschelverlag Kunst und Gesellschaft, 1989), esp. 56–79.

80. Kosel also proposed a theory that considered scientific and technological research as a "productive force." Gerhard Kosel, *Produktivkraft Wissenschaft* (Berlin: Verlag Die Wirtschaft, 1957).

81. Christine Hannemann, *Die Platte: Industrialisierter Wohnungsbau in der DDR*, 3rd ed. (Berlin: Schiler, 2005), 75–83.

82. "Weltweite Zusammenarbeit sozialistischer Bauleute," *Neues Deutschland*, 26 May 1957.

83. "Stenografisches Protokoll," 27 May 1957, BArch DH 1/44994.

84. Compare the Albanian and North Korean reports of the meeting: "Doklad Albanskoi delegatsii" and "Doklad Koreiskoi delegatsii," May 1957, BArch N 2504/197.

85. Kaser, *Comecon*, 134; Raymond Stokes, *Constructing Socialism: Technology and Change in East Germany, 1945–1990* (Baltimore: Johns Hopkins University Press, 2000), 124.

86. "Bericht über die Entwicklung der Mittel der Mechanisierung im Bauwesen," BArch DH 1/45576.

87. "Zur internationalen Tagung über Typenprojektierung," *Deutsche Architektur* 6, no. 4 (special supplement) (1957): 1–16; Gerhard Kosel, handwritten note, 12 November 1992, BArch N 2504/193.

88. On the Albanian response to the Berlin meeting: "Projekt-vendim rreth problemeve të ngritura në kongresin ndërkombëtar të projekteve tip në Berlin (21–31 maj 1957)," n.d., AQSH, f. 499, v. 1957, dos. 80, fl. 1 10.

89. Soviet officials reviewed the working plans. "Aktennotiz," 23 July 1958, BArch DH 1/8087. Notably, the Albanian 1958 delegation included two architects with prewar Western credentials (Gjovalin Gjadri and Anton Lufi). Office of the Prime Minister to Secretariat of the Central Committee (Secret), 8 March 1958, AQSH, f. 14/AP, OU, v. 1958, dos. 28, fl. 74.

90. "Besichtigung des Großplattenbauwerkes Hoyerswerda," 27 August 1958, BArch DH 1/8087.

91. Kosel to Schneidratus (Abteilung Städtebau und Dorfplanung), 20 August 1958, BArch DH 1/8087.

92. "Bericht über die konstituierende Tagung der Ständigen Kommission Bauwesen des Rates für gegenseitige Wirtschaftshilfe," 17 October 1958, BArch DH 1/8084.

93. Sektion "Projektierung und Typung" der Ständigen Kommission Bauwesen des Rates für gegenseitige Wirtschaftshilfe, 27 August 1958, BArch DH 1/8087; "Plan der Maßnahmen zum Arbeitsplan 1959–1960 der Sektion Entwurfslösungen, Typenprojektierung und Normen (ETN) der Ständigen Kommission Bauwesen des RfgW, 13 June 1959, BArch DH 1/39186.

94. "Protokoll der 1. Sitzung der Sektion Gebietsplanung und Städtebau der Ständigen Kommission Bauwesen," December 1958, BArch DH 1/8087.

95. "Einschätzung der Arbeit der Ständigen Kommission Bauwesen," 18 November 1958, BArch DH 1/8087.

96. "Verzeichnis der Tafeln für die Ausstellung zur 2. Internationalen Tagung über Typenprojektierung in Leningrad," 09.06.1959, BArch DH 1/8085.

97. "Protokoll" (Vertrauliche Dienstsache), n.d. [1959], BArch DH 1/8085.

98. There were over fifty meetings of the Comecon construction committee from inception to the early 1980s. At the 1982 meeting, for example, Cuba, Mongolia, and Yugoslavia also participated. Yemen was an observer. "Information über die 54 Tagung der Ständigen Kommission des RGW für die Zusammenarbeit auf dem Gebiet des Bauwesen," 18 November 1982, SAPMO-BArch DY 30/27081.

99. "Weiterentwicklung der Plattenbauweise zur Raumzellenbauweise," 18 May 1960, and "Arbeitsplan der Zusammenarbeit der Deutschen Bauakademie mit der Akademie für Bauwesen und Architektur der UdSSR," 15 December 1960, BArch DH 2/20159; "Bericht über die Städtebaukonferenz in Moskau," n.d. [1960], BArch DH 2 21698; "Bericht," December 1962, BArch DH 2/21108.

100. On East German-Polish collaboration, see "Bericht," [1958], DH 1/9408.

101. Výzkumný ústav pozemních staveb to Deutsche Bauakademie, 27 November 1963, BArch DH 2/21109.

102. *Report of the Study Tour of Building Technologists from Latin America, Africa, Asia and the Middle East to the Union of Soviet Socialist Republics* (New York: United Nations, 1964).

103. Zarecor, *Manufacturing a Socialist Modernity*, 224–94; Virág Molnár, *Building the State: Architecture, Politics, and State Formation in Post-War Central Europe* (London: Routledge, 2013), 69–103; "Vervollkommnung des Großplattenbaus," n.d. [1962], and "Komplexe Bewertung der verschiedenen Herstellungsverfahren und der Montage großformatiger Stahlbetonelemente," December 1962, BArch DH 2/21112.

104. "O nekotorykh nedostatkakh v organizatsii kul'turnykh i nauchnykh sviazei mezhdu SSSR i stranami narodnoi demokratii" (Top Secret), 3 September 1955, RGANI, f. 5, op. 28, d. 286, ll.179–80.

105. "Wirtschaftspolitische Direktive für die Delegation der DDR zur Arbeitstagung der Vertreter der zentralen Organe Bauinformation der Teilnehmerländer des RGW," n.d., BArch DH 1/8085.

106. "A hazai és külföldi panelos és öntött épitési rendszerek értékelése," March 1963, BArch DH 2/21114; "Bericht," November 1967, BArch DH 2/21710.

107. "Raport mbi aktivitetin e delegacionit Ministrisë së Ndërtimit të R.P. Shqipërisë në Republikën Çekosllovake," 24 June 1957, AQSH, f. 499, v. 1957, dos. 98, fl. 45ff; "Urdhër," 17 July 1957, AQSH, f. 499, v. 1957, dos. 110/1, fl. 10–16; "Informacion i shkurtër mbi punën dhe propozimet e delegacioneve që vajtën për eksperiencë në R.D. Gjermane, R.P. Çekosllovake, R.P. Rumune dhe R.P. Bullgare," 21 August 1957, AQSH, f. 499, v. 1957, dos. 98, fl. 130–133 verso.

108. Czechoslovak Embassy (Tirana) to Prague, "Mimoriadna politická zpráva o návšteve u s. Envera Hodža, prvého tajomníka ÚV ASP" (Secret), 4 October 1957, NA, KSČ-ÚV-100/3, sv. 23, a.j. 81, 100. One Czechoslovak prefabrication specialist then joined the state university. "Informacion për shokun Spiro Rusha mbi takimet që bëhen me të huajt," dated by hand 10 December 1960, AQSH, f. 490, v. 1960, dos. 1129, fl. 50.

109. "Informacion mbi vërejtjet që i u bënë planit tematik 10–15 vjeçar të Universitetit Shtetëror të Tiranës nga Akademia e Shkencave të B.S.," forwarded 3 June 1960, AQSH, f. 499, v. 1960, dos. 103, fl. 2–13.

110. "Projekt. Thirrje e konferencës kombëtare të punonjësve të ndërtimit," 29 June 1958, AQSH, f. 499, v. 1958, dos. 483, fl. 60.

111. In addition to the Stakhanovites and norm-breakers we have encountered earlier, there were the examples of individuals like Sali Vata, a miner in Selitë who was referred to as "the lion of the tunnels." Ibrush Pasho, a worker from the plain of Myzeqe, had reportedly dug some seventeen cubic meters of earth in under eight hours—even though one of his arms had been half amputated—thus earning the nickname "the bulldozer of Myzeqe." See "Ndërtimet t'ona gjat gjashtë vjetë të pushtetit popullor," n.d., AQSH, f. 499, v. 1951, dos. 56, fl. 4.

112. A Politburo decision following the June 1958 construction conference hailed the transfer of blueprints, prototypes, and prefab technology from the Eastern bloc. "Vendim no. 214 mbi përdorimin e materialeve të bashkëpunimit tekniko-shkencor dhe përhapjen e eksperiencës së përparuar në prodhim," 4 July 1958, AQSH, f. 14/AP, OU, v. 1958, dos. 16, fl. 135–39.

113. "Mbi gjendjen e ndërtimit të banesave dhe detyrat," June 1958, and "Mbi parafabrikimet në ndërtim," n.d., AQSH, f. 499, v. 1958, dos. 445, fl. 18–25, 66–69.

114. "Relacjon teknik mbi sekcionet tip të banesave për vitin 1959," 25 February 1959, AQSH, f. 499, v. 1959, dos. 566, fl. 29.

115. "Projekt-vendim," May 1960, AQSH, f. 490, v. 1960, dos. 963, fl. 5. For earlier references to monotony: "Relacion teknik. Mbi studimin për variante banesash me seksjone tip," 27 October 1958, AQSH, f. 499, v. 1958, dos. 84, fl. 14–18.

116. "Raport," May 1960, AQSH, f. 490, v. 1960, dos. 963, fl. 81.

117. "Relacion mbi punimet për ndërtimin e banesave nga N.SH.N. '21 Dhjetori' për vitin 1961," 17 January 1962, AQSH, f. 490, v. 1961, dos. 895, fl. 40–41.

118. The security police reported that some enterprises refused to execute *tipizime* and were instead preoccupied with achieving individual targets. "Mbi mos realizimin e planit në ndërtimin e disa objekteve" (Top Secret), 14 June 1961, AQSH, f. 490, v. 1961, dos. 890, fl. 2.

119. "Urdhër," dated by hand 28 October 1958, AQSH, f. 490, v. 1958, dos. 893, fl. 144–46.

120. "Società Anonima Fabbriche Fiammiferi ed Affini," *La ricerca scientifica ed il progresso tecnico nell'economia nazionale* 11, no. 12 (December 1940): xix–xx.

121. Antonio Spinosa, *Starace: L'uomo che inventò lo stile fascista* (Milan: Mondadori, 2002), 260; Indro Montanelli and Mario Cervi, *Storia d'Italia*, vol. 8, *1936–1943* (Milan: RCS Libri, 2006), 425–426.

122. "Udhëzim mbi prodhimin dhe ndërtimin me qerpiç," dated by hand 3 July 1955, AQSH, f. 499, v. 1955, dos. 362, fl. 22–26. Specialists also planned to experiment with other industrial remnants and reeds. "Relacion mbi nevojat për të ndërtuar rreth 250.000 m2 ndërtesa banimi, si shtesë plani gjatë vjetëve 1958–1960," 26 February 1958, AQSH, f. 490, v. 1958, dos. 893, fl. 71–76.

123. "Raport mbi punën e delegacionit të Ministrisë së Ndërtimit në Itali," n.d. [November 1958], AQSH, f. 490, v. 1958, dos. 896, fl. 18–26.

124. "Mbi disa çështie lidhur me ndërtesat e banimit," 24 June 1958, AQSH, f. 490, v. 1958, dos. 893, fl. 106–13.

125. "Vendim no. 403 mbi përcaktimin e llojeve të materialeve të ndërtimit për vende të ndryshme të Republikës," 20 September 1960, AQSH, f. 499, v. 1960, dos. 236, fl. 1–6.

126. "Vendim no. 65, mbi suvatimin e ndërtesave të reja në rrugët kryesore të disa qyteteve," 6 March 1958, AQSH, f. 490, v. 1958, dos. 893, fl. 80. By 1961, however, many newly erected structures still featured unfinished façades. So the government issued yet another directive. "Relacion mbi suvatimin e ndërtesave shtetërore në Fier," 20 April 1961, and "Vendim no. 135 mbi suvatimin e ndërtesave të reja në rrugët kryesore të disa qyteteve, 10 May 1961, AQSH, f. 490, v. 1961, dos. 173, fl. 1, 6.

127. "Mbi bojatisjen e ndërtesave," 26 December 1961, AQSH, f. 490, v. 1961, dos. 173, fl. 11.

128. "Analiza mbi regjistrimin e ndërtesave të banimit," 22 September 1959, AQSH, f. 499, v. 1959, dos. 345, fl. 1–18 verso.

129. "Vendim no. 440 mbi numrin e kateve dhe lartësinë midis kateve në ndërtesat e banimit," 4 December 1961, AQSH, f. 490, v. 1961, dos. 393, fl. 6.

130. On the continued problem of low dwellings and the struggle to enforce urban planning: "Gjendja si dhe masat për zgjidhjen e problemeve që ngrihen në informacionin e Lidhjes së Shkrimtarëve dhe Artistëve të Shqipërisë mbi takimin kombëtar të arkitektëve," forwarded 14 September 1971, AQSH, f. 490, v. 1971, dos. 303, fl. 31.

131. "Vendim mbi aprovimin e projekt/ides të stufave ekonomike dhe mobilimin e mbrendshëm të kuzhinave," 28 August 1958, and "Relacion mbi ndërtimin në vend të stufave ekonomike dhe mobilimin e mbrendshëm të guzhinës," 21 October 1958, AQSH, f. 490, v. 1958, dos. 893, fl.117, 124–26.

132. "Proces verbal," 23 April 1955, and "Relacion," 6 September 1955, AQSH, f. 567, v. 1955, dos. 182, fl. 5–6 verso.

133. "Ndryshim projekti," 12 February 1962, AQSH, f. 499, v. 1962, dos. 420, fl. 90.

134. "Disa vërejtje reth apartamenteve të reja që janë ndërtuar e po ndërtohen në Tiranë," forwarded 30 March 1961, AQSH, f. 499, v. 1961, dos. 239, fl. 2. Tirana-based furniture enterprises had already established direct contacts with counterpart enterprises in East Germany. "Aufnahme," 27 July 1959, BArch DE 1/26906.

135. "Relacjon i anketave mbi banesat e reja të ndërtuara në v. 1958," 30 May 1959, AQSH, f. 499, v. 1958, dos. 445, fl. 32–36.

136. "Raport," May 1960, AQSH, f. 490, v. 1960, dos. 963, fl. 99ff.

137. "Relacjon teknik mbi sekcionet tip të banesave për vitin 1959," 25 February 1959, AQSH, f. 499, v. 1959, dos. 566, fl. 27–30.

138. "Relacion mbi një problem funksional me ndërtesat e banimit," n.d., AQSH, f. 499, v. 1956, dos. 439, fl. 12.

139. "Relacion teknik. Mbi studimin për variante banesash me seksjone tip," 27 October 1958, AQSH, f. 499, v. 1958, dos. 84, fl. 15.

140. "Proçes-verbal mbajtur në mbledhjen e Sekretariatit të KQ të PPSH" (Secret), 16 December 1961, AQSH, f. 14/AP, OU, v. 1961, dos. 59, fl. 349–53.

141. Letter (Reuters, Belgrade) to Salisbury, 10 March 1958, Harrison Salisbury Papers, box 306, folder 18.

142. "Proçes-verbal mbajtur në mbledhjen e Sekretariatit të KQ të PPSH" (Secret), 16 December 1961, AQSH, f. 14/AP, OU, v. 1961, dos. 59, fl. 351.

143. "Protokoll i mbajtur në mbledhjen e Byrosë Politike të K.Q. të PPSH" (Secret), 6 June 1959, AQSH, f. 14/AP, OU, v. 1959, dos. 18, fl. 8–9; "Studim mbi industrializimin e prodhimit të materialeve të ndërtimit për pesëvjeçarin e III-të," n.d., AQSH, f. 499, v. 1960, dos. 775, fl. 34–38.

144. "Über die Arbeit der Ständigen Kommission Bauwesen im Jahre 1960," n.d. BArch DH 2/20181; Dragoti to Kosel, 3 November 1961, BArch DC 20 (Ministerrat der DDR)/12068, 6.

145. "Kurzinformation—Unterstützung der Volksrepublik Albanien beim Aufbau der Baustoffindustrie," 19 June 1961, BArch DE1/25484.

146. In correspondence with the deputy premier, Kosel accused the Albanian side of misrepresenting facts. Kosel to Stoph (Vertrauliche Verschlußsache), 14 December 1961, BArch DC 20/12068, 2–3. See also "Protokoll der V. Tagung der Sektion Gebietsplannung und Städtebau der Ständigen Kommission Bauwesen," 12–18 September 1961, BArch DH 2/20159.

147. "Evidenca e realizimit apartamenteve për 10/mujorin 1961," n.d. [December 1961], AQSH, f. 14/AP, OU, v. 1961, dos. 59, fl. 304.

148. "Informacion," n.d., AQSH, f. 499, v. 1964, dos. 27, fl. 5–16; "Projekt-plani për bashkëpunimin kultural me vendet e tjera për vitin 1966" (Secret), 5 May 1965, AQSH, f. 499, v. 1965, dos. 77, fl. 1–5 verso.

149. "Mbi dërgimin e specialistëve jashtë shtetit për vitin 1971 në Zvicër, Danimarkë e Suedi me mardhënie kulturale me botën e jashtme," dated by hand 4 January 1971, AQSH, f. 499, v. 1971, dos. 267, fl. 6.

150. Duanfang Lu, *Remaking Chinese Urban Form: Modernity, Scarcity and Space, 1949–2005* (London: Routledge, 2006), 122.

151. Albanian Embassy (Pyongyang) to Tirana, "Relacion. Mbi disa të dhëna për ndërtimet e banesave me blloqe të parafabrikuara prej betoni," 10 June 1961, AQSH, f. 490,

v. 1962, dos. 1142, fl. 38–41; Albanian Embassy (Pyongyang) to Tirana (Top Secret), 12 December 1961, AMPJ, v. 1961, dos. 182, fl. 72–74; "Aktiviteti në fushën e B.T. Shkencor të Ministris Ndërtimit në vitin 1964," [date unclear], AQSH, f. 490, v. 1964, dos. 1190, fl. 7; "Relacion mbi projektin e godinës së banimit me 5 kate dërguar nga R.P.D. e Koresë," dated by hand 8 September 1965, AQSH, f. 499, v. 1965, dos. 83, fl. 2–3.

152. "Njerëz dhe . . . çelik!" *Miqësia*, September 1964, 14–15.

153. Kapo to Havana, 23 April 1963, AQSH, f. 14/AP, DJ, v. 1963, dos. 834, fl. 1–6.

154. "Përshtypje dhe mendime mbi arkitekturën e Kubës," n.d., AQSH, f. 490, v. 1963, dos. 916, fl. 29.

155. Pedro Ignacio Alonso and Hugo Palmarola, "A Panel's Tale: The Soviet KPD System and the Politics of Assemblage," *AA Files,* no. 59 (2009): 30–41.

156. "Kërkesa në fushën e B.T. Shkencor për mbledhjen e VI-të të Komisjonit të përbashkët Shqiptaro-Korean dhe mbledhjes së I-rë që do të bëhet në R. e Kubës," dated by hand 13 March 1964, AQSH, f. 490, v. 1964, dos. 1199, fl. 22–23; "Mbi një fabrikë për panele të gatëshme," dated by hand 29 August 1969, AQSH, f. 499, v. 1969, dos. 177, fl. 2; "Mbi caktimin e punonjësve që do të specializohen në R.P. të Kinës" (Secret), dated by hand 1 November 1971, AQSH, f. 499, v. 1971, dos. 267, fl. 46. One architect recalled that the panels coming out of the Chinese-funded factory were initially full of defects, creating more problems to be solved. Bego, *Skeda arkitekture*, 58–59.

157. "Konkluzione të Byrosë Politike të Komitetit Qendror të PPSH 'Mbi thjeshtimin e ndërtimeve për t'i bërë ato më pak të kushtueshme,'" forwarded 4 May 1971, AQSH, f. 490, v. 1971, dos. 303, fl. 23–26.

158. "Relacion. Mbi punën e grupit të specialistëve që vizituan R.P. Bullgarisë, të Rumanisë për problemin e Paneleve vertikale për godina banimi," 2 April 1971, AQSH, f. 499, v. 1971, dos. 142, fl. 1–6; "Analiza e shkallës mekanizimit dhe parafabrikimit në vitin 1973," n.d., AQSH, f. 499, v.1973, dos. 300, fl. 1–11; "Mbi disa të meta në objektet e Tiranës" (Sekret), 27 July 1974, AQSH, f. 499, v. 1974, dos. 261, fl. 1–3; Enver Faja, "Urbanistika e qyteteve të reja të ndërtuara pas çlirimit dhe blloku i banimit" (unpublished thesis, Tirana, 1984).

159. Throughout the bloc (and elsewhere), architects feared that industrialization would bring about the "deskilling and automatization of their expertise." Molnár, *Building the State*, 81.

160. Khrushchev, *Memoirs,* 2:276–77, 287.

6. THE GREAT LEAP

1. "Protokoll i mbledhjes së Byrosë Politike të KQ të PPSH," 18 December 1958, AQSH, f. 14/AP, OU, v. 1958, dos. 24.

2. Relacion. Mbi ndërtimin e Pallatit Kulturës," forwarded 12 August 1959, AQSH, f. 499, v. 1959, dos. 448, fl. 3.

3. "Marrveshje midis qeverisë Republikës Popullore të Shqipërisë dhe qeverisë së Bashkimit të Republikave Sovjetike Socialiste mbi ndërtimin e Pallatit të Kulturës në Shqipëri" (Secret), 3 July 1959, AQSH, f. 499, v. 1959, dos. 173, fl. 1–4.

4. Maks Velo, "Qendra e Tiranës, shkretëtira e tartarëve dhe teoria e shesheve të vegjël," *Shekulli,* 16 April 2006.

5. Each side blamed the other. "Informacion mbi marëdhëniet me palën sovjetike për ndërtimin e Pallatit të Kulturës Tiranë," 17 May 1961, AQSH, f. 499, v. 1961, dos. 110, fl. 1–9. One Soviet diplomat told an East German counterpart that the Albanian side was at fault for trying to go bigger than the original Soviet plans. Tschanter to Opitz, 16 May 1961, BArch DE 1/25476, 20–21; "Information" (Strictly confidential), 16 May 1961, PA AA, MfAA, C 274/75, 38–40.

6. "Raport informativ mbi gjendjen politike në qytetin e Tiranës" (Top Secret), 17 June 1961, AQSH, f. 14/AP, OU, v. 1961, dos. 55, fl. 60.

7. "Relacion mbi fondet që nevojiten për ngritjen e katër sektorëve (guroreve) për prodhimin e blloqeve të gurve dekorativ për veshjen e Pallatit të Kulturës, 9 April 1953, AQSH, f. 499, v. 1963, dos. 724, fl. 4–4 verso.

8. The building was initially supposed to host an exhibition about "the achievements of the people's economy of the USSR." See "Marrveshje" (Secret), 3 July 1959, AQSH, f. 499, v. 1959, dos. 173, fl. 1. The Soviet design was featured in *Arkhitektura SSSR,* no. 11 (1960): 63–65.

9. "Të dashur shokë," n.d., AQSH, f. 490, v. 1966, dos. 386, fl. 12.

10. "Vermerk über eine Besichtigung des neuen Kulturpalasts Tirana am 6.10.66," 11 October 1966, PA AA, MfAA, C 607/78, 12.

11. Noteworthy studies of the Sino-Soviet split include Jeremy Friedman, *Shadow Cold War: The Sino-Soviet Competition for the Third World* (Chapel Hill: University of North Carolina Press, 2015), and Lorenz M. Lüthi, *The Sino-Soviet Split: Cold War in the Communist World* (Princeton: Princeton University Press, 2008); Donald S. Zagoria, *The Sino-Soviet Conflict, 1956–1961* (Princeton, NJ: Princeton University Press, 1962); William E. Griffith, *Albania and the Sino-Soviet Rift* (Cambridge, MA: M.I.T. Press, 1963). See also Vladislav Zubok and Constantine Pleshakov, *Inside the Kremlin's Cold War: From Stalin to Khrushchev* (Cambridge, MA: Harvard University Press, 1996); Odd Arne Westad, ed., *Brothers in Arms: The Rise and Fall of the Sino-Soviet Alliance, 1945–1963* (Washington, DC: Woodrow Wilson Center Press, 1998); Chen Jian, *Mao's China and the Cold War* (Chapel Hill: University of North Carolina Press, 2001). The later years of the crisis are captured in Sergey Radchenko, *Two Suns in the Heavens: The Sino-Soviet Struggle for Supremacy, 1962–1967* (Stanford: Stanford University Press, 2009).

12. Tony Judt, *Postwar: A History of Europe since 1945* (New York: Penguin, 2005), 422.

13. "O polozhenii s ispol'zovaniem kreditov, predostavliaemykh Albanii Sovetskim Soiuzom i stranami narodnov demokratii" (Secret), 24 September 1956, RGANI, f. 5, op. 28, d. 391, l. 194.

14. "Nekotorye sovety Albanskim druz'iam" (Top Secret), 24 September 1956, RGANI, f. 5, op. 28, d. 391, ll. 191–92. There were also suggestions to develop a new radio service devoted to broadcasting propaganda in medium waves to the Middle East. "Relacion mbi vajtjen e delegacionit të radios shqiptare në Moskë," 17 December 1957, AMPJ, v. 1957, dos. 56, fl. 28. Moscow sent an Arabic speaker to Radio Tirana to help with these broadcasts. Albanian Embassy (Moscow) to Tirana (Top Secret), 12 March 1958, AMPJ, v. 1958, dos. 63, fl. 14.

15. "Nga fjalimi i shokut N.S. Hrushov në drekën e shtruar për nder të delegacionit të qeverisë dhe të partisë të RPSH," n.d., AQSH, f. 14/AP, M-PK(b)BS, v. 1957, dos. 2.

16. Khrushchev, *Memoirs,* 3:516.

17. "Wichtiger Nachtrag zu dem Schreiben an Kollegin Rath vom 8 Mai 1957" (Top Secret), 13 May 1957, BArch DC 1/4230.

18. Czechoslovak Embassy (Tirana) to Prague, "Mimoriadna politická zpráva o návšteve u s. Envera Hodža, prvého tajemníka ÚV ASP" (Secret), 4 October 1957, NA, KSČ-ÚV-100/3, sv. 23, a.j. 81, 98.

19. The Sudanese diplomat accredited to Tirana scoffed in a meeting with a US representative the following year that "Albania had no particular appeal in the Middle East, the majority of whose people and leaders didn't even know what Albania was." US Embassy (Rome) to Department of State (Confidential), 16 September 1958, in *Records of the Department of State Relating to the Internal Affairs of Albania, 1955–1959*, record group 59, decimal file 767 (Wilmington, DE: Scholarly Resources, 2002?).

20. Nevertheless, Tirana asked Berlin for information about East Germany's relations with the Arab world in 1959. "Aktenvermerk," n.d. [April 1959], SAPMO-BArch DY 30/ IV 2/20/94, 116–17.

21. "Të dashur shokë" (handwritten letter), 6 April 1949, AQSH, f. 14/AP, M-PK(b) BS, v. 1949, dos. 19, fl. 3. "Stalin's words are golden," the party chief wrote at the time, "profound, orienting, the only way forward for us."

22. "Protokoll i mbledhjes së Byrosë Politike të KQ të PPSH," 18 December 1958, AQSH, f. 14/AP, OU, v. 1958, dos. 24, fl. 16.

23. Between 1953 and 1956, the number of persons "being processed" (*në përpunim*) by security operatives doubled. It then tripled by 1959. The data are drawn from an internal security police study contained in AMPB, bound undated book, n.d. [likely after 1972], p. 97.

24. Tirana to all missions abroad (except Belgrade), no. 1037 (Top Secret), 24 November 1956, AMPJ, v. 1956, dos. 16, fl. 163; "Zapis' besedy V. F. Nikolaeva s G. Georgy-Dezhem o pozitsii Iugoslavii po voprosu ob I. Nade i ego gruppe i merakh, neobkhodimykh dlia normalizatsii v Vengrii" (Top Secret), 26 November 1956, in *Sovetskii Soiuz i vengerskii krizis 1956 goda*, ed. V. K. Volkov et al. (Moscow: ROSSPEN, 1998), 694.

25. "Proçes-verbal i mbledhjes të Byrosë Politike të K.Q. të P.P.SH.," 27 April 1957, AQSH, f. 14/AP, OU, v. 1957, dos. 10, fl. 1–35. "Mbi takimet 'për çështje partie,' Moskë," 15 April 1957, and handwritten notes by A. Kostallari (translator), "Nga fjala e shokut N.S. Hrushov në bisedimet me delegacionin tonë në prill të vitit 1957 në Moskë," AQSH, f. 14/AP, M-PK(b)BS, v. 1957, dos. 2.

26. "Proçes-verbal i mbledhjes të Byrosë Politike të K.Q. të P.P.SH.," 27 April 1957, AQSH, f. 14/AP, OU, v. 1957, dos. 10, fl. 23.

27. GDR Embassy (Tirana) to Berlin, 8 May 1957, and "Wichtiger Nachtrag," 13 May 1957, BArch DC 1/4230.

28. The Czechoslovak ambassador's account of Hoxha's report is contained in "Informatívna zpráva z porady u s. Envera Hodžu, prvého tajomníka ÚV ASP" (Secret), 2 July 1957, NA, KSČ-ÚV-100/3, sv. 23, a.j. 81, 83–96

29. "O politicheskom polozhenii v NR Albanii" (Secret), 4 October 1956, RGANI, f. 5, op. 28, d. 388, l. 187.

30. "Plenumi i Komitetit Qendror të PPSH të dates 20 qershor 1958," 20 June 1958, AQSH, f. 14/AP, OU, v. 1958, dos. 3. The party plenum affirmed "waging a war without compromises in order to politically and theoretically unmask and defeat modern revisionism."

31. "Protokoll i mbledhjes së Byrosë Politike të KQ të PPSH," 18 December 1958, AQSH, f. 14/AP, OU, v. 1958, dos. 24, fl. 16.

32. "Raport i Ministrisë së Punëve të Brendshme mbi veprimtarinë e armiqve të jashtëm e të brendshëm dhe mbi aktivitetin e organeve të punëve të brendëshme për vjetin 1958" (Top Secret), 10 March 1959, AQSH, f. 14/AP, OU, v. 1959, dos. 11.

33. "Shokut Nikita Sergejeviç Hrushov, Kremlin—Moskë" 19 May 1959, AQSH, f. 14/AP, M-PK(b)BS, v. 1959, dos. 18.

34. "Protokoll mbajtur në mbledhjen e Byrosë Politike të K.Q. të P.P.SH," 19 May 1959, AQSH, f. 14/AP, OU, v. 1959, dos. 17, fl. 1–6.

35. "Protokoll i bisedimeve të zhvilluara midis delegacionit të Partisë Komuniste dhe Qeverisë së BRSS dhe delegacionit të Partisë së Punës dhe Qeverisë së Republikës Popullore të Shqipërisë në Tiranë," 25 May 1959, AQSH, f. 14/AP, M-PK(b)BS, v. 1959, dos. 24.

36. "Promemoria mbi disa çështje të ekonomisë së Republikës Popullore të Shqipërisë," n.d., AQSH, f. 14/AP, M-PK(b)BS, v. 1959, dos. 22, fl. 1–24.

37. "Protokoll," 25 May 1959, AQSH, f. 14/AP, M-PK(b)BS, v. 1959, dos. 24; "Disa kërkesa të K.Q. të P.P.SË [*sic*] Shqipërisë dhe të Këshillit të Ministrave të shtruara N.S. Hrushçov," 20 May 1959, AQSH, f. 14/AP, M-PK(b)BS, v. 1959, dos. 25, fl. 1–7.

38. "Protokoll mbajtur në mbledhjen e Byrosë Politike të K.Q. të P.P.SH," 6 June 1959 (Secret), AQSH, f. 14/AP, OU, v. 1959, dos.18, fl. 1–12.

39. "Karakteristikat e ndërmarrjeve bujqësore shtetërore dhe kooperativave bujqësore që parashikohet të vizitojë delegacioni sovjetik," n.d., AQSH, f.14/AP, M-PK(b)BS, v. 1959, dos. 21, fl. 62ff.

40. "Vrejtjet e bëra në bisedimet" (Top Secret), AQSH, f. 14/AP, M-PK(b)BS, v. 1959, dos. 23, fl. 1–18.

41. Letter to the Soviet, Polish, Czechoslovak, East German, Romanian, Hungarian, and Bulgarian parties, 1 February 1960, contained in AQSH, f. 14/AP, M-PK(b)BS, v. 1960, dos. 11, fl. 1–4. Shortly before the meeting of Communist parties in Bucharest that year, Moscow agreed to push back loan repayments for ten to fifteen years. The letter signed by Khrushchev, dated 25 April 1960, is contained in AQSH, f. 14/AP, M-PK(b)BS, v. 1960, dos. 11, fl. 9–10.

42. "Protokoll mbajtur në mbledhjen e Byrosë Politike të Komitetit Qendror të P.P.SH." (Top Secret), 11 February 1960, AQSH, f. 14/AP, OU, v. 1960, dos. 8. At the June meeting, Hoxha let it be understood that they had insisted that Moscow and Beijing solve their problems among themselves. "Proçes-verbal i mbledhjes së Byrosë Politike të KQ të P.P.SH.," 6 June 1960, AQSH, f. 14/AP, OU, v. 1960, dos. 14, fl. 1–12. He made the same point later that summer: "Proçes-verbal i mbledhjes së Plenumit të Komitetit Qendror të P.P.SH.," 11–12 July 1960, AQSH, f. 14/AP, OU, dos. 2, fl. 36.

43. "Komitetit Qendror të Partisë së Punës të Shqipërisë," 2 June 1960, AQSH, f. 14/AP, M-PK(b)BS, v. 1960, dos. 2.

44. "Shënime nga bisedimet e zhvilluara midis delegacionit të RPSH dhe udhëheqësve të qeverisë kineze," 2 June 1960, AQSH, f. 14/AP, M-PKK, v. 1960, dos. 1, fl. 2; "Bisedimi me shokët udhëheqësa kinczë," 4 June 1960," AQSH, f. 14/AP, M-PKK, dos. 2, fl. 10–14.

45. Ana Lalaj, "Ndarja me sovjetikët dhe aleatja e fundit e Shqipërisë komuniste," *Studime historike*, no. 3–4 (2010): 239–57 (esp. 241).

46. "Proçes-verbal i mbledhjes së Byrosë Politike të KQ të P.P.SH.," 6 June 1960, AQSH, f. 14/AP, OU, v. 1960, dos. 14, fl. 9.

47. "Vetërm shokëve Liri dhe Gogo" (Very Urgent), AQSH, f. 14/AP, M-PKK, v. 1960, dos. 2.

48. Author interview with Liri Belishova, 28 October 2008, Tirana.

49. "Proçes-verbal i mbledhjes së Plenumit të Komitetit Qendror të P.P.SH.," 11–12 July 1960, AQSH, f. 14/AP, OU, v. 1960, d. 2, fl. 39ff.

50. "Protokoll mbajtur në mbledhjen e Byrosë Politike të Komitetit Qendror të P.P.SH.," 22 June 1960, AQSH, f. 14/AP, OU, v. 1960, dos. 16, fl. 1–10.

51. "Proçes-verbal i mbledhjes së Byrosë Politike të K. Qendror të P.P.SH," 24 June 1960, AQSH, f. 14/AP, OU, v. 1960, dos. 17, fl. 2.

52. "Proçes-verbal i mbledhjes së Byrosë Politike të Komitetit Qendror të P.P.SH.," 7 July 1960, AQSH, f. 14/AP, OU, v. 1960, dos. 18.

53. "Proçes-verbal i mbledhjes së Plenumit të Komitetit Qendror të P.P.SH.," 11–12 July 1960, AQSH, f. 14/AP, OU, v. 1960, d. 2, fl. 33.

54. "Shënime nga takimi midis shokut Mehmet Shehu dhe shokut Van Dun, i ngarkuari me punë ad interim dhe sekretar i parë i ambasadës së Republikës Popullore të Kinës në Shqipëri në datën 1 gusht 1960," 1 August 1960, AQSH, f. 14/AP, M-PKK, v. 1960, dos. 5, fl. 1.

55. Lüthi, *The Sino-Soviet Split*, 173, citing Mao Zedong, *Jianguo yilai Mao Zedong wengao*, vol. 9 (Beijing: Zhongyang wenxian chubanshe, 1996).

56. "Raport në Plenumin e Komitetit Qendror të PPSH mbi qëndrimin në kundërshtim me vijën politike e ideollogjike të partisë të sh. Liri Belishova," 3 September 1960, AQSH, f. 14/AP, OU, v. 1960, dos. 3, fl. 76–81.

57. GDR Embassy (Tirana) to Berlin (Top Secret), "Bemerkungen," 20 September 1960, SAPMO-BArch DY 30/IV 2/20/97, 35.

58. "Ultimately, Hoxha's pro-Chinese policy was not the result of ideological concord but of intra-party struggles and Khrushchev's strong-arm tactics," writes Lüthi, inexplicably denying the importance of ideology in Tirana even as he painstakingly establishes it for the Chinese. See his *The Sino-Soviet Split*, 202. Decades earlier, William Griffith had speculated that the split was due to some Moscow-initiated coup. Griffith, *Albania and the Sino-Soviet Rift*, 47. No evidence has emerged about a Soviet-designed coup.

59. Shpati to Shehu (New York), 6 October 1960, AMPJ, v. 1960, dos. 532/18.

60. Shpati to Shehu (New York), 9 October 1960, AMPJ, v. 1960, dos. 532/18, fl. 84/1.

61. Shehu (New York) to Hoxha, 9 October 1960, AMPJ, v. 1960, dos. 532/18, fl. 85.

62. "Takimi i delegacionit të P.P.SH. me përfaqësuesit e P.K. të B.S., Moskë, Kremlin," 12 November 1960, AQSH, f. 14/AP, M-PK(b)BS, v. 1960, dos. 24, fl. 23–35.

63. Peking to Tirana (Top Secret), no. 5401, 13 September 1960, AMPJ, v. 1960, dos. 114, fl. 90; untitled memo to deputy prime minister, minister of foreign affairs, minister of trade, n.d., AMPJ, v. 1960, dos. 114, fl. 98; "Memorandum of Conversation with Zhou Enlai," 2 February 1961, *Cold War International History Project Bulletin*, no. 16 (Fall 2007–Winter 2008): 197–200.

64. Westad, *The Global Cold War*, 69.

65. "Nga biseda e sh. Hysni dhe sh. Ramiz me delegacionin kinez," 1 December 1960, AQSH, f. 14/AP, M-PKK, v. 1960, dos. 10, fl. 32.

66. In his memoirs, Hoxha later noted that the "conspirators admitted everything with their own mouths" but did not mention the tortures that had been inflicted on them. See his *The Khrushchevites: Memoirs* (Tirana: 8 Nëntori, 1980), 471.

67. "Njëzet vjetë jetë dhe luftë revolucionare," printed in Enver Hoxha, *Vepra*, vol. 22 [October 1961–December 1961] (Tirana: 8 Nëntori, 1976), 127.

68. "Bisedim i zhvilluar më 18 nëntor 1971, në pritjen që i bëri kryetari i Këshillit të Ministrave, Mehmet Shehu, delegacionit qeveritar ekonomik të RP të Kinës, të kryesuar nga Ministri për Lidhje Ekonomike me Botën e Jashtme, Fan Ji," 18 November 1971," AMPJ, v. 1971, dos. 149, fl. 92–116 (at 101).

69. "Teza mbi disa çështje për të biseduar me shokët udhëheqës të P.K. të Kinës," 29 August 1963, AQSH, f. 14/AP, OU, v. 1963, dos. 12, fl. 27–55; "Takim i tretë me shokun Ten Hsiao Pin në Pekin," 24 September 1963, AQSH, f. 14/AP, M-PKK, v. 1963, dos. 7, fl. 64–91.

70. "Ökonomische Beziehungen der VR Albanien zu den anderen sozialistischen Ländern," n.d. [most likely September 1960], PA AA MfAA, A 4.525, 16.

71. "Information über die derzeitige innere und außere Lage der Volksrepublik Albanien" (Confidential), 13 June 1962, PA AA, MfAA, A 17.155, 95.

72. "Qëllimi i vajtjes së delegacionit," n.d. [discussed in Politburo meeting on 11 July 1962], AQSH, f. 14/AP, OU, v. 1962, dos. 11, fl. 36.

73. "Informacion," n.d., AMPJ, v. 1960, dos. 123, fl. 10–11.

74. A memorandum of a meeting between the Albanian ambassador in Pyongang and Kim Il Sung, dated 11 May 1961, is contained in AMPJ, v. 1961, dos. 182, fl. 18. Kim's son, the country's future leader, similarly reassured Albanian students in Pyongyang that they were on the right side of the dispute. Albanian Embassy (Pyongyang) to Tirana (Top Secret), 26/27 July 1961, AMPJ, v. 1961, dos. 182, fl. 32. "The revisionists are trembling because of the Communist Party of China," declared Hoxha two years later, "because of us, Korea, Vietnam, and now also Romania, which has openly opposed Khrushchev." "Proces-verbal i mbledhjes së Sekretariatit të KQ të PPSH," 10 May 1963, AQSH, f. 14/AP, OU, v. 1963, dos. 19, fl. 343.

75. "Qëllimi i vajtjes së delegacionit," n.d., AQSH, f. 14/AP, OU, v. 1962, dos. 11, fl. 47ff.

76. "Proçes-verbal i mbledhjes së Byrosë Politike të Komitetit Qendror të PPSH" (Top Secret), 11 July 1962, AQSH, f. 14/AP, OU, v. 1962, dos. 11.

77. *Miqësija*, March 1961, 2.

78. Central Committee to local party committees (Secret), 1 November 1961, AQSH, f. 14/AP, str., DAP, v. 1961, dos. 114, Fl. 2.

79. Central Committee to local party committees (Secret), 29 December 1961, AQSH, f. 14/AP, OU, v. 1961, dos. 59, fl. 137–51.

80. "Raport informativ. Mbi gjendjen politike në qytetin e Tiranës" (Top Secret), 17 June 1961, AQSH, f. 14/AP, OU, v. 1961, dos. 55, fl. 55–70.

81. "Monat der Albanisch-Sowjetischen Freundschaft," 4 September 1961, PA AA, MfAA, A 4.421, 129.

82. East German Embassy (Tirana) to Berlin, 12 May 1961, PA AA, MfAA, A 4.422, 8.

83. "Program i qartë për të ardhmen e ndritur," Miqësia, August 1962, n.p.

84. Two recent memoirs capture the contradictions, hopes, and disillusionment produced by the Sino-Soviet split. Spartak Ngjela, Përkulja dhe rënia e tiranisë shqiptare, 1957–2010 (Tirana: UET Press, 2011), esp. 337ff; Kadare, Kohë e pamjaftueshme, esp. 101ff.

85. Rolf Italiaander, Albanien—Vorposten Chinas (Munich: Delp'sche Verlagsbuchhandlung, 1970), 8.

86. "Relacion mbi bisedimet e zhvilluara nga shokët tanë me bullgarë, lidhur me mbledhjen e Moskës dhe dekllaratën" (Secret), 3 February 1961, AQSH, f. 14/AP, str., DJ, v. 1961, dos. 446, fl. 2–6.

87. A conversation between the Albanian and Chinese ambassadors in Warsaw, for example, touched on the idea that the well-known Soviet ambassador there did not support Khrushchev's line. "Relacion mbi dy bisedime të zhvilluara me ambasadorin kines shokun Vang Ping Nan," 21 September 1961, AQSH, f. 14/AP, str., DJ, v. 1961, dos. 499, fl. 8.

88. "Proces-verbal i mbledhjes së Sekretariatit të KQ të PPSH të dates 19 qershor 1961" (Secret), 19 June 1961, AQSH, f. 14/AP, OU, v. 1961, dos. 54, fl. 225.

89. On the Albanian Telegraphic Agency and radio propaganda directed at foreign countries: "Mbi propagandën për jashtë të ATSH-s dhe Radio-s," dated by hand 15 July 1961, AQSH, f. 14/AP, OU, v. 1961, dos. 55, fl. 72.

90. "Relacion mbi gjendjen e kuadrit të Ministrisë së Punëve të Jashtme dhe të përfaqësive diplomatike për vitin 1961," dated by hand 16 December 1961, AQSH, f. 14/AP, OU, v. 1961, dos. 59, fl. 202–210/1.

91. Arabic-language broadcasts were twice as long as those in other languages. "Mbi propagandën për jashtë të ATSH-s dhe Radio-s," dated by hand 15 July 1961, AQSH, f. 14/AP, OU, v. 1961, dos. 55, fl. 73.

92. "Vendim no. 222 mbi përmirësimin e propagandës me botën a jashtme në Radio Tirana dhe agjensinë Telegrafike Shqiptare" (Secret), 15 July 1961, f. 14/AP, OU, v. 1961, dos. 55, fl. 79; Vendim no. 383 mbi krijimin e emisionit për punonjësit e Bashkimit Sovjetik në Radio Tirana" (Secret), 3 November 1961, AQSH, f. 14/AP, OU, v. 1961, dos. 59, fl. 11. Another call for expansion came in 1965, when party officials recommended improving programs targeted at countries in Asia, Africa, and Latin America. "Vendim no. 38 mbi disa masa për forcimin e luftës kundër propagandës së armikut, detyrat e kundër-propagandës dhe forcimin e propagandës në botën e jashtme" (Secret), 10 February 1965, AQSH, f. 14/AP, OU, v. 1965, dos. 4, fl. 139–41.

93. "Vermerk über den Empfang des ghanesischen Botschafters, Suljeman Tandoh, am 13.3.1962, um 13.00 Uhr, auf dem Flugplatz Rinas bei Tirana" (Top Secret), 20 March 1962, PA AA, MfAA, A 17.155, 62.

94. "Information über ein Zusammentreffen der Geschäftsträger der sozialistischen Länder Europas am 6.2.1962 im Botschafterwohnhaus" (Top Secret), 9 February 1962, and "Vermerk über eine Zusammenkunft der Geschäftsträger der Vertretungen der sozialistischen Länder Europas in der Botschaft der Rumänischen Volksrepublik am 16.3.1962," 16 March 1962, PA AA, MfAA, A 17.155, 28–29, 56.

95. "Aktenvermerk," 2 September 1961, PA AA, MfAA, A 4.422, 11–12.

96. "Mein lieber Richard" (handwritten letter), 28 February 1962, SAPMO-BArch DY 30/IV 2/20/94, 132–133 verso.

97. "Entwurf eines Antwortbriefes an Jaho," n.d., SAPMO-BArch DY 30/IV 2/20/94, 137.

98. "Lieber Siegfried," n.d., SAPMO-BArch DY 30/IV 2/20/94, 139–140.

99. "Vendim no. 129 mbi martesat e shtetasve shqiptarë me shtetasit e huaj" (Secret), 2 April 1959, and related protocol of the discussion of the Politburo, AQSH, f. 14/AP, OU, v. 1959, dos. 11.

100. "Proçes-verbal mbajtur në mbledhjen e Byrosë Politike të Komitetit Qendror të P.P.SH." (Top Secret), 5 December 1961, AQSH, f. 14/AP, OU, v. 1961, dos. 47.

101. Ana Lalaj, "Ndarje të trishtuara. Një vështrim historik-juridik mbi martesat midis shtetasve shqiptarë dhe të huaj," *Studime historike*, no. 1–2 (2010): 155–65 (esp. 163–64).

102. Maks Velo, *Historia e një cope guri: rrëfime* (Elbasan: Sejko, 2006), 75.

103. "Nëpër BRSS," *Miqësia*, November 1962, n.p.; "Pesë ditë—pasë kate!" *Miqësia*, March 1963, 19.

104. Ngjela, *Përkulja dhe rënia e tiranisë shqiptare*, 312–20; Juliane Fürst, *Stalin's Last Generation: Soviet Post-War Youth and the Emergence of Mature Socialism* (New York: Oxford University Press, 2010), 229.

105. Khrushchev, *Memoirs*, 2:232.

106. "Relacion. Mbi përkthimin dhe botimin e veprave kryesore të K. Marksit dhe F. Engelsit në gjuhën shqipe dhe mbi masat që duhet të merren për këtë punë," dated by hand 15 July 1961, and "Vendim no. 227 mbi përkthimin dhe pregatitjen për në shtyp të veprave të zgjedhura të shokut Mao Ce Dun," 15 July 1961, AQSH, f. 14/AP, OU, v. 1961, dos. 55, fl. 135–39, 153.

107. "Raport informativ. Mbi gjendjen politike në qytetin e Tiranës" (Top Secret), 17 June 1961, AQSH, f. 14/AP, OU, v. 1961, dos. 55, fl. 61. Consider also the role of the security police. Back in 1953, Hoxha had explained that he would rather staff its ranks with men who had spent years fighting with the partisans in the mountains than with professors and teachers and other middle-class elements. "Protokoll no. 3 i mbledhjes së Byrosë Politike të KQ të PPSH," 26 January 1953, AQSH, f.14/AP, OU, v. 1953, dos. 8, fl. 111–14.

108. In April 1962, one Albanian escapee to Trieste (through Yugoslavia) told a Radio Free Europe interviewer a version of the Albanian-Soviet break that closely mirrored the official narrative, centered on antiparty elements and conspirators. Obviously, this person had no reason to parrot the party line in Trieste. But his testimony shows how deeply the party-controlled narrative permeated Albanian society, in which information in the 1960s still circulated by word of mouth. "Intervista con A.N.," 22 April 1962, Radio Free Europe/Radio Liberty broadcast records, Hoover Institution Archives, box 264.

109. "Proçes-verbal i mbledhjes së Sekretariatit të KQ të PPSH" (Secret), 15 July 1961, AQSH, f. 14/AP, OU, v. 1961, dos. 55, fl. 395.

110. "Proçes-verbal mbajtur në mbledhjen e Byrosë Politike të Komitetit Qendror të PPSH" (Top Secret), 19 January 1965, AQSH, f. 14/AP, OU, v. 1965, dos. 3, fl. 143–208.

111. Examples are contained in the Central Committee Foreign Department correspondence, AQSH, f. 14/AP, str., DJ, v. 1960, dos. 727. Relatives of purged party officials similarly constituted primary targets. Two young women, for example, were singled out because their father was known to have family connections with Belishova. "Relacion mbi dërgimin e studentëve jashtë shtetit për të vazhduar studimet dhe mbi prerjen e bursës për jashtë disa prej tyre," dated by hand 7 August 1961, AQSH, f. 14/AP, OU, v. 1961, dos. 43, fl. 18–27.

112. "Memorandum of Conversation, ALP Delegation with Mao Zedong," 29 June 1962, in *Cold War International History Project Bulletin*, no. 16 (Fall 2007–Winter 2008): 256.

113. "Proçes-verbal i mbledhjes së Byrosë Politike të Komitetit Qendror të PPSH" (Secret), 7 August 1961, AQSH, f. 14/AP, OU, v. 1961, dos. 43, fl. 93; "Vendim no. 247 mbi sistemimin në shkollat e larta të vendit të studentëve që ndiqnin studimet jashtë shtetit dhe mbi dërgimin e një pjese prej tyre për të vazhduar studimet" (Top Secret), 7 August 1961, AQSH, f. 14/AP, OU, v. 1961, dos. 43, fl. 28–29/1.

114. "16 Jahre Wirtschaftshilfe der SU für Albanien," n.d., BArch, DE 1/25481, 409–12.

115. Office of the Prime Minister, untitled instruction, 19 April 1962, AQSH, f. 490, v. 1962, dos. 1150, fl. 1; "Shokut Koço Theodhosi, shokut Abdyl Këllëzi," and "Shokut Behar Shtylla," 2 April 1962, AQSH, f. 490, v. 1962, dos. 1153, fl. 1–5.

116. "Mbi shfrytëzimin e dokumentacioneve të B.T.SH.-së," 20 August 1962, AQSH, f. 490, v. 1962, dos. 1146, fl. 4.

117. "Raport mbi zbatimin e planit të masave për shfrytëzimin e materialeve të ardhura në vendin t'onë nëpërmjet B.T.SH.-së," n.d., AQSH, f. 490, v. 1962, dos. 1146, fl. 20–23.

118. "Pyeteni se çfarë bëhet me disa dokumentacione të rëndësishme të maruna kohë më parë në rrugën e B.T.SH.," n.d., AQSH, f. 490, v. 1962, dos. 1146, fl. 25.

119. Hamm, *Albania*, 33.

120. "Vijon shkresa e jonë Nr. 391 datë 9/VI/1961," 5 August 1961, AQSH, f. 490, v. 1961, dos. 673, fl. 20–22.

121. "Bisedë me sekretarin kinez të Komitetit Solidaritetit Afro-aziatik shokun Jang Chi më datën 28. Shkurt 1963," 20 February 1963, AQSH, f. 14/AP, str., DJ, v. 1963, dos. 785, fl. 2.

122. "Vendim no. 99 mbi aprovimin e specialistëve kinezë që do të vinë në Republikën Popullore të Shqipërisë dhe praktikantëve shqiptarë që do mësojnë në Republikën Popullore të Kinës për veprat industriale" (Secret), 28 March 1963, AQSH, f. 499, v. 1963, dos. 426, fl. 2.

123. "Bericht über ein Informationsfahrt am 15. und 16.4.1962" (Top Secret), 3 May 1962, PA AA, MfAA, C 607/78, 30–31.

124. "Njoftojmë mbi materialet e ardhura nëpërmjet B.T.SH. në ish Drejtorinë Ekonomisë Komunale," 11 June 1965, AQSH, f. 490, v. 1965, dos. 964, fl. 13–16.

125. Instruction to ministries, dated 30 January 1965, are contained in AQSH, f. 490, v. 1964, dos. 1199, fl. 30.

126. Lüthi, *The Sino-Soviet Split*, 204. Estimating Chinese assistance is complicated by the fact that both sides claimed substantially different figures (and by whether military aid is included). Chinese sources claim anywhere between 3 billion RMB in the 1960s (excluding military aid) and 10 billion by the late 1970s (roughly 5 billion US dollars at the time). Fan Chengzuo, "Wo qinli de zhong A liang dang guanxi de qiu dong jijie," *Zhonggong dangshi yanjiu*, no. 4 (2006): 92; Wang Taiping (ed.), *Zhonghua renmin gongheguo waijiao shi, 1957–1969* (Beijing: Shijie zhishi, 1998), 344. A close observer of Albanian economic affairs put total Chinese aid at 838 million US dollars. Kaser, "Economic System," 302n47.

127. "Takim i shokëve Hysni Kapo dhe Ramis Alia me kryetarin e Këshillit të Shtetit të Republikës Popullore të Kinës, shokun Çu En Lai," 27 June 1962, AQSH, f. 14/AP, M-PKK, v. 1962, dos. 7, fl. 26.

128. In one example, Albanian officials kept insisting that a sodium hydroxide factory had to be located in Vlorë, despite Chinese protests that the zone was prone to earthquakes. Koleka, "Mbi gjendjen e punimeve pregatitore për hartimin e projekteve për 25 veprat që do të na jepen nga RP e Kinës," 10 January 1962, AQSH, f. 14/AP, OU, v. 1962, dos. 6, fl. 5–6.

129. "Proçes-verbal i mbledhjes së Byrosë Politike të Komitet Qendror të P.P.SH." (Top Secret), 15–16 June 1965, AQSH, f. 14/AP, OU, v. 1965, dos. 8, fl. 206.

130. "Proçes-verbal" (Top Secret), 27–29 March 1965, AQSH, f. 14/AP, M-PKK, v. 1965, dos. 4, fl. 99–150. "Sometimes our Albanian friends had too big an appetite for Chinese assistance," a Chinese participant in Sino-Albanian discussions later recalled. Fan Cheng-zuo's recollections are contained in *China and Eastern Europe, 1960s–1980s: Proceedings of the International Symposium: Reviewing the History of Chinese–East European Relations from the 1960s to the 1980s*, ed. Xiaoyuan Liu and Vojtech Mastny (Zürich: Center for Security Studies, 2004), 184. Recalling the hefty requests, one Albanian negotiator is quoted as saying that he had felt "ashamed," adding, "When we needed anything, we just asked the Chinese." Quoted in Jung Chang and Jon Halliday, *Mao: The Unknown Story* (New York: Knopf, 2005), 462.

131. In a 1962 interview, one Albanian exile favorably contrasted the Chinese specialists, who did not command high salaries and special privileges, with the Soviets, whom he criticized for having acted "like occupiers." The Chinese specialists, he observed, ate in the same canteens as their Albanian colleagues. "Intervista con A.N.," 22 April 1962, Radio Free Europe/Radio Liberty broadcast records, Hoover Institution Archives, box 264.

132. "Mbi disa çështje të B.T.SH.," 8 October 1962, AQSH, f. 490, v. 1962, dos. 1142, fl. 12–12 verso. The following year, government officials acknowledged that rumors about disaffected Chinese specialists had "spread all the way to China." One Chinese official reportedly complained that the Albanian side had paid much more for Soviet and Eastern bloc specialists. Indeed, Tirana incurred far fewer costs in keeping Chinese specialists than had been the case with Soviet specialists (let alone the Czechs). "Njoftim" and "Për një përmirësim të madh të trajtimit të specialistëve kinez që gjenden në vendin tonë duke dhënë ndihmë teknike," 21 January 1963, AQSH, f. 490, v. 1963, dos. 1056, fl. 33–38.

133. "Mbi sigurimin e transportit të specialistëve kinezë, etj.," 18 January 1965, AQSH, f. 490, v. 1965, dos. 819, fl. 23–24.

134. "Informacion mbi strehimin dhe ushqimin e specialistëve kinez të veprës no. 6333," n.d., AQSH, f. 490, v. 1965, dos. 819, fl. 37–40.

135. "Informacion," 23 July 1963, AQSH, f. 490, v. 1963, dos. 931, fl. 38.

136. "Kërkesa në fushën e B.T. Shkencor për mbledhjen e VI-të të Komisjonit të përbashkët Shqiptaro-Korean dhe mbledhjen e I-rë që do të bëhet në R. e Kubës," 13 March 1964, AQSH, f. 490, v. 1964, dos. 1199, fl. 22; "Dërgohen disa dokumentacione Koreane t'ardhura në rrugën e B.T.SH," 22 January 1965, AQSH, f. 499, v. 1965, dos. 54, fl. 6.

137. "Zëv. Kryeministrit," 23–30 April 1962, and related communication on the Korean specialists, 5 December 1962, AQSH, f. 490, v. 1962, dos. 1142, fl. 29–30, 47–48. Some early Albanian visitors to China, on the other hand, were not accustomed to Chinese food, which they nevertheless found preferable to the North Korean food. "Raport," n.d. [1961], AQSH, f. 511, v. 1961, dos. 82, fl. 5–8.

138. "Relacion mbi gjendjen e kuadrit përkthyes dhe masat për pregatitjen e tij," n.d., AQSH, f. 14/AP, OU, v. 1963, dos. 19, fl. 137.

139. "Relacion mbi përkthimin dhe pregatitjen për në shtyp të veprave të zgjedhura të sh. Mao Ce Dun," dated by hand 15 July 1961, f. 14/AP, OU, v. 1961, dos. 55, fl. 151.

140. On the informality of the elite-driven Sino-Albanian relationship, see Elez Biberaj, *Albania and China, 1962–1978: A Study of an Unequal Alliance* (Boulder: Westview, 1986), 48.

141. Committee for Cultural and Friendly Relations with Foreign Countries to Ministry of Education and Culture, 23 July 1963, AQSH, f. 511, v. 1963, dos. 87.

142. "Biseda e shokut Mao Ce Dun me delegacionin e Ushtrisë Popullore të Shqipërisë të kryesuar nga shoku Beqir Balluku," 2 October 1963, AQSH, f. 14/AP, M-PKK, v. 1963, dos. 8, fl. 2.

143. "Bisedë me shokët e Byrosë të komiteteve të partisë në rrethe" (Top Secret—to be destroyed after use), 1 November 1964, AQSH, f. 14/AP, M-PKK, v. 1964, dos. 39, fl. 10–15.

144. "Proçes-verbal i mbledhjes së Sekretariatit të Komitetit Qendror të PPSH" (Secret), 30 October 1964, AQSH, 14/AP, OU, v. 1964, dos. 27, fl. 182ff.

145. "Proces verbal i mbledhjes së Byrosë Politike të Komitetit Qendror të PPSH" (Top Secret), 31 October 1964, AQSH, f. 14/AP, OU, v. 1964, dos. 13.

146. Ibid.

147. "Proçes-verbal i mbledhjes së Byrosë Politike të Komitet Qendror të P.P.SH." (Top Secret), 15–16 June 1965, AQSH, f. 14/AP, OU, v. 1965, dos. 8, fl. 244.

148. "Takimi i sekretarit të parë të Komitetit Qendror të Partisë së Punës të Shqipërisë, shokut Enver Hoxha, me ambasadorin e Republikës Popullore të Kinës në Republikën tonë Popullore," 4 April 1966, AQSH, f. 14/AP, M-PKK, v. 1966, dos. 1, fl. 3.

149. "Bashkëbisedimet midis delegacionit të P.P.SH. dhe delegacionit të P.K. të Kinës," 28 April 1966, AQSH, f. 14/AP, M-PKK, v. 1966, dos. 2, fl. 3.

150. "Relacion mbi punën e shoqatave të miqësisë me Shqipërinë në vendet kapitaliste," dated by hand 19 June 1961, and "Vendim no. 170 mbi punën e shoqatave të miqësisë me Shqipërinë në vendet kapitaliste edhe masat për përmirësimin e tyre" (Secret), 19 June 1961, AQSH, f. 14/AP, OU, v. 1961, dos. 54, fl. 135–37, 140.

151. "Proçes-verbal i mbledhjes së Sekretariatit të Komitetit Qendror të PPSH" (Secret), 30 October 1964, AQSH, 14/AP, OU, v. 1964, dos. 27, fl. 182–233.

152. "Relacion mbi punën politike për sqarimin e problemeve ndërkombëtare në rrethet Vlorë dhe Pogradec," 19 October 1964, and "Relacion mbi punën politike për sqarimin e problemeve ndërkombëtare në rrethin e Vlorës," n.d., AQSH, 14/AP, OU, v. 1964, dos. 27, fl. 107–9, 111–13.

153. "Die Haltung der Bevölkerung zur Politik der Parteiführung," dated by hand 15 April 1964, PA AA, MfAA, C 614/78, 22.

154. "Relacion mbi marrëveshjen kulturale të përfunduar me Algjerinë," forwarded 15 February 1964, AQSH, f. 490, v. 1964, dos. 500, fl. 2; "Relacion mbi nënëshkrimin e planeve kulturale dhe mbi shkëmbimet kulturale me vendet e tjera," forwarded 1 August 1964, AQSH, f. 490, v. 1964, dos. 366, fl. 2; "Kërkesa në fushën e B.T. Shkencor për vitin 1966," forwarded 21 April 1965, AQSH, f. 499, v. 1965, dos. 54, fl. 13–18.

155. "The Fourth Anniversary of the First 'Sparks,'" B.R.P.SH. Information Bulletin, March 1963, 2.

156. B.R.P.SH. Information Bulletin, October 1963, 1.

157. "Java e kulturës kubane," Miqësia, April 1965, 22–23.

158. Cited in Willard Scott Thompson, Ghana's Foreign Policy, 1957–1966: Diplomacy, Ideology and the New State (Princeton: Princeton University Press, 1969), 399. See also "Act of receiving and consigning of document," n.d., AQSH, f. 490, v. 1964, dos. 1184, fl. 10.

159. Relacion mbi gjendjen e fondit special në dispozicion të Komitetit Qendror të PPSH dhe propozimet për vitin 1966," 19 March 1966, and "Vendim no. 61 mbi përdorimin e fondit special në dispozicion të Komitetit Qendror të PPSH" (Top Secret), 21 March 1966, AQSH, f. 14/AP, OU, v. 1966, dos. 28, fl. 91–92, 95.

160. "Vendim no. 298 mbi dhënien e një ndihme shokëve polakë" (Secret), 29 September 1964, AQSH, f. 14/AP, OU, v. 1964, dos. 26, fl. 54; "Vendim no. 315 mbi dhënie ndihmë Partisë Komuniste të Kolumbisë" (Secret), 24 October 1964, AQSH, 14/AP, OU, v. 1964, dos. 27, fl. 43; "Vendim no. 389 mbi dhënien e një ndihme Partisë Komuniste të Perusë" (Top Secret), 31 December 1964, AQSH, f. 14/AP, OU, v. 1965, dos. 14, fl. 46.

161. "Vendim no. 343 mbi ardhjen në Shqipëri të 15 shokëve iranianë" (Secret), 21 November 1964, and "Vendim no. 348 mbi ardhjen për studime në Shkollën e Partisë 'V. I. Lenin' të 5 shokëve nga P.K. Indoneziane" (Secret), 5 December 1964, AQSH, 14/AP, OU, v. 1964, dos. 28, fl. 39, 59; "Vendim no. 215 mbi disa shpenzime për shokët indonezianë që

kanë ardhur për pushime në Shqipëri" (Secret), 23 June 1964, AQSH, f. 14/AP, OU, v. 1964, dos. 23, fl. 53. Tirana's state university also enrolled small numbers of Vietnamese, Chinese, Indonesian, Peruvian, Bolivian, Syrian, and Sudanese students. "Relacion për punën me studentët e huaj," n.d., AQSH, f. 14/AP, str., Sektori i Jashtëm (SJ) (Foreign Section), v. 1969, dos. 272, fl. 21ff.

162. "Raport mbi veprimtarinë e armikut kundra R.P. të Shqipërisë gjatë viteve 1963–1964 dhe punën e organeve të Sigurimit të Shtetit" (Top Secret), 23 November 1964, AQSH, f. 14/AP, OU, v. 1965, dos. 3, fl. 42.

163. Stavro Skendi, "Albania," in *East Central Europe and the World: Developments in the Post-Stalin Era*, ed. Stephen Kertesz (Notre Dame, IN: University of Notre Dame Press, 1962), 216.

164. A Central Committee letter on atheist-scientific propaganda and on combating religious prejudices, dated 16 March 1964 and marked "Secret," is contained in AQSH, f. 490, v. 1964, dos. 722, fl. 6–7.

165. "Tezat e sekretarit të parë të KQ të PPSH, shokut Enver Hoxha, në mbledhjen e Byrosë Politike më 21 dhjetor 1965 në lidhje me luftën kundër burokracisë dhe për një metodë dhe stil revolucionar në punë," n.d. [from Politburo meeting of 21 December 1965], and "Proçes-verbal i mbledhjes së Byrosë Politike të Komitetit Qendror të PPSH," 21 December 1965, AQSH, f. 14/AP, OU, v. 1965, dos. 12, fl. 8–17. A valuable overview is Nicholas Pano, "The Albanian Cultural Revolution," *Problems of Communism* 23, no. 4 (July–August 1974): 44–57.

166. Any doubts about Hoxha's continued Stalinist orientation are dispelled by a reading of his handwritten "theses" for the Fifth Party Congress: "Teza për Kongresin V," 7 September 1965, AQSH, f. 14/AP, OU, v. 1966, dos. 1, fl. 43–54.

167. One author observed that Mao's Cultural Revolution served to heighten the ambition of Hoxha's revolutionary measures but also helped make them "less dependent on purely coercive methods." Anton Logoreci, *The Albanians: Europe's Forgotten Survivors* (London: Victor Gollancz, 1977), 165.

168. The Chinese Communist Party, as Arne Westad has argued, was fundamentally shaped by war: a crucial need for organization, hierarchy, and enforcement of rules. There was, he writes, "almost no time to stop fighting and study texts." Odd Arne Westad, *Restless Empire: China and the World since 1750* (New York: Basic Books, 2012), 286.

169. "Takimi me shokun Mao Ce Dun," 5 May 1966, and "Bisedimi që u zhvillua gjatë darkës që shtroi shoku Mao Ce Dun më datën 5 maj 1966," AQSH, f. 14/AP, M-PKK, v. 1966, dos. 3, fl. 1–21.

170. Institute of Marxist-Leninist Studies at the Central Committee of the Party of Labor of Albania, *History of the Party of Labor of Albania* (Tirana: Naim Frashëri, 1971), 612–47.

171. The speech, delivered at a meeting of party organizations in Kërrabë, was published in the party daily on 7 February 1967. An English-language translation was published as "The Further Revolutionization of the Party and Government," in Enver Hoxha, *On Further Revolutionizing our Party and the Life of our Country as a Whole (Speeches, 1967–1968)* (Tirana: 8 Nëntori, 1974), 3–57. A key document in the history of the 1967 movement is a communication from the Durrës party committee following Hoxha's speech: "Vendim no. 85. Mësimet e shokut Enver 'mbi revolucionarizimin e mëtejshëm të partisë e të pushtetit' për zhvillimin në thellësi të inisiativave të masave në luftë kundër zakoneve prapanike dhe mbeturinave fetare," 17 February 1967, AQSH, f. 14/AP, str., Sektori i Edukimit (SE) (Education Section), v. 1967, dos. 192, fl. 2–10.

172. "Komiteteve të partisë të rretheve" (Top Secret), 27 February 1967, AQSH, f. 511, v. 1967, dos. 20, fl. 2–10.

173. Korçë Episcopate to the Directorate of the Autocephalous Orthodox Church of Albania, 24 February 1967, AQSH, f. 536, v. 1967, dos. 1371, fl. 4.

174. "Informacion mbi zëvendësimin e gazetave të murit në fletë rrufe" (Sekret), n.d., AQSH, f. 14/AP, str., SE, v. 1967, dos. 226, f. 2.

175. "Komiteteve të partisë të rretheve" (Top Secret), 27 February 1967, AQSH, f. 511, v. 1967, dos. 20, fl. 3.

176. Ibid., fl. 9.

177. "Relacion mbi shkurtimin e numrit të monumenteve fetare," forwarded 17 October 1967, AQSH, f. 511, v. 1967, dos. 58, fl. 1–3. There seem to have also existed hundreds of religious structures not in use. For example, a report from earlier that summer observed that authorities had taken over a total of 2,169 religious buildings, including 740 mosques, 608 Orthodox churches and monasteries, 157 Catholic churches, and 530 Bektashi structures. "Raport informativ mbi rezultatet e para të luftës kundër fesë dhe disa masa për thellimin e mëtejshëm të saj," 7 July 1967, AQSH, f. 511, v. 1967, dos. 20, fl. 23.

178. "Mbi zëvendësimin e praktikave dhe zakoneve fetare të jetës së përditshme të njerëzve me ceremoni dhe festa socialiste," forwarded 10 May 1967, AQSH, f. 511, v. 1967, dos. 20, fl. 12–20.

179. State Archives Directorate to Central Committee and Office of the Prime Minister, 2 August 1967, AQSH, f. 14/AP, str., SE, v. 1967, dos. 193, fl. 1–3.

180. "Informacion mbi disa komente armiqësore" (Top Secret), 17 April 1967, AQSH, f. 14/AP, Grupi i instruktorëve (GI) (Instruction), v. 1967, dos. 37, fl. 6.

181. "Shënim," 30 March 1967, AQSH, f. 14/AP, str., SE, v. 1967, dos. 190, fl. 12.

182. Letter signed "Nga grat e Mirditës," 17 February 1969, AQSH, f. 14/AP, Sektori i përgjithshëm (SP) (General Sector), v. 1969, dos. 439, fl. 1.

183. Examples of personal letters addressed to Hoxha are contained in AQSH, f. 14/AP, SP, v. 1967, dos. 330, fl. 1–14. One problem, for example, was the ongoing battle over the question of what constituted proper socialist dress. Some provincial authorities did not want inhabitants to continue to wear traditional Albanian dress. Aggrieved peasants sent complaints to Hoxha, asking him for a personal intervention.

184. Ministry of Foreign Affairs to Ministry of Education and Culture, 20 July 1967, AQSH, f. 511, v. 1967, dos. 125, fl. 74; Tirana to Albanian Embassy (Beijing) (Top Secret), 20 September 1967, and 23 September 1967, AMPJ, v. 1967, dos. 64, fl. 69–70. On the sources of ritualized speech during the Cultural Revolution: Roderick MacFarquhar and Michael Schoenhals, *Mao's Last Revolution* (Cambridge, MA: Harvard University Press, 2006), 262–68. On the global reception of the Mao cult: Alexander C. Cook, ed., *Mao's Little Red Book: A Global History* (Cambridge: Cambridge University Press, 2014).

185. "Relacion mbi udhëtimin tonë për në Republikën Popullore të Kinës dhe vizitën nëpër Kinë," 22 February 1968, AQSH, f. 511, v. 1967, dos. 124, fl. 28–32.

186. One example: Red Guards ("The Great School of Mao Zedong Thought," Shanghai) to Hoxha, January 1967, AQSH, f. 14/AP, SP, v. 1967, dos. 462, fl. 5.

187. In 1966, the party's Secretariat resolved to publish the complete works of the party chief. "Vendim no. 136 mbi botimin e veprave të plota të shokut Enver Hoxha," 31 August 1966, AQSH, f. 14/AP, OU, v. 1966, dos. 33, fl. 93. During one visit to China in 1968, a musical ensemble brought two thousand portraits and twenty busts of Hoxha, in addition to porcelain works, photo albums, and hundreds of red badges. "Informacion mbi punën e propagandës me jashtë gjatë periudhës 1967–1968," 20 April 1968, AQSH, f. 511, v. 1968, dos. 8, fl. 12. His fiery Moscow speech from November 1960, on the other hand, was translated into English in small-format pocket-size booklets—much like Mao's portable teachings had been—to be disseminated around the world. Enver Hoxha, *Reject the Revisionist Theses of the XX Congress of the Communist Party of the Soviet Union and the Anti-Marxist Stand of Khrushchev's Group! Uphold Marxism-Leninism! Speech Delivered at the Meeting of 81 Communist and Workers' Parties in Moscow on November 16th, 1960* (Tirana: Naim Frashëri, 1969).

188. "Bisedim," 7 July 1967, AQSH, f. 490, v. 1967, dos. 246, fl. 6.

189. "Proces-verbal i mbledhjes së Byrosë Politike të Komitetit Qendror të PPSH," 30 June 1967, AQSH, f. 14/AP, OU, v. 1967, dos. 12, fl. 194–278.

AFTERWORD

1. *La nave dolce: Un incredibile viaggio verso la libertà*, directed by Daniele Vicari (Cecchi Gori, 2013), DVD.

2. "Procesverbal i mbajtur në mbledhjen e Presidiumit të Kuvendit Popullor më datën 31 gusht 1990, ditën e premte, ora 9.00," 31 August 1990, AQSH, f. 489, v. 1990, dos. 169, fl. 5.

3. One author pointed out that "it took the Albanian economy until 1973 to achieve the same level of relative efficiency as in 1959, and until 1969 to exceed 95%, as it had done in 1958." Adi Schnytzer, "Industry," in Grothusen, *Albanien*, 326.

4. Back in 1961, Albanian representatives had pleaded with Pyongyang for assistance, only to be told that North Korea faced hardships of its own. "Both of our countries are dealing with difficulties," a Korean Politburo member said at the time, "and that is why we ought to work harder in order to become economically independent." Albanian Embassy (Pyongyang) to Tirana (Top Secret), 12 December 1961, AMPJ, v. 1961, dos. 182, fl. 74.

5. "Bisedë e shokut Enver Hoxha, sekretar i parë i KQ të PPSH me shokun Li Hsien Nien kryetar i delegacionit të partisë dhe qeverisë të RP të Kinës," 27 November 1969, AQSH, f. 14/AP, M- PKK, v. 1969, dos. 17, f. 6.

6. "Proçesverbal i mbledhjes së Byrosë Politike të Komitetit Qendror të PPSH," 2 August 1971, AQSH, f. 14/AP, OU, v. 1971, dos. 45/2, fl. 20–55.

7. "Mbi ndërtimin e plotë të televizionit tonë me ndihmën e R.P. të Kinës," 9 August 1969, AQSH, f. 490, v. 1972, dos. 390, fl. 11–15.

8. To see the Sino-Soviet struggle exclusively through the angle of diplomatic history is to overlook cultural continuities in socialism. Consider, for example, that in the mid-1970s, just as they continued to rail against the Moscow revisionists, Albanian officials tried to get the Chinese to help them obtain Soviet newspapers and literature, which they otherwise could not obtain directly from Moscow. "Mbi mundësinë e sigurimit të shtypit dhe të librave sovjetikë nëpërmjet korporatës kineze për importin e literaturës së huaj 'Vaiven Shudian,'" 17 May 1975, AQSH, f. 511, v. 1975, dos. 8, fl. 17.

9. *Kushtetuta e Republikës Popullore Socialiste të Shqipërisë* (Tirana: 8 Nëntori, 1977).

10. In 1969, the Belgrade-based correspondent of Agence France-Presse observed "holes dug into the hills, cliffs and mountains of the country, to shelter Chinese-made air-to-air or air-to-ground missiles." He also saw "sharp-eyed young girls parading, in ranks of 15, with submachine-guns at their sides." Georges-Albert Salvan, "China's New Weapon for Albania," 2 June 1969, newspaper clipping, Hoover Institution Archives, Frederick Nossal Papers, box 23.

11. Ismail Kadare, *Linja të largëta: Shënime udhëtimi* (Tirana: Naim Frashëri, 1971). Cf. Philippe Delaroche, "Ismail Kadaré."

12. Lubonja, *Nën peshën e dhunës*, 68–71.

13. Shehu's wife, a member of the Central Committee, was put on trial and imprisoned. One son committed suicide. Bashkim Shehu, *Vjeshta e ankthit: Esse* (Tirana: Albinform, 1994).

14. "Bisedim i zhvilluar më 18 nëntor 1971, në pritjen që i bëri kryetari i Këshillit të Ministrave, Mehmet Shehu, delegacionit qeveritar ekonomik të RP të Kinës, të kryesuar nga Ministri për Lidhje Ekonomike me Botën e Jashtme, Fan Ji," 18 November 1971," AMPJ, v. 1971, dos. 149, fl. 101–2. Decades later, some of Albania's Chinese-supplied ammunition stock would end up in Afghanistan, by way of shady US Department of Defense contractors based in Miami. C. J. Chivers, "Supplier under Scrutiny over Arms for Afghans," *New York Times*, 27 March 2008.

Bibliography

ARCHIVES

Berlin

Bundesarchiv

Stiftung Archiv der Parteien und Massenorganisationen der DDR im Bundesarchiv

Politisches Archiv des Auswärtigen Amts—Ministerium für Auswärtige Angelegenheiten

College Park, Maryland

National Archives and Records Administration

London

The National Archives of the United Kingdom
School of Slavonic and East European Studies Library

Moscow

Gosudarstvennyi Arkhiv Rossiiskoi Federatsii
Rossiiskii Gosudarstvennyi Arkhiv Ekonomiki
Rossiiskii Gosudarstvennyi Arkhiv Noveishei Istorii

New York

Rare Book and Manuscript Library, Columbia University

Prague

Národní archiv

Rome

Archivio Centrale dello Stato
Archivio Fondazione Istituto Gramsci
Archivio Storico Diplomatico del Ministero Affari Esteri

Stanford, California

Hoover Institution Archives

Tirana

Arkivi i Agjencisë Telegrafike Shqiptare
Arkivi i Ministrisë së Punëve të Brendshme

Arkivi i Ministrisë së Punëve të Jashtme
Arkivi Qendror Shtetëror

Fondi 14/AP (formerly Arkivi Qendror i Partisë së Punës të Shqipërisë)

Arkivi Qendror Teknik i Ndërtimit

COLLECTIONS OF DOCUMENTS

Békés, Csaba, Malcolm Byrne, and János Rainer, eds. *The 1956 Hungarian Revolution: A History in Documents*. Budapest: CEU Press, 2002.
Ercolani, Antonella. *L'Albania di fronte all'Unione Sovietica nel Patto di Varsavia, 1955–1961*. Viterbo: Sette città, 2007.
Fursenko, A. A., ed. *Prezidium TsK KPSS: 1954–1964*. 3 vols. Moscow: Rosspen, 2002–8.
Kaba, Hamit, and Ethem Çeku, *Shqipëria dhe Kosova në arkivat ruse: 1946–1962*. Prishtinë: Brezi 81, 2011.
Kramer, Mark, ed. "Declassified Materials from CPSU Central Committee Plenums: Sources, Contexts, Highlights." *Cold War International History Project Bulletin*, no. 10 (March 1998): 7–25.
Lalaj, Ana, Christian F. Ostermann, and Ryan Gage. "'Albania Is Not Cuba': Sino-Albanian Summits and the Sino-Soviet Split." *Cold War International History Project Bulletin*, no. 16 (Fall 2007–Winter 2008): 183–337.
Plasari, Ndreçi, and Luan Malltezi. *Marrëdhëniet shqiptaro-jugosllave 1945–1948, Dokumente*. Tirana: Drejtoria e Përgjithshme e Arkivave, 1996.
United States Department of State. *Foreign Relations of the United States 1946*. Vol. 6. Washington, DC: United States Government Printing Office, 1969.
——. *Records of the Department of State Relating to the Internal Affairs of Albania*. Microfilm. Wilmington, DE: Scholarly Resources, 1987–2002?
Volkov, V. K. et al., eds. *Sovetskii Soiuz i vengerskii krizis 1956 goda*. Moscow: ROSSPEN, 1998.
Volokitina, T.V., T. M. Islamov, G. P. Murashko, A. F. Noskova, and L.A. Rogovaia, eds. *Vostochnaia Evropa v dokumentakh rossiiskikh arkhivov 1944–1953 gg.* 2 vols. Moscow: Sibirskii khronograf, 1997–8.
Volokitina, T. V., G. P. Murashko, O. V. Naumov, A. F. Noskova, and T. V. Tsarevskaia, eds. *Sovetskii faktor v Vostochnoi Evrope, 1944–1953*. 2 vols. Moscow: ROSSPEN, 1999–2002.

NEWSPAPERS AND PERIODICALS

Agitatori (Tirana)
Architettura: Rivista del Sindacato Nazionale Fascista Architetti (Milan)
Arkhitektura SSSR (Moscow)
Bashkimi (Tirana)
Berliner Zeitung (Berlin)
Bota e re (Tirana)
B.R.P.SH. Information Bulletin (Tirana)
Deutsche Architektur (Berlin)
Die Wirtschaft (Berlin)
Jeta e re (Tirana)
Kolkozjani sovjetik (Tirana)

Märkische Union (Potsdam)
Messaggero di Roma (Rome)
Miqësia/Miqësija (Shqipëri B.R.S.S.) (Tirana)
Ndërtuesi (Tirana)
Neues Deutschland (Berlin)
New York Times
Përpara (Korçë)
Pravda (Moscow)
Punëtori sovjetik (Tirana)
Rinia (Tirana)
Rivista d'Albania (Rome)
USSR Information Bulletin (Washington, DC)
VOKS Bulletin (Moscow)
Zëri i Popullit (Tirana)

OTHER SOURCES

Abrahams, Fred C. *Modern Albania: From Dictatorship to Democracy in Europe*. New York: NYU Press, 2015.

Alexander, Joseph Aloysius. *In the Shadow: Three Years in Moscow*. Melbourne: Herald and Weekly Times, 1949.

Alonso, Pedro Ignacio, and Hugo Palmarola. "A Panel's Tale: The Soviet KPD System and the Politics of Assemblage." *AA Files*, no. 59 (2009): 30–41.

Åman, Anders. *Architecture and Ideology in Eastern Europe: An Aspect of Cold War History*. Cambridge, MA: MIT Press, 1992.

Antic, Ana, Johanna Conterio, and Dora Vargha. "Beyond Liberal Internationalism." *Contemporary European History* 25, no. 2 (2016): 359–71.

Apor, Balázs, Péter Apor, and E. A. Rees, eds. *The Sovietization of Eastern Europe*. Washington, DC: New Academia, 2008.

Appadurai, Arjun. *Modernity at Large: Cultural Dimensions of Globalization*. Minneapolis: University of Minnesota Press, 1996.

Applebaum, Anne. *Iron Curtain: The Crushing of Eastern Europe, 1944–1956*. New York: Doubleday, 2012.

Applebaum, Rachel. "The Friendship Project: Socialist Internationalism in the Soviet Union and Czechoslovakia in the 1950s and 1960s." *Slavic Review* 74, no. 3 (Fall 2015): 484–507.

Armstrong, Charles K. *The North Korean Revolution, 1945–1950*. Ithaca: Cornell University Press, 2003.

——. *Tyranny of the Weak: North Korea and the World, 1950–1992*. Ithaca: Cornell University Press, 2013.

Austin, Robert. *Founding a Balkan State: Albania's Experiment with Democracy, 1920–1925*. Toronto: University of Toronto Press, 2012.

Azarov, T. "Problems in Coordinating the Scientific and Technical Research of Comecon Countries." *Eastern European Economics* 2, no. 4 (Summer 1964): 11–16.

Babiracki, Patryk. *Soviet Soft Power: Culture and the Making of Stalin's New Empire, 1943–1957*. Chapel Hill: University of North Carolina Press, 2015.

Ballinger, Pamela. "Borders of the Nation, Borders of Citizenship: Italian Repatriation and the Redefinition of National Identity after World War II." *Comparative Studies in Society and History* 49, no. 3 (2007): 713–41.

Banac, Ivo. *With Stalin against Tito: Cominformist Splits in Yugoslav Communism*. Ithaca: Cornell University Press, 1988.

Barany, Zoltan. "Soviet Takeovers: The Role of Advisers in Mongolia in the 1920s and in Eastern Europe after World War II." *East European Quarterly* 28, no. 4 (1995): 409–33.

Bauman, Zygmunt. "East European and Soviet Social Science: A Case Study in Stimulus Diffusion." In *The Influence of East Europe and the Soviet West on the USSR*, edited by Roman Szporluk, 91–116. New York: Praeger, 1976.

Bego, Mauricio. *Skeda arkitekture: 1965–2004: Në kronikën e një jete të dallgëzuar.* Tirana: DEA, 2009.

Behrends, Jan C. *Die Erfundene Freundschaft: Propaganda für die Sowjetunion in Polen und in der DDR.* Cologne: Böhlau, 2006.

Beissinger, Mark. R. *Scientific Management, Socialist Discipline, and Soviet Power.* Cambridge, MA: Harvard University Press, 1988.

Ben-Ghiat, Ruth. *Fascist Modernities.* Berkeley: University of California Press, 2001.

Berend, Iván T. *An Economic History of Twentieth Century Europe: Economic Regimes from Laissez-Faire to Globalization.* Cambridge: Cambridge University Press, 2006.

Biberaj, Elez. *Albania and China, 1962–1978: A Study of an Unequal Alliance.* Boulder, CO: Westview, 1986.

Boden, Ragna. *Die Grenzen der Weltmacht: Sowjetische Indonesienpolitik von Stalin bis Brežnev.* Stuttgart: Franz Steiner, 2006.

Brydan, David. "Axis Internationalism: Spanish Health Experts and the Nazi 'New Europe,' 1939–1945," *Contemporary European History* 25, no. 2 (2016): 291–311.

Brzezinski, Zbigniew. *The Soviet Bloc: Unity and Conflict.* Cambridge, MA: Harvard University Press, 1967.

Bykov, Aleksandr Naumovich. *Nauchno-tekhnicheskie sviazi stran sotsializma.* Moscow: Mysl', 1970.

Castillo, Greg. *Cold War on the Home Front: The Soft Power of Midcentury Design.* Minneapolis: University of Minnesota Press, 2010.

Chakrabarty, Dipesh. "The Muddle of Modernity." *American Historical Review* 116, no. 3 (June 2011): 663–75.

Chang, Julian. "The Mechanics of State Propaganda: The People's Republic of China and the Soviet Union in the 1950s." In *New Perspectives on State Socialism in China*, edited by Timothy Cheek and Tony Saich, 76–124. Armonk, NY: M.E. Sharpe, 1997.

Chang, Jung, and Jon Halliday. *Mao: The Unknown Story.* New York: Knopf, 2005.

Chen Jian. "China, the Third World, and the Cold War." In *The Cold War in the Third World*, edited by Robert J. McMahon, 85–100. New York: Oxford University Press, 2013.

——. *Mao's China and the Cold War.* Chapel Hill: University of North Carolina Press, 2001.

Chivers, C. J. "Supplier under Scrutiny over Arms for Afghans." *New York Times*, 27 March 2008.

Chuvakhin, D. S. "S diplomaticheskoi missiei v Albanii, 1946–1952 gg." *Novaia i noveishaia istoriia*, no. 1 (1995): 114–31.

Ciucci, Giorgio. *Gli architetti e fascismo: architettura e città, 1922–1944.* Torino: Einaudi, 1989.

Clavin, Patricia. "Defining Transnationalism." *Contemporary European History* 14, no. 4 (November 2005): 421–39.

Colton, Timothy J. *Moscow: Governing the Socialist Metropolis.* Cambridge, MA: Belknap Press of Harvard University Press, 1995.

Connelly, John. *Captive University: The Sovietization of East German, Czech and Polish Higher Education, 1945–1956.* Chapel Hill: University of North Carolina Press, 2000.

Conrad, Sebastian. *Globalisation and Nation in Imperial Germany.* New York: Cambridge University Press, 2010.

Cook, Alexander C., ed. *Mao's Little Red Book: A Global History.* Cambridge: Cambridge University Press, 2014.

Cooper, Frederick. "Writing the History of Development." *Journal of Modern European History* 8, no. 1 (January 2010): 5–23.

Council for Mutual Economic Assistance. *A Survey of 20 Years of the Council for Mutual Economic Assistance.* Moscow: CMEA Secretariat, 1969.

Cresti, Carlo, ed. *Gherardo Bosio: Architetto fiorentino, 1903–1941.* Florence: A. Pontecorboli, 1996.

Danylow, Peter. "Sieg und Niederlage der Internationale: Die Sowjetisierung der Kommunistischen Partei in Albanien." In *Gleichschaltung unter Stalin? Die Entwicklung der Parteien im östlichen Europa 1944–1949,* edited by Stefan Creuzberger and Manfred Görtemaker, 239–64. Paderborn: Ferdinand Schöningh, 2002.

David-Fox, Michael. "The Iron Curtain as Semipermeable Membrane: Origins and Demise of the Stalinist Superiority Complex." In *Cold War Crossings: International Travel and Exchange across the Soviet Bloc, 1940s–1960s,* edited by Patryk Babiracki and Kenyon Zimmer, 14–39. College Station: Texas A&M University Press, 2014.

——. "Multiple Modernities vs. Neo-Traditionalism: On Recent Debates in Russian and Soviet History." *Jahrbücher für Geschichte Osteuropas* 54, no. 4 (2006): 535–55.

——. *Showcasing the Great Experiment: Cultural Diplomacy and Western Visitors to the Soviet Union, 1921–1941.* New York: Oxford University Press, 2012.

Davies, R. W. "The Builders' Conference," *Soviet Studies* 6, no. 4 (1955): 443–57.

Dedijer, Vladimir. *Jugoslovensko-albanski odnosi (1939–1948)* Belgrade: Borba, 1949.

de Grazia, Victoria. *Irresistible Empire: America's Advance through 20th Century Europe.* Cambridge, MA: Belknap, 2005

Delaroche, Philippe. "Ismail Kadaré: 'La littérature et la vie sont des mondes différents, deux mondes en lutte,'" *Lire,* no. 380 (November 2009): 96–101.

Dervishi, Kastriot. *Shërbimi sekret shqiptar 1922–1944.* Tirana: "55," 2007.

——. *Sigurimi i Shtetit: 1944–1991. Historia e policisë politike të regjimit komunist.* Tirana: "55," 2012.

Dimitrovgrad. Sofia: Nauka i iskustvo, 1959.

Djilas, Milovan. *The New Class: An Analysis of the Communist System.* New York: Praeger, 1957.

Ehrenburg, Il'ia. *European Crossroad: A Soviet Journalist in the Balkans.* New York: Knopf, 1947.

Eksperienca e novatorëve sovjetikë në punimet e ndërtimit. Tirana: Ministria e Ndërtimit, 1955.

Engerman, David C. "The Second World's Third World." *Kritika: Explorations in Russian and Eurasian History* 12, no. 1 (Winter 2011): 183–211.

Engerman, David C., and Corinna R. Unger. "Introduction: Towards a Global History of Modernization." *Diplomatic History* 33, no. 3 (June 2009): 375–85.

Faja, Enver. "Urbanistika e qyteteve të reja të ndërtuara pas çlirimit dhe blloku i banimit." Unpublished thesis, Tirana, 1984.

Fan Chengzuo. "Wo qinli de zhong A liang dang guanxi de qiu dong jijie." *Zhonggong dangshi yanjiu,* no. 4 (2006): 88–93.

Fejtő, François. *A History of the People's Democracies: Eastern Europe since Stalin.* New York: Praeger, 1971.

——. "La deviazione albanese." *Comunità,* no. 107 (1963): 18–32.

Fidelis, Malgorzata. *Women, Communism, and Industrialization in Postwar Poland.* New York: Cambridge University Press, 2010.

Filtzer, Donald A. *Soviet Workers and Late Stalinism: Labour and the Restoration of the Stalinist System after World War II.* Cambridge: Cambridge University Press, 2002.

Fischer, Bernd J. *Albania at War, 1939–1945.* West Lafayette, IN: Purdue University Press, 1999.

——. "Enver Hoxha and the Stalinist Dictatorship in Albania." In *Balkan Strongmen: Dictators and Authoritarian Rulers of Southeast Europe,* edited by Bernd J. Fischer, 239–68. West Lafayette, IN: Purdue University Press, 2007.

——. *King Zog and the Struggle for Stability in Albania.* Boulder, CO: East European Monographs, 1984.

Fitzpatrick, Sheila, ed. *Stalinism: New Directions.* London: Routledge, 2000.

Forty, Adrian. *Concrete and Culture: A Material History.* London: Reaktion, 2012.

Frashëri, Agron. "One Day in Albania." *New Central European Observer* 4, no. 23 (1951): 365.

Frashëri, Kristo. *Historia e lëvizjes së majtë në Shqipëri dhe e themelimit të PKSh-së, 1878–1941: Vështrim historik me një shtojcë dokumentare.* Tirana: A.SH. SH., 2006.

Friedman, Jeremy. *Shadow Cold War: The Sino-Soviet Competition for the Third World.* Chapel Hill: University of North Carolina Press, 2015.

Fuller, Mia. *Moderns Abroad: Architecture, Cities and Italian Imperialism.* London: Routledge, 2007.

Fursenko, A. A., and Timothy J. Naftali, *Khrushchev's Cold War: The Inside Story of an American Adversary.* New York: Norton, 2006.

Fürst, Juliane. *Stalin's Last Generation: Soviet Post-war Youth and the Emergence of Mature Socialism.* New York: Oxford University Press, 2010.

Gati, Charles. *The Bloc That Failed: Soviet-East European Relations in Transition.* Bloomington: Indiana University Press, 1990.

Gibianskii, Leonid. "Forsirovanie sovetskoi blokovoi politiki." In *Kholodnaia voina, 1945–1963 gg: Istoricheskaia retrospektiva. Sbornik statei,* edited by N. I. Egorova and A. O. Chubar'ian, 137–86. Moscow: OLMA-PRESS, 2003.

——. "Ideia balkanskogo ob"edieniia i plany ee osushchestvleniia v 40-e gody XX veka," *Voprosy istorii,* no. 11 (November 2001): 38–56.

Gilbreth, Frank Bunker. *Bricklaying System.* New York: M.C. Clark Publishing Co., 1909.

Gilburd, Eleonory. "The Revival of Soviet Internationalism in the Mid to Late 1950s." In *The Thaw: Soviet Society and Culture during the 1950s and 1960s,* edited by Denis Kozlov and Eleonory Gilburd, 362–401. Toronto: University of Toronto Press, 2013.

Ginzburg, Carlo. *Threads and Traces: True False Fictive.* Berkeley: University of California Press, 2012.

Gitelman, Zvi Y. "The Diffusion of Political Innovation: From East Europe to the Soviet Union." In *The Influence of East Europe and the Soviet West on the USSR,* edited by Roman Szporluk, 11–67. New York: Praeger, 1976.

Giusti, Maria Adriana. *Albania: Architettura e città, 1925–1943.* Florence: Maschietto, 2006.

Gorsuch, Anne, and Diane Koenker, eds. *The Socialist Sixties: Crossing Borders in the Second World*. Bloomington: Indiana University Press, 2013.

Gresleri, Giuliano, Pier Giorgio Massaretti, and Stefano Zagnoni, eds. *Architettura Italiana d'oltremare: Atlante iconografico*. Bologna: Bononia University Press, 2008.

Griffith, William E. *Albania and the Sino-Soviet Rift*. Cambridge, MA: MIT Press, 1963.

Gross, Jan T. *Revolution from Abroad: The Soviet Conquest of Poland's Western Ukraine and Western Belorussia*. Princeton: Princeton University Press, 1988.

——. "Social Consequences of War: Preliminaries to the Study of Imposition of Communist Regimes in East Central Europe." *East European Politics and Societies* 3, no. 2 (Spring 1989): 198–214.

Grothusen, Klaus-Detlev, ed. *Albanien*. Göttingen: Vandenhoeck & Ruprecht, 1993.

Guppy, Shusha. Interview, "Ismail Kadaré, The Art of Fiction," *Paris Review* 147 (Summer 1998): 195–217.

Halfin, Igal. *Terror in My Soul: Communist Autobiography on Trial*. Cambridge, MA: Harvard University Press, 2003.

Hamm, Harry. *Albania—China's Beachhead in Europe*. New York: Praeger, 1963.

Hannemann, Christine. *Die Platte: Industrialisierter Wohnungsbau in der DDR*. 3rd ed. Berlin: Schiler, 2005.

Harris, Steven E. *Communism on Tomorrow Street: Mass Housing and Everyday Life after Stalin*. Washington, DC and Baltimore: Woodrow Wilson Center Press and Johns Hopkins University Press, 2013.

Havel, Václav. *Redevelopment, or, Slum Clearance*. London: Faber and Faber, 1990.

Hellbeck, Jochen. *Revolution on My Mind: Writing a Diary under Stalin* (Cambridge, MA: Harvard University Press, 2009).

Hibbert, Reginald. *Albania's National Liberation Struggle: The Bitter Victory*. London: Pinter Publishers, 1991.

Hobsbawm, Eric. "Guessing about Global Change." *International Labor and Working-Class History*, no. 47 (Spring 1995): 39–44.

Hoffman, David L., and Yanni Kotsonis, eds. *Russian Modernity: Politics, Knowledge and Practices, 1800–1950*. New York: Macmillan, 2000.

Hopkins, A. G. ed., *Globalization in World History*. New York: Norton, 2002.

Hoxha, Enver. *The Khrushchevites: Memoirs*. Tirana: 8 Nëntori, 1980.

——. *On Further Revolutionizing Our Party and the Life of Our Country as a Whole (Speeches, 1967–1968)*. Tirana: 8 Nëntori, 1974.

——. *Reject the Revisionist Theses of the XX Congress of the Communist Party of the Soviet Union and the Anti-Marxist Stand of Khrushchev's Group! Uphold Marxism Leninism! Speech Delivered at the Meeting of 81 Communist and Workers' Parties in Moscow on November 16th, 1960* (Tirana: Naim Frashëri, 1969).

——. *The Titoites: Historical Notes*. Tirana: 8 Nëntori, 1982.

——. *Vepra*. Vol. 22. Tirana: 8 Nëntori, 1976.

Institute of Marxist-Leninist Studies at the Central Committee of the Party of Labor of Albania. *History of the Party of Labor of Albania*. Tirana: Naim Frashëri, 1971.

Instituti i Studimeve Marksiste-Leniniste. *Historia e Partisë së Punës të Shqipërisë*. Tirana: 8 Nëntori, 1981.

Iriye, Akira. *Cultural Internationalism and World Order*. Baltimore: Johns Hopkins University Press, 1997.

Italiaander, Rolf. *Albanien—Vorposten Chinas*. Munich: Delp'sche Verlagsbuchhandlung, 1970.

Jersild, Austin. *The Sino-Soviet Alliance: An International History*. Chapel Hill: University of North Carolina Press, 2014.

——. "The Soviet State as Imperial Scavenger: 'Catch Up and Surpass' in the Transnational Socialist Bloc, 1950–1960." *American Historical Review* 116, no. 1 (February 2011): 109–32.

Josephson, Paul. "'Projects of the Century' in Soviet History: Large-Scale Technologies from Lenin to Gorbachev." *Technology and Culture* 36, no. 3 (July 1995): 519–59.

Judt, Tony. *Postwar: A History of Europe since 1945.* New York: Penguin, 2005.

Kadare, Helena. *Kohë e pamjaftueshme: kujtime.* Tirana: Onufri, 2011.

Kadare, Ismail. *Ftesë në studio.* Tirana: Naim Frashëri, 1990.

——. *Le crépuscule des dieux de la steppe.* Paris: Fayard, 1981.

——. *Linja të largëta: Shënime udhëtimi.* Tirana: Naim Frashëri, 1971

——. *Lirika.* Moscow: Izdatel'stvo inostrannoi literatury, 1961.

——. *Muzgu i perëndive të stepës.* Tirana: Onufri, 2006.

——. *The Palace of Dreams.* New York: Morrow, 1993.

——. *Vepra.* 20 vols. Tirana: Onufri, 2007–9.

Kaser, Michael. *Comecon: Integration Problems of the Planned Economies.* 2nd ed. Oxford: Clarendon Press, 1967.

——, ed. *The Economic History of Eastern Europe 1919–1975.* Vol. 3. Oxford: Oxford University Press, 1986.

Kasoruho, Amik. *Një ankth gjysmëshekullor.* Tirana: Çabej, 1996.

Kenney, Padraic. *Rebuilding Poland: Workers and Communists, 1945–1950.* Ithaca: Cornell University Press, 1997.

Khrushchev, Nikita. *Memoirs of Nikita Khrushchev.* Edited by Sergei Khrushchev. 3 vols. University Park: Pennsylvania State University Press, 2004–7.

Kołakowski, Leszek. *Main Currents of Marxism: Its Origin, Growth, and Dissolution.* 3 vols. Oxford: Clarendon Press, 1978.

Kolevica, Petraq. *Arkitektura dhe diktatura.* Tirana: Logoreci, 2004.

Kongresi I-rë i Shoqërisë për lidhje kulturale midis R.P. të Shqipërisë dhe B.R.S.S. Tirana: Shoqëria për lidhje kulturale midis R.P. të Shqipërisë dhe B.R.S.S., 1948.

Konrád, György. *The City Builder.* New York: Harcourt Brace Jovanovich, 1977.

Kopalin, Il'ia, dir. *Novaia Albaniia.* Order of the Red Flag Central Studio of Documentary Films and Committee of Arts and Culture of the People's Republic of Albania, 1948.

Kosel, Gerhard. *Produktivkraft Wissenschaft.* Berlin: Verlag Die Wirtschaft, 1957.

——. *Unternehmen Wissenschaft: Die Wiederentdeckung einer Idee: Erinnerungen.* Berlin: Henschelverlag Kunst und Gesellschaft, 1989.

Kotkin, Stephen. *Magnetic Mountain: Stalinism as a Civilization.* Berkeley: University of California Press, 1995.

——. "Modern Times: The Soviet Union and the Interwar Conjuncture." *Kritika: Explorations in Russian and Eurasian History* 2, no. 1 (Winter 2001): 111–64.

——. "Mongol Commonwealth? Exchange and Governance across the Post-Mongol Space." *Kritika: Explorations in Russian and Eurasian History*, 8, no. 3 (Summer 2007): 487–531.

——. *Stalin.* Vol. 1. New York: Penguin, 2014.

Kramer, Mark. "The Early Post-Stalin Succession Struggle and Upheavals in East-Central Europe: Internal-External Linkages in Soviet Policy Making." *Journal of Cold War Studies* 1, no. 1 (Winter 1999): 3–55.

——. "Stalin, Soviet Policy, and the Consolidation of a Communist Bloc in Eastern Europe, 1944–1953." In *Stalinism Revisited: The Establishment of Communist Regimes in East-Central Europe*, edited by Vladimir Tismaneanu, 51–102. Budapest: Central European University Press, 2009.

——. "Stalin, the Split with Yugoslavia, and Soviet-East European Efforts to Reassert Control, 1948–1953." In *Stalin and Europe: Imitation and Domination,*

1928–1953, edited by Timothy Snyder and Ray Brandon, 295–315. New York: Oxford University Press, 2014.

Kulić, Vladimir. "The Scope of Socialist Modernism: Architecture and State Representation in Postwar Yugoslavia." In *Sanctioning Modernism: Architecture and the Making of Postwar Identities*, edited by Vladimir Kulić, Timothy Parker, and Monica Penick, 37–62. Austin: University of Texas Press, 2014.

Kulikov, Andrei. *Për ndërtimin e shtëpijave për banim*. Tirana: Botim i Këshillit Qendror të B.P.S., 1949.

Kushtetuta e Republikës Popullore Socialiste të Shqipërisë. Tirana: 8 Nëntori, 1977.

La ricerca scientifica ed il progresso tecnico nell'economia nazionale. Consiglio Nazionale delle Richerche, 1940.

Lalaj, Ana. "Detanta e parë dhe Shqipëria." *Studime historike*, no. 3–4 (2009), 337–43.

——. "Ndarja me sovjetikët dhe aleatja e fundit e Shqipërisë komuniste." *Studime historike*, no. 3–4 (2010): 239–57.

——. "Ndarje të trishtuara. Një vështrim historik-juridik mbi martesat midis shtetasve shqiptarë dhe të huaj." *Studime historike*, no. 1–2 (2010): 155–65.

——. "Shqipëria dhe Informbyroja." *Studime historike*, no. 3–4 (2009): 103–38.

Lebow, Katherine. *Unfinished Utopia: Nowa Huta, Stalinism, and Polish Society, 1949–56*. Ithaca: Cornell University Press, 2013.

Leffler, Melvyn P., and David S. Painter, eds. *Origins of the Cold War: An International History*. 2nd ed. New York: Routledge, 2005.

Liu, Xiaoyuan, and Vojtech Mastny, eds. *China and Eastern Europe, 1960s–1980s: Proceedings of the International Symposium: Reviewing the History of Chinese- East European Relations from the 1960s to the 1980s*. Zurich: Center for Security Studies, 2004.

Logoreci, Anton. *The Albanians: Europe's Forgotten Survivors*. London: Victor Gollancz, 1977.

Lu, Duanfang. *Remaking Chinese Urban Form: Modernity, Scarcity and Space, 1949–2005*. London: Routledge, 2006.

Lubonja, Todi. *Nën peshën e dhunës*, 2nd ed. Tirana: Mësonjëtorja, 1998.

Lüthi, Lorenz. *The Sino-Soviet Split: Cold War in the Communist World*. Princeton: Princeton University Press, 2008.

MacFarquhar, Roderick, and Michael Schoenhals, *Mao's Last Revolution*. Cambridge, MA: Harvard University Press, 2006.

Marko, Petro. *Intervistë me vetveten (Retë dhe gurët)*. Tirana: OMSCA, 2000.

Markov, Georgi. *The Truth That Killed*. New York: Ticknor & Fields, 1984.

Mastny, Vojtech. *The Cold War and Soviet Insecurity: The Stalin Years*. New York: Oxford University Press, 1996.

Mazower, Mark. *Governing the World: The History of an Idea*. New York: Penguin, 2012.

——. *Hitler's Empire: How the Nazis Ruled Europe*. New York: Penguin, 2008.

Mbi miqësinë shqiptaro-sovjetike (përmbledhje dokumentash e materialesh kushtuar 40 vjetorit të Revolucionit të Madh Socialist të Tetorit). Tirana: Universiteti Shtetëror i Tiranës; Instituti i Historisë së P.P.SH; Shoqëria e Miqësisë Shqipëri-B.R.S.S., 1957.

Miano, Giuseppe. "Florestano di Fausto from Rhodes to Libya." *Environmental Design: Journal of the Islamic Environmental Design Research Center*, no. 9–10 (1990): 56–71.

Mëhilli, Elidor. "Defying De-Stalinization: Albania's 1956." *Journal of Cold War Studies* 13, no. 4 (Fall 2011): 4–56.

——. "The Socialist Design: Urban Dilemmas in Postwar Europe and the Soviet Union." *Kritika: Explorations in Russian and Eurasian History* 13, no. 3 (Summer 2012): 635–65.

Miłosz, Czesław. *The Captive Mind*. Translated from the Polish by Jane Zielonko. New York: Knopf, 1953.

Milward, Alan S. *The Reconstruction of Western Europe 1945–51*. London: Routledge, 1984.

Mňaćko, Ladislav. *Albanská reportáž*. Bratislava: Pravda, 1950.

——. "When Liri Grows Up." *New Central European Review* 4, no. 1 (1951): 287.

Molnár, Virág. *Building the State: Architecture, Politics, and State Formation in Post-War Central Europe*. London: Routledge, 2013.

Montanelli, Indro. *Albania una e mille*. Torino: Paravia & Co., 1939.

Montanelli, Indro, and Mario Cervi, *Storia d'Italia*. Vol. 8. Milan: RCS Libri, 2006.

Morgan, Peter. *Ismail Kadare: The Writer and the Dictatorship, 1957–1990*. London: Legenda, 2010.

Musaraj, Shevqet. *Njëzet ditë në Bashkimin Sovjetik*. Tirana: Naim Frashëri, 1950.

Naimark, Norman M. *The Russians in Germany: A History of the Soviet Zone of Occupation, 1945–1949*. Cambridge, MA: Belknap Press of Harvard University Press, 1995.

Naimark, Norman, and Leonid Gibianskii, eds. *The Establishment of Communist Regimes in Eastern Europe, 1944–1949*. Boulder, CO: Westview, 1997.

Neubacher, Hermann. *Sonderauftrag Südost 1940–1945: Bericht eines fliegenden Diplomaten*. Göttingen: Musterschmidt-Verlag, 1956.

Neuwirth, Hubert. *Widerstand und Kollaboration in Albanien 1939–1944*. Wiesbaden: Harrassowitz, 2008.

Ngjela, Spartak. *Përkulja dhe rënia e tiranisë shqiptare, 1957–2010*. Vol. 1. Tirana: UET Press, 2011.

Nolan, Mary. *The Transatlantic Century: Europe and America, 1890–2010*. New York: Cambridge University Press, 2012.

O'Rourke, Kevin H., and Jeffrey G. Williamson. *Globalization and History: The Evolution of a Nineteenth-Century Atlantic Economy*. Cambridge, MA: MIT Press, 1999.

Osterhammel, Jürgen, and Niels P. Petersson. *Globalization: A Short History*. Princeton: Princeton University Press, 2005.

Pano, Nicholas C. "Albania." In *The Columbia History of Eastern Europe in the Twentieth Century*, edited by Joseph Held, 17–64. New York: Columbia University Press, 1992.

——. "The Albanian Cultural Revolution." *Problems of Communism* 23, no. 4 (July–August 1974): 44–57.

Perović, Jeronim. "The Tito-Stalin Split: A Reassessment in Light of New Evidence." *Journal of Cold War Studies* 9, no. 2 (Spring 2007): 32–63.

Péteri, György, "Nylon Curtain—Transnational and Transsystemic Tendencies in the Cultural Life of State-Socialist Russia and East-Central Europe." *Slavonica* 10, no. 2 (November 2004): 113–23.

Pipa, Arshi. *Albanian Stalinism: Ideo-Political Aspects*. New York: Columbia University Press, 1990.

——. *Libri i burgut*. Rome: Apice, 1959.

Plamper, Jan. *The Stalin Cult: A Study in the Alchemy of Power*. New Haven: Yale University Press, 2012.

Pollo, Stefanaq, and Arben Puto. *The History of Albania: From Its Origins to the Present Day*. London: Routledge & Kegan Paul, 1981.

Potapova, Nina. *Gjuha ruse (Metodë)*. Moscow: Shtëpia Botonjëse e Letërsisë në Gjuhë të Huaja, 1951.

Pribichevich, Stoyan. "Albania: Key to the Adriatic." *Current History* 50, no. 1 (March 1939): 40–42.

Prifti, Peter R. "Albania's Expanding Horizons." *Problems of Communism*, January–February 1972, 30–39.

Pula, Besnik. "Becoming Citizens of Empire: Albanian Nationalism and Fascist Empire, 1939–1943." *Theory and Society* 37 (2008): 567–96.

——. "State, Law and Revolution: Agrarian Power and the Nation-State in Albania." PhD diss., University of Michigan, 2011.

Rabinow, Paul. ed., *The Foucault Reader*. New York: Pantheon, 1984.

Radchenko, Sergey. *Two Suns in the Heavens: The Sino-Soviet Struggle for Supremacy, 1962–1967*. Stanford: Stanford University Press, 2009.

Rajak, Svetozar. *Yugoslavia and the Soviet Union in the Early Cold War: Reconciliation, Comradeship, Confrontation, 1953–1957*. New York: Routledge, 2011.

Reid, Susan E. "The Khrushchev Kitchen: Domesticating the Scientific-Technological Revolution." *Journal of Contemporary History* 40, no. 2 (2005): 289–316.

Reinisch, Jessica. "Agents of Internationalism." *Contemporary European History* 25, no. 2 (2016): 195–205.

Report of the Study Tour of Building Technologists from Latin America, Africa, Asia and the Middle East to the Union of Soviet Socialist Republics. New York: United Nations, 1964.

Rifkind, David. "Gondar: Architecture and Urbanism for Italy's Fascist Empire." *Journal of the Society of Architectural Historians* 70, no. 4 (2011): 492–511.

Rodogno, Davide. *Fascism's European Empire: Italian Occupation during the Second World War*. Cambridge: Cambridge University Press, 2006.

Roselli, Alessandro. *Italy and Albania: Financial Relations in the Fascist Period*. London: I.B. Tauris, 2006.

Rugg, Dean S. "Communist Legacies in the Albanian Landscape." *Geographical Review* 84, no. 1 (January 1994): 59–73.

Sanchez-Sibony, Oscar. *Red Globalization: The Political Economy of the Soviet Cold War from Stalin to Khrushchev*. Cambridge: Cambridge University Press, 2014.

Santoianni, Vittorio. "Il Razionalismo nelle colonie italiane 1928–1943. La 'nuova architettura' delle Terre d'Oltremare." PhD diss., Università degli Studi di Napoli Federico II, 2008.

Sauvy, Alfred. "Trois mondes, une planète." *L'Observateur*, 14 August 1952.

Schaefer, Henry W. *Comecon and the Politics of Integration*. New York: Praeger, 1972.

Schmidt-Neke, Michael. "Zwischen Kaltem Krieg und Teleologie: Das kommunistische Albanien als Objekt der Zeitgeschichtsforschung." In *Albanische Geschichte: Stand und Perspektiven der Forschung*, edited by Oliver Jens Schmitt and Eva Anne Frantz, 131–47. Munich: R. Oldenbourg Verlag, 2009.

Scott, James. *Seeing Like a State: How Certain Schemes to Improve the Human Condition Have Failed*. New Haven: Yale University Press, 1998.

Seton-Watson, Hugh. *The East European Revolution*. New York: Praeger, 1951.

Shehu, Bashkim. *Vjeshta e ankthit*. Tirana: Albinform, 1994.

Shen Zhihua. *Sulian zhuanjia zai zhongguo, 1948–1960*. Beijing: Zhongguo guoji guangbo chubanshe, 2003.

Shen Zhihua and Yafeng Xia. *Mao and the Sino-Soviet Partnership, 1945–1959*. Lanham, MD: Lexington Books, 2015.

Shostakovich, Dmitri. *Testimony: The Memoirs of Dmitri Shostakovich*. Edited by Solomon Volkov. New York: Limelight, 2004.

Siegelbaum, Lewis H. *Stakhanovism and the Politics of Productivity in the USSR, 1935–1941*. New York: Cambridge University Press, 1988.

Sinani, Shaban, Ismaïl Kadaré, and Stéphane Courtois, *La dossier Kadaré*. Paris: Odile Jacob, 2006.

Skendi, Stavro. "Albania." In *East Central Europe and the World: Developments in the Post- Stalin Era*, edited by Stephen Kertesz, 197–228. Notre Dame, IN: University of Notre Dame Press, 1962.

——. "Albania within the Slav Orbit: Advent to Power of the Communist Party." *Political Science Quarterly* 63, no. 2 (1948): 257–74.

Smirnova, Nina D. *Istoria Albanii v XX veke*. Moscow: Nauka, 2003.

Snyder, Timothy, and Ray Brandon, eds. *Stalin and Europe: Imitation and Domination, 1928–1953*. New York: Oxford University Press, 2014.

"Società Anonima Fabbriche Fiammiferi ed Affini," *La ricerca scientifica ed il progresso tecnico nell'economia nazionale* 11, no. 12 (December 1940): xix-xx.

Società per lo sviluppo economico dell'Albania. *Un decennio di vita della "S.V.E.A." Relazione presentata all'assemblea generale degli azionisti del 15 maggio 1936-XIV*. Rome: La libreria dello stato, 1936.

Spinosa, Antonio. *Starace: L'uomo che inventò lo stile fascista*. Milan: Mondadori, 2002.

Stokes, Raymond. *Constructing Socialism: Technology and Change in East Germany, 1945–1990*. Baltimore: Johns Hopkins University Press, 2000.

Stone, David R. "CMEA's International Investment Bank and the Crisis of Developed Socialism." *Journal of Cold War Studies* 10, no. 3 (Summer 2008): 48–77.

Stone, Randall. *Satellites and Commissars: Strategy and Conflict in the Politics of Soviet-Bloc Trade*. Princeton: Princeton University Press, 1996.

Taylor, Frederick Winslow. *The Principles of Scientific Management*. New York: Harper & Brothers, 1911.

Thirje e pjesëmarësve të konferencës së ndërtonjësve, arkitektave, punonjësve të industrisë së materialeve të ndërtimit, të prodhimit të maqinerisë së ndërtimit dhe rrugëve, t'organizatave të projektimit dhe kërkimeve shkencore të B. Sovjetik, organizuar nga Komiteti Central i Partis Komuniste të B. Sovjetik dhe Këshillit të Ministrave të B.R.S.S. për të gjithë punonjësit e industrisë së ndërtimeve. Tirana: Ministria e Ndërtimit dhe Komunikacioneve, 1955.

Thompson, Willard Scott. *Ghana's Foreign Policy, 1957–1966: Diplomacy, Ideology and the New State*. Princeton: Princeton University Press, 1969.

Tismaneanu, Vladimir. *Stalinism for All Seasons: A Political History of Romanian Communism*. Berkeley: University of California Press, 2003.

Tiukhin, Vasilii. "Ismail' Kadare: 'Mne snilas' Moskva,'" *Sankt-Peterburgskie vedomosti*, 21 February 2007, 4.

Todorova, Maria. "The Trap of Backwardness: Modernity, Temporality and the Study of Eastern European Nationalism," *Slavic Review* 64, no. 1 (Spring 2005): 140–64.

Vehbiu, Ardian. *Kulla e Sahatit*. Tirana: K&B, 2003.

——. *Shqipja totalitare: Tipare të ligjërimit publik në Shqipërinë e viteve 1945–1990*. Tirana: Çabej, 2007.

Velo, Maks. *Historia e një cope guri: Rrëfime*. Elbasan: Sejko, 2006.

——. *Paralel me arkitekturën*. Tirana: Njeriu, 1998.

——. "Qendra e Tiranës, shkretëtira e tartarëve dhe teoria e shesheve të vegjël," *Shekulli*, 16 April 2006.

Vicari, Daniele, dir. *La nave dolce: Un incredibile viaggio verso la libertà*, Cecchi Gori, 2013.

Villari, Giovanni. "A Failed Experiment: The Exportation of Fascism to Albania." *Modern Italy* 12, no. 2 (June 2007): 157–71.

Volokitina, T. V., G. P. Murashko, and A. F. Noskova. *Narodnaia Demokratiia: Mif ili real'nost'? Obshchestvenno-politicheskie protsessy v Vostochnoi Evrope, 1944–1948 gg*. Moscow: Nauka, 1993.

Volokitina, T.V., G. P. Murashko, A. F. Noskova, and T. A. Pokivailova. *Moskva i Vostochnaia Evropa: Stanovlenie politicheskikh rezhimov sovetskogo tipa, 1949–1953*. Moscow: ROSSPEN, 2002.

Vukmanović-Tempo, Svetozar. *Revolucija koja teče: Memoari*. Vol. 2. Zagreb: Globus, 1982.

Wang Taiping, ed. *Zhonghua renmin gongheguo waijiao shi, 1957–1969*. Beijing: Shijie zhishi, 1998.

Weiner, Amir. *Making Sense of War: The Second World War and the Fate of the Bolshevik Revolution*. Princeton: Princeton University Press, 2001.

Westad, Odd Arne, ed. *Brothers in Arms: The Rise and Fall of the Sino-Soviet Alliance, 1945–1963*. Washington, DC: Woodrow Wilson Center Press, 1998.

———. *The Global Cold War: Third World Interventions and the Making of Our Times*. Cambridge: Cambridge University Press, 2005.

———. *Restless Empire: China and the World since 1750*. New York: Basic Books, 2012.

———. "Struggles for Modernity: The Golden Years of the Sino-Soviet Alliance." In *The Cold War in East Asia, 1945–1991*, edited by Tsuyoshi Hasegawa, 35–62. Washington, DC and Stanford: Woodrow Wilson Center and Stanford University Press, 2011.

Wilczynski, Jozef. *The Economics of Socialism after World War II*. New Brunswick, NJ: AldineTransaction, 2008.

Wiles, P.J.D. *Communist International Economics*. New York: Praeger, 1969.

Zagoria, Donald S. *The Sino-Soviet Conflict, 1956–1961*. Princeton: Princeton University Press, 1962.

Zarecor, Kimberly Elman. *Manufacturing a Socialist Modernity: Housing in Czechoslovakia, 1945–60*. Pittsburgh: University of Pittsburgh Press, 2011.

Životić, Aleksandar. *Jugoslavija, Albanija i velike sile: (1945 1961)*. Belgrade: Arhipelag, Institut za noviju istoriju Srbije, 2011.

Zubok, Vladislav. *Zhivago's Children: The Last Russian Intelligentsia*. Cambridge, MA: Harvard University Press, 2009.

Zubok, Vladislav, and Constantine Pleshakov. *Inside the Kremlin's Cold War: From Stalin to Khrushchev*. Cambridge, MA: Harvard University Press, 1996.

Index

Page numbers in *italics* indicate illustrations.

CPSIA information can be obtained
at www.ICGtesting.com
Printed in the USA
BVOW09*0130061017
496595BV00001B/1/P